DATE DUE

MAR 22 '78			

Studies in Legal History

Published in association with the American Society for Legal History

Editor: Stanley N. Katz

Editorial Advisory Board

John D. Cushing
John P. Dawson
Lawrence M. Friedman
Charles M. Gray
Oscar Handlin
George L. Haskins
J. Willard Hurst
S. F. C. Milsom
A. Arthur Schiller
Joseph H. Smith
L. Kinvin Wroth

American Lawyers in a Changing Society, 1776-1876

Maxwell Bloomfield

Harvard University Press
Cambridge, Massachusetts
and
London, England
1976

Publication of this volume has been aided by a grant from the
Andrew W. Mellon Foundation.

Library of Congress Cataloging in Publication Data

Bloomfield, Maxwell H
   American lawyers in a changing society, 1776-1876.

   (Studies in legal history)
   Includes bibliographical references and index.
   1. Law—United States—History and criticism.
2. Lawyers—United States—Biography.   I.   Title.
KF366.B5   340'.0973   75-14172
ISBN 0-674-02910-0

To my parents

Preface

Anyone who has ventured very far into the wilderness of nineteenth-century legal biography must acknowledge a sense of frustration closely akin to that described by an anonymous law writer of the Civil War years:

> Of all the distinguished members of the American Bar, how brief a record remains, when they have once shuffled off the mortal coil of daily and nightly toil! A stale joke, a brilliant repartee, an adroit evasion, or an ingenious checkmate, it may be, tells the brief story of their history, in the very halls made eloquent with their words, for half a century. And how impossible it is to catch the nice shades of character and talent, of thought and feeling, of look and gesture, which made up the sum of their greatness and power, while here among the moving scenes of life! How little, how less than nothing it seems, as we look upon the mere skeleton of life, which we have been able to catch and confine to paper, of thoughts that breathe and words that burn; of all which went to make the life and fame of him, whose history we essay to write! (*American Law Register* [1863])

For all the elusiveness of the legal personality, however, it seems essential to me that some serious effort be made to comprehend the practitioners of the past in their totality: to approach them, that is, not merely from the standpoint of their professional competence and achievements, but in terms of their broader involvement in the everyday life of their local communities, whose mores they necessarily shared to a greater or lesser degree. In the pages that follow, therefore, I have chosen to focus, as far as possible, upon the interaction between law, lawyers, and American society, taking into account not only the influence that bench and bar wielded over the lay public, but also the equally important restraints that societal norms imposed upon the thinking and behavior of the professional classes.

Other writers—notably, Charles Warren, Roscoe Pound, J. Willard Hurst, Anton-Hermann Chroust, and, most recently, Lawrence M. Friedman—have dealt in a more systematic way with the evolution of the American bar during these same years, and to their pioneer labors I am immensely indebted. But the comprehensive scope of such pathbreaking works inevitably prevented their authors from giving adequate consideration to a host of significant legal and cultural problems that deserve extended treatment in their own right. The present volume is designed to fill that gap in part and, I hope, will encourage further interdisciplinary research into the social history of the American legal profession.

I would like to thank the American Bar Foundation for a Fellowship in Legal History that, together with a matching grant from The Catholic University of America, enabled me to devote one full year to travel and research. The staffs of the following institutions were uniformly courteous and helpful, and I acknowledge with thanks permission to quote from their respective manuscript collections: Columbia University Library; Columbia County Historical Society (Kinderhook, New York); New York Historical Society; Historical Society of Pennsylvania; Library of Congress; Maryland Historical Society; William L. Clements Library (Ann Arbor, Michigan); Cincinnati Historical Society; Barker Texas History Center (Austin, Texas); and Erastus Milo Cravath Library (Fisk University). To Mrs. Clara M. Jacobs and Mrs. Wayne King of the South Caroliniana Library, Columbia, South Carolina, and to Robert C. Park of the Rosenberg Library, Galveston, Texas, I owe special thanks for extraordinary services rendered. It is a pleasure also to record the generous hospitality and friendly assistance of Dr. and Mrs. LeRoy J. Holbert, of Kinderhook, New York; Mr. and Mrs. Ralph F. Puck, of Cincinnati, Ohio; and Ruby Bowdoin Bloomfield and the late Benjamin M. Bloomfield, of Houston, Texas, and Readfield, Maine.

Portions of chapters 3, 5, 7, and 9 have appeared as articles in the following journals: "William Sampson and the Codifiers: The Roots of American Legal Reform, 1820-1830," *American Journal of Legal History*, 11 (1967): 234-252; "Law vs. Politics: The Self-Image of the American Bar (1830-1860)," ibid., 12 (1968): 306-323; "Lawyers and Public Criticism: Challenge and Response in Nineteenth-Century America," ibid., 15 (1971): 269-277; "Frederick Grimké and American Civilization: A Jacksonian Jurist's Appraisal," *Ohio History*, 76 (Winter/Spring 1967): 5-16, 89; and "John Mercer Langston and the Rise of Howard Law School," in Francis Coleman Rosenberger, ed., *Records of the Columbia Historical Society of Washington, D.C.*, 48 (1971-72): 421-438. I am indebted to the editors of those journals for permission to reprint this material here.

A number of friendly critics read parts of the manuscript from time to time and called attention to my most egregious blunders. I have profited greatly from the constructive suggestions of Hugh F. Rankin, Donald Roper, Philip Detweiler, Joseph M. Hernon, David H. Flaherty, Herman Belz, Arthur A. Ekirch, Jr., Charles Fairman, V. Jacque Voegeli, Stanley N. Katz, Morton J. Horwitz, and the late Adrienne Koch. My colleagues at The Catholic University of America—Harold D. Langley, Edward C. Carter II, Joseph N. Moody, Jon L. Wakelyn, Thomas Reed West, and E. Clinton Bamberger, Jr., dean of the Columbus School of Law—have likewise offered valuable criticism and advice, while the entire manuscript has benefited from the careful scrutiny of Aida DiPace Donald of the Harvard University Press. Stanley I. Kutler deserves special mention for his continuing interest and encouragement from a very early stage of the work, as does my wife, Helen, whose contributions would require a separate volume to detail.

Contents

American Lawyers in a Changing
Society, 1776-1876

There are no reasons from which it can be
shown, that a man may not in *principle*
adhere to the old government as well as support the new, and the rule against neutrality in
civil wars, necessarily admits it.
Observations on the Banishing Act (1778)

1 Peter Van Schaack and the Problem of Allegiance

The role of the moderate in an
age of violence is seldom enviable. Committed by training and
temperament to a belief in orderly change, a moderate finds
himself ill equipped to combat the impassioned activism of
those who urge an immediate and drastic solution to long-standing social ills. Inevitably the tide of events engulfs and sub-
merges him, until only his adversaries—the unequivocal heroes
and villains of the day—remain in possession of the field. Such
was the fate of Erasmus and More in the days of the Protestant
Reformation and of Mirabeau and Lafayette during the French
Revolution of 1789. Such, too, was the experience of many
Americans in 1776 whose self-doubts and lack of militancy have
caused them to be woefully neglected by admirers of our "revolutionary tradition."

Today, when the nonhero looms so large in the popular
imagination, we may expect a rebirth of interest in these forgotten figures. Their very ambivalence speaks to the modern

temper and sheds an unfamiliar glow over the stirring events they witnessed. Particularly is this true in the case of Peter Van Schaack, a New York lawyer who measured wartime policies against the preservation of legitimate human rights, and found both sides wanting. In his ringing defense of the inviolability of the individual conscience, even in the midst of a disintegrating society, Van Schaack touched upon a theme which in its continuing importance transcends that of the Revolution itself.

The village of Kinderhook lies some twenty miles southeast of Albany, New York, on a plateau that slopes steeply down to the banks of the Hudson. In the mid-eighteenth century it was still considered a frontier community, although the first settlers had arrived from Holland almost a hundred years earlier. Conspicuous among the local Dutch families were the Van Schaacks—Cornelius, Lydia, and their seven children—who lived on the outskirts of town in an old house that had once served as a wilderness fort. Allied by marriage with the powerful Schuyler clan of Albany, Cornelius Van Schaack could congratulate himself upon his rise from obscurity to a position of moderate wealth and status among his neighbors. An elder of the Dutch Reformed Church, a successful merchant and landowner, a magistrate and colonel in the provincial militia, he typified the kind of social mobility that existed within colonial society for those with the right connections. And his numerous progeny promised to extend the Van Schaack influence still further into the political and economic life of the countryside.

Peter, the youngest member of the family, was earmarked for one of the liberal professions from the day he was born in March 1747.[1] Despite a native shyness that made classroom recitations a recurrent nightmare, he found himself compelled to attend the classes of the village schoolmaster—a crotchety character—until he had exhausted the latter's limited store of knowledge. Then his parents shipped him off to Staten Island for two successive winters (1762-63) to round out his studies under the guidance of Richard Charlton, an Episcopal clergyman and graduate of Dublin's famed Trinity College. From Charlton young Peter imbibed a lifelong enthusiasm for the classics and sufficient general knowledge to enter the freshman class of King's College, New York, in the fall of 1763.

By that time he had outgrown his adolescent dreams of becoming a soldier like his dashing brother Henry, a veteran of the French and Indian War. King's College, besides, had ample compensatory excitements of its own to offer a lad fresh from the western country. Here was a meeting ground for the wealth and talent of the entire province—an arena whose bloodless combats tested the mettle of many a future leader of the colonial Establishment, and of some who would help to pull down that Establishment, such as Peter's close friends and classmates Egbert Benson, Gouverneur Morris, and John Jay. Spurred on by such competitors, Van Schaack made rapid progress in his studies and soon rose to first place in his class. He also found time to fall in love with Elizabeth Cruger, daughter of a wealthy New York merchant and one of the most eligible heiresses of Manhattan. Anticipating parental opposition, the young couple eloped in 1765 and were married in a private ceremony. (In the sequel their precautions were fully justified: on hearing the news old Henry Cruger, the bride's father, hurled his wig into the fire and swore that the newlyweds would never set foot in his house again—a bit of eighteenth-century mummery that scarcely survived the birth of his first grandchild the following year.)

With a family to support, Peter dropped out of college at the end of his third year to begin the study of law as a clerk in the office of his brother-in-law, attorney Peter Silvester of Albany. But his plans soon took another turn when the Supreme Court of the Province of New York announced a new rule for admission to the bar as part of a continuing campaign to restrict the profession to men of wealth and station. Hitherto a clerkship period of five years—coupled with an exorbitant tuition fee of two hundred pounds—had been required of all candidates. Now the scales were further weighted in favor of an educated elite: beginning in 1767 college graduates had to clerk for only three years, while a seven-year apprenticeship was imposed upon all others. Hurriedly Peter returned to New York, established himself in the law office of William Smith, Jr., on a part-time basis, and resumed his college studies. He received his B.A. degree in the spring of 1768 and wasted no time in applying to take the qualifying bar examinations, although he still lacked five months of prescribed office training.

To Peter Silvester he candidly outlined his reasons for haste:

Mr. C[ruger] told me the other Day that if I were in the Practice now I sho^d have the advantage of managing a good Deal of the deceased Mr. Walton's Estate as also the *Treasurers*, thro' means of the old Mayor his B^r who is one of the Trustees—He says if I co^d get a Licence & Mr. Smith agreed he shod like me to do some little uncontroverted Jobs to furnish me with *Paper & Quills* . . . I must say that my Friends seem anxious to advance me—& I flatter myself I shall find the Advantage of a very extensive Connection by keeping up my Friendship with my Relations here.[2]

The supreme court agreed to overlook minor irregularities in Van Schaack's case and admitted him to practice in January 1769 at the age of twenty-one. Few fledgling lawyers embarked upon their professional careers with better prospects of success. Tall and personable, with patrician manners and a ready wit, he was admirably calculated to win the regard of the mercantile oligarchy that governed New York. Aided by retainers from Peter Silvester and the Crugers, he soon built up a lucrative general practice centering about probate matters, the collection of debts, and, above all, disputed land titles.

Whole communities, including Kinderhook, were at this time involved in protracted boundary disputes that grew out of the vague descriptions of lands conveyed by early royal patents. Descendants or assignees of the original proprietors seized every opportunity to assert quasi-feudal privileges against the settlers on their vast manorial tracts. The result was a multiplicity of lawsuits and occasional outbreaks of violence by the embittered small farmers of the Hudson Valley.

Through his personal involvement as counsel in several important land contests, Van Schaack became convinced that the insecurity of property rights in real estate transactions posed as great a threat to the welfare of the province as any of England's tax measures. "The encouragement of old dormant claims can never be advantageous to a community," he warned, particularly where vast tracts of land lay uncultivated or unimproved as a result. In a public statement drafted around 1773, he called upon the legislature to appoint qualified boundary commissioners to arbitrate all outstanding title controversies once and for all.[3]

A similar concern for the general improvement of the law led the young attorney to take an active part in the deliberations of the Moot. Begun in 1770, this organization of twenty prominent New York lawyers brought old and young practitioners together on a basis of equality to thrash out disputed legal questions. Members met regularly at various taverns where, after a good dinner, they debated the wisdom of the latest supreme court decisions and other matters of professional interest. Their conclusions carried much weight with both bench and bar; by 1775, when the approaching Revolution disrupted their proceedings, the Moot reputedly enjoyed the virtual authority of a court of last resort for the province. William Smith, Jr., was vice-president of the club, while his protégé Van Schaack— whom he proudly described as "the first genius of all the young fellows at New York"[4]—acted as its secretary and kept the records.

Van Schaack's growing professional reputation, abetted by the political influence of his wife's uncle John Cruger, Speaker of the New York Assembly, led to his appointment as reviser of the laws of New York in 1772. The office conferred great prestige on its recipient, along with an intolerable work load; for it required that he collect, revise, edit, and index all the laws of the province of New York from 1691 forward. Undaunted, Van Schaack plunged into the task with characteristic thoroughness. A year later his compilation—a masterful synthesis of colonial jurisprudence—was ready for the press. But his painstaking scholarship left his vision permanently impaired, and he was reduced to a state of partial blindness within a few years. Meanwhile the political crisis with the mother country steadily worsened, and he found it more and more difficult to maintain that intricate web of loyalties—to family, friends, government, and profession—which had hitherto contributed to his advancement.

The structure of New York politics in the 1770s made it almost impossible for an ambitious man to remain uncommitted. As in other colonies, power was divided between rival family-centered oligarchies that waged interminable feuds, as fierce at times as those that once wracked the republics of Renaissance Italy. A Whig faction generally supported greater power for the elected assembly, which it controlled through a restricted franchise; while the Conservative opposition tended to work through the governor and his appointed council. But in New York, where the contending forces were evenly matched, the situation was more complex. Here the conservative De Lancey faction won control of the assembly after 1768, and secured for John Cruger the post of Speaker.

Yet it would be misleading to impose any rigid ideological patterns upon these amorphous clan groupings, which were held together principally by personal loyalties. On most questions of imperial policy, for example, the merchants who constituted the backbone of the De Lancey party shared the sentiments of their opponents. Thus the Crugers voiced little opposition when their kinsman Peter Van Schaack entered the law office of William Smith, Jr., founder of the Whig Club of New York and a most articulate critic of the transgressions both of Great Britain and the De Lanceys.

Under Smith's tutelage, Van Schaack imbibed a strong admiration for the constitutional techniques employed during the Stamp Act crisis of 1765—that "meritorious opposition," as he once termed it,[5] which combined dignified parliamentary protest with effective economic sanctions. The formula seemed foolproof so long as enlightened self-interest prevailed among politicians and the American masses did not get out of hand. Smith had been willing to use the Sons of Liberty and their rowdy followers in his campaign against the stamp tax, but since then the merchants of New York had grown fearful of social revolution and repudiated all connection with the mob. The vagaries of British policy, however, brought these strange bedfellows together once more in the stormy aftermath of the Boston Tea Party.

News of the closing of the port of Boston and other Coercive Acts of the British government reached New York on May 12, 1774. Four days later, at a mass meeting for which the propertied classes turned out in strength, a Committee of Fifty was elected to work out appropriate retaliatory measures, in concert with similar ad hoc groups in other colonies. Van Schaack attended the gathering and, as an acknowledged disciple of William Smith, easily won a place on the committee.

At the time his view of the American position was all that any patriot could demand. "The measures of government, so strongly indicating a determination to establish the supremacy of Parliament over these colonies, are truly alarming," he wrote on May 13 to his college classmate John Vardill, who had gone to England to be ordained an Episcopal minister:

When claims are so inconsistent, indeed, it would be chimerical to expect a decision of them upon the principles of reason merely. An appeal to the sword I am afraid is inevitable . . . An absolute exemption from Parliamentary taxation in every case whatever, is what the colonies will never recede from. Indeed, if that is not their *right*, they do not enjoy the privileges of British subjects. That it *is* their right, is a concession we cannot expect from England, until necessity shall compel them to it.[6]

Yet in his work on various subcommittees through the spring and summer of 1774, Van Schaack never looked beyond the mild expedients of nonimportation and nonexportation agreements to bring the home government to its knees. These, he assumed, would be the ultimate weapons employed by the intercolonial congress scheduled to convene at Philadelphia in September. The New York committee had been the first to propose this gathering, as a means of preventing more militant action by its own radical minority. The decorous Stamp Act Congress served as an obvious model, and with William Smith, Jr., acting as unofficial adviser to the committee, history seemed about to repeat itself.

When the group met to elect delegates to the First Continental Congress, however, the radicals took over the proceedings and forced the rejection of conservative nominees. Van Schaack walked out in protest at what he regarded as high-handed electioneering tactics and the refusal of the radicals to submit their choices to the general public for confirmation. But he continued to pin his hopes on the collective wisdom of the forthcoming congress, where he believed "cool and dispassionate" judgments would again prevail.[7]

Seldom have precedents been more misleading: in fact the radicals proved as effective at Philadelphia as they had been in New York. Instead of a diplomatic statement of grievances, the congress early adopted the inflammatory Suffolk Resolves, which bluntly denounced recent British measures and called upon the American people to arm themselves for the future. After such militant rumblings the endorsement of additional economic boycotts appeared anticlimactic. And direct appeals for relief to King George and the English people did little to soothe the ruffled feelings of Parliament. Van Schaack confessed his disappointment at these developments to John Vardill:

I dare say you have been equally surprised, instead of a Petition or Memorial to *Parliament*, to find a warm address to the *Nation* at large. There must be some fatal Distemper in the Body politick which can render such a Remedy justifiable or necessary—an Appeal to the People from the Supreme Power of the Empire seems to imply the actual Dissolution of the Government. This the Tyrany of Govt. may render necessary, but certain it is It was the Measure adopted by the infamous Parliament in the last Century with Respect to their Sovereign the unhappy Charles.[8]

Ironically, as his misgivings multiplied Van Schaack came to play an ever larger role in the revolutionary movement. In November 1774 he was unanimously reelected to a new Committee of Sixty formed to carry out the nonintercourse policies of the First Continental Congress. The committee enforced the boycott provisions of the Continental Association with a heavy hand, using the threat of mob violence to intimidate dissident New York merchants and consumers. But Van Schaack managed to ignore occasional broken windows and cracked heads in his zeal for the success of a full-scale program of economic retaliation. The association was "a peaceable mode of obtaining redress," he explained to his brother David. "It should have a fair trial."[9]

Events moved too swiftly for such temporizing, however. On April 23, 1775, New Yorkers learned of the first bloody skirmishes at Lexington and Concord, and the effect was instantaneous. By the following day, noted William Smith, Jr., in his diary, "The Populace had seized the City Arms after demanding the Key & the Magazine . . . and taken out 12 hundd-Weight of Powder & threatened to attack 406 Soldiers under the Command of Major Hamilton."[10] Moderate politicians felt the ground slipping from under them and hurriedly engineered a coalition Committee of 100 to keep the peace of the city. Van Schaack helped to draft the "Association" of this body, a policy statement which pledged that the committee would "adopt and endeavor to carry into execution whatever measures may be recommended by the Continental Congress, or resolved upon by our Provincial Convention, for the purpose of preserving our Constitution and opposing the execution of the several arbitrary and oppressive Acts of the British Parliament."[11] He was also named to a special Committee of Correspondence and Intelligence along with some of the leading radicals of New York.

The ambiguities of his position had now grown almost intolerable. While he sincerely believed in the justice of colonial claims, he hesitated to enforce them at the expense of open rebellion. Neither theory nor practice seemed to him to warrant such a dangerous expedient. A century earlier John Locke had argued that citizens had a duty to overthrow a tyrannical government that attempted to invade their inalienable natural rights to life, liberty, and property. With this formula Van Schaack the Whig had no quarrel. But Locke also made it clear that only genuinely oppressive acts of government could ever

justify a people in resorting to this ultimate "right of revolution." He wrote as an apologist for Parliamentary power and
vigorously asserted the need for a single paramount legislative
authority in every society.

With less equivocation history, too, seemed to confirm
Locke's cautionary pronouncements against untimely revolutions. From his classical studies Van Schaack derived a horror
of those civil wars that so often accompanied the collapse of
empires and left once proud nations defenseless against their
foreign enemies. Historical precedents of this sort strengthened
his regard for existing institutions, under which, to be sure, he
and his brothers had prospered.

But the greatest stumbling block to his full acceptance of the
patriot position lay in his continued faith in the good will of
British statesmen. Through his extensive correspondence with
Vardill and several other Americans resident in England,
including his brother-in-law Henry Cruger, Jr., Van Schaack
found it impossible to believe that the British were engaged in
any deliberate effort to subvert American liberties. Bumbling
bureaucrats they undoubtedly were, but not tyrants. His
opposition therefore lacked emotional fervor; while others
welcomed the first bloodshed as a signal for their abandonment
of any lingering doubts, Van Schaack continued to play the
judge, carefully weighing the advantages and disadvantages of
union as if he were dealing with a purely legal problem. Fragments of private memoranda reveal his tortuous introspection,
as well as his determination to maintain a balanced viewpoint:

If the line between authority and dependence has never been drawn,
will it not render the offence less heinous if the Parliment has trans-
gressed it? . . . I perceive that several of the acts exceed those
bounds, which, of right, ought to circumscribe the Parliament. But,
my difficulty arises from this, that taking the whole of the acts complained of together, they do not, I think, manifest a system of slavery, but may fairly be imputed to human frailty, and the difficulty
of the subject. Most of them seem to have sprung out of particular
occasions, and are unconnected with each other, and some of them
are precisely of the nature of other acts made before the commencement of his present Majesty's reign, which is the era when the supposed design of subjugating the colonies began . . . Our undefined
Rights while we actually *enjoyed* the greatest liberty was better than
the precarious Issue of a Contest for the ascertaining of them . . .
What is to be obtained by the Contest on our Part? The utmost is

perhaps 3 Pages in the Stat. Book, for in *Fact* we have been as happy as it is possible for us to be.[12]

These were hardly the sentiments of a revolutionary, yet Van Schaack shrank from an open rupture with the Committee of 100. His closest friends, such as Jay and Gouverneur Morris, still adhered to the patriot cause, and he dreaded their reaction to his apostasy. Besides, he could truthfully say that his sympathies in the abstract had not changed, although his conscience would not allow him to cooperate in any of the war-like measures which were sure to come from the Second Continental Congress.

As partisan pressures became unendurable in New York, Van Schaack looked elsewhere for relief from total commitment. The illness of his wife and two of his children, combined with his own failing eyesight, offered a plausible pretext for removal to the country. He sounded out his brothers, who responded to the idea with enthusiasm. "I by all means approve of your coming up here," wrote David Van Schaack from Kinderhook. "If anywhere, we shall preserve peace here. We are, and have been, very circumspect for a long while."[13] The prospect was too tempting to resist. In mid-May 1775 Peter abandoned his New York practice and set sail with his family for the peace and quiet of Kinderhook Village.

"I never expected to see such Days," wrote Elizabeth Van Schaack to her father a few months later.[14] There was no place, it seemed, where one could escape the absolute demands of war. When her husband attempted to resume his practice locally, a Committee of Correspondence from the neighboring town of Pittsfield, Massachusetts, promptly censured him for pressing the claims of "Tories" against "Friends of the Country." His letters from England were opened by order of the Provincial Congress, and whole passages were read publicly before that body at its sessions in Albany. Peter affected to treat such annoyances as a joke, but it was clear that they presaged more dangerous inquisitions to come.

In September 1776 the revolutionary government of New York set up a special committee to detect and defeat "all conspiracies, which may be formed in this State against the liberties of America." Members were clothed with broad authority to compel the attendance of witnesses and the production of records; to call out the militia to suppress insurrections; "to apprehend, secure or remove persons whom they might judge dangerous to the safety of the State"; to conduct their inquiries with maximum secrecy; "and, in general, to do every act and thing whatsoever necessary to execute the trust reposed in them."[15] Subcommittees at the county level acted as primary enforcement agencies and carried out their mandate with a vengeance. Soon unwary residents found themselves in serious trouble for criticizing the war effort or for refusing to accept depreciated Continental paper money at par value in the discharge of bonds and mortgages.

Kinderhook, already reputed to be "the place of Tories," came under the special scrutiny of the Albany County committee. Since the beginning of the war the village had been a haven for dissenters—both full-fledged British partisans and those who, like Van Schaack and his brothers, still preserved a precarious neutrality. Strong feelings divided the community and exploded at times into open violence. Tories, according to local gossip, burned the house of patriot John C. Wynkoop and murdered one Abraham Van Ness; in retaliation a gang of rebels from the surrounding countryside staged a midnight raid that sent prominent Kinderhook Loyalists scurrying for safety to nearby woods and caves. Such incidents further polarized public opinion and intensified the revolutionary drive against subversives. In Kinderhook even militia officers were not above suspicion, and the acknowledged influence of the Van Schaack family inevitably made its members prime targets for investigation.[16]

On December 30, 1776, Peter and his brother David were summoned before the Albany committee to answer charges that they had "long maintained an equivocal neutrality in the present struggles" and were "in general supposed unfriendly to the American cause."[17] No witnesses appeared against them, no incriminating facts were established, nor were any defenses admitted. The committee had only one question to ask: Did the suspects consider themselves to be subjects of the state of New York or of the king of Great Britain? If they declared themselves patriots and took a prescribed oath of allegiance, they might go free. Otherwise, as security risks, they incurred the penalty of banishment from the state for an indefinite period.

Both men declined to answer and were ordered to leave for Boston under guard within ten days. Peter appealed for additional time to settle his affairs, but his request was denied.

Angrily he protested to the full convention, then in session at Fishkill. How, he demanded, could an oath of allegiance be imposed before a regular government was even established? New York as yet had no constitution to secure the rights of its citizens. Unlimited power was vested in a single amorphous legislative body which operated through ad hoc committees. The evils of such a system needed no elaboration. Had not Montesquieu himself, the favorite philosopher of the Continental Congress, once declared that the union of legislative, executive, and judicial powers in the same body of men "puts an end to liberty"? A punitive test oath under existing circumstances violated the logic of the entire revolutionary argument.

As a close student of John Locke, Van Schaack fully appreciated the rationale behind the Declaration of Independence. The tyrannical acts of King George III, that document alleged, had dissolved the social compact and destroyed forever the constitutional ties that bound England to her American colonies. While Van Schaack disagreed with these premises, he drew from them some embarrassingly orthodox conclusions: "Upon this principle, I conceive that we were reduced to a state of nature, in which the powers of government reverted to the people, who had undoubtedly a right to establish any new form they thought proper; that portion of his natural liberty which each individual had before surrendered to the government, being now resumed, and to which no one in society could make any claim until he incorporated himself in it."

The disappearance of the old order, in other words, left each man free to determine his future allegiance for himself. He could not be forced to join any other political grouping without his express consent. Until stable societies again emerged from the chaos of war, the conscience of the individual took precedence over the demands of the majority. Hence the New York convention had no right to offer a Hobson's choice to those residing within the borders of the state:

> Should I deny subjection to Great Britain, it would not follow that I must necessarily be a member of the State of New York; on the contrary, I should still hold that I had a right, by the "immutable laws of nature," to choose any other State of which I would become a member. And, gentlemen, if you think me so dangerous a man, as that my liberty at home is incompatible with the public safety, I now claim it at your hands as my right, that you permit me to remove from your State into any other I may prefer, in which case, I reserve to myself the power of disposing of my property by sale or otherwise.

Van Schaack concluded with an eloquent denunciation of the arbitrary procedures employed by the committee on conspiracies. He had done nothing disloyal or illegal, he affirmed; his only offense lay in his allegedly dangerous opinions. But the board refused to allow him to explain these opinions or to confront his accusers. In the midst of a war for the preservation of individual rights, he demanded some respect for the principle of due process: "I expected at least that my informers and judges should have been under oath; and if a test was necessary, I expected it would be in consequence of some *general law*, putting all men who are in the same class in the same situation, and not that it should be left at the discretion of particular men to tender it to such individuals as malevolence, or party, family, or personal resentment should point out."[18]

These thrusts at the underside of the patriot cause apparently produced some effect, for the convention soon abandoned the use of a general test oath, admitting its impropriety in the absence of a regularly constituted government. Meanwhile administrative delays hampered a final determination of Van Schaack's case, and he was not recalled from exile until early April. He then appeared in person before the convention, which permitted him to return to his family in Kinderhook on his parole that he would "neither directly or indirectly do or say any thing to the prejudice of the American cause."[19]

Through the darkest days of the war he remained unmolested at home. The summer months brought a reign of terror to the valley, as Burgoyne, St. Leger, and their Indian allies launched a massive campaign in upper New York. Only in October, with the battle of Saratoga, did American prospects brighten. Thereafter the French government belatedly agreed to an alliance, and by the spring of 1778 there was open talk of peace.

For Van Schaack, however, such speculation was marred by private grief. His wife, Betsey, who had been in failing health for several years, went into a serious decline in March. Local doctors advised a change of scene, and she begged to be taken back to New York to see old friends once more and to receive the last rites of the Anglican church. Desperately her husband sought permission to make the trip. Governor George Clinton was sympathetic, but he refused to issue a pass while the city remained in British hands. Even the services of an outside specialist—an English doctor taken prisoner at Saratoga—were denied at the insistence of the Albany Committee of Safety.

Betsey Van Schaack died of consumption in April 1778 after hours of agonizing deathbed appeals that left her husband physically and emotionally shattered.

To complete his circle of woe, he now feared that he would soon be completely blind. No sight remained in his right eye, while in his left he detected a growing dimness. After much hesitation he resolved to consult a foreign oculist about the possibility of an operation, and obtained permission from Governor Clinton to travel to England for this purpose as soon as circumstances should permit.

The trip in fact took place ahead of schedule, thanks to the interference of the New York legislature. On June 30, 1778, that body enacted a measure, popularly known as the Banishing Act, which struck at everyone who still resisted the revolutionary ideology. Pursuant to its provisions, "commissioners of conspiracies" were required to tender a loyalty oath to "all persons of neutral and equivocal characters in this State, whom they shall think have influence sufficient to do mischief in it." The oath was ironclad in its demands for intellectual conformity to the patriot creed:

> I, A B, do solemnly, and without any mental reservation or equivocation whatever, swear and call God to witness; or if of the people called Quakers, affirm, that I do believe and acknowledge the State of *New-York* to be of right, a free and independent State. And that no authority or power can of right be exercised in or over the said State, but what is, or shall be granted by, or derived from the people thereof. *And further*, That as a good subject of the free and independent State of *New-York*, I will, to the best of my knowledge and ability, faithfully do my duty; and as I shall keep or disregard this oath, so help and deal with me Almighty God.

Nonjurors faced a battery of harsh mandatory punishments. They were to be removed behind enemy lines, and their perpetual banishment recorded in the office of the secretary of state; the lands they owned or might subsequently acquire in New York were forever subject to double taxation; and if they attempted to return to the state at any time, they might be prosecuted for the crime of "misprision of treason."[20]

Although several of the commissioners were personal friends of Van Schaack, they carried out their official duties with disconcerting rigor. A liberal reading of the preamble might have exempted him from the provisions of the act; so undoubtedly would a general knowledge of his prior negotiations with Clinton. But the governor was at Poughkeepsie, the commissioners at Albany, and Van Schaack fell victim to the communications gap between them—to that administrative inefficiency which, far more than deliberate malice, so often accounts for the arbitrariness of revolutionary regimes.

Summoned to Albany in mid-July, he refused the oath, and the penalties followed automatically. Before he could obtain a written statement from the governor he learned that all proceedings against him had been completed. The order for his banishment bore the signature of one of his own former law clerks, Leonard Gansevoort, Jr. To him Van Schaack responded with characteristic stoicism: "Leonard! you have signed my death warrant; but I appreciate your motives."[21]

From the decision of the board there was no appeal, and he began immediate preparations for his departure. The commissioners agreed that he might sell any part of his estate and take the proceeds with him. But he chose to leave the bulk of his property in the hands of a New York attorney, as trustee for himself and his three young children. These he resolved should not share his punishment but should continue to be raised as American citizens under the protection of various relatives and friends.

In defense of his own position he drew up a private memorandum in which he reexamined the entire loyalty issue. Again he distinguished between conduct and belief, arguing that the state might legitimately prohibit treasonable acts but had no right to coerce private opinions. The "good of society" alone could justify "acts of severity towards individuals," he maintained, and the public derived little benefit from compulsory oath taking: "The tendering of an oath, involving in it certain speculative principles, and matters of opinion in a contested question, under the penalty of banishment and confiscation of property, is a severe attack upon the weakness of human nature, and lays a strong temptation for perjury."

Unscrupulous men would swear as a matter of course, while even an honest fellow, to save his family from ruin, might end by disavowing his real principles. In the latter case, Van Schaack contended, the oath would not be binding in conscience, and one who attempted to fulfill its requirements while believing them to be unlawful would compound his moral guilt.

The loyal citizen, on the other hand, incurred no added

obligation to the state through *his* oath, which at most confirmed an existing commitment. Nor could the New York legislature claim any overriding "state necessity" for its program.
Dissenters no longer posed any serious danger to the conduct of
the war, which many well-informed sources predicted would
soon be over. Yet the lawmakers chose this moment to
inaugurate their most drastic witch-hunt, which threatened
alike the integrity of the individual and the entire liberal creed:

> We are called before a board for punishing conspirators, when we
> are acknowledged to be no conspirators; before a board unknown
> to the constitution of this State, to be condemned without a trial,
> and to be punished without a crime. The utmost extent of all that is
> alleged, amounts to no more than a difference in opinion, and that
> in a case wherein I have a right, and by the eternal laws of God am
> bound, to exercise my private judgment, and wherein I should vio-
> late the most sacred obligations if I acted against the light of my
> own conviction.

More humane security measures were surely possible. Even a
modified oath, relating solely to actions, would be acceptable,
Van Schaack suggested. He pointed to the guidelines established
for religious dissenters by the state constitution. Article 38
guaranteed the "free exercise and enjoyment of all religious
professions without discrimination" and held minority groups
liable only for licentious acts or practices inconsistent with the
safety of the state. Such toleration, he insisted, might safely be
extended to political heretics as well. Indeed, during civil wars
all questions of political orthodoxy had to await a final determination on the battlefield. Until then, honest men might differ
in their principles and each side claim to be right. So long as a
man remained neutral in practice, therefore, he should not be
punished for errors of judgment. Still less should his family suffer for his ideological sins through a vindictive confiscation
policy.[22]

These views, which Van Schaack reiterated in his personal
correspondence, found an echo among moderates in the patriot
camp. His old friends—now occupying influential posts in the
revolutionary government—assured him of their continued
regard and did what they could to cushion the impact of his
approaching exile. Theodore Sedgwick, one of the leading
Whigs of western Massachusetts, went furthest in his atten-
tions by proposing to take charge of Van Schaack's eldest boy,

twelve-year-old Harry, and to raise him as his own son. In a remarkable letter that points up the insufficiency of conventional Whig-Tory stereotypes, Sedgwick went on to outline his own convictions:

> It is with extreme pleasure I reflect, that during the *turbulency* of the times, I have preserved entire my friendship and esteem for the *worthy*, who have been opposed to me in their political creed; nor do I imagine that it is possible to select from the *aggregate* of human follies and bigotry, a more sure and incontestable evidence of the weakness of head and depravity of heart, than that narrow and confined policy, which has for its end a uniformity of opinions, whether political or religious. I wish my country happy, great, and flourishing; I wish her independent; but that she may be happy under the last, it is necessary that she become wise, virtuous, and tolerant. There is one way most certainly to know whether a state is or is not actuated by a spirit of freedom: let the constitution be violated, in the person of a subject obnoxious to popular resentment, or let his happiness be in any way sported with; if *this* gratifies popular, malignant malice, and no murmurings or disturbances ensue, it is a sure indication that not only the flame, but that every spark of liberty is extinct.[23]

In mid-August 1778 Van Schaack said his last farewells to family and friends at Kinderhook and embarked for New York, there to take ship for England. Like the typical Tory refugee of the war years, he arrived full of admiration for the culture and institutions of the mother country, but a closer acquaintance left him disillusioned. Despite six years of residence in the British Isles he remained invincibly American in his outlook—a product of the Puritan ethic combined with legal rationalism.

Almost from the moment he landed at Cork, he found himself confronted by glaring social inequalities that he did not like. The extremes of wealth and poverty—of luxury and vice—which he subsequently witnessed at London further shocked his middle-class sensibilities. "Amusement and dissipation predominate to excess," he complained, "and the ancient spirit of the country, like the manly virtues of Rome, seems to have dwindled into Italian virtu."[24]

Only in the provinces did he discover something of that more open and robust quality of life he had known in America. The manners of the "principal families" of New York corresponded to those of the English townspeople, he noted in his diary, while

New England farmers were almost indistinguishable from their country cousins across the Atlantic. Even so, the pretensions of the squirearchy disturbed him, and he positively shuddered at the sensuousness of some of the paintings and sculpture on display in manorial halls. Admittedly, he remarked, they were faithful reproductions of nature and carried artistic technique to a degree of perfection he had not thought possible: "It may be doubted, however, whether there is not in some of them rather too much of *nature*, not to interfere a little with the rules of decency, for it will be difficult to view those strong resemblances with an eye abstracted altogether from the objects in nature which they imitate; and unless, on those occasions, we can resume the purity and innocence of Eden, a fig leaf at least ought not to be dispensed with." Decadence in the arts, like venality in government, seemed but one more proof of a general "licentiousness of manners" among the English people.[25]

In London, where he spent most of his time, Van Schaack regularly attended the parliamentary debates, especially those relating to the war. Neither the politicians nor their speeches impressed him. Most, he decided, were second- or third-rate party hacks, and even the few genuine orators, such as Burke and Fox, were too "vehement" and lacking in dignity. Under a hopelessly corrupt electoral system "men of merit" from the middle class stood no chance of winning office, which went instead to the proprietors of "venal boroughs, which are bought and sold like the ancient villeins." Ministers and their subservient majorities seemed willing to embrace the most contradictory policies to retain power, and Van Schaack looked in vain for that disinterested leadership in which he had once believed.[26]

The shabbiness of parliamentary schemes became more apparent as British military efforts in the colonies flagged. Returning commanders like Sir William Howe blamed their defeat on a united and resolute American population and had special words of censure for the poor support they had received from professed Loyalists. Committees of inquiry accepted these explanations, to the anger of all political refugees. Van Schaack in retaliation drew up a long and circumstantial account of Howe's tactical blunders for the London papers. He charged that the war had never been prosecuted with zeal or efficiency, and praised the Loyalists for their steady adherence to principle.[27] By the summer of 1779, convinced that no "rational hope of success" remained for British arms, he looked forward with confidence to the early termination of hostilities. "The American contest certainly is at an end with respect to the original object of it," he observed. "This is given up. There seems to be no idea of bringing her back to submission, and the only plan is to prevent her being an accession to France."[28] But again the ministry tacked, adopting a new hard line that threatened, in Van Schaack's eyes, to convert the struggle into a naked war of aggression.

A fresh crisis of conscience ensued in which he reexamined the justice of the war with the same deliberateness he had employed at its inception—and with comparable results. As he had once argued himself out of commitment to the Revolution, he now repudiated his allegiance to the Establishment: "I do not think an *American* bound to promote the views of Great Britain, when they are directed only to weaken, to cripple America, and not to recover her; or when that recovery is only hoped for, from the ruin and destruction, by conflagration, pestilence and famine, of America." To his English friends, who found these refinements somewhat bewildering, he protested that he had never deviated in his principles. The difficulty, as always, lay in applying fixed principles to a changing set of facts: "A man forming his idea of the rectitude of a government from what he knows at the time, may change it in consequence of facts coming afterwards to his knowledge, without impeachment of his firmness, or the rectitude of his principles, for what can we reason from but what we *know*?"[29]

In America Van Schaack had steadfastly rejected rumors of a parliamentary conspiracy against the colonies; in London he soon discovered one. After a "fair investigation" he concluded that British statesmen had never been sincere in their professions of principle; that from the beginning they had plotted to extort a "substantial, solid revenue" from the colonies; that they had backed down only when forced to; that their compromises were intentionally couched in equivocal terms, so that they might retract them when occasion offered; and that "the real design was to enhance the influence of the Crown, by multiplying officers dependent on it." If the American leaders had rushed into war too quickly, without exhausting all possible avenues of nonviolence, their British counterparts had been equally guilty, for they had long courted conflict through their obsessive efforts to establish in the colonies the same system of corruption that prevailed in England. A countervailing policy might have developed if the British constitution had remained a vital force; but, Van Schaack asserted, "it is clear to me that it has no longer an existence." The national character had become "so depraved" that Englishmen lacked the spirit to rescue their government from its destructive course.[30]

Still less could the English appreciate the painful moral dilemma in which a revolutionary crisis placed the conscientious citizen: "Those who have submitted to the New Govts. are here not only excused but justified and I find the Doctrine of Allegiance is explained away so as to make it only a Tye while it remains *convenient*, a Tye of Interest not of Duty. Hudibras (not his *Author*) is become the very standard of political Orthodoxy & Power is contended to be the only Rule & Measure of Right."[31]

Under such circumstances Van Schaack considered his own political obligations "dissolved," and formally renouncing his British allegiance proclaimed himself henceforth a "citizen of the world."[32] A curious stance for one who, several years earlier, had trembled at the very idea of anarchy! Yet his intellectual detachment was no pose, as his wartime correspondence amply demonstrates. "I cannot help the defects of my understanding," he declared, "but I can subdue the errors of my heart, in which revenge never had a place."[33] Although banished forever from his native state, he never ceased to regard himself as de facto an American citizen. While he actively aided his fellow exiles in their efforts to obtain reparations from the British government, he claimed none for himself, requesting only a small sum (sixty pounds per year) to help defray his immediate expenses. This modest allowance, coupled with scattered legal fees, provided him with the necessities of life. During the last years of the war he supplemented his income in a more regular fashion by acting as executor of the estate of his father-in-law, Henry Cruger, Sr., who died at Bristol in 1780, leaving behind considerable assets on both sides of the Atlantic. Unlike most upper-class refugees, Van Schaack bore his reduced circumstances with equanimity and early announced his intention of returning to America at the close of the war, regardless of which side won.[34]

Meanwhile he continued to urge moderation upon his relatives and friends overseas. "I beseech you not to indulge any resentment for what I have suffered in the unhappy civil wars which have distracted our country," he wrote to his son Harry.

In such scenes, distress is a common lot. But I wish you to be well acquainted with the origin and history of this great contest, which will make an era not only in the annals of our own country, but of Europe, and perhaps, in its consequences, of every quarter of the globe. Study it therefore attentively; not with the heat of a bigot, but dispassionately, like a philosopher. Suffer not yourself to be warped even by my conduct or sentiments relative to it. Hear all, — judge for yourself.[35]

As the tempo of peace negotiations quickened, Van Schaack sought to counteract anti-American propaganda in London. His transatlantic correspondents supplied him with optimistic reports of postrevolutionary economic and political conditions which he retailed at private parties and occasionally in the public press. Soon he was promoting emigration to the former colonies and fretting over the weakness of the Confederation Congress. He longed to see his children again and would willingly have sailed for New York even before the articles of peace were formally ratified. "Power has no such charms to me as to make me care much who possesses it," he assured his brother Henry. "For my part . . . I shall be as good a subject of the new government as I ever was of the old."[36] Unfortunately, in real life the problem of commitment was charged with an emotionalism that no reading of Locke, however authoritative, could convey. Van Schaack had yet to experience the full consequences of his alienation from the majority will. For two more years he dallied in London, waiting for popular passions to subside, while the Whig elite of New York politics maneuvered behind the scenes to help him recover his lost citizenship.

"Having been very well assured that the conduct of Peter Van Schaack (and others) had been perfectly unexceptional and that they had not associated with the abominable Tory Club of London, I received and returned their visits," noted circumspect John Jay in 1783. The rapprochement occurred while Jay was in Europe serving on the American peace commission. He promised to do all that he could to facilitate Van Schaack's return to his homeland, observing that only "the *faithless and the cruel*" deserved permanent exile. At the same time Jay warned against any precipitate action: "There is a tide in all human affairs, and while it runs too hard against us to be stemmed, it would be imprudent to weigh anchor."[37]

The personal risks in Van Schaack's case remained critical, despite the benevolent provisions of the Treaty of Paris. That document barred any further prosecution of Loyalists and pledged that Congress would "earnestly recommend" to the various state legislatures a full restoration of Loyalist rights and properties. Arguably, however, sentence had already been passed on Van Schaack under the Banishing Act, and he could expect to be treated as a convicted criminal if he returned.[38]

Indeed, the New York legislature seemed bent on vengeance, regardless of what the diplomats had agreed. On May 12, 1784, four months after the formal ratification of the peace treaty, an act "to preserve the freedom and independence" of the state was passed, disfranchising all persons who had not been friendly to the Revolution. An earlier law, which had decimated the old New York bar by requiring a stringent loyalty oath of all practitioners, likewise remained in effect. Even without a doubtful criminal charge hanging over him, therefore, Van Schaack could not hope to vote, hold office, or practice his profession under the postrevolutionary government.[39] But he refused to give up his plans for repatriation or to join the Loyalist exodus to Canada, where influential acquaintances assured him of an appointment to high executive or judicial office. "For a moment I am captivated with these suggestions," he confessed, "but my heart still turns to my friends and connections."[40] At last, in 1785, his patience was rewarded. Jay and Egbert Benson, after lengthy consultations with Governor Clinton, Chief Justice Richard Morris, and others, concluded that the danger of personal reprisals against Van Schaack had all but disappeared. He accordingly sailed from Falmouth in June, arriving in New York on July 20, after an exile of nearly seven years.

Jay boarded the ship as soon as it anchored in the harbor and personally escorted Van Schaack to a meeting with the governor and other dignitaries, at which further assurances of his personal safety were presumably given. These backstage negotiations received official sanction the following year when a new legislature, after repealing the attorney's test oath and other discriminatory measures, specifically enacted "that . . . Peter Van Schaack, Richard Bartlett, Theophilus Nelson, and Zebulon Walbridge, shall be, and they are hereby respectively restored to all their rights, privileges and immunities, as citizens of this State, from and after such time as the said persons respectively shall in any court of record of this State take the oath of abjuration and allegiance prescribed by law, any thing in any former law contained to the contrary thereof notwithstanding."[41] In April 1786 Van Schaack appeared before the supreme court in Manhattan's city hall, swore to uphold the state government, and was readmitted to the bar. "I am happy among my associates, who treat me with great politeness and attention," he reported to his son Harry,[42] and doubtless he could have resumed the threads of his earlier career with little effort. His revised statutes continued in force under the new state constitution, while New York society stood ready to lionize the man who had known Samuel Johnson, Mrs. Siddons, Lord Mansfield, and other transatlantic celebrities. But Van Schaack turned his back on the metropolis to devote himself to a country practice in Kinderhook.

His failing eyesight no doubt influenced his decision, although it was not a crucial factor. During the six years in which he had consulted European specialists, he had repeatedly refused an operation, fearing that it might result in total blindness. His left eye, which he once believed to be as permanently damaged as the right, seems rather to have improved somewhat after an initial crisis in 1780. At any rate, his docket books at Kinderhook reveal that he engaged in active legal practice from 1786 to 1817. In the peak period between 1789 and 1805 he averaged thirty-five cases a year,[43] a practice that he might have carried on quite as well in New York had he desired it.

Probably his habitual shyness, intensified by the embarrassment of exile, prompted him most strongly toward semiretirement. He had never felt at ease in a crowd; his modest experience as a public figure during the early stages of the Revolution could scarcely be called satisfactory, and while convinced of his own integrity, he shrank from having his wartime principles impugned by strangers. "I trust I shall be allowed to begin *de novo*, and to be tested by my *future* conduct, without a retrospect to what is past," he declared. The chances of this were far better in Kinderhook, where people knew and respected him regardless of his political views. He soon established himself in a "pretty little box" next to the mansion of his brother David, on the main street of the village. There he brought a second wife—Elizabeth Van Alen, the daughter of a local farmer—and settled down to the life of a country gentleman: "building, farming, lawyering," as he happily described it.[44]

His contacts with the outside world remained strong, nonetheless. In the early years lawyers and judges regularly sought his advice on proposed innovations in the legal institutions of the state. Cumbersome rules of British practice seemed ill suited to the simpler needs of an agrarian republic, but jurists hesitated to tamper with traditional common-law forms. Since Van Schaack had observed the courts of Westminster Hall in practical operation, his suggestions carried much weight. And he invariably championed the cause of legal reform.

As a refugee in London he had been sadly disappointed at the caliber of the English bench and bar: "I found arguments arose about questions not of the greatest nicety; and the length of those arguments and the hesitation of the judges, convinced me that *they* had exaggerated who taught me to expect . . . something superior to what I could conceive from the abilities of my own countrymen."[45] Now he prodded those countrymen at every opportunity to a greater display of self-reliance. In a typical exchange he warned Judge Robert Yates of the New York Supreme Court against using unfamiliar British terms in the newly created court of exchequer:

> I will cheerfully write to England if you think it necessary, which, however, I do *not*. Their cobweb niceties and refinements do not, in my opinion, suit us. In old countries, they are unavoidable to counteract those evasions and subterfuges to which we are as yet strangers. Like the ceremonial laws of the Jews, they are punishments for sins we are not yet contaminated with. I would as soon suppose the flannels and crutches of a gouty debauchee to be necessary for a robust American, or the appendages of an old dowager's toilette ornamental to the bloom of nineteen, as that the complex subtleties of their practice would be proper for the simplicity of our courts. Let us not attempt to transplant the tree; but let the trunk grow out of our own soil, and if we can get a few foreign grafts, suited to that and to our climate, it is, I think, all we want.[46]

Through his practice in Albany and Columbia counties Van Schaack came to know almost all the important lawyers who pleaded in the courts of eastern New York between 1786 and 1830. His own forte was real estate law, a field he had begun to mine prior to the Revolution. As his records indicate, he represented the local landlords in a variety of actions against tenants and debtors: ejectment and trespass suits; debt, covenant, and partition proceedings; and probate matters. Despite his stiffness before juries he proved so successful at trial work that he enjoyed in time a reputation as the Great Lawyer of his area. Even so demanding a critic as Alexander Hamilton expressed admiration for his dispassionate style and closely reasoned arguments.

But Van Schaack exerted his greatest influence as a lawyer through the school that he set up in his home in 1786. There he trained over two generations of New York practitioners, including the sons of such notables as Rufus King, Chancellor James Kent, Theodore Sedgwick, William W. Van Ness, and Ambrose Spencer. While Kinderhook never attained the prestige of Litchfield, Connecticut, where Judge Tapping Reeve had established the first private American law school two years earlier, Van Schaack left a durable imprint upon the jurisprudence of his own state. From 1786 until he gave up teaching in 1828 (at the age of eighty-one) he was never without one or more students; nearly a hundred young men in all clerked for him, attended his lectures, and carried his political conservatism into the age of Andrew Jackson.

That he was a dedicated teacher appears incontestable. Even before the Revolution he had trained his clerks in a much more systematic fashion than any of his fellow practitioners deemed necessary, or he himself had enjoyed, under the traditional apprenticeship system. "Believe me," he observed in 1769, looking back over his own clerkship experience, "I know not above one or two [lawyers] in town that do tolerable justice to their clerks. For my part, how many hours have I hunted, how many books turned up for what three minutes of explanation from any tolerable lawyer would have made evident to me! It is in vain to put a law book into the hands of a lad without explaining difficulties to him as he goes along."[47]

When the first American edition of Blackstone's *Commentaries* appeared in 1771, Van Schaack hailed it as a brilliant compendium of common-law principles and ever afterward recommended it enthusiastically to beginning students. But he directed his own teaching primarily toward the practical application of those principles in an American setting. Method was his obsession, and former students gratefully acknowledged that the most important lesson they had learned from him was how to study. For his classes at Kinderhook he prepared an "Analysis of the Practice of the Supreme Court," which traced the progress of a typical case, step by step—a schematic presentation that he supplemented with illustrative details drawn from his own professional experience. The utilitarianism of the approach has a distinctly modern ring, while the problems that Van Schaack propounded were likewise designed to produce accomplished technicians: "Suppose a person inclined to purchase a farm in the County of Westchester was to give you a fee for your advice, how he should find out, whether there were any incumbrances upon the land. What instructions would you give him?"[48]

The students he taught came from middle- or upper-middle-class backgrounds. Although Van Schaack's son and biographer asserts that he took in many poor clerks without compensation, there is no evidence that he ever accepted a genuine charity case. His clerkship accounts for the years 1801 through 1814 indicate that the only pupils who paid no fees were the sons of specially favored friends, such as Theodore Sedgwick. Most of the others paid a flat sum of $250 for presumably three years of clerkship and tuition. If they remained at Kinderhook a shorter time, the figure was scaled down accordingly, though never below a minimum of $50. By 1809 Peter's real and personal estate was valued for tax purposes at £3,100—a figure that placed him among the wealthiest 2 percent of the community's property owners. The enhanced socioeconomic status that he enjoyed in the new nation doubtless contributed in no small way to the intense political partisanship of his later years.[49]

"I returned to my country with a fixed determination to keep out of public life," he remarked with some unction in 1789. "I am persuaded that as a private citizen I can do more good than I could do in any official character."[50] To the end of his life he held himself aloof from the rough and tumble of party battles, preferring to act as backstairs strategist and informal adviser to his less fastidious political friends. The role enabled him to preserve his own principles untarnished without sacrificing entirely the fierce joys of partisan infighting.

Like Jay, Morris, and other conservative Whigs, Van Schaack cherished a passion for order, in politics as in law. Always a "friend to government," he, too, had once dreamed of a powerful American parliament directing the destinies of the New World within a Commonwealth framework. That the Revolution failed to produce such an institution early filled him with apprehension. "The United States will be a rope of sand, if some controlling, superintending power is not maintained," he complained in 1783,[51] and a few months after he returned to Kinderhook his worst fears seemed about to be realized, with the outbreak of Shays's Rebellion. This abortive uprising of debt-ridden farmers in western Massachusetts threatened for a time the lives and property of the creditor classes of the area, in which the Van Schaack family had large landholdings. The rebels took over the courthouses in several towns, prevented the judges from sitting to hear foreclosure suits, and, in a bid for greater power, launched a large-scale attack upon the poorly defended United States arsenal at Springfield. Ultimately the state militia under General Benjamin Lincoln restored order, but not before many insurgents fled across the border into neighboring New York.

To prevent further flare-ups from that quarter, General Lincoln appealed to Van Schaack to mediate with the fugitives in his neighborhood, and promise them amnesty if they would put down their arms and return to their former allegiance. Van Schaack willingly complied—helping to scotch a rising of the masses could not have been an uncongenial assignment for him—but he feared the true crisis of authority was yet to come, in the absence of a strong central government. Many other old-line Whigs shared these forebodings, which lent a greater urgency to the deliberations of the impending federal convention in Philadelphia. Summoned to correct the deficiencies of the existing Articles of Confederation, the delegates resolved instead to rear a "more perfect Union" on the ruins of the old revolutionary settlement. The constitution they drafted conferred broad coercive powers on an enlarged national government and set up an elaborate system of checks and balances to thwart any direct expression of the popular will.

Van Schaack was delighted with the conservatism of the document and campaigned actively for its ratification in Columbia County. "A frame of government held out to the people at large for discussion, is a phenomenon in political annals," he informed his young nephew Harry Walton. "You cannot conceive what agitation it has occasioned . . . I have mounted the rostrum several times, and harangued the multitude on law, government and politics." For the *Hudson Weekly Gazette* he wrote a series of articles in defense of the Constitution which, according to contemporaries, rivaled the productions of his friends Jay and Hamilton in lucidity and persuasiveness. He even ventured, for the one and only time since the

Revolution, to enter the political lists himself, seeking election as a delegate to the ratifying convention at Poughkeepsie. But anti-Federalist sentiment ran strong in his district and he was soundly beaten at the polls. The experience confirmed his already dim view of mass political behavior: "The popular tide was against us, that is, (to be sure,) against what was *right* and *good.*"[52]

Not even the subsequent adoption of the Constitution and the inauguration of President George Washington restored his faith in a virtuous electorate. Many malcontents, he predicted, would seek to obstruct the new administration and prevent its enjoying a "fair and liberal" trial. As a full-fledged opposition party did in fact develop in response to the French Revolutionary crisis and Hamilton's domestic program, Van Schaack's anxieties multiplied. "Surely," he declaimed to his brother-in-law in 1796, "a systematic Opposition to a Government or an Administration, constituted by the People or emanating from them, must be political Heresy, or all the Ideas of Benefit from Union [and] Concord must be rejected, as ancient Prejudices which ought to vanish before the Light of the 'new order of Things.' "[53]

Yet he had not always set such a high value on the virtues of "Union" and "Concord." As an aspiring youngster in prerevolutionary New York, he had found much to admire in a two-party system. Especially when the contending groups were equally matched, he then wrote, they lent stability to the state and prevented political abuses; for, "where each Party continues formidable to the other & upon an equal Footing neither will dare to attempt because neither *can* oppress."[54] In those early days, to be sure, the parties were balanced socially as well as politically. Gentlemen vied for office with their peers; wealth and talent were the passports to power; and the lower classes deferred to their natural leaders. Now the pretensions of an aristocratic leadership were being challenged, even at the village level. Van Schaack and the "high-toned" Federalists felt their influence slipping away into the hands of pothouse politicians who did not scruple to beg for votes from an ever expanding electorate. Too proud to bend and too stubborn to yield, the old elite fought a savage rear guard action to maintain their prerogatives against what seemed to them a massive conspiracy to subvert the principles of "true" republicanism.

The paranoid style of Federalist politics is quite evident in the most remarkable of Van Schaack's later writings, an essay entitled "Political Parties" that he prepared, probably for the newspapers, in the 1790s. Here, besides a talent for vituperation, he displayed a surprising willingness to mythologize the American Revolution, in defiance of his own experience. The Jeffersonians, he charged, were trying to stigmatize their Federalist opponents as "Tories" when in fact the Federalists were the only genuine heirs of a monolithic Whig tradition:

> "Whoever is not for us, is against us," was the current Language & acknowledged Standard of Whigism & Toryism in *Seventy five*. Let the Jacobin, the Antifederalist, the Democrat, & the exclusive Republican undergo a little self Examination, by this Criterion. It will be a wholesome discipline, but it must be performed without Evasion, or secret Reservation. Let him not deceive himself by saying, that he is for his Country, but opposed to its Government, or that he is for the Government, but opposed to its Administration, or that being opposed to all he is still a Republican. Let him, if he should lay claim to the character of a Whig, recollect that the Spirit of Seventy Six was, not to excite disunion, but *"unite or die"*; not to scatter pitiful suspicions & base Jealousies, but to inculcate a manly and even unbounded Confidence in those whom the People had chosen to act for them; not to resist or contravene, but to pay implicit obedience to the Acts & even Recommendations of Congress; not like Frenchmen, capriciously to raise & pull down, but like Americans steadily to support their tried & approved Servants, their Washington, their Adams, Jay &c.
> If the Tory was criminal for dissenting from the Measures of Congress, while the Country was in a State of Revolution, what must be the Man, who professing to have been a Whig opposes the Measures of Congress, after the object of the Revolution has been fully accomplished. If it was criminal not to join in rearing the Fabric of our Independence, what must he be, who claiming the Merit of wresting it from Britain, now claims the Right of prostrating it at the Feet of France.[55]

Effective as propaganda, the piece offers an ironic commentary on the durability of political dissent. Once the champion of intellectual heresy, Van Schaack ended by becoming a zealous partisan of the "old Washington school." He strongly supported the repressive Alien and Sedition Acts, agreeing with the sentiment of his friend Loring Andrews, editor of the Stockbridge, Massachusetts, *Western Star*: "Those infernal engines of deception, the antifederalist papers, ought to be quelled."[56]

From a narrowly logical viewpoint, of course (and Van Schaack was ever the casuist in interpreting his own motives), there was no necessary inconsistency between witch-hunting and a healthy regard for individual rights. Van Schaack had always drawn a line between privately held beliefs and any attempt to act upon them. The state, he argued, might never coerce the individual conscience through such devices as loyalty oaths, but it had a duty to protect itself against all subversive actions—including, it now appeared, the publication of dissenting literature. Only on the emotional side did his position lack consistency, for his earlier spirit of toleration and respect for contrary opinions had conspicuously evaporated by the end of the century.

And to little avail, as matters turned out. The Federalists failed to silence their opponents or to find any road back to the structured society of prewar days. Instead, Van Schaack and his circle, like so many others of the revolutionary generation, lingered like revenants in a world whose more egalitarian values they neither shared nor appreciated. For the last ten years of his life the Great Lawyer was totally blind and seldom left his home, except on election days, when he tottered to the polls to vote against all democratic candidates. Martin Van Buren was his special bête noire, although the two men somehow managed to remain personal friends despite their irreconcilable ideological differences. ("In respect to the latter we never made an approach toward accord," Van Buren commented wryly in his *Autobiography*.) Nevertheless, when Van Schaack lay dying he made a special point of sending for his Democratic neighbor to bid him a last farewell. Van Buren, who had just returned from a diplomatic mission to London for President Andrew Jackson, hurried over to the old lawyer's bedside for what proved to be a poignant leave taking:

I found [Van Schaack] lying upon a temporary bed in his library, where he desired to die, and where I had so often seen him in the full possession and exercise of his powerful mental faculties. As soon as I entered, he had himself raised in his bed, extended his hand to me, and expressed his satisfaction at seeing me. He said he was going through his last change, and upon my expressing a hope that such might not prove to be the case, he stopped me, and said "No!" he had lived out the full measure of his days, and could not be too thankful that his mental faculties had been preserved till his last moments. It so happened that I had made myself familiar with the place of his residence during his exile in London, and he listened with interest to my description of its present condition. He spoke kindly and considerately of the relations that had existed between us, and I was struck with the evident desire to make the civil things his gentlemanly disposition induced him to say conform strictly to the fact without reviving unpleasant recollections. In bidding me farewell forever he said: "I am happy, Sir, to think we have always been——" *friends* he seemed about to add, but pausing a moment he continued—*"that you have always come to see me when you visited Kinderhook."*[57]

A purist to the end, Peter Van Schaack breathed his last on September 27, 1832. He had reached the age of eighty-five and wrestled with many problems that cast a shadow across succeeding generations of American lawyers. One in particular was suggested by that final confrontation between the Little Magician and the Old Roman. Given a choice between public life and private service to clients, where did one's paramount professional duty lie? Later practitioners continued to argue the question, as they strove with varying success to reconcile their skills with the demands of a democratic society.

Downfall to Monarchy,
And Aristocracy;
    Let Man be free!
Repeat it o'er and o'er,
Let ev'ry voice encore—
Tyrants shall rule no more,
    Man shall be free!
"To Liberty," *Philadelphia Minerva* (1795)

2   Antilawyer Sentiment in the Early Republic

Utopianism has been a recurrent theme in American history since the days of the earliest explorers. The age of discovery implied an age of faith as well for many Europeans, who looked to the West for escape from the burdensome restraints of a crumbling feudal order. Columbus himself best expressed the millennial yearnings of his time when he wrote of his epic voyages: "God made me the messenger of the new heaven and new earth, of which he spoke in the Apocalypse of St. John . . . and He showed me the spot where to find it."[1] The vision of an Edenic life attainable in the transatlantic wilderness assumed many forms in the centuries that followed, but it was generally tied to the ideal of a voluntary, self-regulating society. Lawyers found little place in such thinking; at best they were tolerated as a necessary evil. The American Revolution sharpened the unresolved tensions between the millennial spirit and the common law, and led to an explosive encounter between lawyers and populace in some states, as republican pamphleteers called for a social order that would not require an organized bar.

The legal profession had come of age in most colonies by the middle of the eighteenth century. Lawyers shared political power with mercantile and landed elites; study in a law office (or, for the favored few, in the English Inns of Court) had become an established norm for practitioners; courts and some local bar associations, as in New York, helped to control admission standards and internal police. Most important of all, as John R. Aiken has argued, the "Common Law image of man" had replaced earlier utopian views for the average citizen.[2]

Such a symbolic shift of values was almost a precondition to the rise of a professional bar in America. The English settlers who made up the bulk of the colonial population in the seventeenth century often brought with them an intense dislike for the class-conscious laws of their homeland, and a determination to set up more equitable modes of social control in the wilderness. Two legendary systems provided them with alternative models to a common-law form of government: one was embodied in the egalitarian golden age described by Ovid and other ancient writers; the other was found in the biblical commonwealths of the Old Testament. Incompatible in their underlying philosophies, both of these constructs at least envisaged societies in which lawyers would play no meaningful role.

The classical golden age suggested a state of nature, in which men lived together in democratic simplicity, sharing in common the fruits of a bounteous earth. Government and laws did not exist; men were wise and good and settled all quarrrels with brotherly kindness. During the Middle Ages Ovid's myth became fused with the Christian concept of a Garden of Eden, but the materialistic elements of the tale continued to predominate. Men still dreamed of a land of plenty—an unspoiled natural paradise somewhere in the West—where peace and justice would reign and simple arbitration procedures would settle all the problems of an innocent rural population.

Far more sophisticated were the religious utopias of Isaiah and Jeremiah. Here law rather than anarchy prevailed—a law that reflected the strict moral standards which Jehovah demanded of his people. Patriarchal judges administered the system, hearing claimants in person and settling disputes according to ethical considerations. Since the laws were required to be read repeatedly "before all Israel in their hearing," every man knew his rights and had little need for hired lawyers, whom the Scriptures denounced as artful liars and hypocrites.

The American colonists, in framing their early codes and statutes, borrowed freely from both of these societal patterns. They often relied upon compulsory arbitration and "khadi justice" (to borrow Max Weber's phrase) to settle their controversies. Professional lawyers were actively discouraged—either by express prohibition or, more frequently, by provisions allowing a relative or friend of a litigant to appear for him as an "attorney-in-fact." Lay judges attempted to render substantial justice to both parties, regardless of common-law niceties. They avoided unnecessary formality, employing straightforward inquisitorial methods to uncover the moral factors involved in each case. Such rough-and-ready tactics, which mirrored the practices of certain English local courts, worked well enough so long as communities remained small and economically self-contained. Everyman might safely act as his own lawyer while society stood ready to protect his moral as well as his legal rights. The utopian image of man—stressing his corporate nature, subordinating his total behavior to community norms, and judging his transgressions by absolute moral standards—provided an essential foundation for early American jurisprudence.

By the end of the seventeenth century, however, this image was waning. The increased complexity of land and mercantile transactions, coupled with the demands of foreign trade and investment, made necessary a degree of precision and predictability that the discretionary modes of summary justice could not supply. Community concerns, by outgrowing the knowledge of local inhabitants, encouraged a resort to more technical common-law doctrines and procedures. As formal pleading replaced judicial paternalism and attorneys-in-fact yielded to trained practitioners, a view of the individual litigant developed that was better suited to a burgeoning capitalist economy.

"The image in the Common Law," writes Aiken, "was one of self-interest, of pressing one's legal rights against any individual or against society, *in personam* and *in rem*, regardless of the morality of one's cause. It is the image of a man not bound by any ethical or moral consideration, but only the law."[3] Once held to ideal standards of behavior, the individual was now required to be no better than the average member of his species: the "normal person," the "typical man," the "reasonable and prudent man." He might do whatever the law did not forbid, without fear of judicial interference; moral obligations were no longer enforceable at law. But if freed from community surveillance and restraints, he was equally deprived of community protection. The letter of the law remained his only safeguard in the courtroom, and to avail himself of it he had to call upon skilled attorneys whose self-interest fully matched his own. The result was a continuing tension in lawyer-client relations, with neither side fully trusting the other, although both were indispensable to the common-law system of justice.

The utopian spirit of the early sectarians and gold seekers had long spent its force when the American Revolution set men once more to dreaming of ideal polities. Fought primarily over bread-and-butter economic and political issues, the long struggle with Great Britain had its moralistic side as well. Wartime propaganda—especially the Declaration of Independence—held out glowing promises of social justice for all citizens once British power was overthrown. With the return of peace the victorious rebels set out to redeem these humane pledges, as a lesson not merely to Englishmen but to all mankind. Self-consciously dissociating themselves from the corrupt influences of the Old World, they proposed to erect model republics in the widerness—inaugurating a "new order of the ages," as they proclaimed on their Great Seal, beneath the design of an unfinished pyramid inscribed 1776. The times, it appeared, were ripe for the emergence of an American-style millennium, in which age-old dreams of human happiness would at last be realized.

"The mouldering works on yonder hills, while they recall the sad remembrance of many of our hapless heroes, teach me to realize the importance of our emancipation from tyranny," commented one journalist in a typical vein. "The banners of liberty wave unmolested in these happy climes, and rouse the enterprizing genius of American sons. They feel themselves situated in a smiling land that courts rather the sickle than the plough. They find their extensive sea coasts washed by the prolific Atlantic, and their immense country penetrated and enriched by innumerable genial rivers." The inexhaustible natural resources of the American continent invited exploitation and banished forever the specter of poverty and a permanently depressed lower class: "indeed by becoming an inhabitant of America a man becomes wealthy."[4]

Yet even while extolling the relative effortlessness of life in the American Eden, writers continued to demand industry and frugality of their fellow citizens. Labor alone conferred value upon property, they urged, and every man had a duty to provide for himself and his family. Beyond a modest sufficiency, however, the accumulation of wealth posed grave dangers for republican virtue. A taste for luxury had destroyed popular governments in the past, as citizens grew lazy and effeminate, without the moral fiber to defend their heritage. The best hope for the preservation of an American arcadia lay in the sturdy, independent yeoman: "View the honest, guileless farmer, when, fatigued with the business of the day, he retires to his humble cot, the residence of health, peace, and competency, to enjoy the social eve with his virtuous partner, surrounded with a blooming train of dutiful children, and say, does not this scene exhibit a more pleasing prospect of happiness, than all the cloying pleasures of the luxurious and the gay?"[5] Lest one should write off such effusions as the work of a small body of literary hacks schooled in the classics, consider the corroborating accounts of independent witnesses. Crusty old Henry Van Schaack, merchant and farmer, was anything but a man of letters or a sentimentalist; yet in describing his neighbors in 1784 he remarked: "I never in my life saw any people come so nearly to the morality of Swift's Hounheims as my present townsmen . . . During my residence in Richmond [Massachusetts], I never was a witness to swearing, drunkenness, or a breach of the Sabbath; or, in short, any flagrant trespass upon morality. A purse of gold hung up in the public streets, would be as safe from our inhabitants as it used to be in the great Alfred's time. Beggars and vagrants we are strangers to, as well as overbearing, purse-proud scoundrels. Provisions we abound in."[6]

Other commentators discovered the same rustic virtues at work in the large cities of the nation. The French traveler J.P. Brissot de Warville marveled at the austerity of life in Boston during a visit there in 1788. Even at Sunday church services he observed no affectation of manner or dress among the congregation, while in day-to-day intercourse no man dared to assume "important airs" with his neighbor. The leading figures of the Revolution, such as John Adams and General Heath, had retired to the solitude of their farms, in the tradition of the "best ages of Rome and Greece." Simplicity, Brissot concluded, was the first of republican virtues: "a virtue born with the Americans, and only acquired with us."[7] In Philadelphia, Peter DuPonceau, scholar and jurist, recorded similar impressions of the postrevolutionary scene in which he began his distinguished career: "Those were the patriarchal times of our country, the days of innocent pleasures, which are never to return." His friends—the elite of Philadelphia society—made no attempt to ape the manners of foreign aristocrats, or to indulge in "extensive and showy" amusements. "Everything was then in the plain republican style," a condition that DuPonceau attributed to the relative poverty of the country and the survival of colonial habits.[8]

For several decades after the Revolution, indeed, America remained primarily an underdeveloped agricultural area, in which the arcadian myth could flourish as an analogue to the realities of republican government. Democratic manners, for example, did exist, although hostile critics saw in them less of antique virtue than of frontier crudity and barbarism. The other mythic components of the American Eden likewise had their real-life approximations, which included a pervasive distaste for societal restraints inherited from the Revolution. To foreign observers the permissiveness of life in the early Republic seemed almost overwhelming. The Irish émigré William Sampson voiced a typical reaction when he hailed America as uniquely the land of liberty: "The government here makes no sensation. It is round about you like the air, and you cannot even feel it." Nor was greater energy displayed in the execution of the laws. One constable with a staff, Sampson remarked, could handle twenty prisoners—a striking contrast to those Old World monarchies where "every man has a soldier to watch him with a musket."[9]

The republican creed itself demanded a maximum freedom of action for every citizen, and practical politicians often addressed their constituents in language borrowed from the heroic ages. Robert Williams, governor of the Mississippi Territory, admonished the members of the general assembly in 1805 that their laws should "breathe the spirit of moderation, justice and virtue"; and further that it was "conducive to the public weal and the peace and quiet of the people that there should be as few laws as possible. Many laws indicate the depravity of society, for they are not made for the virtuous, but for the vicious, and to protect and enforce the rights of the former against the attacks and injustice of the latter." Similar sentiments were expressed the following year in more sophisticated Boston, where Governor Caleb Strong told his listeners that the well-being of a people depended not upon laws and government but upon the strength of private virtue: "Government is necessary to preserve the public peace, and protect the persons and property of individuals; but our social happiness must chiefly depend upon other causes; upon simplicity and purity of manners; upon the education that we give our children; upon a steady adherence to the customs and institutions of our ancestors; upon the general diffusion of knowledge, and the prevalence of piety and benevolent affections among the people."[10]

Such republican idealism permeated all social classes, including the professional. Even the most urbane legal practitioners were no proof against the blandishments of the simple life. Thus the erudite New York lawyer James Kent early announced his determination to practice virtue, work hard, and "lay up a Stock of knowledge & Property sufficient to enable me to live all the better half of my future Life . . . in some rural retirement."[11] The same theme runs with monotonous insistence through the memoirs of his contemporaries at the bar, most of whom also viewed the good life through the prism of a middle-class mythology:

> No feudal ties the rising genius mar,
> Compel to servile toils or drag to war;
> But free each youth his fav'rite course pursues,
> The plough paternal or the sylvan Muse.
> For here exists once more th' Arcadian scene,
> Those simple manners and that golden mean:
> Here holds society its middle stage,
> Between too rude and too refin'd an age;
> Far from that age when not a gleam of light,
> The dismal darkness cheer'd of gothic night,
> From brutal rudeness of that savage state—
> As from refinements which o'erwhelm the great,
> Those dissipations which their bliss annoy,
> And blast and poison each domestic joy.[12]

The vision, to be sure, was appealing; but what need had such a virtuous society for lawyers?

Legal historians have been somewhat puzzled at the popular hostility toward the bar that appeared in the wake of the Revolution. Recalling the prominent role which many lawyers played in support of that struggle, later commentators have tended to explain the profession's unsavory postwar reputation in terms of a dramatic shift in public opinion. Having outgrown their original disfavor, the argument runs, lawyers rose rapidly in public esteem until they became the acknowledged leaders of the revolutionary movement. Their prestige began to decline only in the troubled postwar depression days, when their professional duties brought them into collision with the debtor classes and helped to revive ancient prejudices. An elegiac note permeates the discussion, as modern researchers echo the lament of an anonymous poet of the 1780s:

> Where's now, that reverential awe,
> Once paid the sages of the law?[13]

But perhaps the query itself is misleading, for at no time in their history have the American people shown much disposition to revere their lawyers. At best their approval of the profession has been qualified, and the case was no different in the eighteenth century. Ample evidence indicates that the public continued to cherish certain basic suspicions of the legal fraternity, even while relying upon its membership for political guidance. To cite only one illustration, drawn from the presumed peak period of lawyer-community rapport: almost every other delegate to the Congress that adopted the Declaration of Independence was a lawyer. Yet on July 25, 1776—only three weeks after the passage of that long-awaited measure, whose sponsors had become popular heroes—Timothy Dwight warned the graduating class of Yale College against the evils to be found in legal practice: "That meanness, that infernal knavery, which multiplies needless litigations, which retards the operation of justice, which, from court to court, upon the most trifling pretences, postpones trial to glean the last emptyings of a client's pocket, for unjust fees of everlasting attendance, which artfully twists the meaning of law to the side we espouse, which seizes unwarrantable advantages from the prepossessions, ignorance, interests and prejudices of a jury, you will shun rather than death or infamy."[14] Almost the only standing complaint omitted from Dwight's list was that which ridiculed the meaningless jargon and quibbles in which attorneys indulged.

Together, such charges formed the core of a traditional body of antilawyer criticism handed down from the seventeenth century. Their vintage flavor may be detected in a homespun assault upon legal "gabble" that appeared in a Philadelphia newspaper of 1736. The writer there alleged that attorneys at the bar prosed interminably, striving to make the simplest issues appear complex, while they sinned even more flagrantly in their written pleadings: "when you find how little there is in a Writing of vast Bulk, you will be as much surpriz'd as a Stranger at the Opening of a *Pumpkin*."[15] Such unvarnished distrust of legal mores remained conspicuous in popular journalism throughout the eighteenth century; after the Revolution, as before, the same accusations continued to appear in the public prints. They were reinforced, however, by certain new attitudes which grew directly out of the American struggle for independence. That contest had been waged in large part to escape the restraints of British law, and many rebels looked forward to a personal liberation from the trammels of unwanted lawsuits, especially those brought by creditors. The notorious "horse jockey" who so enraged honest John Adams in 1775 voiced a widespread feeling when he predicted the permanent disappearance of all courts of justice.

To such enthusiasts lawyers seemed a counterrevolutionary force, blocking the emergence of a truly free republic by their stubborn adherence to prewar forms and ceremonies. Even their dress proclaimed the distance that separated them from their guileless fellow citizens. In the 1780s pomp and circumstance still attended the opening of court in Boston, as "the Honourable the Judges arrayed in their scarlet robes, the Attorney General and other Barristers at Law, in their proper habits," marched in procession from State Street to the county courthouse. And Philadelphia attorneys long continued to appear at the bar with powdered hair and formal black attire—survivals of prerevolutionary decorum that ill suited the innovative temper of the new nation.[16]

That temper, as we have seen, repudiated the establishments of the past in the name of republican virtue; and by doing so posed a fundamental challenge to the very existence of a legal profession. For in the face of a primitivist ideology, the lawyer of the early republic represented, above all else, the force of civilization. Armed with his Blackstone and Coke, he invaded the wilderness to impose artificial constraints upon the anarchy of nature, transferring to frontier areas all the machinery of coercion familiar to the most sophisticated European governments. "Under his influence," intoned one western jurist, "new governments are established, courts erected, laws passed, obedience inculcated and enforced, and the great principles of English law and liberty administered in the forests, as on the banks of the Thames or in Westminster Hall."[17] The maintenance of these Old World refinements in the midst of the American Eden provided perhaps the strongest psychological irritant to good community relations in the postrevolutionary years.

A mass of ephemeral literature testifies to the public's concern over the unnatural wiles of its lawyers and their rapid rise to positions of power within state and national governments. "Their subtle arts direct the nation, and fire the rising generation," lamented the anonymous author of "The Republic of Beasts," a lengthy verse parable that marks the most ambitious literary effort to deal with the "lawyer question" during the Confederation period. In this account the Lawyer-Foxes, who served the cause of tyranny in the days of monarchical rule, manage to maintain their ascendancy in republican America by preying upon the innocence of their fellow citizens:

> When sires, whom patriot virtues warm,
> Assembled government to form,
> Then note, the *Foxes* too were there,
> With learned and important air;
> The fabricators in debate,
> Of ev'ry mystic turn of state;
> So intricate to grovel thro'
> That none but they can find the clue.
> They rack'd their oratorial might
> That spreads a mist, or holds up light;
> Can fright by terror-feign'd extremes,
> Or fasenate by golden dreams;
> Can make the just corruption's tools,
> And sages oft the dupes of fools:
> For still the wise and good we find
> Of noble unsuspecting kind.[18]

Once entrenched in the postrevolutionary power structure, the Foxes promote their self-interest at the expense of the general welfare. By multiplying their governmental jobs and functions and concealing their chicanery behind "mystick forms abstruse," they seek to perpetuate themselves as an elite ruling class within a nominally democratic society. But an aroused public opinion may be counted upon to frustrate their betrayal of the republican dream:

> Divisions unto mean and great,
> Are bane to ev'ry virtuous state;
> Shall we invite the fett'ring bands
> Of other old corrupted lands?
> To you each brute should be prefer'd,
> Of all the stupid honest herd;
> In judgment or in legislation,
> To rule or represent the nation. [19]

While lawyers had often been denounced in earlier ages for truckling to the will of powerful minorities, their position in the young Republic was singularly anomalous. Since the Tory exodus (which included roughly one-fourth of all prerevolutionary practitioners), an aristocratic class—or at least one with professed aristocratic pretensions—was virtually nonexistent. This group had been the focal point of middle-class discontent for several decades, and its sudden disappearance left a void in the national mythology. It may well be that every society, and especially one just emerging from the trauma of revolution, needs some stereotyped version of "the enemy" by which to measure its own character and achievements. Lawyers served this purpose for a time in republican thinking because they were the only social group that appeared to defy direct popular control. The citizens of New Braintree, Massachusetts, bore witness to widespread popular suspicions of this kind when they warned their representative to the state assembly in 1786: "With regard to the Practitioners of the Law in this Commonwealth, daily experience convinces us of the horrid extortion, tyranny and oppression, practised among that order of men, who, of late years, have amazingly increased in number, opulence, and grandeur, . . . and we think there is much to fear from so powerful and numerous a body of men as the practitioners of the law are now become, if they are suffered still to proceed on, without any check or controul." [20]

Conspiracy theories, formerly reserved for the Tory elite, were refurbished and adapted to the activities of the bar. Critics read sinister implications into the very idea of the lawyer-politician, charging that an inevitable conflict of interest must exist when the same men both made the laws and profited from their ambiguities in private legal practice. No matter how one turned the picture, the public remained in peril: if not enslaved by professional lawmakers, citizens stood to lose their shirts to the pettifoggers who infested their courts. And where local bar associations existed, their potential for evil left imaginative commentators gasping:

> Suppose, for instance, (and I will not affirm that it has not already taken place) *that the lawyers should meet every quarter, and correspond with their brethren throughout the State: That they should determine the business of every Court by previous consultation, whether to close a cause at the next term, or defer it to another: That the determinations at their conventions should be minutely entered in their* BAR-BOOK, *and the whole business dealt out in Court agreeable to their pre-determined resolutions.* Suppose *a Grand Secretary should be chosen, to keep a particular account of all proceedings, and each one should be sacredly bound to adhere to what was transacted at this meeting.* Also, *a Committee should be appointed to examine all candidates, who should adhere strictly to the rules of this convention.* In a word, suppose this "order," at their quarterly meetings, *should establish a perfect Star-Chamber jurisdiction, as to all Court proceedings.*[21]

These exaggerated fears—flowing from the vision of an unholy alliance between lawyers, judges, and legislators—had some foundation in objective conditions. Attorneys *were* profiting from the distress of the times through their heavy involvement in contract cases, debt collections, and land transactions, which made up the lion's share of their practice. Furthermore, the harsh provisions of English insolvency laws remained in force throughout the former colonies, leaving debtors entirely at the mercy of their creditors in legal proceedings. The lack of a homestead exemption meant that a poor man's family might be turned into the streets with nothing but the clothes on their backs, while the man himself faced subsequent imprisonment if the sale of his property did not raise sufficient funds to pay off his indebtedness. And if he appealed to the legislature for relief in the form of stay laws or an inflated currency, he usually got nowhere. Small wonder, then, that he felt trapped at times in a vast web of legal chicanery and denounced those who had constructed it.

But the vehemence of popular protest against the bar should not obscure its essentially conservative character. Campaigns to "get the lawyers" represented no Marxist struggles between opposing economic groups, no risings of the propertyless masses against an oppressive capitalist order. Most of the malcontents were sturdy middle-class types who were bent upon protecting their property rights against what they conceived to be a new form of tyranny. Far from demanding extensive changes in the content of the laws, they were chiefly incensed over the high costs and burdensome machinery of litigation—a continuing complaint that makes the middle class in the twentieth century still bitterly critical of the profession.[22] The position of the middle-class litigant was well described by a newspaper writer in 1805:

If a debt is due recourse must be had to a professional man, who is alone viewed by the law as competent to point out the legal remedy required. In most instances before his advice can be obtained, a fee must be given, seldom less than three or four dollars, and rising in proportion to the magnitude of the cause. The lawyer frequently resides at a distance of twenty or thirty miles from the party aggrieved; and consequently one or two days will be consumed in reaching him, and in afterwards returning home.

Court costs and administrative delays further embarrass the thrifty bourgeois, who finds himself victimized by the very system which purports to promote the claims of the common-law man. "Do [such burdens] not entirely sap the principle of equal rights? . . . Do they not necessarily create distinctions among men; between the rich and the poor? Do they not give power to the former, while they deny it to the latter?"[23] If the argument suggests a strong class animus, recall that the "poor man" of the example is also a creditor who seeks to use the legal system for his personal ends.

To remedy the deficiencies of middle-class justice, agitators proposed either the "annihilation" or socialization of the American bar. The first alternative, besides sounding more dramatic, had obvious affinities with the contemporary cult of virtue and simplicity. Its antecedents stretched back to the legal utopianism of the previous century, and it was no accident that the most militant antiprofessional propaganda came from Massachusetts and Pennsylvania, two areas in which the earlier idealism had taken strongest root.

Benjamin Austin, the leading spokesman for New England radicalism, was a Boston merchant who urged the state legislature to abolish the "order" of lawyers and permit the parties in all civil actions to substitute arbitration procedures for lawsuits. If litigants preferred to take a case to court they might still do so, but without the need of professional assistance or the fear of professional wiles. In the absence of hired pleaders, a paternal judge, representing the community interest, would hear the evidence of the parties and instruct the jury in the appropriate legal principles involved. While this seems to mark a return to the days of khadi justice, Austin modified the utopian tradition in several important respects. His judges were not to be untutored laymen who dispensed a "law of the heart" as conscience dictated. Besides requiring of them a thorough knowledge of common-law doctrines, he planned to recruit them from the ranks of a wealthy elite rather than from among the common people:

> If no practitioners were allowed in our Courts, the important study of law, would be followed solely with a view of doing justice; and gentlemen of fortune, who meant to serve their country as *Judges*, would make the public good their chief object. They would not take up the profession as a set of *needy persons*, who meant by chicanery and finesse, to get a living by their practice; but they would make a point of duty, so to understand the laws, as to distribute equal justice to the rich and poor; each individual would receive the benefit of the laws, and by a speedy and impartial determination, every man would have his cause decided without the imposition of enormous Court charges, and lawyers fees.[24]

Austin relied upon two additional safeguards to keep his judges incorruptible: their salaries would be fixed and paid by the state, and any misconduct on their part would be punished by impeachment at the hands of the people. Since the judges were to be few in number and their duties performed in full view of the public, an alert citizenry might detect the slightest hint of venality and remove its servants from office. Even under the existing system, judges were held to the mark by such considerations: "So far from any complaint against the present Bench, every individual is satisfied with their conduct."[25]

Although lay referees and disinterested judges might be expected to answer all the normal needs of a just society, Austin also revived the attorney-in-fact for use on special occasions. If a party desired to be represented by counsel (a right guaranteed to him by the constitution of Massachusetts), he might choose a friend to present his case in court. This unskilled advocate would remain a public servant, however, receiving only a nominal fee from the government for his services. (In proof of his good faith, he would be required to swear *"that he had not received, and that he did not expect to receive any reward from the parties for his services."*) If he violated his trust he would incur a "very heavy penalty" and be excluded from all government employment thereafter. By removing the profit from legal business and encouraging every man to state his own cause in nonadversary proceedings, Austin hoped to forestall the rise of a new class of pettifoggers in his utopia, where he prayed

> That all the opposing elements of life,
> The gales of rage and hurricanes of strife,
> Might cease; and waft our barks on silken sail,
> And on life's ocean one vast calm prevail!
> That mutual passions, mutual charms might lend,
> *And each to each be Neighbour, Father, Friend.* [26]

The dream of a golden age reborn figures even more prominently in the work of Jesse Higgins, a well-to-do Delaware landowner whose unhappy experiences in a chancery court inspired him to write the most influential antilawyer tract that appeared in the Middle States. The interminable title of his book offers a good index to its major preoccupations: *Sampson against the Philistines; or, The Reformation of Lawsuits; and Justice Made Cheap, Speedy and Brought Home to Every Man's Door: Agreeably to the Principles of the Ancient Trial by Jury, before the Same Was Innovated by Judges and Lawyers.* Published in Philadelphia in 1805, *Sampson* was immediately appropriated by the Jeffersonian Republicans, who used it as a weapon in their struggle to oust the Federalists from their entrenched positions in the state judiciary. But Higgins's argument transcended narrow party lines, as he himself insisted, and his pamphlet remains of interest as the ablest early defense of a legal system based entirely upon compulsory abritration.

Sampson begins with an elaborate excursion into history, as

Higgins traces the institution of the jury back to the days of Good King Alfred and his Saxon warriors. In those heroic times, as even Blackstone admitted, lawyers and judges were unheard of, and a virtuous yeomanry referred all disputes to their friends and neighbors for settlement. Alfred, in keeping with the egalitarian spirit of Germanic military life, established a highly decentralized civil government which was administered through innumerable local courts. These tribunals of the people functioned as arbitration boards on which local residents sat to resolve all neighborhood quarrels according to the principles of natural justice. Each court was autonomous; no levels of jurisdiction existed; and disappointed suitors enjoyed no right of appeal from the decision of a "jury" save, in exceptional cases, to Alfred's "parliament." This admirable democratic system flourished until the Norman Conquest, when William and his successors began a process of ruthless centralization that included the introduction of superior courts and royal judges at Westminster Hall. In time the new agencies of monarchical control wrested power from the people's courts and reduced the jury to a mere fact-finding body in litigation controlled by undemocratic judges and their professional colleagues at the bar. From these premises Higgins drew an irresistible conclusion: the American people must recapture their lost Anglo-Saxon heritage by restoring the ancient trial by jury in its pristine vigor.

Such a restoration implied, of course, the demise of bench and bar, but Higgins assured his readers that their passing would be painless. A single legislative act compelling arbitration at the option of either party to a lawsuit would reopen the way to the good society. Once men learned that they might claim justice at the hands of their honest neighbors—a procedure long favored by merchants, methodists, and George Washington—they would abandon their old courts, transforming them into "undisturbed monuments of usurped innovation."

Since Higgin's animus extended to judges as well as lawyers, he went farther than Austin in defending the right of the uneducated man to pass judgment on his fellows. Civil suits involved personal or property rights, he noted, and these every man understood because they were his inalienable birthright, conferred upon him by nature herself without the need of additional sanctions. The judicious Saxons, who had no written laws whatever, relied exclusively upon intuitive natural-law

precepts to settle their disputes. Yet they seldom erred, Higgins
asserted, especially in property matters, where they protected
the claims of individual proprietorship with all the zeal of an
eighteenth-century bourgeois. Furthermore, even in sophisticated societies,

> all those laws which relate to property, and the common inter-
> course among men, which are just and ought to be valid, are in
> every age and every country, the simplest rules, and fitted to the
> plainest capacities, with few exceptions; insomuch that any and
> every ignorant man, who has barely a knowledge of the truth, and
> of right and wrong, can decide any question agreeable to law,
> although he never heard a law read during his life . . . Is it not the
> law of the land, that every man should hold his own property; and
> would not such be the decision of the most ignorant man in society?
> Is not the same the case with respect to a reasonable compensation
> for services performed, for damage sustained, &c . . . God never
> intended his creature man, should be under the necessity to carry a
> written book in his pocket, or a lawyer by his side, to tell him what
> is just and lawful; he wrote it on his mind.[27]

Although he drew some distinction between rights and remedies
and admitted that laymen might profit from reading a few
general digests of common-law principles, Higgins directed his
best efforts toward burying formal law learning in the same
grave with a professional bar.

Thereafter, he predicted, with the people once more in control of the legal process, America might look forward to an era
of fraternal justice which should surpass the achievements of
the ancients:

> In this state of society, no man would think of doing a wrong, when
> a week, or a month would force him to do right, and expose his
> wrong doing. Shame, and disgrace would follow every wilful
> wrong; and a peaceable, cheap, and speedy settlement, every real
> disagreement. Disputes must in such a state be very rare, when two
> willing minds could not, and would not settle them themselves.
> Probity would then be not only the interest but the necessary course
> of every man. Every one would deal with confidence. Credit would
> be as nearly equal to cash, as a note in bank is to bank notes. Delay
> of payment would be attended with little other loss than interest; as
> every prudent man could get credit, or cash on loan. Young men
> would thrive, and old men live in peace. Virtue would abound, and

a crime would seldom be heard of. The industrious, and virtuous of other communities would flock to this, and none but the lazy, and vicious would quit it.[28]

The proposals of Austin and Higgins represented an extreme solution to the problem of the American lawyer. Other reformers favored the retention of a small professional bar, paid and controlled by the state. These government lawyers would be assigned to civil cases at the request of individual litigants, but, like Austin's attorneys-in-fact, they would remain public servants whose chief function would be to assist the jury to a clearer understanding of the issues involved. What better way to have your cake and eat it too, writers asked. Through a socialized bar the administration of justice might be democratized without forfeiting the special skills of the trained practitioner. In the absence of private fees, rich and poor alike would stand equal at the bar of justice, where each might demand without cost the best legal talent available. Similarly, defendants under criminal indictment would be entitled to the services of a public defender or "advocate-general" appointed and paid by the state.

Behind the facade of this extensive welfare program lay the familiar image of a prudent and responsible citizenry whose quarrels would seldom reach the courtroom without the prompting of self-interested pettifoggers. Socialization would weed out the shysters and their unconscionable profits, leaving behind only a skeleton cadre of reliable practitioners to handle all legal duties at minimal cost to the public. Occasionally writers got down to specific figures for the new establishment. One Massachusetts critic suggested that the number of attorneys in his state might profitably be reduced from eighty to twenty-five. The resulting work force could then be apportioned among the counties on a population basis and elected to office, like other government personnel, for short terms. A few judges, too, might be elected from the ranks of the lawyers to complete a socially responsible system in which practitioners would be stimulated to remain always on their best behavior and to "use the persons well for whom they do business." Contrary to the typical socialization scheme, fees would continue to be paid by individual litigants, but they would be strictly defined and regulated by legislative fee tables, which would guarantee to the public the benefit of law learning at one-third to one-fourth the prevailing cost. Lawyers would no longer be able to accumulate princely fortunes to the scandal of simple republicans; "yet, by being attentive to their business, and conducting well, would they not be pretty sure of a decent and genteel living, as good as reputable and learned Clergymen obtain? And why should this not content them?"[29] (The question was not entirely rhetorical, since the author confessed to being a "young clergyman" himself.)

Although antilawyer prejudice existed throughout the nation, it seems to have been somewhat less intense in the South and West. Neither of these areas produced a polemicist of the stature of Higgins or Austin, and a random sampling of early publications reveals little abuse of the profession aside from that found in standard lawyer jokes and anecdotes, which were everywhere in demand as filler material. The subject has yet to claim the attention of serious scholars, although a fully documented account of the lawyer's reputation in either of these regions would add a fascinating chapter to American social history. Meanwhile we are forced to rely upon fragmentary evidence to guide us further in our inquiry.

We know that a vigorous antilawyer sentiment flourished in the North Carolina of Justice James Iredell, as well as in post-revolutionary Georgia. But these states remained, to a considerable extent, frontier areas whose attitudes did not necessarily reflect a regional consensus. Elsewhere in the South the lawyer was apparently accepted as a potentially useful member of a structured agrarian society. The antiprofessionalism of the layman perhaps made less stir in a setting in which attorneys themselves regarded the law as a secondary pursuit, a sideline to their major interest in politics and farming. The distinctive life-style of the southern lawyer was a holdover from colonial times when, as Philip Detweiler has remarked, "The young man of good family, anticipating the role of responsible leadership in the community, came to look on the study of law as a natural preliminary to his work as a provincial statesman."[30] Even when he journeyed to England for his legal training the southerner tended to utilize the experience primarily to enhance his position as a member of the colonial ruling class. South Carolina sent more of her sons to the Inns of Court than any other colony, yet of the thirty-odd "Carolina Templars" who received their legal education during the quarter century preceding the Revolution, only a few took up law as a full-time profession on their return to America.[31] And in the postrevolutionary era, which witnessed a breakdown of class barriers and the opening of the bar to talented individuals from every social stratum, the law continued to serve as a stepping-stone to other, more attractive employments.

The typical southern lawyer, immersed in the details of plantation management and neighborhood politics, was thus better calculated to appeal to community sympathies than his more professionalized northern prototype. One of the few favorable portraits of the early practitioner comes from a South Carolina magazine of 1806, and it points up the interweaving of legal and social aspirations in the South. The writer purports to be describing the members of a fashionable Charleston club:

> My greatest favourite in the society is MR. VERDICT, the proprie-
> tor of a small plantation, not far from town. He was bred to the
> law, received his education in England, and on his return to his
> native country, continued in the practice of the profession for sev-
> eral years. He has been known to refuse a fee, when the cause of his
> client was evidently bad; though he seldom failed in settling it by
> arbitration; and so acknowledged was the integrity of his character,
> that he was generally chosen, on such occasions, the judge or
> umpire of both parties. By the death of a near relation, he became
> owner of a plantation in a distant part of the state, which he after-
> wards sold, and purchased that which he now possesses. MR.
> VERDICT is a man of the most liberal education and sentiment. He
> is aware, without the price of experience, that property never
> thrives so well as when the proprietor is on the spot; and for this
> reason, he settled on his estate immediately after the bargain was
> concluded, and now scarcely ever comes to town but on club
> nights.[32]

From the account it is difficult to say whether Mr. Verdict should be applauded more for his exemplary legal practice or for his abandonment of law in favor of farming. Perhaps, for many southerners, a golden age already existed, and the lawyer-planter figured in their thinking as the natural defender of a system that, as it grew more dependent on slave labor, would make ever stronger demands upon the instrumentalities of order.

But if southern lawyers achieved a measure of acceptance

through their connection with an agrarian heritage, practitioners on the western frontier profited from the absence of any traditional establishments in dealing with their public. The best available surveys indicate that most pioneer attorneys came from poor or middle-class backgrounds, had only a limited education beyond the common-school level, and found little difficulty in casting their arguments in a homespun style familiar to their audiences.[33] Since bar associations seldom existed and fees (even when not subject, as they generally were, to stringent legislative regulation) remained trifling and payable in commodities or services, western clients experienced few of the major irritants that disgruntled their neighbors to the east. Lawyers did involve themselves heavily in frontier politics, but their success depended more upon their oratorical abilities than upon any pretensions to technical expertise. Much the same might be said of courtroom practice: although recent studies attest to the high level of competence displayed by the members of several "circuit bars" in the West, it is clear that personality counted at least as much as book learning in attracting clients. Indeed, to a sparse and culturally deprived population the courtroom typically functioned as an entertainment center, where neighbors gathered to enjoy the theatrical talents of backwoods spellbinders, such as the attorney who concluded his defense of an accused horse thief with the stirring appeal: "True, he was rude—so are our bars; true, he was rough—so air our buffalers. But he was a child of freedom; and his answer to the despot and the tyrant was, that his home was in the bright setting sun!"[34]

Westerners had no dearth of grievances against the law, to be sure, in spite of its popular trappings. A whole body of folklore testifies to the persistent efforts of rugged individualists to evade the restraints of common-law justice. But frontier hostility tended to focus upon specific persons and practices; it represented less a reasoned assault upon the profession than a visceral explosion—a violent gut reaction to the immediate threat of mortgage foreclosers, debt collectors, and their intimidating scraps of paper. The simple anti-intellectualism and self-help techniques of the frontiersman are well conveyed through the experience of one Dirck Gardenier, a young Dutchman sent to serve an ejectment notice on a farmer in upstate New York in 1787. "I went yesterday unarmed to Mr. Selah

Abbots," Gardenier reported to his formidable old lawyer-uncle Peter Van Schaack.

> I found a Number of People at work for him in Harvest. I gave his wife the Eject^t. & Read the letter of Mr. Stout. I Tould her besides the Contents & then Made to the Door. She Desired I^d stay untill her Husband came home who was in sight. I went on my Horse & then stopt. When he came up he asked me what I left that paper for. I tould him I had no further use for it. He foamed at the mouth his Limbs shook his Voise faltered. Seized hold of my Bridle & Tould me to take back the paper or he would send me into Eternaty in a Moment with Many Bitter oaths to inforce a belief. I was obliged to take back the paper as I saw a number Making up towards the hous. When I had the paper he let lose the Rains. I Trowed Down the paper & put speed to my Departure. He Called for his horse & ordered the Rest to follow his Example. I had got the start of him some. My horse not being of the best we Measured the ground as fast as we could and at Maj^r Duglas's they overtook me to the number of about fifteen. However I got in the House before them & fastned the Door. They Demanded admittence which Maj^r Duglas Refused. They Brandished their Clubs swore they would have me Dead or alive, or I must go & Take the Eject^t back. I Tould them I would not go back but if He would send for it I w^d Take it back. It is Needless for me to Tell you all the Tretning I Received in which you was not forgot. I think we staid four Hours untill The sun set. The Major advised me to Come to some truce with them or it might be Dangerous in the Night as they Might black & Disfigure themselfs & he believed they w^d Tare Down his House if Nothing was Done to Appease them—at Last we agreed that the Copy should be sent for & I give up Boath to Mr Abbot & write on the back of them that the sarvice was good for Nothing & of no Effect, which I Did *But* previous to this I went aside & Drew an other Copy which I here present you with every Circumstance attending the same. Only this, that after I had wrote on the back, I again Read Mr. Stout's Letter to him & advised him to appear at Albany and Defend the same & then gave boath the Declarations which he took with him. The other I send you attested to.[35]

For all the sound and fury of the episode, the resolute Mr. Abbot scored only a Pyrrhic victory over his adversaries. They would return in time, fortified with other court orders, to impose their abstractions once more on the smiling face of nature. Abbot's personal frustration symbolized the general failure of antilawyer efforts to achieve enduring results in these years. Despite opposition the serpents continued to thrive in the garden—a circumstance quite as remarkable in its way as the impassioned drive to eradicate them.

An anonymous poetaster commented in 1789, with perhaps greater insight than he realized, on the "Multitude of Lawyers":

> I wonder William, Harry said,
>> From whom have all those Lawyers bread?
>
> Quoth Will, I wonder at the same:
>> But Harry we are both to blame;
>> The more the Dogs the more the Game.[36]

Indeed, a middle-class public, cherishing the ideals of competition, utilitarianism, and self-advancement, found itself unwilling to forego the advantages of an individualistic legal system in favor of some more equitable communitarian experiment.

In politics lawyer-community relations followed much the same pattern after as before the Revolution: a torrent of colorful abuse from the press did not deter the electorate from elevating attorneys to the highest positions of public trust. Massachusetts offers perhaps the best illustration of the postwar trend. Here an intense antilawyer campaign culminated in the short-lived Shays's Rebellion of 1786. Inspired in part by Austin's writings, voters elected an unprecedented number of nonlawyers to the General Court; irate mobs of farmers seized control of the courthouses in several towns and closed them down; and only the timely exertions of the governor and the state militia averted the threat of civil war. Yet no sooner was order restored than the profession regained political favor. Two of the four Massachusetts delegates to the federal convention of 1787 were lawyers, and in the First Congress of the United States both of the state senators had been admitted to the bar, as well as five out of eight representatives. (Theodore Sedgwick of Stockbridge, one lawyer-representative, had been an outspoken opponent of the Shaysites and had taken an active part in putting down the disturbances in his neighborhood.) At the state capital a similar situation prevailed. Lawyer-politicians quickly recovered from the setback they had experienced at the height of the antilawyer movement, as the following table demonstrates:

Lawyers Elected to the Massachusetts General Court

Year	Senators	Representatives
1784	6	13
1785	5	15
1786	3	8
1787	2	11
1788	3	16
1790	4	19
1800	6	20

Source: Gerard W. Gawalt, "Massachusetts Lawyers: A Historical Analysis of the Process of Professionalization, 1760-1840" (Ph.D. diss., Clark University, 1969), table 1, p. 239.

Voters may have been inclined to separate the politician from the lawyer in their thinking, and to rely upon their power to control any elected official in his public duties. But a candidate's legal skills often operated as a positive factor, inducing even hard-bitten lay critics to acknowledge (however grudgingly) that some trained professionals were needed to help frame their laws. No man, for example, kept in closer touch with the popular pulse than Jonathan Roberts, a self-made Jeffersonian politician from Pennsylvania. Roberts was a loyal friend and supporter of Jesse Higgins, and the kindest comment he ever made about the bar was, "I will not say the professions of Law & Divinity *necessarily* make men worse." Yet, once elected to the state senate, he began to court favor with one of the few lawyers (and a Federalist, too!) in that body, explaining, "I had just motives to conciliate him. He had had a good Law education. It was my interest to avail myself of his knowledge in that branch. He answer'd all my inquiries, with patience and good humor. This saved much study, & accelerated my progress to usefulness."[37]

Ambivalence thus continued to define the public's response to its lawyers, and made illusory all threats of socialization or worse. Austin's followers did score a short-lived victory of sorts in Massachusetts with the passage in November 1786 of "An Act for rendering processes in Law less expensive within this Commonwealth." The measure removed the existing four-pound limit on the jurisdiction of justices of the peace, giving them cognizance of all civil suits except those involving real estate titles. Plaintiffs might still take their cases to a county court for trial, but only after conferring with a justice of the peace, who was required by law to stress the economic advantages to be gained by submitting all disputes to referees for arbitration. Where court trials did take place, the law further stipulated that each party might employ only one lawyer to represent him. Proponents of the act hoped that arbitration procedures would completely replace costly court actions and that lawyers would be reduced to handling only criminal cases and those involving realty. For several years the number of new actions brought in the various courts of common pleas did decline considerably, but complaints soon mounted against the incompetence of many lay justices and arbitrators, and a corrective statute of 1789 restored to litigants direct access to all inferior state courts. By the following year most causes were again being tried in court, with the assistance of lawyers. All attempts to regulate lawyers' fees more effectively suffered a similar fate during these years. The most notable effort—a strong proposal to establish an ironclad fee schedule in 1787—twice failed to pass the Massachusetts legislature.[38]

In Pennsylvania the ideas of Jesse Higgins were embodied to a limited extent in a statute of 1809 that opened to arbitration all civil suits involving less than one hundred dollars. Subsequently the system was extended to permit justices of the peace to determine suits for larger amounts where both parties desired it. This was a far cry from the general compulsory arbitration law envisaged by Higgins, and it provoked no irresistible enthusiasm for lay justice among litigants. While one twentieth-century scholar has concluded that arbitration became a popular technique for settling lesser disputes, it seems to have appealed chiefly to the rural population. "In Philadelphia," confessed a leading supporter of the new system, "they had to abandon it from the abuse of arbitration, making a trade of it by protracting their sittings, & holding short sessions on several actions the same day."[39] As in Massachusetts, laymen proved no more trustworthy than professionals when it came to selling their judicial services cheap.

Although nonlawyers were appointed to the bench in many states and flourished even at the state supreme court level, their presence did little more to reestablish the utopian spirit in jurisprudence. They spoke the language of a golden age, to be sure. John Dudley, trader and farmer, who held the post of associate justice of the Supreme Court of New Hampshire from 1785 to 1797, was wont to harangue a jury in these terms:

> You have heard, gentlemen of the jury, what has been said in this case by the lawyers, the rascals! . . . They talk of law. Why, gentlemen, it is not law that we want, but justice. They would govern us by the common law of England. Trust me, gentlemen, common sense is a much safer guide for us; —the common sense of Raymond, Epping, Exeter, and the other towns which have sent us here to try this case between two of our neighbors. A clear head and an honest heart are worth more than all the law of all the lawyers . . . There was one good thing said at the bar. It was from one Shakspeare, an English player, I believe. No matter. It is good enough almost to be in the Bible. It is this: "Be just and fear not." That, gentlemen, is the law in this case, and law enough in any case. "Be just and fear not." It is our business to do justice between the parties, not by any quirks of the law out of Coke or Blackstone, books that I never read, and never will, but by common sense and common honesty as between man and man. That is our business; and the curse of God is upon us, if we neglect, or evade, or turn aside from it.[40]

For all his fervent disclaimers, though, Dudley paid attention more often than not to the arguments of counsel in reaching his decisions, as did most other lay judges of the period. Adversary proceedings still shaped the course of litigation and helped to prevent a return to the arbitrary ways of khadi justice. In the absence of accessible American precedents—the first book of reports appeared in Connecticut in 1789, but most states did not authorize the printing of judicial decisions until after the turn of the century—all judges faced the task of constructing a body of reasonable principles out of materials drawn largely from a common-law heritage and argued out in courtroom debate. In this winnowing process nonprofessionals often proved as discriminating as their trained contemporaries—a point conceded by Theophilus Parsons, the learned Massachusetts jurist, when he described Dudley without irony as "the best judge I ever knew in New Hampshire."[41]

Whether on the bench or not, American laymen found it virtually impossible to resist the common-law image of man. To Crèvecoeur's famous query "What is an American?" one might well reply that in the eighteenth century he was a creature of the common law and, by implication, of the common lawyer. Although the liaison between practitioner and public was a troubled one at best, it was stamped with inevitability. Clients might rail at pettifoggery and profiteering and attorneys denounce in turn the materialism of a bourgeois society (a standard theme in nineteenth-century legal writing), but both groups were indispensable to a system based upon individual initiative and enterprise. Even in the remotest parts of the country a mutual interest bound them together in uneasy partnership. Charles Watts, just beginning a practice in the bayou parishes of Louisiana, noted: "I am cheerful and in good spirits. I am doing well in business and if I keep my health doubt not to succeed to my utmost reasonable expectations . . . There is a vast deal of litigation. No man pays without being sued and every man is in debt . . . I read, write, ride, walk and give advice. I associate with the parish Judge, the Clerk of the Court, the Sheriff and one or two other folks and am looked up to as an oracle."[42] In retrospect the image seems peculiarly appropriate. To the postrevolutionary public the American lawyer did represent, above all else, an oracular force, to be consulted though not always understood or trusted.

As to occupation I have too much, but of fees too little. We are obliged I assure you nowadays to work hard for small profits. The law is of no use now but to knaves and they do not put themselves in the hands of the most honest lawyers. The delays and obstructions are all the people know of the laws, and they vent their spleen upon the profession. Somewhat must be done. *Jawbone* must do it if nothing else will.

Sampson to Peter DuPonceau, April 24, 1825

3 William Sampson and the Codification Movement

The zealous partisanship of the Jeffersonian years, when Republican politicians regularly assailed the obstructionism of Federalist judges and their English-oriented law, gave way to a more equable brand of consensus politics following the War of 1812. Andrew Jackson's victory over the British at New Orleans aroused in most Americans a heightened awareness of national identity and purpose that set the tone of political discourse for more than a decade. Lawyers as a class profited from the general euphoria that accompanied business expansion and a rising standard of living in the Era of Good Feelings. Although popular attacks upon the bar did not altogether cease—even Austin's *Observations* enjoyed a new lease on life when reprinted for a younger generation of readers during the short-lived depression of 1819—lay criticism tended to be highly localized and ineffective, compared to the growing prestige that attached to a successful legal practice.

Yet at the very time that outside interference was reduced to a minimum, the profession was wracked by internal dissensions that put in issue the credibility not merely of the American lawyer but of the basic administrative norms of common-law justice. Promoted by liberal practitioners with no political axes to grind, the codification movement of the 1820s sought to close the gap between legal dogmatism and the changing needs of a democratic society. In a wide-ranging debate that spilled over from law journals to newspapers and literary magazines, reformers raised fundamental questions about the nature of the judicial process, the relative merits of courts and legislatures as policymaking agencies, and the feasibility of legislative planning for the general welfare. As in any large movement, a complex interaction of circumstances and personalities contributed to the final outcome of the codification effort, but in its impact upon popular opinion it owed a unique debt to the tireless public relations work of one man—the flamboyant Irish émigré lawyer William Sampson (1764-1836). More than any of his contemporaries, Sampson dramatized the issues of legal dissent for a lay audience, initiating a continuing dialogue on the uses of juridical power whose end is not yet in sight.[1]

To an English statesman of the mid-eighteenth century plagued by reports of increasing militancy among American colonists, the latest dispatches from Ireland must have come as a welcome relief. In that neighboring island dependency a close-knit Anglo-Irish oligarchy of landlords and bureaucrats ruled with an iron hand, ruthlessly repressing all efforts by the native population to secure civil or political rights. Although numerically an insignificant minority, the so-called Anglican "ascendancy" owned five-sixths of all Irish lands, controlled the Irish Parliament at Dublin, and monopolized key administrative positions within the government and the established Church of Ireland. Through a battery of harsh penal laws—a by-product of England's climactic battlefield victories of the previous century—the Roman Catholic "natives," who made up three-fourths of the Irish population, were reduced to the status of a permanently depressed tenantry. Forbidden to vote or to hold public office, to attend a university or to enter a profession, to purchase land or to practice their religion, the Irish Catholics were more viciously exploited on the whole than any comparable social group in Western Europe prior to the French Revolution. Discriminatory regulations extended to the smallest details of private life and sought to instill in the Irish masses a consciousness of their inherent inferiority to the Protestant elite groups above them. Besides the tiny Anglican aristocracy at the top of the social pyramid, a middle strata of some one million Presbyterians—merchants, tradesmen, linen weavers, artisans, and farmers—shared the ruling-class mystique, even as they chafed under lesser political and religious disabilities that were still imposed upon Dissenters throughout the British Isles. With each class insulated from the others by law, custom, and religion, Ireland thus formed a model caste system, in which, as one nineteenth-century historian remarked, a few "griping borough-mongers" tyrannized over the Presbyterian bourgeoisie and, "by way of recompense, encouraged the Protestants to gratify the worst passions of human nature, by triumphing over the Catholics."[2]

Into this closed and seemingly unshakable society William Sampson was born on January 17, 1764. The son of an Anglican clergyman, he had every reason to court favor with the Establishment, as other members of the family had been doing with marked success ever since old John Sampson sailed from England a century earlier to settle the Irish lands granted to him by Queen Elizabeth I. Under normal circumstances William would doubtless have continued the ancestral tradition and found for himself a comfortable niche in the Church, the army, or the bureaucracy. But the times were anything but normal, and the rising generation, caught up in a vortex of revolutionary political upheaval, had no choice but to confront endemic social ills that earlier elites had managed to ignore.

For William the legitimacy of the Irish power structure became an open question long before he reached manhood. Growing up at Londonderry in northern Ireland, where the Presbyterians formed a compact majority, he was early exposed to the Dissenters' hostile view of bishops and landed aristocrats as well as to that heritage of republican idealism that stretched back to John Knox and the covenanters of the seventeenth century. The outbreak of the American Revolution three months after his eleventh birthday provided an object lesson in democratic nation-building and fired him with enthusiasm for the cause of "liberty" and electoral reform at home. As he later noted approvingly, the transatlantic rebels "had reduced the theories of the great philosophers of England, France, and other countries into practice; and persecutors began to find themselves surprised like owls overtaken by the day."³

Middle-class Irishmen responded to the American example by organizing in 1778 an armed militia, the Irish Volunteers, to wrest major concessions from the hard-pressed English government. Commanded by liberal aristocrats such as Henry Grattan, the Protestant Volunteers enjoyed for a time unparalleled popular support, even among the Catholic masses. As British troops suffered one setback after another on the battlefields of North America, Irishmen of every description rejoiced at the prospect of their own impending national liberation. By 1782, when Sampson at eighteen joined the Volunteers as a commissioned officer, the organization numbered 80,000 potential fighting men, and the war-weary English, unwilling to engage in a new police action, acceded to Irish demands for legislative autonomy without a struggle. Thereafter Grattan's Parliament exercised complete control over domestic policy-making through the rest of the century, while Ireland retained a privileged trade position within the British Empire. (Ironically, it was this very commonwealth status that American statesmen had unsuccessfully urged as their alternative to revolution a decade earlier.)

Once the victory celebrations died down in Dublin, however, the old divisions within Irish society speedily reasserted themselves. Political reformers secured a few piecemeal civil rights for Catholics and Dissenters, but all moves toward Catholic emancipation or agrarian relief encountered a solid wall of conservative resistance. While the franchise was broadened somewhat to include a slightly larger proportion of middle-class property owners, the entrenched Anglo-Irish aristocracy stubbornly pursued its traditional shortsighted policies with even greater irresponsibility than before. The Irish Volunteers, who had begun to recruit Catholic members, were soon denounced as dangerous radicals and forced to disband, but many held on to their weapons as they watched with mounting bitterness the worsening state of Irish political life.

In these troubled transition years Sampson completed his education and settled down into family life and a professional career. After attending classes at Dublin's Trinity College (from which his father had graduated with honors a generation earlier), he married into a well-established family and traveled to London to pursue the study of law, "keeping his terms" at Lincoln's Inn. On his return to Ireland in 1791 he was promptly admitted to the Irish bar and began a promising practice in Belfast, then a bustling seaport as well as the intellectual capital of the country.

Although in retrospect he always insisted that he "never was inclined to political contention," he found himself drawn almost at once into the ranks of antigovernment activists, for his debut as a lawyer virtually coincided with a fresh crisis in Irish affairs. Too long had Grattan's Parliament dragged its heels in matters of reform; now, with the great changes wrought in France by the Revolution of 1789 before their eyes, Irish liberals found further procrastination intolerable and began to reorganize for a new assault upon their caretaker regime. Again leadership was provided by the alienated sons of the Anglican elite, strongly supported by the middle classes, but this time the reformers sought from the outset to create a mass base by appealing directly to the Catholic natives. So was born the Society of United Irishmen, founded in Belfast late in 1791 by Sampson's friend Theobald Wolfe Tone to work toward the twin objectives of complete religious toleration and universal manhood suffrage in Ireland.

At first an open and orderly pressure group, the United Irishmen spread reform ideas to the remotest parts of the country through the pages of their official organ, the Belfast *Northern Star*, one of the most significant democratic newspapers of the English-speaking world at the time. Published twice a week at less than twopence a copy, the *Star* soon attracted more than four thousand regular subscribers, outstripping all other Irish journals in circulation. Each issue included much material on the progress and achievements of the French Revolution (reprinted from the leading Jacobin papers of France), along with original broadsides from Irish reformers. Sampson was an important contributor, as well as the paper's legal counsel, from its beginnings down to its final suppression by the government in 1797.[4] His barbed satires ranged widely over the abuses of the existing political system, but he scored his greatest success with a series of articles attacking legal obscurantism as a major obstacle to the emergence of popular government among his countrymen.

This theme—which was to remain a lifelong preoccupation with him—received its finest early expression in a burlesque piece that he brought out in 1794 (and republished in the United

States a decade later). Here he ridiculed the unintelligible jargon of English criminal law, as he envisaged a trial in which a hurdy-gurdy stood charged with criminal libel for daring to play the inflammatory "Ça ira" along with its other tunes. (The situation was not as fanciful as one might think, since the music of a hurdy-gurdy did form part of the evidence used to convict one Thomas Muir of sedition during these years.) While Sampson zestfully demolished the pretentious formalities of courtroom procedure, he struck his most telling blows at the partisanship of Irish judges, in whose hands an ambiguous law could be transformed into a powerful bulwark of the ruling classes. Whenever the law was oracular, he maintained, judges usurped the functions of both jurors and legislators. Trials then became mere puppet shows, with jurors forbidden even to reason about the facts, "but on the contrary they are to hear with the *law's ear*, see with the *law's eye*, speak with the *law's voice*, of which law the court are alone to judge."[5]

These apprehensions concerning judicial power (which were later to be revived in a New World setting) stemmed directly from personal experience. Sampson practiced on the Northeast Circuit, which included the most militant counties of Ireland, and as the associate and protégé of the brilliant defense counsel John Philpot Curran he early became involved in some of the most famous political trials of the decade. William Orr, Joseph Cuthbert, the Reverend William Jackson, and Michael Egan figured among his clients, as did scores of others charged with treason, sedition, or libel. But the chances of winning an acquittal almost disappeared with the passage of increasingly repressive legislation and the vesting of broad discretionary power in the bench over the conduct of causes and the fixing of punishments. The United Irish Societies were outlawed and driven underground after England went to war with France, and by 1797 mere membership in the organization was punishable by death. Sampson, who regarded himself as a moderate and had for tactical reasons refused to join the Irish underground, now felt compelled to side openly with the cause of his clients:

> It shocked me to see hundreds of thousands of my countrymen, among whom were many possessing all the purity and all the virtue that could adorn their species, branded as traitors, and living at the mercy of the veriest and the vilest traitors. Manhood could nor ought not to endure it; and seeing the crisis at hand, when there

could be no more neutrality, I took, in open court, the oath of the United Irishmen, repeating it from the very document on which my client then stood upon his trial for his life or his death . . . I did not do this in a spirit of bravado or romance, but because I hated dissimulation, and felt a consciousness that I was doing what became me, and I have never repented of it.[6]

Thereafter he was a marked man in the eyes of the authorities, who considered him a self-confessed conspirator and possible ringleader in the growing movement to establish an independent Irish republic. Actually he was a most reluctant rebel, never comfortable in the presence of violence, and convinced that the government was deliberately prodding the nation toward revolution, in a calculated bid for stronger military support from England. The events that sparked the abortive "rebellion of '98" seemed to demonstrate the truth of this proposition, as they made it impossible for him ever to regain that middle ground he had once prized so highly.

"Nothing but terror will keep them in order," wrote the commander of the Irish garrison to his British superiors late in 1797. For months fresh troops had been arriving from England to help keep the peace against the dual threat of Irish insurrection and a combined naval invasion from France, where Wolfe Tone and other United Irish leaders had gone to work out the details of a projected military alliance. An Insurrection Act passed by the Dublin Parliament the previous year placed all Ireland under virtual military rule and sanctioned the most extreme measures of repression under the plea of necessity. So was launched an official reign of terror that grew in scope and intensity as time passed. Agents provocateurs infiltrated the United Irish Societies and reported their plans to the authorities; suspected militants were arrested without warrant and imprisoned without trial; illegal searches and seizures became commonplace, as did looting, arson, and various forms of physical torture. To add to the confusion, secret farm societies (such as the Catholic Defenders and the Protestant Peep-of-Day Boys) plundered the countryside at intervals, for reasons of their own, while a host of Orange Lodges sprang up in Ulster to combat the United Irishmen on their home ground, in the name of a virulent anti-Catholicism.

Early in 1798 the government began a systematic roundup of

all remaining radical leaders, as rumors circulated that a vast expeditionary force—Napoleon's shadowy *Armée d'Angleterre*—was being assembled on the channel coast of France. Mass arrests took place in Dublin on March 12, with Sampson's name on the list of the accused. Forewarned, he went into hiding, after notifying the authorities that he would give himself up as soon as he was officially assured of a speedy trial.[7] The charges of high treason against him were, so far as he could tell, wild fabrications: a militiaman who had searched his rooms claimed to have turned up a commission appointing him a lieutenant general in the French army, as well as a list of individuals marked for assassination in Ireland! Sampson could not believe that the government seriously proposed to prosecute him on such trumped-up grounds; the real design, he reasoned, was to imprison him indefinitely without bail, thereby depriving his clients of legal counsel and cutting short his work on a projected history of the times, for which he had begun to collect documentary evidence of military atrocities committed against the peasants in the southern counties. After waiting in vain for some official response to his offer of conditional surrender, he managed to take ship for England disguised as a female passenger, but midway in the crossing someone spotted him shaving, and he was arrested as soon as he set foot on English soil at Whitehaven.

Several weeks later, on May 5, he was returned to Dublin under guard. By that time the long-awaited Irish rebellion had broken out in earnest, and heavy fighting was under way in Wexford and other areas. As Sampson passed through Dublin Castle on the way to his place of confinement he noticed a pile of captured enemy weapons whose crude workmanship told better than any dispatches what the probable outcome of the struggle must be. They were mostly green crooked sticks cut from hedges and topped with long spikes, nails, knives, or scythe blades to form homemade pikes—fit emblems of a popular but desperate cause. Deprived in advance of their best leaders, who were either on the Continent or in British jails, the insurgents wore themselves out in uncoordinated local actions, which were put down by the military in piecemeal fashion. Any hope of effective French aid vanished with Napoleon's fateful decision on May 19 to divert his armada to the conquest of Egypt, but still the Irish rebels maintained a stubborn resistance that forced the government to increase its troop strength to unheard-of levels. In the end it took 140,000 fighting men to put down the rebellion. Half of these were Irish militiamen or yeomanry of varying degrees of reliability, but the other half were trained British regulars—twice the number of British soldiers that fought on the Continent against the French Republic and Empire from 1793 through the battle of Waterloo.

By July, in the face of these impressive odds, most of the rebels had surrendered, but the fierce ethnic and religious hatreds nourished by the conflict made any genuine pacification impossible. To a matter-of-fact Englishman like Charles Cornwallis, who had been thrust somewhat reluctantly upon the scene as commander of all British forces, the perfervid emotionalism of the Irish crisis dwarfed anything in his previous experience, including the American Revolution. "The whole country is in such a state that I feel frightened and ashamed whenever I consider that I am looked upon as being at the head of it," he confessed to a brother officer.

> Except in the instances of the six state trials that are going on here, there is no law either in town or country but martial law . . . conducted by Irishmen heated with passion and revenge. But all this is trifling compared to the numberless murders that are hourly committed by our people without any process or examination whatever. The yeomanry are in the style of the Loyalists in America, only much more numerous and powerful, and a thousand times more ferocious. These men have saved the country, but they now take the lead in rapine and murder. The Irish militia, with few officers, and those chiefly of the worst kind, follow closely on the heels of the yeomanry in murder and every kind of atrocity.[8]

Resolved to set an example of clemency for others to follow, Cornwallis gave his support to a compromise arrangement involving Sampson (whom he considered one of the "principal criminals") and the other prisoners who were still awaiting trial. They were guaranteed their freedom if they testified fully concerning the United Irish organization and agreed to exile in some European country not then at war with England. To save the life of a condemned fellow prisoner, all accepted these terms. Sampson, whose health had begun to break during his months of confinement, chose Portugal as his place of asylum and, after many frustrating delays, reached Oporto in March 1799.

"Good God!" he mused later, in looking back over his refugee years on the Continent. "Will there never be a period of civilization, when humanity will emerge from darkness and barbarity?"⁹ His *Memoirs* read much like a picaresque novel today, but at the time his misadventures seemed far more sinister than amusing. He had scarcely settled down at the country home of a hospitable English merchant when he was arrested by the Portuguese government on vague charges, the exact nature of which he could never discover. Since his papers were repeatedly ransacked, however, he guessed that the English minister was somehow responsible for this "persecution," which must have been expected to turn up fresh subversive writings. Shuttled from one jail to another for the next two months, he experienced at first hand the uncertainty and helplessness that made daily life a Kafkaesque nightmare for those enmeshed in an arbitrary criminal process:

> The whole science of criminal jurisprudence in Portugal is this: to throw the suspected person into a secret dungeon, which is aptly called in their judicial phrase, *Inferno* (Hell). Here the wretch remains until he is reported fit to be examined. If he confesses, he is put into irons, and either condemned as a slave, to work in chains, or sent to Goa or the American plantations. If he does not confess he remains in his dungeon. I mentioned to one of the gaolers my sense of this hardship, as an obstinate guilty person might deny the truth, whilst an innocent one, less courageous, might very readily, to relieve himself from such a state of misery, make a false confession: his answer was laconic, *"logo confesse,"* "they soon confess."¹⁰

After an absurd hearing before a Portuguese judge who could not speak English, Sampson was left largely to his own devices. He spent long hours reading or playing the flute, drawing charcoal designs on his prison walls or composing romantic notes to a dark-eyed young girl whose balcony he could see from his window. (These billets-doux he then lowered, with commendable Irish resourcefulness, in a hollowed-out orange fastened to the end of a stocking thread.) Just as these random activities were settling down into a fixed routine he was abruptly released and transported to a miserable fishing boat about to weigh anchor in Lisbon harbor. Only when well out to sea did he learn for the first time that he was being officially deported to France as an undesirable alien. Despite the monumental incompetence of captain and crew, which led to a near shipwreck on the coast of Spain, he managed in due course to reach Bayonne, where his reputation for once assured him of a friendly reception.

During the next six years (June 1799-May 1805) he remained in France as a prisoner of war—first at Bordeaux, then in Paris, where his wife and two children (whom he had not seen since he left Ireland) joined him early in 1802. Despite the almost continuous state of hostilities with England, he was permitted to move about freely (for who could doubt his ardent Anglophobia?) and even to criticize, from the high ground of revolutionary principle, the growing authoritarianism of Napoleon's rule. Spending his summers at the fashionable spas of Montmorency and his winters in the capital, he hobnobbed with the great and near-great of French society, including Josephine and her redoubtable mother-in-law, Letizia Bonaparte. In some respects this was the most pleasant period of his life, a lotus-eating interlude in an otherwise combative career, but it also marked a crucial stage in his professional development. As his imprisonment by the Portuguese had intensified his concern for the rights of the accused in criminal cases, so his lengthy sojourn in France set him to thinking about broader issues of legal reform—about nothing less, in fact, than the total restructuring of the Anglo-American legal system.

An interested foreign observer could scarcely have chosen a better time to study the mechanics of societal evolution at close range. Under Napoleon all France was transformed into a vast social laboratory, in which government planners labored to provide the postrevolutionary public with a set of stabilizing institutions. Rationalization achieved its most impressive results in the area of jurisprudence, where the comprehensive Code Napoleon supplanted the divergent usages of local *parlements* after March 1804. Sampson watched the progress of the codification experiment with growing admiration, and a personal acquaintance with several French statesmen and jurists made him even more appreciative of the merits of a code system, as opposed to the uncertainties of judicial precedent. Years later he would renew these Old World ties in an unexpected way, for according to his daughter's testimony "after the restoration of the Bourbons, several eminent French emigrants, and amongst others Joseph Buonaparte, settled in the United States; most of these united in choosing Mr. Sampson as their legal adviser;

some of them had befriended him when an exile, and he now more than repaid the obligation."[11]

In the spring of 1805 Sampson left Paris for the neutral port of Hamburg, armed with a prisoner-of-war passport from the French War Department. He hoped that less compromising surroundings might induce the British Government to grant his long-standing request for permission to return to Ireland long enough to wind up his affairs before embarking permanently for the United States. (With Jefferson in the White House, even "Irish Jacobins" were now welcome there for the first time.) But, although several old friends held high posts in the coalition government of Charles James Fox, official British policy toward him remained what it had always been: no deals. For almost another year he waited in vain for some positive response to his repeated applications, as he busied himself, in true *philosophe* fashion, with the education of his eleven-year-old son—tutoring him in the rudiments of prose composition, art, and modern languages as they strolled for hours each day along the quais. Finally the advance of Napoleon's armies accomplished what no amount of paper work had been able to do. In the face of the impending military occupation of Hamburg by French forces, the resident British minister reluctantly issued an emergency passport to Sampson and his family, enabling them to board one of the last vessels bound for England.

Their subsequent appearance in London created as much joy in official circles as a visitation of the plague. After trading insults for more than an hour with His Majesty's first lord of the admiralty, Sampson was placed under house arrest, to be shipped off to America at the earliest possible opportunity. This came some three weeks later, in mid-May, when he boarded the packet *Windsor Castle* at Falmouth. Once more he was separated from his wife and children, under peculiarly trying circumstances, for he was ill again (with yellow jaundice this time), and he seriously doubted that he could survive the voyage. But seven weeks at sea revived his spirits, until he felt almost a new man by the time his ship arrived in New York harbor on July 4, 1806. An auspicious date to begin life in the New World, he thought. By the time he got ashore it was late, but scattered bonfires were still blazing and the mayor and other dignitaries were out celebrating in the streets with their constituents. Best of all, there were no troops around to repress popular enthusiasm. Here at last, it seemed, was a "land of peace and liberty" where reason prevailed over force and the institutional forms of Old World corruption had not taken root.

Sampson was forty-two years old when he arrived in America—a somewhat advanced age to begin afresh the practice of a profession he had been forced to abandon eight years earlier. Besides the usual difficulties of adjustment, he encountered much personal ill will from a legal community that still remained largely Federalist and antirevolutionary in character. Only a short time earlier James Kent and other bar leaders had voiced strong objections to the very idea of permitting a "fugitive jacobin" like Sampson's friend Thomas Addis Emmet to practice in the New York courts. While Emmet did manage to obtain a counselor's license in February 1805 under a ruling of the New York Supreme Court that his alien status did not bar him from pursuing a legal career in the state, a strong conservative faction of lawyers continued to oppose the admission of any other Irishmen. When Sampson applied for his license in August 1806 the controversy reached a climax. It was finally decided that he should be admitted under the Emmet precedent, but at the same time the supreme court renounced any further flirtation with European radicalism by ruling "that hereafter no person, not being a natural born or naturalized citizen of the *United States*, shall be admitted as an attorney or counsellor of this court."[12]

In the early years of his practice Sampson found the silent ostracism of his colleagues a potent force in keeping clients from his door. "I am getting on through hard and adverse beginnings," he reported to a friend in the summer of 1808,[13] by which time the social climate had begun to thaw. Yet even after he achieved full acceptance in legal circles he never managed to build up a very large or lucrative American practice. One reason—perhaps the chief reason—for his qualified professional success lay in his own quixotic personality. To his contemporaries he seemed, above all, a figure of fun—a warmhearted, gregarious Irishman whose infectious good humor few could resist. Even those like Chancellor Kent, who thought "his notions of law & Government were utopian, & wild, & radical,"[14] came in time to relish his wit and polished manners and to seek out his company on social occasions. His very physical appearance projected a kind of theatrical charm, a hint of bravura performance. A portrait of 1807 shows him seated at a portable writing desk, quill in hand: a large oval face above a white stock; dark wavy hair brushed negligently over a high forehead; shrewd, piercing eyes, suggestive alike of boldness and suppressed mirth; prominent nose and ears; and a wide, sensuous mouth. Despite the stiffness of the pose, there is no mistaking the romantic soul within: an appropriate treatment of one who could describe American women as "fair-haired Dryads of the woods" while criticizing their haughty European rivals for having "cheeks of brass and eye-balls of stone." Such hyperbole went over much better in after-dinner conversation than in courtroom pleading, but Sampson all too often indulged his muse regardless of occasion, so that his oral arguments mirrored both the brilliance and the frivolity of his table talk.

In his penchant for the picturesque phrase he was, of course, by no means unique. Most lawyers and judges of the time, however they declaimed in favor of "chaste" and restrained eloquence, liked nothing better than to wallow in sentimentality when occasion offered. (Did not even Webster and Marshall reportedly shed tears over the proprietary claims of little Dartmouth College?) Yet in an age of long-winded oratory, when many other practitioners thought that "getting back to first principles" meant starting with Genesis and working their way up, Sampson was in a class by himself. For one thing, he was not limited to classical, biblical, or Shakespearean allusions; he could (and did) drag the manifold wrongs of oppressed Ireland into his cases, whether the issue was rape, fraud, or the proper interpretation of a contract. His apprenticeship years with Curran had left their mark here, it seems; although Sampson, after listening to one of his mentor's interminable harangues, had once likened him—with fair accuracy—to a rampaging river that swept heedlessly over everything in sight,

> Leaving nothing he could find
> But his client's cause behind.

American legal commentators were soon to echo such complaints against the émigrés of '98 and to warn beginning law students against the "florid eloquence of the Irish school."[15]

But Sampson's courtroom flamboyance, however unprofessional, fitted into a larger pattern of divided loyalties, since he remained at heart a publicist as well as a lawyer. In America, to be sure, he rarely engaged in the kind of partisan polemics that had made him notorious in Ireland. He saw little need for such broadsides, since he adhered to a consensus theory of American politics that minimized party differences on most issues. Only in 1812 did his admiration for Jefferson (with whom he carried on an intermittent correspondence for some ten years) lead him to publish anonymously two small pamphlets in which he defended Republican policy and lashed out at England's violations of international law.[16] Otherwise he contented himself with propaganda of quite another kind, for which the courtroom became his forum and the published transcripts of sensational trials his pamphlet literature.

He had first taken up shorthand as a fledgling Irish lawyer, to preserve for posterity the moving speeches of John Philpot Curran in defense of the United Irishmen, and in the United States he became a pioneer court reporter whose stenographic skills enabled him to produce for the public authentic accounts of celebrated cases, in several of which he had taken part as counsel. Looking back over a dozen of these published reports, commentators have concluded that he did a thriving and prestigious business at the American bar, but exactly the opposite inference would be closer to the truth. He went to the trouble of publishing his cases partly for ideological reasons and partly to supplement the inadequate income he obtained from his practice.[17]

A less distorted picture of the scope and nature of that practice may be gleaned from the printed reports of all New York tribunals during a sample five-year period (1816-1820), in which Rogers' *New York City-Hall Recorder* reported many municipal court decisions not ordinarily available in printed form. Sampson appeared in only thirty of these cases, and three-fourths of them were below the appellate level. (Compare the record of his more distinguished colleague Thomas Addis Emmet, who in the same years argued 141 cases, 73 of them before the New York Supreme Court or the New York Court of Errors.) The reports further demonstrate that besides being primarily a trial lawyer Sampson tended to specialize to a great extent in civil rights litigation, and that a substantial proportion of his clients came from foreign-born or low-income groups. His private correspondence confirms this profile: although he liked to describe himself to friends as a "ready

money lawyer" whose inflexible motto was "no counsel without
fee," he found it virtually impossible to turn down a needy
client with a meritorious cause—from the Catholic priest who
refused to testify about things he had learned in the confessional
to the Eskimo family whose members had been abducted from
their homeland by a Barnum-type ship captain and were being
exhibited like animals to New York audiences.[18] Even in later
years, when he pleaded on four separate occasions before the
United States Supreme Court, the libertarian aspects of his
practice remained conspicuous. In *Ogden* v. *Saunders* (1827),
his most famous case, he joined a galaxy of renowned cocounsel
(William Wirt, Edward Livingston, David B. Ogden, and
Walter Jones) to vindicate the constitutionality of New York's
bankruptcy legislation, while in *U.S.* v. *Nicholl* (1827) he helped
to prosecute in the public interest the surety of a Treasury agent
who had misappropriated government funds.[19] The ideological
components discernible in many individual cases were linked to
broader questions of legal reform in his stenographic publications. One reported trial in particular pointed up the need for a
massive restructuring of American law along more democratic
lines. The *Case of the Journeymen Cordwainers of the City of
New York* (1809) marked one of the earliest attempts to establish the legality of collective bargaining in America. A group of
workers had formed an association to improve their lot and
sought to enforce a demand for higher wages through strike
activity. While no American statute prohibited such conduct, it
stood condemned as an illegal conspiracy at common law.
Should English doctrine on this point control the decision of a
New York judge? Sampson argued that it should not.

The common law, he observed, had never been adopted in
full by the American colonies. Even Blackstone acknowledged
that the colonists took with them only those legal precepts and
institutions that were suited to conditions in the New World.
And now that independence had been achieved it was more
important than ever to guard against any foreign doctrines that
might impair the growth of a democratic society. English conspiracy statutes, directed against working-class organizations,
had no place in a free America. "We might as well prevent
parents from conspiring to marry their children, indict landlords for refusing to let their house at the usual rents, or
merchants from following the rates of the markets," Sampson
maintained. He attacked the class bias of English legislators and

judges, whose reactionary pronouncements, he claimed, were held in superstitious awe by American jurists. Such blind adherence to common-law precedents could undermine the very ideals for which the Revolution had been fought, as in a recent workmen's case in Philadelphia where

> his honor said it was improper to inquire whether or not the application of the common law to our concerns would operate as an attack upon the rights of man . . . But the constitution of this State is founded on the equal rights of men; and whatever is an attack upon those rights is contrary to the constitution. Whether it is, or is not, an attack upon the rights of man, is, therefore, more fitting to be inquired into, than whether or not it is conformable to the usages of Picts, Romans, Britons, Danes, Jutes, Angles, Saxons, Normans, or other barbarians, who lived in the night of human intelligence . . . The more I reflect upon the advantages this nation has gained by independence, the more I regret that one thing should still be wanting to crown the noble arch—a NATIONAL CODE.[20]

Sampson's oratory failed, however, to convince the court to reconsider the reasonableness of common-law doctrines adopted as the basis of New York jurisprudence by the framers of the state constitution of 1777. For all the local interest aroused by his cases, he remained a minor critic of the law—indistinguishable from other shadowy agitators in Ohio, Kentucky, and Pennsylvania—until a chance invitation to address the New York Historical Society in December 1823 brought him and his ideas at last to the attention of a nationwide audience.

"I have sent you a copy of a discourse upon the Common Law which I delivered on the anniversary of the historical society," Sampson informed his friend David Baillie Warden, a former American consul general at Paris who had chosen to remain in France after his tour of duty as a kind of one-man cultural exchange agency. "I have much matter ready if there was encouragement enough for a very grave work on this subject on which I have meditated since I first became a lawyer, but the occasion for promulgating such opinions was never ripe till now . . . The subject is an important one in this country and . . . I have at heart the good it may do."[21] His essay, which contained the most devastating critique of common-law idealism ever written in America, relied less upon erudition than upon wit and irony to achieve its effects. By tracing legal history back to the customs of barbaric German tribes, Sampson sought to dispel forever the myth that a golden age of English jurisprudence had existed prior to the Norman Conquest. This was no exercise in pedantry, for the "Saxon idols" still held a firm place in American legal folklore. Even such a staunch opponent of Blackstone and Mansfield as Thomas Jefferson professed a sentimental loyalty to the "pure" institutions and practices of the Saxon era.[22]

But what relevance had the Saxon experience for nineteenth-century America? Sampson queried. Were not these ancient Britons less civilized even than the Iroquois Indians of the New World? Of modern commercial transactions they had no inkling; their criminal laws did not progress beyond the brutalities of the *lex talionis;* and there was little evidence to suggest that they originated the jury system, which they seldom employed in comparison with the trial by water or red-hot ploughshares. Yet their primitive codes, with all their deficiencies, proved more humane than the legal system subsequently imposed upon them by their Norman conquerors. It took centuries after the Battle of Hastings for judges to reestablish the rights of the individual citizen, by resorting to a series of awkward fictions that made the law unintelligible to the average man.

Was it not high time to discard such mummery and pretense and place the law upon a rational and scientific footing? "The well-being of society requires that a subject of such vital importance should be brought to the test of reason in the open light of day," Sampson urged. "Having adopted the common law of England, so far as it is not repugnant to our constitutions, we have a mighty interest to know clearly what it is, and from what stock it comes. We must either be governed by laws made for us, or made by us."[23]

Since history demonstrated that no part of the common-law tradition deserved special veneration, it was all the more imperative that every doctrine be tested by the principles of "natural reason, universal justice, and present convenience."[24] In championing the cause of innovation, however, Sampson was by no means simply following a course already mapped out by earlier reformers; in fact a wide gap separated him from even the politically oriented Jeffersonian agitators of the pre-1812 years. Those men, as loyal party cadre, had typically attacked the law as an instrument of class domination in America. They had tried to stir up the feelings of backwoods "republicans" against a privileged establishment of urban lawyers and judges whose mastery of abstruse legal doctrines enabled them to promote the ends of a wealthy elite at the expense of the democratic masses. Such partisan tactics proved most effective in frontier areas such as Ohio or the western parts of Pennsylvania, where the labels Republican and Federalist often became interchangeable with "jacobin" and "aristocrat" in the popular mind.[25]

But it was precisely this element of class antagonism that Sampson and his adherents rejected in the 1820s. They worked for reform *within* the legal profession, looking to the scholar rather than the demagogue to carry through their program. Sampson thought of himself as a latter-day Luther, called to purge the law of its superstitious and irrational features so that it might be reestablished on a basis of sound principles intelligible to the average man. Far from desiring to uproot accepted doctrines recklessly, he conceded that "the English reports contain, amidst a world of rubbish, rich treasures of experience, and that those of our own courts contain materials of inestimable worth, and require little more than regulation and systematic order."[26] The task of culling useful precepts from a mass of conflicting court decisions could only be entrusted to the legislature, however, because judges were disinclined by temperament and training to challenge past authorities. Indeed, as Sampson pictured them, judges were little more than slaves to precedent. Whenever a case arose, he argued, the doctrine of stare decisis required that a judge suspend his own views and seek instead to fit the facts into some line of previously reported opinions. Since these opinions were both voluminous and at variance with one another, a litigant had no way to predict the outcome of his case. Even where the circumstances proved unique, and a judge found himself compelled to render a verdict on the basis of his own beliefs, one of the parties necessarily fell victim to the announcement of the new rule.

By its very nature, then, judicial policymaking could lead only to arbitrary and highly personal results; yet Sampson was careful to avoid imputing any sinister or undemocratic motives to the judges themselves. It was the system that was at fault, he insisted, a system adapted to the needs of a society in which the masses could neither read nor write and had therefore to rely upon haphazard decisions from the bench to determine their lawful rights. But in America, where popular education was the rule, each citizen had an obligation to study and comprehend the law for himself. A legislative code modeled upon the Code Napoleon would provide comprehensive guidelines for both lawyers and laymen and would insure popular control over any future changes of policy.

To reduce the amorphous bulk of the law to a system of scientific axioms would prove an immense task, of course, but the first steps in the process had already been taken. Most states periodically revised and digested their written statutes; why not complete the picture by systematizing court decisions as well? Present conditions appeared peculiarly ripe for such an experiment. While European nations still suffered from wars and domestic tyranny, the United States had entered upon an era of unprecedented peace and prosperity, in which the fierce party feuds of the Jeffersonian years seemed buried forever. Citizens of all political faiths could now unite behind the labors of enlightened jurists who would reform the law with a "tender, patient, kindly, and experienced hand."[27]

The *Discourse* was widely noted in the newspaper and periodical press of the time and, especially after its publication in pamphlet form early in 1824, created a predictable hullabaloo among reviewers. Although no purely legal journals existed in America at that moment, lawyers contributed extensively to more general publications, which always contained a healthy smattering of articles dealing with current trends and problems in the law. Attorney Henry D. Sedgwick, writing for Boston's influential *North American Review*, praised Sampson's bold attack upon judicial servility to "precedents not consonant to the spirit of the age" and urged that "at least some of the larger and more wealthy states of the Union should cause their laws to pass under a general revision, and to be formed into *written codes*." Conservative reviewers in Philadelphia and New York, on the other hand, denounced the *Discourse* as shallow satire and suggested that any visionary tampering with the law would destroy one of the strongest bonds of union between the states.[28]

Sampson was frankly delighted at the hornet's nest his essay had stirred up. "Its success has been beyond my anticipations," he chortled. "When it came out it scared the night birds. They are now hushed and in public opinion the point is already carried and I think given up."[29] On the advice of his good friend

Peter DuPonceau of Philadelphia he sent a complimentary copy to the editor of the *Revue encyclopédique,* one of France's foremost literary journals, where it soon received a favorable review. And in England the Radical publicist Richard Carlile reprinted the complete text under circumstances that guaranteed it instant notoriety. "This writer [Carlile] is in gaol," Sampson told a correspondent, "and angry, very naturally, and a sharp saucy fellow . . . [He] was not content with praising me and my discourse to the skies, but he publishes a letter which he sent to the King with a copy telling him very gravely who William Sampson was and how he had been persecuted by Castlereagh. You may well believe how I was surprised but it is hard to be angry with those that praise us."[30]

Encouraged by the public's response to his general propositions, Sampson now launched a promotional campaign designed to point up in greater detail the practical advantages of codification. For two years (1824-1826) he maintained an active correspondence with politicians and jurists throughout the Union, spreading his ideas through local newspapers and national magazines.[31] The cream of this correspondence reappeared in book form in 1826, by which time legal reform had become a commonplace topic of discussion in literary periodicals and a source of increasing comment among foreign observers.[32]

Sampson and his supporters were ardent Francophiles who looked to the Code Napoleon as a model for American legislators. In their eyes the French experience demonstrated the limits of improvement possible under a code system. While they agreed that no set of general principles could answer all human problems, they believed that the wisest precedents of the past might be summarized in definitive fashion as a guide to the future. Then, noted the South Carolinian jurist Thomas Cooper, "the labor of reading and of citing the cases which form the basis of the principles enacted . . . will have been taken away, and if much labor still remains, much has been saved." Instead of acting as a deterrent to further social change, every code would necessarily have to be revised from time to time to incorporate new rights and remedies. "But is it nothing," Cooper argued, "that we have, or can have if we please, a new starting place every half century, leaving behind us the accumulated rubbish of years' proceedings?"[33]

Such laborsaving considerations had special meaning for practicing lawyers in the 1820s, who found themselves confronted with an ever increasing mass of reported decisions. In 1824 Caleb Cushing remarked that the number of volumes of American reports alone had leaped from 8 to 198 during the previous twenty years.[34] Codification provided at least one answer to the rising cost of a lawyer's library, as it likewise promised to speed up significantly the preparation of cases for trial. But the general public would reap the greatest benefits under a code system, according to its proponents, since law would cease to be a mysterious science beyond the ken of the masses. Once reduced to fixed moral principles, its methods and objectives could be appreciated by the average layman, who would find the printed code an indispensable textbook of social ethics. A wiser and more responsible citizenry had reportedly emerged in France since the enactment of the Code Napoleon, while in Louisiana, where a civil code had recently gone into effect, the transplanted New York attorney Charles Watts observed: "The planters and well informed men have the code in their hand, and discuss it as a branch of politics; while, on the contrary, the community here [in New York] are involved in Egyptian darkness."[35]

If laymen were to play a more meaningful role in legal deliberations, however, that did not imply the destruction of a professional bar. The codifiers compared the law to a skilled trade whose practitioners required specialized talents and training. Could every man be his own cobbler? they asked. Obviously not. Yet the principles of shoemaking were known to all, and a customer could readily detect the difference between a good pair of shoes and those of inferior quality. So it would be with the law: a thorough grounding in basic principles would enable the average man to exercise a healthy check upon legal fraud and mysticism, as the Reformation had established popular control of religion without lessening the need for trained ministers. Codes could never produce a lawyerless utopia, for litigation was rooted in the selfish nature of man. But the caliber of the bar would be immensely improved under a code system that would eliminate the uncertain precedents and archaic technicalities that played into the hands of the shyster class of common-law pleaders.

In emphasizing the limited aims of their reform program, Sampson and his colleagues were seeking to dissociate themselves from the radicalism of Jeremy Bentham, the English proponent of codes whose propagandist labors for more than thirty years had made his name synonymous with the codification cause in both Europe and America. Bentham was an eccentric reformer who cherished a rather personal hatred of the English judiciary and of what he regarded as the sentimentality of the natural rights school of jurisprudence. In his view a citizen could claim only such rights as were guaranteed to him by positive legislation. To speak of imaginary states of nature conferring inalienable liberties upon the individual was absurdly romantic. Personal freedom could not exist without specific governmental sanctions. Only a code of laws defining in detail the scope of individual action could protect the average man from designing politicians and judges.[36]

Bentham looked upon such written codes as the sole determinant of rights and duties within a state. They were to cover every conceivable problem that might arise among men, embodying solutions in the form of general principles that all men might grasp. An eighteenth-century faith in the inherent rationality of mankind led Bentham to insist also that each article of a code be followed by an explanatory justification, so that citizens might not only know what the law was, but why it had been framed. On this account he sharply criticized the Code Napoleon, alleging that if the true nature of many of its provisions had been revealed to the French people, they would have rebelled against the Corsican's arbitrary rule.[37]

Most American codifiers, on the other hand, considered the brevity of the French code one of its prime attractions. Nor were they ready to abandon the natural law philosophy of John Locke which had inspired the revolutionists of '76 and now held sway over their sons. Lockean theory and French legislative practice formed the twin foundations upon which Sampson and his adherents proposed to erect *their* codes, which should not supplant preexisting rights but rather supplement and strengthen them.

In rebuttal the opponents of codification, deprived of a favorite whipping boy in Benthamite radicalism, turned their full energies toward discrediting the Code Napoleon. "What kind of legislation is this for all the various and multiform concerns of a whole community?" demanded a writer in the Charleston *Mercury* of July 28, 1825.[38] The French experience, he maintained, merely confirmed the futility of trying to compress human behavior into rigid categories. Without a plethora of judicial interpretations the stifling restraints of the code would long since have acted to check economic and social progress in France. Other critics agreed, charging that many articles were already being superseded by court decisions and that in twenty or thirty years such judicial glosses would constitute the sole source of authority for Frenchmen.[39]

To counter these attacks, which struck at the heart of his program, Sampson appealed directly to one of the most distinguished practicing lawyers of France, André Dupin, for a firsthand account of legal conditions in his country. Dupin's reply, which was published in both the United States and England, supplied an indispensable link in the codification argument. After rehearsing the advantages which France derived from abolishing divergent customs in favor of a uniform national code, Dupin observed:

> It is not true, sir, that the authority of precedents has at all prevailed against the text of our codes, nor that we are threatened, in the most distant manner, with the disappearance of the letter of the law under the heap of interpretations. In every discussion, the text of the law is first resorted to, and if the law speaks, then *non exemplis sed legibus judicandum est.* If the law has not clearly decided on the particular case under discussion, doubtless, it being silent or deficient, the defect is supplied by the judges; but where is the system in which the judgments have not necessarily furnished the complement of legislation.[40]

Judicial construction of doubtful code provisions remained a far cry in his view from judicial control of policymaking, such as existed in common-law countries, where the bench regulated the tempo and nature of legal change through "the exercise of arbitrary power."[41]

Dupin confined his remarks to the French codes, voicing only a hesitant faith in America's readiness for a similar experiment. But from another Frenchman, Count Pierre François Réal, came enthusiastic support for Sampson's labors, coupled with some practical suggestions for setting up and working with a code commission. Réal was uniquely qualified to offer such advice. As a jurist and personal friend of Napoleon he had played a major role in drafting the French codes. His unshakable loyalty to the emperor, whom he served as prefect of police during the

Hundred Days, caused him to be banished from France in 1815 by the restored government of Louis XVIII. Thereafter he emigrated to America and settled in upstate New York, from which refuge he wrote to Sampson in 1824, urging:

> Do as we did, but do it better, profiting by our mistakes. Let four or five good heads be united in a commission, to frame in silence the project of a code. It is not so difficult a task. It is only to consult together, and to select . . . what is best from your best authors. You have ample materials. We had Pothier always in our hands, and above all his Treatise on Obligations. We compared and weighed; we tried to settle what was in doubt, and fix what was uncertain, and were often guided by his solutions, which we did little more than reduce into articles . . . As long as nothing is written, nothing will be done; but you gain something the moment that you have a written text for the groundwork of your discussions, how imperfect soever it may be at first. Our code was far from being adopted, as it was originally proposed in the entire. I doubt whether one hundred articles were preserved in the form in which they were presented. It will require ardent hearts, and cool heads, and resolved industry, for such a work. With these, I think, you will not fail of complete success.[42]

The publication of his *Correspondence with Various Learned Jurists* in 1826 signaled the end of Sampson's active involvement in the codification movement. He was sixty-two years old and his health, long precarious, began to decline perceptibly until his death a decade later. "I feel that years have at length begun to exercise their empire over me," he confessed to Warden in 1829. "I have labored under so much indisposition from reiterated attacks of fever and ague and its consequences that I have done little or no business for two years and more."[43] While he continued to practice law on occasion into the early 1830s, he resisted all temptation to re-engage in controversial public debate of any kind. "In late years," recalled the Irish physician who attended him in his final illness, "his habits were so retired, and his occupations so domestic, that his name seldom came before the public, and his society was only enjoyed by a small circle of intimate friends."[44]

Meanwhile the fortunes of his fellow codifiers fluctuated erratically with the changing political temper of the nation.

For all their dreams of authoritative national codes that

should bring order and coherence to state jurisprudence—much as the Constitution, as interpreted by the Supreme Court, had rationalized federal criminal law by abolishing all nonstatutory crimes—the exponents of codification were tied to the vagaries of twenty-four separate legislative bodies for the realization of their program. (In this respect they closely resembled their twentieth-century counterparts, the Commissioners of Uniform State Laws, whose model statutes, transmitted to the states through the American Bar Association, have seldom been approved by a majority of legislatures.) The obstacles in the way of any concerted state action were further augmented in the antebellum years by the rift between slave and free states, since legislation drafted by a proslavery jurist like Thomas Cooper was apt to contain many features unacceptable to New England lawmakers, and vice versa. Still, at the time of Sampson's retirement in 1826, the prospects for some kind of impending breakthrough seemed bright, and he, who had never aspired to draft a code himself, could look back at his propagandist labors with some satisfaction. In Louisiana, a Civil Code and a Code of Practice had been adopted by the legislature the previous year; New York had commissioned three lawyers to review the inadequacies of her existing statutes as a possible first step in the direction of a general code; significant codification movements were afoot in Pennsylvania and South Carolina; and the American bar in general was sharply divided over the issue, with influential spokesmen arrayed on either side. "Codes are to be proposed, discussed, assailed, defended, throughout the Union," predicted William H. Gardiner to readers of the *North American Review* in January 1827, "and we look to see the day, when *codifiers* and *anti-codifiers* will wage a war as fierce and interminable, as that which raged of yore between the Doctors of Admiralty and his Majesty's servants of King's Bench."[45]

Within a decade, however, the energies of the codification party were either neutralized or diverted to other ends by the advent of Jacksonian Democracy. The most influential legal reformers of the 1830s, such as Robert Rantoul, resurrected the old shibboleths of monopoly and class privilege, damning not only the common law but the common lawyer as well. Popular distrust of the expert during the Jackson years militated against the success of any scheme to employ salaried professionals to reconstruct the content of the law.[46] Yet the undemocratic features of the existing system seemed to cry all the more urgently for correction.

The Jacksonians met the challenge with a variety of ad hoc measures designed to bring the administrators of the law under more direct popular control. Mississippi inaugurated one important trend in 1832 by adopting a constitutional provision that called for the election of all state judges for a term of years. Soon a majority of states espoused the principle of limited tenure in some form, abandoning the older practice by which judges had been appointed to the bench for life. Similarly, in an effort to "democratize" the bar, many legislatures redefined professional standards, scaling down educational requirements for lawyers or eliminating them altogether in such states as New Hampshire, Wisconsin, and Indiana, where every "citizen" or "resident" of "good moral character" was entitled by statute to engage in legal practice. And new procedural rules in some jurisdictions gave laymen a more decisive role in the outcome of jury trials, as judges were forbidden to comment on the evidence or otherwise to assist the jury in reaching a verdict.[47]

In such an egalitarian atmosphere the professionalism of the old-style codifiers was foredoomed to defeat. Yet their program suffered also from internal contradictions that no overall assessment can fail to acknowledge. Logically Sampson and his colleagues fell between two stools. They preached emancipation from English legal tutelage in the name of a militant nationalism, while clinging to an eighteenth-century faith in the efficacy of unvarying moral principles. To extol the uniqueness of American conditions was one thing; to bury national peculiarities within general formulas was something else again. For code provisions, once enacted, tended to represent absolute values, largely independent of time and place. And in challenging the common-law tradition reformers encountered a line of defense much better attuned to the romantic xenophobia of the age.

Champions of the judiciary insisted that court decisions mirrored the changing mores of a people more faithfully than uniform laws, which took account only of extreme variations in popular attitudes or behavior. Litigation, on the other hand, served as an accurate barometer to measure the slightest fluctuations in the national character. As customs altered within a state, the common law, grounded upon the collective experience of the citizen body, altered in turn.[48] Such considerations appealed to the jingoism of post-1812 America; coupled with the fact that most state legislatures in the 1820s and 1830s were still dominated by lawyers trained in the black-letter school, they created an insurmountable barrier to the success of any program of general codification.

Yet if the codifiers had clearly lost their major battle by the mid-thirties, in one important respect they won the war. Even the most prominent defenders of judicial power, such as Joseph Story and James Kent, admitted the need for comprehensive legislation to update and rationalize certain branches of the law. Their utilitarian sympathies owed little to Bentham or Napoleon, however, but derived instead from an unimpeachably respectable source: the writings of William Paley, an archdeacon in the Church of England and the foremost "moral philosopher" of his time. Paley's seminal work, *The Principles of Moral and Political Philosophy*, first appeared in London in 1785 and was at once hailed as a peculiarly happy blend of Lockean idealism, biblical piety, and Enlightenment common sense. Public opinion is the foundation of all civil authority, Paley affirmed, and laws, to be effective, must be clearly defined, conformable to moral precepts, and designed to promote the general welfare, since "the obligation of every law depends upon its ultimate utility."[49] Citizens obey the law for reasons of expediency; hence every rule must be tested by its consequences and outmoded regulations revised in timely fashion, to keep the law abreast of the public interest and prevent popular outbursts against the system. With his blunt persuasive prose and his strong faith in the power of creative legislation to remodel the environment, Paley soon won a large audience on both sides of the Atlantic, and nowhere was his vogue greater than among American lawyers, who found their instinctive pragmatism now sanctioned by the highest religious considerations.

As early as 1790 James Wilson was expounding Paley's arguments with enthusiasm to law students in Philadelphia; at Columbia College three years later James Kent began his course of law lectures with Paley's *Principles;* and thereafter the work became a standard college text, as familiar to the average undergraduate in antebellum America as Webster's spellers or McGuffey's readers were to the child in elementary school.[50] Both liberals and conservatives, then, were predisposed by the 1820s—through temperament or training or both—to recognize at least *some* merit in the codification argument, and Sampson's strictures against the technicalities of common-law pleading and the hoary fictions of Anglo-American property law did succeed in launching a series of limited reforms that vitally altered the shape of American jurisprudence by the end of the century.

As a direct result of his labors, the New York legislature passed a statute in 1828 that revolutionized the real-property law of the state, forming in effect a partial code. Other states in turn began to explore the possibilities of systematizing certain branches of their law by taking into account not only prior statutes but related judicial decisions as well. The new trend assumed major proportions after 1848, when New York abolished the intricate common-law rules of pleading and practice in a Code of Civil Procedure that was soon adopted by twenty-three other states and territories.[51]

Under the guise of legislative revision the codification movement achieved respectability, and Sampson and his adherents slipped into the mainstream of the American reform tradition. "A few years ago," declared the influential *American Jurist* in April 1835,

> *codification* had a direful import to the conservative party in jurisprudence; and not wholly without reason; since some of its early champions were sturdy radicals in legal reform. In this view codification was another name for juridical revolution . . . But the alarm has subdued . . . and the doctrine seems to be now acquiesced in, by a general consent, that a code must be more a digest and arrangement of existing laws, than a body of new enactments made *per saltum* . . . The substitution of the terms *revision* and *consolidation* of statutes, for that of *codification*, has contributed, in no small degree, to the change of thinking on this subject.[52]

Partial codification thus emerged as the answer of the professional bar to the mounting clamor for changes in the law after 1828. As laymen struggled to democratize the bench, lawyers worked to reestablish confidence in judicial integrity by eliminating the most glaring anachronisms of common-law doctrine. Out of the ferment of these years developed a continuing reform impulse that restructured American law in significant ways through the rest of the century. The process was gradual and piecemeal, but it did establish a more realistic balance between legal traditionalism and the expanding needs of a modern democracy.

Across the Atlantic, too, the early codifiers inspired foreign observers with a new respect for American jurisprudence that led in time to a fruitful interchange of ideas and information between scholars and legal reformers in Europe and the United States. Innovations of any kind seemed doubly appealing to European liberals during a period of reaction, when conservative regimes everywhere on the Continent stubbornly resisted all popular pressures for change. More than ever the United States in the 1820s appeared a "model nation" to reformers abroad who used every facet of the American experience (including the legal) to support their arguments against the status quo.

In England the Benthamite *Westminster Review* thoroughly canvassed the work of Edward Livingston and other American codifiers, as did the reform-minded London *Jurist*; in France the *Revue encyclopédique* printed every scrap of information available on American laws and institutions, while the internationally acclaimed legal magazine *La Thémis* carried progress reports on codification in the United States to the farthest corners of the Continent. This widespread and generally enthusiastic interest in all things American was a temporary phenomenon, of course. It tended to evaporate rather quickly in the wake of the successful revolutions of 1830 on the Continent and the passage of the Reform Bill of 1832 in England. Once the American example proved no longer essential to the polemical needs of European liberals it was soon disregarded,[53] but by that time the codification controversy had helped to create durable transatlantic ties within the international legal community.

One can see the process at work in the private papers of such figures as Peter DuPonceau and James Kent. Just as Sampson had established contact with Dupin and other French jurists, the anticodifiers in England (where codification posed an equally serious threat to the common-law tradition) sought support for their views from American practitioners. DuPonceau's mild critique of Sampson's arguments in his *Dissertation on the Nature and Extent of the Jurisdiction of the Courts of the United States* (1824) thus evoked a warm response from C. P. Cooper, an English barrister employed by the Parliamentary Commission on the Reform of Real Property law, who wrote:

> [Your work] soon discovered to me how much already we have to learn from you, and the few [American] publications which I have since had the good luck to meet with, have strengthened that impression. At this period I had no occasion to use the[se] valuable materials, and my friend [J. J.] Park informing me that he was about to write upon the subject of codification I urged him to seek for facts and arguments, not in England only, but in France & America also, and furnished him with nearly every book he cites, and I am glad to find that justice is likely to be at last done to the great talent which he has displayed in the use of the information that he obtained.[54]

Park's book was published in 1828 as *A Contre-projet to the Humphreysian Code*, and, like Cooper, he also became a regular correspondent of DuPonceau. The three men exchanged views and publications in a highly systematic fashion, even acting on occasion as press agents for one another in their respective countries.

Similarly, Chancellor Kent's four-volume *Commentaries on American Law* (1826-1830), written in large part to refute the charge that the common law of the several states was hopelessly muddled and contradictory, secured for him a wide circle of admirers abroad. One of them was the English publicist Jabez Henry, who lamented the narrow vision of most of his fellow legal reformers: "I cannot help expressing my surprise that our Commissioners have never once thought of enquiring what has been done in our Colonies and also in your American States where the simplicity of new institutions would have been a great help to them. Had they so enquired they would have found many of their propositions of reform already anticipated and acted upon and their path almost cleared, but the time is not yet come though fast approaching when our lawyers will be forced to study foreign laws and institutes, if they wish to keep pace with their neighbors."[55]

Henry's prophecy was largely verified in 1844, when the Society for Promoting the Amendment of the Law was founded in London to institutionalize contacts with foreign jurists and to provide a clearinghouse of information for legal reformers around the world. Henry Brougham served as first president of the society; Kent and Story were among its earliest corresponding members in the United States, along with Guizot and Dupin in France, Savigny in Berlin, and Mittermaier in Heidelberg.[56] To this select company a much younger and more controversial figure was likewise soon admitted—the American reformer David Dudley Field, who combined the promotional zeal of Sampson with the technical craftsmanship of Edward Livingston to become the world's foremost exponent of codification during the next half century and one of the towering legal personalities of the Victorian age.

Field explicitly acknowledged his debt to Sampson in these later years, but otherwise the genial Irishman was almost totally forgotten by posterity. Even the next generation of New York lawyers knew little of him, as Irving Browne discovered when he tried to work up a biographical sketch toward the end of the century. There was an imposing monument to Thomas Addis Emmet in the churchyard of Old Saint Paul's on Broadway, Browne reported, but nowhere could he find a comparable memorial to Sampson.[57] None in fact existed, although Sampson's memory was preserved in a modest way on Long Island, the favorite haunt of his last years, when he loved to load a small boat with family and friends and sail up the East River to Bowery Bay, the country home of his colleague John L. Riker. There, as his ship approached the dock, he would strike up a merry tune on his flute to alert his hosts, and there the Rikers insisted that he should be laid to his final rest in their own family plot. He was eventually interred in a white marble tomb, on which were inscribed a dozen words that summed up the labors of a lifetime:

AN UNITED IRISHMAN,
HE DEFENDED THE CAUSE OF CIVIL AND RELIGIOUS
LIBERTY.

There is a reciprocal action and reaction constantly, though almost invisibly, existent, between government and our firesides; and, if insubordination reigns in either, it is very certain, in a short time, to obtain in both.
David Hoffman, *Miscellaneous Thoughts on Men, Manners, and Things; by Anthony Grumbler, of Grumbleton Hall, Esq.* (1837)

4 The Family in Antebellum Law

On his now famous journey through the United States in the early 1830s, Alexis de Tocqueville remarked that a new (and, by European standards, a radically egalitarian) family structure had developed in America, thanks to the inexorable progress of the democratic principle. Law, as well as the New World environment, had helped to democratize domestic relations, Tocqueville asserted, citing the abolition of entail and primogeniture as one example of legal change that in his view had undercut the economic basis of paternal authority within the home, and encouraged children to establish separate households of their own at a much earlier age than was customary on the Continent. Where the power of the father, rooted in Roman and civil law sanctions, still held the European family together in a web of extended kinship obligations, Americans, it seemed, relied upon mutual affection and democratic decision making to harmonize the disparate interests of husband, wife, and children. The results in either case were mixed: European family life often tended to be overly rigid and authoritarian, while Americans were prone to be too mobile and atomistic, heedless of their roots in the past or of loyalties to collateral relatives.[1]

Tocqueville's analysis of the democratic family allowed for no significant class or regional variations. Like a good logician he followed his deductive insights to their ultimate conclusion, and that was that. In terms of actual family behavior, his abstract schema applied best to middle- and upper-middle-class groups, whose mores he had been able to observe at first hand. An Irish working-class family was apt to cling more tenaciously to traditional notions of male dominance and authority, while a patriarchal style of life still flourished among the plantation aristocracy of the Old South and the great landed proprietors of the Hudson Valley. But such sociological considerations were irrelevant from a legal standpoint, in any event. The law did not distinguish between "nuclear" and "extended" families; it recognized only one principle of classification—that which separated the poor household from the nonpoor.

By ignoring the impact of the poor laws upon American family life, Tocqueville told only half the story. His democratization thesis, in a modified form, still goes far to explain the constructive changes wrought by antebellum lawmakers and judges in the domestic relations of self-sustaining families. But the destitute lived by a different and contradictory set of rules. For those on relief the law was in no sense a liberating influence, but an increasingly repressive agency of social control and regimentation. At the very time that middle-class wives were gaining greater power over their property and persons, the women of the poor found their freedom of movement curtailed and saw their children taken from them by order of public officials. A dual system of family law, stretching back to the colonial era, reached its apogee in the years before the Civil War, as the poor were effectively insulated from the rest of society behind institutional walls or a screen of bureaucratic regulations. The unhappy results of such a policy of class segregation are all too apparent a century later.

American family law in the seventeenth and eighteenth centuries derived from several distinct sources: the English common law, the marital regulations of the established Church of England, parliamentary and colonial statutes, and the workaday conditions of life on a transatlantic frontier. In general, it may be said that the doctrines and attitudes of common-law judges most strongly influenced the private law of domestic relations, while families on welfare were governed by legislative norms. But any policy formulated in England, whether legislative or judicial in origin, inevitably suffered a marked sea change in its transit from the Old World to the New.

The marriage ceremony itself illustrates the point. Ecclesiastical courts had jurisdiction over marriage and divorce in England, where the law required that every marriage be solemnized by a minister of the Anglican church. No such church courts were ever established in the American colonies, however, and the religious Dissenters who settled New England and Pennsylvania had no intention of conforming to the ritual of a church they had long since repudiated. Instead, Puritans and Quakers tended to espouse the view of Continental religious reformers that marriage was properly a civil contract, whose validity did not depend upon any prescribed church service. Religious ceremonies were not discouraged, of course; in New England it became customary for parties to be married first by a lay magistrate, then by a minister in a church wedding. But the religious sanction added nothing to the legal efficacy of the marriage. By the time of the Revolution the civil ceremony had been introduced by statute into every colony outside the South as a legitimate secular form of marriage.[2]

Even more responsive to the folkways of a rude pioneering society was the development in some jurisdictions of the so-called common-law marriage. No formal ceremony, civil or religious, was needed to validate this type of conjugal union. If a man and woman agreed to consider themselves husband and wife and thereafter lived together as such, the law would uphold their verbal contract and recognize their issue as legitimate. Probably no such institution was ever known to the English common law, although the evidence is conflicting and authorities disagree.[3] But there can be no doubt that informal marriages were prevalent throughout the colonies, for a number of reasons: a shortage of clergymen in many areas; the isolation and loneliness of backwoods settlements; an aversion to bureaucratic procedures on the part of half-educated frontiersmen; and the heavy expense that sometimes accompanied a faithful compliance with legal regulations. In eighteenth-century Virginia, for example, where ministers of the Church of England were alone authorized to celebrate marriages, the fees incident to securing a clergyman's services and a license from the county court equaled the cost of some 465 pounds of tobacco.[4] The colonial judge who gave effect to common-law marriages thus sanctioned a widespread social practice that reflected the Spartan quality of life in an undeveloped country.

Daily experience in a New World environment likewise modified the legal relations that had traditionally existed between English husbands and wives. Those relations had been shaped by the needs of a male-dominated, feudal society, in which land was the chief form of wealth and vassals owed military service to their overlords. Feudal law did not recognize the family as such, or assign rights and duties to individuals in accordance with their respective family roles. Instead, property considerations prevailed over personal relationships or natural blood ties, and property rights alone were enforced by the king's courts in disputes involving husband and wife or father and son.[5]

Under a manorial system geared to the omnipresent threat of war, it was scarcely surprising that male heirs were preferred by law or that women and their property were subjected to the protective custody of masculine guardians or husbands. But the decline of feudalism did little to relieve women of their legal disabilities or to weaken the hoary fiction of the "unity" of husband and wife, which was explained at length in a seventeenth-century law tract:

> In this consolidation which we call wedlock is a locking together. It is true, that man and wife are one person; but understand in what manner. When a small brooke or little river incorporateth with Rhodanus, Humber, or the Thames, the poor rivulet looseth her name; it is carried and recarried with the new associate; it beareth no sway; it possesseth nothing during coverture. A woman as soon as she is married, is called *covert*; in Latine *nupta*, that is, "veiled;" as it were, clouded and overshadowed; she hath lost her streame. I may more truly, farre away, say to a married woman, Her new self is her superior; her companion, her master . . . Eve, because she had helped to seduce her husband, had inflicted upon her a special bane. See here the reason of that which I touched before,—that women have no voice in Parliament. They make no laws, they consent to none, they abrogate none. All of them are understood either married, or to be married, and their desires are to their husbands. I

know no remedy, that some can shift it well enough. The common
laws here shaketh hand with divinitye.[6]

In more mundane terms, the husband through marriage
acquired absolute ownership of his wife's personal property and
lifetime control of her lands. If a living child was born to them,
the doctrine of "curtesy" furnished the husband with a continuing life estate in all lands owned by his wife at her death. Any
other income that accrued to a wife during wedlock, such as
wages earned by her labor, likewise fell into her husband's
hands.

These extensive male prerogatives were not matched by any
corresponding legal duties. Although a man was morally
obligated to cherish and support his wife, the common law permitted him to squander her property with impunity, to deprive
her at will of creature comforts, and, if she complained, to
"chastise" her roundly. Judges would interfere in the sensitive
area of domestic relations only to protect a married woman
against the threat of death or serious bodily harm or to compel
her husband to supply her with the necessities of life. Divorce
was out of the question, too, for any cause. If certain canonical
disabilities existed, such as marriage within prohibited degrees
of blood kinship, an ecclesiastical court might issue a decree of
annulment, but in most cases an unhappy spouse could secure
only a qualified divorce from bed and board (a mensa et thoro),
a form of legal separation that did not allow either party to
remarry. The very wealthy did manage on rare occasions to
squeeze a private bill of divorce out of Parliament; in such
exceptional circumstances adultery invariably figured as a principal charge.[7]

By the seventeenth century English equity courts had begun
to concede limited proprietary rights to married women by
enforcing premarital settlements or trust arrangements that
earmarked certain property as a wife's separate estate and
exempted it from husbandly control. Such protective devices,
which generally reflected a father's desire to shield his daughter
against future penury, benefited only the members of the landed
aristocracy in practice. For other wives the standard disabilities
that accompanied marriage remained fully operative. Unlike
single women, they could not make contracts or wills, execute
deeds, sue or be sued in court, administer estates, or act as
guardians of minors. The one significant proprietary right that

they possessed at common law was dower, the female equivalent of curtesy. Through dower a widow became entitled to a life estate in one-third of the lands owned by her deceased husband.

In the American colonies different social and economic conditions helped to enlarge the legal powers of married women in several notable respects. The institution of civil marriage, where it existed in the northern and middle colonies, accustomed people to think of mutual rights and duties on the part of the contracting spouses; a more egalitarian social structure and an abundance of free land diminished the importance of entail, primogeniture, and other discriminatory feudal doctrines (at least outside the South); and everywhere the spur of necessity forced pioneer women to assume occupational roles that in more stable and tradition-bound societies were reserved for men. Legislation in each colony authorized married women to act as "feme-sole traders" and to conduct businesses or manage landed estates in their own interest or on behalf of absent or disabled spouses. As independent entrepreneurs they were empowered to make and enforce their own contracts and could be sued separately by their creditors. Some also represented their husbands in lawsuits, although the practice seems to have died out by the end of the seventeenth century.[8]

Colonial judges likewise proved more liberal than their counterparts in the home country in upholding postnuptial contracts between a man and wife. Even the Court of Chancery in England drew the line at premarital settlements, reasoning from the fiction of marital unity that spouses could not contract with each other or vary the terms of a property settlement they had agreed upon before marriage. But colonial courts were less doctrinaire, and enforced postnuptial, as well as prenuptial, contracts prior to the Revolution. In practice, as Richard B. Morris has remarked, this striking departure from English precedent often permitted a married couple contemplating separation to effect in advance a legally binding division of family property:

> The separation agreement and other types of post-nuptial contracts clearly served a useful purpose in protecting the economic interests of a married woman and her children without necessitating recourse to a divorce action with its attendant unpleasant publicity . . . In England, it was not until 1879 that equity, spurred on by Sir George

Jessel, recognized that economic and social conditions had changed, and clearly upheld such agreements.[9]

Absolute divorce, too, could be obtained in some colonies. Courts and legislatures alike granted such divorces on occasion in New England, for causes that included desertion and cruelty as well as adultery. On the eve of the Revolution the English Privy Council, in response, expressly condemned colonial divorce acts as either "improper or unconstitutional" and disallowed legislative divorces in Pennsylvania, New Jersey, and New Hampshire. Even in the southern colonies, which adhered closely to English divorce law, mistreated wives could secure a decree of separate maintenance under circumstances that would never have moved an English judge.[10]

One must beware of exaggerating the impact of these legal changes in women's rights, however. At most it may be argued that in the colonial period the first tentative steps were taken toward recognizing the wife as a distinct legal personality, whose interests need not always be subordinated to quasi-religious norms of marital unity. Limited advances in the proprietary capacity of married women provoked no corresponding changes in their social or political status, and except where property claims were involved judges were reluctant to intervene in family affairs, even to protect a wife or child from physical abuse. In every colony the value of privacy in domestic relations received strong community support which, as David H. Flaherty has demonstrated, effectively frustrated all legislative attempts to police the private morals of early American settlers.[11] Since the old maxim "a man's house is his castle" was respected by judges no less than laymen, a householder's authority over his wife and minor children was, for most purposes, complete and legally unassailable.

The common-law principles applicable to parent and child in the seventeenth and eighteenth centuries derived historically from the same set of feudal conditions that had dictated the subjection of married women to their husbands. To protect the integrity of landed estates, feudal law singled out one group of children—heirs and heiresses—for special treatment. The heir received his inheritance by virtue of feudal rules that could not be altered by an ancestor's will, and in other respects his interests as a person were subordinated to overriding economic considerations. Thus, by the law of wardship a father was normally entitled to the custody of his child's person and property. In the event of the father's death, however, guardianship devolved not upon the mother but upon the lord of the infant's land—a clear indication that the child's welfare was deemed of less consequence than the preservation of his estate. But paternal guardianship itself was no guarantee of incorruptibility, since many fathers were not above sordid profiteering in their management of a child's patrimony. While the law obliged them to maintain and educate their wards, it left them otherwise free to use the revenues of an estate as they pleased. Many great medieval statutes and other documents, including Magna Charta, sought to curtail the abuses that flourished under a system that treated guardianship and paternal power as merely profitable rights and made the child heir little more than an adjunct to his lands.[12]

For other children, such as the younger brothers or sisters of a minor heir or the offspring of the propertyless classes, the rules governing the parent-child relationship were drawn from English labor law. The child was regarded in certain contexts as a "servant," and the law pertaining to master and servant was applied to family situations. A father, for example, had a right to his child's services and could sue a third party for abducting, enticing away, or injuring the child, just as a master under similar circumstances could bring suit on behalf of an apprentice. But there the analogy pretty well ended, for the child, as against its parent, possessed none of the contractual rights—to wages, shelter, and maintenance during sickness and disability—that a servant habitually enjoyed. The law, to be sure, recognized certain primary duties, such as protection, support, and education, that every parent owed to his children, but these it held to be exclusively moral obligations. Providence, wrote Blackstone, enforced the claims of the child "more effectually than any laws, by implanting in the breast of every parent that . . . insuperable degree of affection which not even the deformity of person or mind, not even the wickedness, ingratitude, and rebellion of children, can totally suppress or extinguish."[13] Long after feudal tenures had been abolished and the protective jurisdiction of chancery courts extended over wealthy young heirs, most children continued to be regarded, for legal purposes, as quasi servants who had no recourse against the mistreatment or neglect of their paternal "masters."

Nor did youngsters enjoy any greater rights in the American colonies. Indeed, in seventeenth-century New England, Puritan lawmakers invoked biblical sanctions against youthful insubordination that exceeded in severity anything known to English law. Thus, Massachusetts and Connecticut provided the death penalty for any rebellious son or for any child who should "smite or curse" its parents.[14] It does not appear that these sanguinary laws were ever enforced, since happily an alternative method of disciplining the young existed in the widespread practice of "putting out," or apprenticeship.

The apprenticeship system, which was equally popular in England, affected all social classes, but its rationale and general utility varied with the economic condition of a child and its parents. Among the well-to-do and artisan groups, as Stephen B. Presser has noted, apprenticeship often served as a substitute for adoption, a mode of child care that did not exist at common law. Parents sometimes provided by will that a child should be placed in the home of a relative or friend for education and Christian upbringing, or arranged with a neighbor that he should take a youngster into his family and train him for a term of years in some special skill. (Girls were likely to be taught "manners" or household management.) The free consent of both natural and surrogate parents characterized such "putting out" agreements, in which a child's welfare was of paramount concern.[15] Since, in the absence of more specialized civic agencies, a colonial family was expected to perform many semi-public functions of acculturation and job training, the apprenticeship experience could (and frequently did) prove invaluable to the young man or woman of "respectable" background. But a different set of priorities governed the apprenticeship of pauper children. Their treatment inevitably reflected the dependent status of their parents and can be understood only in relation to the total impact of the poor laws upon colonial family life.

The family law of the poor presented a reverse image of the common-law doctrines just considered. Influenced by legislatively defined goals of order and economy, the poor laws attempted to control dependency through various forms of public relief that respected neither domestic privacy nor individual rights. In the name of humanitarian uplift children were separated from their parents and forced to work for strangers; fathers were forbidden to seek employment outside the town where they resided; and grandparents were compelled, at the risk of fine or imprisonment, to support grown children and grandchildren out of their own meager resources.

A comprehensive system of poor relief assumed definitive shape with the enactment of the Elizabethan Poor Law of 1601, whose provisions guided the development of welfare programs in England and America for the next three centuries. Although this elaborate code undoubtedly reflected the importance that Tudor and Stuart statesmen attached to government planning in all sectors of the economy, it could in no sense be described as a tightly constructed or innovative product of the bureaucratic mind. It rather represented a patchwork accumulation of previous customs and practices, some of them dating back several hundred years. Two basic concepts nevertheless held this unwieldy mass together: the idea that the sick and disabled must be maintained at public expense, and the no less important idea that the able-bodied indigent must be compelled by public authority to perform some useful labor.[16]

The acceptance by the state of a primary responsibility for the care of the destitute marked a permanent shift away from the medieval tradition of private, voluntary almsgiving. The major sources of such private charity were fast disappearing, in any event, especially since the dissolution of the monasteries under Henry VIII and the concomitant decline of the guilds. But Elizabethan lawmakers, in announcing a substitute program of public assistance, continued to rely upon local officials for the funding and administration of the system. National standards and supervision remained negligible; even the compulsory property tax, the financial mainstay of relief efforts, was determined and assessed at the parish level, in accordance with purely local needs.

Since every community was obliged to provide for its paupers out of its own resources, taxpayers and administrators sought to keep their relief rolls as uncrowded as possible. The law itself supplied them with a welcome loophole in 1662, when settlement and removal provisions were added to the main body of poor law regulations. Justices of the peace were thereafter empowered to return a newcomer to his former place of residence if the local overseers of the poor considered him likely to become a public charge in the future. Such "warning out" procedures, which had been directed in the fourteenth century against rogues and vagabonds, now threatened both the inoffensive pauper and his family, especially in situations where a parent or child managed to acquire a legal settlement different from that shared by other members of the family.

Once an applicant's eligibility for relief had been determined, other legal rules enabled a community to reduce the cost of his maintenance. Every able-bodied man or woman was required by law to work on some sheltered project supervised by the overseers of the poor. Typically, the overseers would supply a needy person with certain raw materials, such as wool, flax, or hemp, to be woven into cloth. The finished product would then be sold, and the proceeds applied to the further care of the individual. If a pauper refused to work or spoiled the materials given to him, he was committed to a "house of correction," where, like a common criminal, he was ordered "to be straightlye kepte, as well in Diet as in Worke, and also punisshed from tyme to tyme."[17]

It was no accident that the poor laws often failed to distinguish between the dependent and dangerous classes of society. Fear of vagrants and vagabonds as potential sources of riots and other civil disorders pervaded Elizabethan England. The rise of large-scale sheep raising, and the subsequent enclosure movement, had driven numbers of marginal farm workers from the land and swelled the floating population of urban areas. Local officials understandably viewed the unemployed with alarm; was not idleness in itself "the mother & rote of all vyces," a personal fault that clamored for correction? In the name of order as well as economy, therefore, the law authorized the construction of one or two workhouses or houses of correction in each county, where the convicted criminal and the recalcitrant pauper might both learn through Spartan discipline to obey the rules laid down for them by their betters.

Special regulations governed the employment of poor children and established procedures that ran directly counter to common-law doctrines of parental control and accountability. Thus, parish officials were empowered to take children away from indigent or neglectful parents and bind them out to serve designated masters in return for their shelter and maintenance. Unlike the apprenticeship of nonpoor youths, compulsion existed on both sides, since unwilling masters were not legally free to refuse the children assigned to them. A pauper child's indenture read much like that of any other apprentice, but his contractual rights to education and support were less likely to be enforced in practice. His master, after all, was relieving the public of an otherwise burdensome charge. Under such circumstances apprenticeship resembled less a humane system of cultural conditioning than a method of recruiting a cheap and docile labor force.[18]

The desire to reduce public welfare costs likewise led the framers of the poor law to impose upon a needy person's relatives support obligations that did not exist at common law. These statutory liabilities attached to the blood kindred of paupers who were too sick or disabled to support themselves in any way through their own exertions. The principle was first announced in 1597, then reenacted as a permanent part of the poor law system established in 1601:

[The parents, grandparents, and the children of] everie poore olde blind lame and impotente person, or other poore person not able to worke, being of a sufficient abilitie, shall at their owne Chardges releive and maintain everie suche poore person, in that manner and accordinge to that rate, as by the Justices of the Peace of that Countie where suche sufficient persons dwell, or the greater number of them, at their generall Quarter-Sessions shalbe assessed; upon paine that everie one of them shall forfeite twenty shillings for everie monthe which they shall faile therein.[19]

As in the case of pauper apprentices, virtually unlimited discretion was vested in the public authorities charged with administering the law, and common-law theories of parental rights and duties were studiously ignored. Other statutory provisions compelled the mother and putative father of a bastard child to contribute financially to its support, or face imprisonment in a jail or workhouse, and made it a criminal offense for indigent parents to desert their children, leaving them a charge upon the parish. Together, such regulations constituted, in Jacobus tenBroek's words, "not only a law *about* the poor, but a law *of* the poor."[20] And it was this same system of class legislation which, in its leading features—local responsibility, settlement and removal, the support obligations of designated relatives, and the apprenticeship of minors—was transplanted to the American colonies and adapted to their varying needs.

Nowhere, of course, did colonial enactments duplicate

exactly the English model. In the southern colonies, where town life was minimal and an agricultural proletariat did not exist, settlement and removal procedures did not come into general use until the eighteenth century. Massachusetts, on the other hand, went beyond English precedent where support obligations were concerned. A Massachusetts statute of 1692, which was copied in New York and several other colonies, added grandchildren to the list of relatives who were legally bound to help pay for the care of the unemployable poor.[21] Every colony, moreover, showed a marked preference for outdoor relief over institutional confinement—a circumstance that reflected some distinctively American assumptions about the nature of poverty.

As David J. Rothman has recently demonstrated, Americans in the colonial era neither feared their poor nor sought to reform them. Poverty was regarded as an inescapable social fact, a permanent and natural condition for which both religion and government made allowances. Protestantism taught that the poor were part of a divinely ordained social structure and that their presence in a community afforded the more prosperous classes a heaven-sent opportunity to dispense Christian benevolence. Secular theory likewise emphasized the necessary place that the poor occupied in a hierarchical, rank-conscious society, in which each class was bound to the others by reciprocal rights and duties. If a poor man accepted his humble status and paid proper deference to those above him, he could count on assistance from the community in time of need. Public officials made little effort to categorize the poor in any way, or to probe the causes of their misfortune. Generally the fact of need was sufficient to justify relief, without calling into question the possible failings of the individual or of society.

Since they never expected to change the poor or to eliminate poverty, colonial Americans were content in most cases to assist the destitute in their own homes, without disrupting their lives or separating them from their families. In exceptional circumstances of old age, widowhood, or debility, arrangements were made to board individuals in neighboring households. Few workhouses or almshouses were constructed prior to the Revolution; those that did exist were to be found mainly in the larger urban centers, such as Boston, Philadelphia, and New York. They served typically to handle extreme cases: homeless strangers, those too ill or disabled to be cared for properly by their families, deserted children and orphans. Even within such institutions, moreover, a family pattern of organization prevailed. The average almshouse resembled a substitute household, in which welfare recipients were treated more like members of a family than inmates. Discipline was lax; paupers wore no special uniforms and moved about freely; they ate their meals together each day, in company with the keeper and his family; and twice a week all joined in common prayer. The buildings in which they lived were indistinguishable architecturally from private dwellings and were usually located well within town limits. The poor, in short, whether institutionalized or not, remained highly visible, and no serious attempt was made to reorder their lives or to segregate them physically from the rest of society.[22]

But there are subtler forms of degradation, which historical revisionists such as Rothman sometimes overlook. If the American colonists avoided the more repressive forms of institutional control sanctioned by the English poor laws, they made up for it in other ways. Colonial court records are full of cases in which one town sued another town under the settlement laws, hoping by a legal technicality to rid itself of an unwanted welfare recipient. Everywhere the qualifications for settlement grew stiffer and more complex with the passage of time, while local authorities redoubled their efforts to keep strangers under effective surveillance. In Massachusetts 6,764 persons were warned out of Worcester County alone between 1737 and 1788.[23] By the mid-eighteenth century it had become a common practice throughout the colonies to require every pauper on relief, as well as his wife and children, to wear on the sleeve of an outer garment, in plain view, a large "P" of red or blue cloth, and the first letter of the place where the pauper was legally settled.[24] No intensive study has yet been made of the effect produced by the settlement laws upon family structure and stability, but it must have been considerable. And it seems equally clear that the colonial poor, although not physically isolated from their neighbors, were nevertheless made to feel their inferiority in other ways as cruel as any dreamed up in the nineteenth and twentieth centuries.

The Revolution did not alter the substantive content of American family law in any perceptible way. Despite the rhetoric of individualism and natural rights that accompanied the struggle, the legal aspects of domestic relations remained the same after the war as before. From 1783 to 1861 the laws governing poor and nonpoor households continued to evolve along parallel tracks, with some major changes occurring in the years just prior to the Civil War. We shall consider first the gradual liberalization of legal docrines relating to those above the poverty line, reserving for later discussion the status of families under the poor laws.

In the early Republic there was general agreement among jurists that the institution of marriage deserved every possible encouragement, for reasons of sound public policy. Kent, Hoffman, and other leading commentators borrowed heavily from the philosophical writings of William Paley to prove that Christian monogamy alone was suited to the needs of a progressive republican state. Indeed, Paley's *Moral Philosophy* probably did more than any other elementary text to establish the guidelines for legal thinking about family matters, as about codification, in America.[25]

The plain-spoken clergyman from Yorkshire, as we have seen, espoused a unique brand of theological utilitarianism. "God wills the happiness of mankind," he declared, "and the existence of civil society, as conducive to that happiness." Lawmakers therefore were charged with a divine mandate to promote the general welfare, a mission they fulfilled by aiding population growth and encouraging productive employment. For Paley, as for Bentham, "happiness" was a democratic principle, capable of objective measurement: if you doubled the number of citizens you increased the quantity of national happiness in the same proportion, provided all classes enjoyed a reasonable level of subsistence. Conversely, population decline betokened spiritual as well as physical degeneracy and was "the greatest evil that a state can suffer."[26]

Demographic considerations thus pointed up the need for sound marriage laws to regulate sexual intercourse in the public interest. Christian monogamy, argued Paley, possessed built-in pragmatic advantages that made it a superior policy tool: "It is only in the marriage union that this [sexual] intercourse is sufficiently prolific. Besides which, family establishments alone are fitted to perpetuate a succession of generations. The offspring of a vague and promiscuous concubinage are not only few, and liable to perish by neglect, but are seldom prepared for, or introduced into, situations suited to the raising of families of their own." The monogamous household further contributed to political stability by cutting off sexual contests for the possession of more than one woman. (Harem intrigues, Paley thought, sufficiently explained the frequency of palace revolts in the Arab world.) Within "civilized" Western societies marriage to a single spouse divided the community into more manageable subunits, each under the control of a responsible master; it also tied parents to fixed habitations and incited them to greater industry during the minority of their offspring. Enlightened statesmanship therefore called for the strengthening of man's naturally monogamous tendencies through the application of appropriate legal sanctions. The state might grant bounties or tax exemptions to the parents of a certain number of legitimate children, for instance, while imposing stiff punishments on adulterers and others guilty of deviant sexual behavior.[27]

Such a utilitarian approach to the institution of marriage goes far to explain the continued judicial acceptance of common-law and other irregular marriages in a majority of American states. The courts that recognized these informal unions were not as a rule staffed by frontier mavericks, nor did they display much sympathy for theories of anarchic individualism. A strong community interest guided their decisions, which legitimized the position of wives and children for inheritance purposes and prevented them from becoming potential public charges. That social conservatism played a large part in shaping the marital policies of the judiciary may be inferred from the fact that the chief supporters of common-law marriage were all members of the upper middle class, cosmopolitan city dwellers who had little interest in, or sympathy for, frontier mores.

Chancellor James Kent of New York did more than any other to entrench self-marriage in American jurisprudence, despite state statutes requiring registration, parental consent for minors, and other procedural formalities. In the landmark case of *Fenton* v. *Reed* (1809) Kent stated his position unequivocally: "No formal solemnization of marriage was requisite. A contract of marriage *per verba de presenti* amounts to an actual marriage, and is as valid as if made *in facie ecclesiae*." Like any other civil contract, marriage depended for its validity solely on a meeting of minds, on the free consent of the parties. And proof of consent was almost axiomatic; for, as Kent made clear in his later *Commentaries*: "The consent of the parties may be declared before a magistrate, or simply before witnesses, or subsequently confessed or acknowledged, or the marriage may even be inferred from continual cohabitation, and reputation as husband and wife."[28]

The Kent doctrine found its way into the leading law texts of the antebellum period. Tapping Reeve, former chief justice of Connecticut, incorporated it into his pioneer treatise on domestic relations (1816); Professor Simon Greenleaf of the Harvard Law School cited it with approval in his classic work on evidence (1842); and Joel Prentiss Bishop refurbished it at mid-century for use in his magisterial *Commentaries on the Law of Marriage and Divorce* (1852). In a majority of jurisdictions judges relied upon these authorities to sustain the most unorthodox matrimonial arrangements against repeated legislative prohibitions. Statutes that imposed uniform marriage requirements were merely directory, the courts held; they set up a legal mode of solemnization (as the established church had once done), but they did not affect the underlying contractual obligation. Hence, in the absence of an express statutory declaration of nullity, a marriage could at the same time violate state law through procedural infractions, yet remain a binding contract between the parties.[29]

This happy logic—which would have delighted the paradoxical mind of a W. S. Gilbert—did not find favor with all American judges, however. A substantial minority, particularly in the New England states, enforced legislative regulations to the letter and charged that a contrary course would require the courts to condone behavior that would otherwise be punishable as adultery or fornication. Chief Justice John J. Gilchrist of New Hampshire spelled out the moral implications of the problem, as well as the need for accurate record keeping, in one of the ablest statements of the opposition case:

> It is singular that the most important of all human contracts, on which the rights and duties of the whole community depend, requires less formality for its validity than a conveyance of an acre of land, a policy of insurance, or the agreements which the statute of frauds requires should be in writing . . . What would be easier than for parties to agree privately that they are husband and wife, and after a cohabitation of a week or less, to separate either from incompatibility of temper or from the less worthy consideration that

they have become tired of each other, galled by even this temporary bond? Such a transformation of a penal offense into matrimony, where the alleged marriage might be dissolved, as it probably in many cases would be, by the caprice of the parties, would often follow, if, at the inception of the contract, nothing but cohabitation were required. And this temptation to illicit intercourse should be guarded against, for the sake of good morals, . . . by requiring some form of solemnization.[30]

The highest court of Tennessee similarly repudiated common-law marriages on moral grounds. In *Grisham* v. *State* (1831) a widow and widower agreed to cohabit as man and wife and swore an oath to that effect, in the presence of witnesses. They were subsequently indicted and convicted of "lewd acts of fornication and adultery . . . to the great scandal of . . . good and worthy citizens." The state supreme court upheld their conviction with little difficulty, remarking that the law must ever be the "guardian of the morals of the people."[31]

But in states where informal marriages had long been recognized, the consequences of overturning a settled custom forced even the most conscientious jurists to swallow their scruples and bow to expediency. "A doctrine which would tend to vitiate a great proportion of the marriages of the country would result in incalculable evils," asserted the Kentucky Supreme Court in 1821, "and can not be admitted to be correct."[32] A decade later Chief Justice John Bannister Gibson of Pennsylvania expressed equal concern at the prospect of strictly enforcing certain matrimonial regulations that had been in the statute books for generations: "It is not too much to say, that a rigid execution of them would bastardize a vast majority of the children which have been born within the state for half a century." To avoid a "conclusion imputative of guilt to the parties, and destructive of the civil rights of their offspring," Gibson held the requirements in question to be merely directory.[33]

A judicial policy of encouraging marriage, even to the point of tolerating in most states informal or irregular unions, did not extend to two groups in antebellum society: Negroes and Indians. No southern court recognized a marriage between Negro slaves as creating any legal rights or obligations for the spouses. Slaves, judges reasoned, were a form of property subject to the will of their owners. A slave accordingly had no capacity to bind himself by any contract, including a marriage agreement, since his power to perform any engagement depended wholly on the assent of his master.[34]

From a moral point of view, of course, it made a great deal of difference whether slaves purported to live together as man and wife or simply engaged in indiscriminate sexual intercourse. Southern jurists were quick to point out the social benefits that occurred when slaveholders encouraged their slaves to settle down with one spouse, permitting a "married" couple to "have a 'cabin and a patch off to themselves' " and allowing a "husband" from a neighboring plantation to "go to his wife's house" at stated times.[35] But all such arrangements were terminable at the pleasure of the master and conferred no civil rights on the spouses.

Despite their blatant callousness, decisions invalidating slave marriages flowed logically from the nature of the master-slave relation. Once that relation ended, however, the possibility arose of legitimizing the marital status of former slaves who continued after emancipation to cohabit as husband and wife. Two early cases did uphold such informal unions, although for different reasons. In *Girod* v. *Lewis* (1819) the Supreme Court of Louisiana in a very brief opinion enunciated a theory of "dormant civil rights":

> It is clear, that slaves have no legal capacity to assent to any contract. With the consent of their masters they may marry, and their moral power to agree to such a contract or connection as that of marriage, cannot be doubted; but, whilst in a state of slavery, it cannot produce any civil effect, because slaves are deprived of all civil rights. Emancipation gives to the slave his civil rights, and a contract of marriage, legal and valid by the consent of the master and moral assent of the slave, from the moment of freedom, although dormant during the slavery, produces all the effects which result from such contract among free persons.[36]

Five years later the highest court of Kentucky sustained an informal marriage between two emancipated blacks by using the same reasoning it applied to the common-law marriages of white persons. After noting that emancipation removed all the contractual disabilities incident to slavery, the court continued: "Whether or not the act of this country concerning marriages, applies to persons of this description, is a question which it is not necessary now to consider; for, to marry is a right common to all the human species, and whenever in fact contracted by persons able and willing to contract, the *feme* becomes subject to the disabilities of coverture, though in form the requisitions of the act of this country may not have been pursued."[37]

The results in these isolated cases did not establish any general trend. Especially after 1830, as southerners adopted a harder line toward the "peculiar institution" and imposed added statutory disabilities upon free Negroes, courts in the slave states seldom mentioned natural rights when ruling upon racial issues of any kind. A North Carolina decision of 1858 typified the sort of judicial thinking that prevailed on the eve of the Civil War, while illustrating as well the close link between common-law marriage and inheritance rights.

There was no dispute over the facts in *Howard* v. *Howard*: a Negro man, while a slave, had married another slave with his master's consent. Soon afterward he was emancipated and in due course purchased his wife from his former master. The couple lived together as man and wife until the woman died, by which time they had raised a family of eight children. Later the widower remarried, in a formal ceremony that fulfilled all legal requirements. His second wife was a "free woman of color," by whom he had four children. When he died intestate, both sets of heirs claimed a share of his estate, and a lawsuit was begun that eventually reached the supreme court of the state.

Although common-law marriages between white persons were condoned in North Carolina, Chief Justice Richmond M. Pearson gave short shrift to the offspring of the slave marriage: "Their parents, having become free persons, were guilty of a misdemeanor in living together as man and wife, without being married, as the law required; so that, there is nothing to save them from the imputation of being 'bastards.' " The second group of heirs was alone entitled to the estate, therefore. Pearson ridiculed the reasoning in the *Girod* case, terming the idea of dormant civil rights for slaves "rather a fanciful conceit . . . than the ground of a sound argument." Perhaps, he conjectured, the marriage relation in Louisiana "is greatly affected by the influence of religion, and the mystery of its supposed dormant rights, is attributable to its divine origin. If so, the case has no application, for, in our courts, marriage is treated as a mere civil institution."[38]

The Civil War shortly rendered the whole problem academic, of course. In the wake of the Thirteenth Amendment, which abolished slavery wherever it existed, the legislature of North Carolina in 1866 passed a statute declaring that former slaves who were then cohabiting as man and wife would be deemed lawfully married. They were required to go before a registrar and acknowledge their cohabitation, but a failure to comply with this procedure would not invalidate their marriage. Other southern states took similar steps to regularize the marital status of their newly freed Negro populations. In this way the principle of consensual marriage was introduced into the jurisprudence of several states, such as Tennessee, that otherwise repudiated common-law marriages.[39]

Like the Negro, the American Indian also ran into peculiar difficulties when he tried to establish the legality of his matrimonial arrangements. While he remained on a reservation, federal treaties guaranteed him the right to a semiautonomous existence under the laws and customs of his tribe. But when he took his family into the white man's world—or, as more commonly happened, when a white man returned to his people with an Indian bride—the legal rights of the spouses fell under the scrutiny of "civilized" judges schooled in the excellencies of an alien culture. Since most tribes permitted parties to dissolve the marriage bond at will, Indian litigants had an uphill fight to prove that they were more than promiscuous heathen. All too often judges not only turned down their claims but lectured them on their immoral behavior as well—ignoring the fact that common-law marriages were likewise geared to the pleasure of the parties.

Perhaps the most elaborate nineteenth-century tirade against "savage" matrimonial practices came from an Indiana judge, who summed up neatly the prevailing cultural assumptions of his time. Explaining why the marriage of two Miami Indians, although lawful by tribal custom, could have no reciprocal legal effect in the state of Indiana, Judge Samuel E. Perkins observed:

The law of nations, or international law, is mainly of modern origin, growing out of increased commercial and social intercourse, and exists only among civilized states. Civilization, it is true, is a term which covers several states of society; it is relative, and has not a fixed sense; but, in all its applications, it is limited to a state of society above that existing among the Indians of whom we are speaking. It implies an improved and progressive condition of the people, living under an organized government, with systematized labor, individual ownership of the soil, individual accumulations of property, humane and somewhat cultivated manners and customs, the institution of the family, with well-defined and respected domestic and social relations, institutions of learning, intellectual activity, etc. We know, historically, that the North American Indians are classed as savage and not as civilized people; and that, in fact, it is problematical whether they are susceptible of civilization.[40]

By the time of the Civil War a more liberal trend was nevertheless discernible in court decisions, as some judges—influenced perhaps by the ethnological studies of such men as Lewis Henry Morgan—no longer insisted rigorously upon the element of permanence to legitimize Indian marriages. Cohabitation for an indefinite period, looking toward the procreation and rearing of children, would constitute a legally binding marriage under the law of nature and "in the sight of God," asserted the Missouri Supreme Court in the leading case of *Johnson* v. *Johnson's Administrator* (1860),[41] and tribunals in most other states adopted a similar line of reasoning. Anglo-Saxon morality thus belatedly came to terms with the mating practices of the red man.

Where postmarital domestic relations were concerned, the law materially improved the position of wives and children in the years before the Civil War. Married women secured a greater measure of economic (and ultimately social) independence with the passage of Married Women's Property Acts in a majority of states. Mississippi enacted the first such statute in 1839, and by mid-century about nineteen other states had followed her example. None of these early laws gave a wife full legal equality in economic matters, but they did enlarge her capacity to deal independently with her property in a number of specific situations. They also simplified conveyance procedures and made unnecessary the cumbersome trust arrangement that had characterized family property settlements in the colonial era. Indeed, as Lawrence M. Friedman has observed, a major, if not controlling, motive behind much of this legislation was the desire to rationalize land transactions so that creditors might be better able to collect debts out of real estate owned by husband,

wife, or both.[42] Lawmakers certainly did not intend to effect
any radical changes in the relations between the spouses; they
sought merely to codify and expand colonial precedents, and to
make available to all women the protective devices formerly
reserved for a wealthy elite. Even these paternalistic designs
were sometimes frustrated by conservative judges, who tended
to construe strictly any statutory provisions that threatened to
impair the common-law rights of married men.

A sampling of representative cases suggests the variety of
judicial responses elicited by the claims of antebellum wives
under specific statutes. In New York Judge Platt Potter of the
state supreme court ruled that legislation passed in 1848 and
1849 had effectively abolished a husband's common-law right
of curtesy in his wife's lands. Remedial statutes ought to be
interpreted liberally, Potter argued, with a rhetorical overkill
reminiscent of William Sampson:

> Why, in this noon of the nineteenth century, and under a free gov-
> ernment, are we solemnly warned against innovations upon the
> common law as it existed, and the legal precedents established in the
> days of the Norman conqueror? Did all knowledge exist in the past?
> . . . For theories which have no support but antiquity I have no ven-
> eration . . . I hold an honest, sensible construction of the statute,
> according to its true intent, to be practical wisdom; and that the
> spirit of justice, befitting the wants of the age, is the soundest phi-
> losophy in a system of law. I regard it as a humiliating admission of
> intellectual decline, and worse than weak superstition, to assume
> that all wisdom existed in the former common law of England, or
> that laws suited to the condition of a free government could only be
> framed by the ancient inhabitants of Britain, whom Blackstone with
> fond partiality calls "our Saxon *princes;*" nor do I believe that it is
> *only* in the annals of *past* ages that we shall look for the wisdom
> necessary to guide us in our own. As changes are wrought in the cir-
> cumstances of a people, or country, it is necessary, not only that
> their laws themselves, but also the spirit of the laws should be
> accommodated.

The New York statutes were meant to eradicate such feudal
excrescences as tenancy by the curtesy, the learned judge concluded, and, if properly construed, they "will become a kind of
magna charta, in the restoration of natural rights, too long and
too unreasonably withheld."[43] Unhappily for the feminist
cause, the same New York tribunal a few months later qualified

Potter's opinion considerably and reasserted a husband's common-law rights of succession to his wife's property. Although admitting that state legislation empowered a married woman to dispose of her property absolutely during her lifetime, the court nevertheless held that if she failed to do so her husband's vested marital rights of succession would become enforceable at the time of her death.[44]

In the neighboring state of New Jersey, where the law authorized a wife to "hold" lands "to her sole and separate use," the courts ruled that she had no power to convey such lands to a third party, since they remained subject to her husband's right of curtesy. She might manage her landed property in her own interest, however, free from the power of her husband or the claims of his creditors.[45]

Careless draftsmanship and ambiguous legislative purpose marred many of the early property acts and invited judges to resist any changes which they feared might alter traditional sex roles within the family. The most glaring example of legislative ambivalence involved the earnings of married women. Virtually no antebellum statute provided in express terms that a wife was entitled to the money or other property that she earned during her marriage. The courts therefore tended to uphold the common-law rights of the husband while indulging in avuncular remarks on the nobility of the American female. In Pennsylvania a statute passed in 1848 declared that "all property, of whatever name or description, which shall accrue to any married woman, by will, descent, deed of conveyance, or otherwise, shall be owned, used, and enjoyed by such married woman as her own separate property." Deceived by such apparently comprehensive coverage, a married woman who ran a boardinghouse sued in *Raybold* v. *Raybold* (1853) to establish her equitable title to some real estate that her husband had purchased out of her rents and savings. But the court turned a deaf ear to her claim, explaining: "Meritorious as her industry and frugality were, they enured to the benefit of her husband . . . He is still entitled to the person and labor of the wife, and the benefits of her industry and economy. Nor is she degraded to the condition of a hireling, which she would be if servants' wages could become her separate property."[46]

From state to state other wifely wage earners lost out to their male protectors with monotonous regularity. Mississippi, the pioneer in women's economic legislation, had provided in 1839 that "any married woman may become seized or possessed of any property, real or personal, by direct bequest, demise [sic], gift, purchase, or distribution, in her own name, and as of her own property, provided the same does not come from her husband after coverture." In *Henderson* v. *Warmack* (1854) an overseer's wife sought unsuccessfully to recover a slave whom she had bought with her own money, given to her by the plantation owners in return for extra services that she performed about the place. Despite the fact that the bill of sale was made out in her name alone, her husband seized the slave against her wishes and mortgaged him to one of his creditors as security for a debt. The court informed the irate wife that she had no legal leg to stand on: since the act did not refer to money earned by a wife during coverture, "such means would, therefore, remain the property of the husband, and a purchase made therewith by the wife would vest in the husband."[47] A like result obtained in Maine, where a statute of 1847 contained a comparable provision. In *Merrill* v. *Smith* (1854) a wife had used her earnings to buy a sleigh, which was attached by her husband's creditors. The court flatly rejected the argument that she had "purchased" the sleigh within the meaning of the statute: "What she earns by her personal labor becomes his and not her property."[48]

Judicial concern over the weakening of long-accepted family relationships, which ran as an undercurrent through many of the property decisions, received its most articulate expression in an unusual and protracted Maryland case. The complaining wife in *Schindel* v. *Schindel* (1858) was a tempestuous southern belle of the Scarlett O'Hara variety, who walked out on her husband after six months of marriage because he allegedly said unkind and cruel things to her. Not content with returning to her mother's home to live, she sought to take all of her property with her, relying upon the terms of several state laws that asserted the economic rights of married women. First she induced her brother-in-law to carry off her furniture, but the husband promptly sued him for trespass, and won.[49] She then brought suit in her own name, asking for an accounting of the use hitherto made of her separate property as well as an injunction against her husband's further management of her estate. Judge Thomas Perry, in rejecting her demands at the circuit court level, made explicit the underlying sexual assumptions that guided most antebellum jurists in their approach to the emancipation of the American housewife.

Is it proper [Perry queried] to give a construction to the law, by which a change is to be made in the social relations of husband and wife, unknown to the common law, and which requires from her that which would do violence to that delicacy and retirement which is so much admired and encouraged, and so essential to the happiness of the marriage state? To give her a title as a *feme sole*, a title independent of, and distinct from her husband, would, as an incident to such right, require her to make all contracts and agreements and perform all the duties usually expected from the other sex, forcing her from the domestic circle to go out into the community to protect the rights to, and secure the profits of her property.[50]

The fear of any drastic reordering of sex roles that might impair the stability of family life manifested itself still more strongly in the argument of attorney Richard H. Alvey, who represented Ms. Schindel's husband in the final stage of the case before the Maryland Court of Appeals. Alvey's strident harangue forecast the difficulties that later generations of legal traditionalists would face in trying to separate limited economic concessions from more fundamental changes in the social and political status of women:

The right sought to be established by this proceeding is an extraordinary one, and goes far beyond anything that has yet been conceded to the cause of woman's rights. To enable the wife to leave her husband at pleasure, and to take with her, in the retreat, all her property, of every kind and description, to be enjoyed by her, and managed and disposed of as her own, apart from and to the entire exclusion of the husband, and in total disregard of the marital rights, is a monstrous proposition, that, among all the wild theories of improvements, has never yet been advocated in a civilized, Christian community, until the bringing of this suit, except by a few erratic and fanatical women, composing what is known as the "Woman's Rights Society." It is true, our legislation for the protection of married women, is of a most liberal character, even to the extent of doubtful propriety; but that it has gone the length of cutting the cords that bind society together, and of virtually destroying the moral and social efficacy of the marriage institution, is a notion not to be entertained for a moment. But such would be the inevitable result, if such a proceeding as this could be sustained. For let it once be understood that a wife, whenever she may become tired of her husband, or moved by any whim or caprice, may leave him, and take with her the whole property that she ever owned, and enjoy it exclusively, and thus become independent of that superiority and controlling power which the law has always wisely recognized in the husband, what incentive would there be for such a wife ever to reconcile differences with her husband, to act in submission to his wishes, and perform the many onerous duties pertaining to her sphere? Would not every wife, with property enough to sustain herself independently of her husband, when becoming impatient of his restraint and control, however necessarily exercised over her, take the refuge such a law would give her, and abandon her husband and her home? And thus the community would be filled with persons maintaining the unenviable character of husbands without wives, and wives without husbands, indulging in mutual hatred and animosity, bringing disgrace upon themselves, and mortification upon their families and friends.[51]

The high court proved predictably responsive to Alvey's reasoning and ruled that Ms. Schindel's capricious separation from her husband gave her no statutory right to separate maintenance or to the independent management of her property.

In the cold light of historical hindsight, the manifold deficiencies of the early Married Women's Property Acts stand out all too plainly. Crudely drafted, ambiguous in important particulars, subjected to rough handling by unsympathetic judges, they yet represented a major turning point in the legal emancipation of American women. If the rights they conceded were limited, and generally agreed to by male lawmakers with a minimum of debate or publicity, they amounted nonetheless to tangible economic gains that were further enlarged with the passage of time. The process was piecemeal and erratic; it was also progressive and irreversible. By 1875 a majority of state legislatures had passed statutes that explicitly gave a wife control of her separate earnings.[52] And, where paternalistic lawmakers led, militant suffragettes soon followed. The old Blackstonian unity of husband and wife, once shattered by antebellum legislation, proved impossible to repair, as seasoned observers such as David Dudley Field were quick to perceive. "An attempt to restore the old laws of marital relations," Field reported to the Law Amendment Society of London in 1857, "would have as little chance of success here, as an attempt to restore the Corn laws would have in England."[53]

Changes in the legal rights of the child during the antebellum years were far less dramatic, but here too some significant inroads were made upon traditional common-law doctrines of paternal power. Improvements occurred in three broad areas: custody and parental support obligations; the control of a minor's services and wages; and the availability of adoption procedures.

Although most courts continued to uphold a father's paramount claim to the custody of his minor children in the absence of a strong showing of misconduct or unfitness on his part, the development of a more child-centered theory of guardianship was clearly discernible among progressive jurists. The new view, destined to prevail in later times, guided the New York Court of Errors in its approach to one of the most famous custody cases that arose in the United States prior to the Civil War. In *Mercein v. People ex rel. Barry* (1840) a husband and wife had separated, pursuant to an agreement that left an infant daughter, in delicate health, permanently in the care of her mother. Later the husband sought to recover custody of the child through habeas corpus proceedings that came before the courts on five different occasions. At one point the court of errors, the highest state tribunal, ruled that the mother might retain possession of the girl, who was only two years old and required special care. "The interest of the infant is deemed paramount to the claims of both parents," declared Senator Alonzo C. Paige, who then went on to outline a theory of the state as *parens patriae* in custody situations:

> By the law of nature, the father has no paramount right to the custody of his child. By that law the wife and child are equal to the husband and father; but inferior and subject to their sovereign. The head of a family, in his character of husband and father, has no authority over his wife and children; but in his character of sovereign he has. On the establishment of civil societies, the power of the chief of a family as sovereign, passes to the chief or government of the nation. And the chief or magistrate of the nation not possessing the requisite knowledge necessary to a judicious discharge of the duties of guardianship and education of children, such portion of the sovereign power as relates to the discharge of these duties, is transferred to the parents, subject to such restrictions and limitations as the sovereign power of the nation thinks proper to prescribe. There is no parental authority independent of the supreme power of the state . . . The moment a child is born, it owes allegiance to the government of the country of its birth, and is entitled to the protection of that government. And such government is obli-

gated by its duty of protection, to consult the welfare, comfort and interests of such child in regulating its custody during the period of its minority.[54]

But matters did not end there, for two years later the husband secured another writ, and the New York Supreme Court then ordered his daughter to be returned to him. Exceptional circumstances no longer existed, since the child was now healthy and the father admittedly capable of giving her a proper upbringing. The qualifications of both spouses being equal, the court held that "by the law of the land the claims of the father are superior to those of the mother."[55]

Despite the final outcome of the *Mercein* case, which was typical of custody decisions in other states, the willingness of antebellum judges to weigh the peculiar needs of the individual child against the claims of either parent marked a necessary transitional stage in the evolution of modern custody practices. Not all judges were so child-oriented, of course; some clung stubbornly to the old formulas of paternal omnipotence.[56] But by 1860 the tide had set in the direction of more humane custody procedures as legislatures, too, began to recognize the importance of consulting a child's wishes and interests in matters of parental guardianship. Massachusetts lawmakers thus passed statutes in 1855 and 1856 that gave judges broad discretionary control over the award of custody in divorce and separation cases, "on the principle that the rights of the parents to their children, in the absence of misconduct, are equal, and the happiness and welfare of the children are to determine the care and custody."[57]

A similar concern for child welfare led some antebellum courts to impose upon parents a legal obligation to support their minor children, where the common law had recognized only a nonenforceable moral duty. New York judges pioneered in the establishment of this principle, which took almost half a century to evolve fully out of scattered and tentative precedents. It was not until 1863 that the New York Supreme Court squarely held that a third party who supplied necessaries to a minor could recover his expenses from the child's delinquent parent in an action at common law. Parental liability in such circumstances, reasoned the court, was analogous to a husband's common-law obligation to provide for his wife: both derived from the essential nature of the marriage relation itself.[58] Although third-party creditors were major beneficiaries of the doctrine in New York and other states, it did provide further needed protection for children whose deprivation might otherwise have gone unrelieved.

Judges also contributed to the economic independence of young workers by qualifying in important ways a father's right as master to the services and earnings of his children. While the law had long recognized that such paternal power might be waived with the express assent of the parent, courts in the antebellum years regularly implied emancipation from external conditions and behavior, ignoring the protests of fathers who insisted that they had never relinquished their rights. Where a man neglected his children, for example, and forced them to shift for themselves, or where he permitted a minor to collect and keep his wages over a period of time, judges ruled that the youngsters had been effectively emancipated and might retain control of their earnings for the future.[59] Emancipation might likewise be achieved through early marriage, as in the colonial period. In states where common-law marriages were still valid, or where the age of consent had not been raised by statute, boys might lawfully marry at fourteen, girls at twelve. Thereupon, by operation of law, they attained adult status, and the old master-servant analogue ceased to apply to them.

Finally, with the passage of the first comprehensive adoption acts around the middle of the nineteenth century, a serious effort was made to give adopted children all of the legal rights formerly enjoyed by natural children alone, including a share of the estate of adoptive parents who died intestate.[60] Since this progressive legislation was directed primarily toward the relief of orphans and destitute young people, its origins and implementation will be considered at greater length in connection with the treatment of children under the poor laws. Before turning to that subject, however, one further aspect of general family law must be explored: the liberalizing of divorce requirements in many states during the antebellum years.

As in the case of marriage laws, the regulations governing divorce varied widely from state to state. South Carolina remained a divorceless society down to the Civil War; New York granted divorces for only one cause, adultery. But most states tended to enlarge upon the limited precedents set in colonial times in two ways: they broadened the range of acceptable legal grounds for divorce, and they democratized divorce procedures so as to bring legal action for the first time within the reach of every taxpayer.

Indiana went further than any other state in multiplying grounds for complaint. Besides the traditional ones, such as adultery, bigamy, and desertion, her statutes recognized cruel treatment, habitual drunkenness, conviction of a felony, and "any other cause for which the Court shall deem it proper that the divorce shall be granted." This open-ended "omnibus clause," coupled with lax residence requirements, made the Hoosier state the divorce capital of the country in the 1850s. She also served as a model for sister jurisdictions in one other respect: her new constitution of 1851 expressly forbade the legislature to meddle in any way with future divorce proceedings, which were left exclusively in the hands of the judiciary.[61]

The shift from private divorce bills to court decrees granted pursuant to general statutes marked one of the most striking developments in antebellum jurisprudence. A nationwide phenomenon, it seems to have reflected in part a real increase in the demand for legal divorces. So much may be gleaned from the reasons officially given by the Georgia legislature in 1835 for vesting complete jurisdiction over divorces thereafter in the state courts. The number of divorce applications had increased alarmingly in recent years, the lawmakers reported, taxing the time and energies of the legislative body and unnecessarily swelling the statute books. While the statistical record scarcely seems appalling to modern eyes, it does reveal a rising frequency curve that substantiates legislative contentions in a modest way. Between 1798 and 1835, only 291 legislative divorces were granted in Georgia, but approximately one-tenth of these occurred in the single year of 1833. State legislators hoped to curb the trend by entrusting divorce matters to the more conservative administration of the courts, asserted Judge Eugenius A. Nisbet in an early decision interpreting the new legislation.[62]

If conditions in Georgia were at all representative of those in other states, logistical considerations played a determining role in the abolition of legislative divorces. But other factors, of a less obvious nature, may also have been operative. Thus, a move toward general divorce laws arguably represented part of a larger crusade against special privilege that moved into high gear with the election of Andrew Jackson to the Presidency in 1828. Just as small businessmen in the antebellum period sometimes demanded and got general incorporation laws from their state legislatures to protect them against the expense and favoritism associated with individual legislative grants, so less affluent householders may have sought general divorce legislation to eliminate the need for costly private bills that catered to the interests of the upper classes. The end results of the process, in any event, were noteworthy: in the early Republic legislative divorces had been common in every state; by 1867 only four states still permitted them.[63]

Despite the comparative ease with which divorces were made available to the masses in these years, however, there was no dramatic rush to take advantage of them. Statistics indicate only a slight rise in the national divorce rate to the time of the Civil War, when the figures leveled off at 0.3 divorces per 1,000 persons, a ratio that remained virtually constant for the next decade. There was much loose talk of a spreading "divorce evil" in newspapers and magazines, of course, and the first divorce novel, T. S. Arthur's *The Hand but Not the Heart*, made its appearance in 1858. But in retrospect the relaxation of divorce requirements, like the passage of the Married Women's Property Acts, appears rather a symbolic gesture—a concession to the temper of a democratic society—than the signal for any revolutionary assault upon the institution of the family.[64]

The libertarian tendencies so strikingly displayed in the family law of the nonpoor did not affect the legal rules governing indigent spouses and their children. For families on relief the antebellum years brought no comparable improvement in the poor laws or their administration. The trend was rather the reverse: instead of obtaining greater civil rights, the poor were subjected to harsher and more repressive regulation. Welfare policies varied in detail from state to state, as in the colonial period, but everywhere relief recipients were dealt with legislatively as a separate and unequal class. A sampling of practices from multiple jurisdictions illustrates the nature of legislative interference with family relationships, especially in the previously defined areas of: settlement and removal procedures;

the imposition of support obligations upon relatives; and the apprenticeship of minor children.

By the 1820s settlement provisions had grown amazingly complex in some states, opening the door to a flood of litigation. The expenses incident to settlement and removal proceedings consumed one-ninth of all funds allocated for poor relief in New York state by 1824, while in Oswego County such legal costs reportedly totaled more than the money actually spent for the maintenance of the local poor.[65] Other states, including Connecticut and Ohio, witnessed a similarly heavy reliance on the courts for the determination of intricate settlement questions arising from the periodic toughening of statutory requirements. Where the term of residence needed to acquire a legal settlement had generally been set at three or four months in the colonial period, it was raised to a year or more in many states by the early nineteenth century. Other stipulations pertaining to the ownership of property or the payment of taxes were also strengthened, as were the penalties assessed against those who brought indigent persons into a community or gave them shelter without reporting their presence to poor law officials.[66]

Under such an expansive network of bureaucratic regulations, obvious opportunities for abuse existed. The integrity of the individual family seemed at first glance to be pretty well protected, however, through the general adherence of judges to the doctrine that a child's legal settlement must follow that of its parents. In defending the social policy served by the rule, the Supreme Court of Ohio commented in 1827:

> If the legal settlement of the child does not follow that of the parent, it might and frequently would so happen that the legal settlement of the child would be in one place, while that of a parent would be in another. And a case might be presented where there are many children that the settlement of the parent and each one of the children would be in separate and distinct townships. Will it be for a moment believed, that such is the policy or meaning of the law? If such is the law, children of the same family, in their tender years, may be separated from their natural guardian, the parent, and from each other, and a statute which is entitled, "an act for the relief of the poor," may be made to operate most oppressively upon that class of the community.

The state legislature never intended that warning-out provisions

should be applied to minor children, concluded Chief Justice
Peter Hitchcock, since "the warning presupposes a right in the
individual concerned to remove from the township," and an
infant "has no legal right to remove, where such removal would
separate him from or place him beyond the control of his
natural guardian."[67]

But five years later the same tribunal exhibited far less concern for the preservation of family ties. In *Trustees of Bloomfield* v. *Trustees of Chagrin* (1832) an indigent mother had
remarried and moved to another township, leaving behind an
infant to be cared for by local poor law administrators. The
court here ruled that the woman's change of residence did not
create a new settlement for her child, so the burden of the
infant's support could not be transferred to the second township.[68]

Exceptions to the principle of family protection flourished in
other states as well, as town and county authorities employed
an endless variety of hairsplitting technicalities to avoid the
fiscal responsibilities of poor relief. Perhaps the most flagrant
example of family disruption occurred in New York in 1819,
when young William Chittenden, an eleven-year-old pauper,
was separated from his mother and other members of his family
and forced to return to the town where he was born. William's
parents, it appeared, had been repeatedly warned out of towns
across the state and had never gained a legal settlement anywhere. Under those circumstances, reasoned the New York
Supreme Court, the doctrine that a child's settlement follows
that of its parents had no relevance. Instead, the boy's birthplace must be regarded as his proper place of settlement and
must bear the expense of his maintenance.[69] Presumably the
court's harsh logic also implied the future dispersal of William's
brothers and sisters, and thus the removal of minor children
from their "natural guardians," which had seemed unthinkable
to one Ohio judge, found a secure niche in the jurisprudence of
a sister state.

Behind the willingness of some judges to countenance the
breakup of indigent families lay a further policy consideration:
a view of the poor as an inferior class whose civil rights were
negligible. This view was seldom openly expressed but may be
glimpsed in a number of settlement cases. In *Otsego* v. *Smith-
field* (1827), for example, the New York Supreme Court ordered

a wife and children to be removed to the woman's maiden settlement, in part to prevent further cohabitation between the spouses. The husband was admittedly a ne'er-do-well, a heavy drinker who did not provide adequately for his family. There was no indication, however, that he physically abused them at any time or that they desired to leave him. "The law will not tolerate the dispersion of families in this way," argued counsel for the town named in the removal order. But Chief Justice John Savage retorted:

> I hope I duly appreciate rights of marriage to the individuals concerned, and to society. But I can see neither reason, propriety, or humanity, in compelling one town to support paupers, having a settlement in another, merely to accommodate a vagabond, intemperate husband, as in this case, with the society of the wife and children, whom he has, by his misconduct, reduced to pauperism; thus enabling him, perhaps, to add to the number of paupers, and the burthens of the town into which he has happened to stray. It is enough that *Smithfield* is compelled to support one idle, useless member of society, casually thrown upon them; and they ought not to be further aggrieved by supporting those who have a settlement elsewhere within the state.[70]

A similar disregard of family feelings in removal cases characterized the decision of the Vermont Supreme Court in *Town of Randolph* v. *Town of Braintree* (1838). Here a widow was separated from her mentally disturbed daughter, with whom she had been living on a small farm for some eight years. The girl was not a violent lunatic; she was fed and cared for by her mother, though she sometimes wandered into town, "to the annoyance of the inhabitants of said Randolph," and she owned part of the farmhouse and some adjoining lands. Nevertheless, the local overseers of the poor, complaining that she was likely to become a public charge in the future, secured judicial authorization for the sale of her property and for her removal to the town where her deceased father had been settled. In approving these proceedings, the supreme court merely noted that an adult lunatic could not acquire a settlement of her own. Chief Justice Charles K. Williams brushed aside all appeals for the protection of the family tie between mother and daughter: "It is wholly immaterial whether she resided with her mother or any other person . . . Why should she not be removed if of full age, incapable of taking care of herself, and likely to become chargeable? Of what consequence is it with whom she resided, or of what family she was a member?"[71]

Such insensitivity to the needs of the poor as human beings reached perhaps its highest point in the "dumping" cases, in which sick, elderly, or dying paupers were transported across boundary lines (town, county, even state boundaries) to relieve the pocketbooks of local taxpayers. The picture was not all one-sided, of course; many courts scrupulously protected the family unit, and legislatures acted from time to time to correct the most palpable injustices of the system. But the indigent everywhere remained peculiarly vulnerable to manipulation under the settlement laws, as a Vermont judge noted in 1830, in contrasting the disabilities of welfare recipients with the rights enjoyed by self-supporting citizens:

> Every person who can support himself without being a public charge should be permitted to take up his abode where his inclination may direct, and seek his living in those places where he can find the best prospects of success in his business or calling, and to consult his fancy or his interest in selecting the place of his residence without being liable to be directed in his choice, except in obedience to the laws of the government. The policy of the law, however, has directed that if from misfortune or fault he becomes unable to maintain himself or family, he may be restricted in his choice, and must remain in that place which the law points out as the place of his settlement. It may be remarked that whenever a person is thus reduced so as to become the subject of a proceeding to ascertain the place of his settlement, he is passive, he has no voice in the proceedings, and however inconvenient or injurious it may be to his feelings or his interest, he has nothing to do but to obey the order, or be removed by a regular warrant.[72]

In addition to the restrictions imposed directly upon paupers and their offspring under the settlement laws, many states continued to require relatives to shoulder the cost of poor relief, wherever possible. Illinois went furthest in this direction during the antebellum years by adding brothers and sisters to the earlier categories of responsible kinfolk that included grandparents, parents, children, and grandchildren. Only in-laws were everywhere excluded from such legislative classification, since there was general agreement that the duty of support followed the blood line. A man therefore could not be compelled to assist his wife's indigent parents, nor could a woman be made to contribute to the maintenance of a pauper daughter-in-law.[73]

But the ascertainment of a person's statutory liability still left many prickly questions to be answered by the courts. What criteria, for example, determined the outer limits of the support obligation for individuals of low or moderate income? The statutes commonly authorized assessments against those "of sufficient ability" to pay; beyond that judges were free to fashion their own tests of solvency. The range of permissible judicial attitudes and responses is well displayed in two representative cases of the antebellum era.

In *Overseers of the Poor of the Town of East Greenwich* v. *Henry Card* (1850) poor law officials in Rhode Island sought to recover from a father the total expenses incident to the care of his lunatic son, who had been confined first in a hospital, then in the local poorhouse. By the time the case was decided the son had died, so that only previous expenditures were in issue. The state supreme court, while sympathetic to the argument for full reimbursement, ordered the father to pay only one-half of the sum claimed by the town, noting: "To order him to pay for the entire maintenance, might have the effect of bringing both father and son upon the town." No other concern was expressed for the plight of the parent, who was reduced to a state of near-dependence through the court's strict construction of the poor laws.[74]

The appellate judiciary of New Hampshire, on the other hand, acknowledged the hardships that the support obligation entailed for relatives of modest means and strove to alleviate them in practice. *Colebrook* v. *Stewartstown* (1854) provides an instructive study in rule making by a "liberal" tribunal. Colebrook, the defendant in the case, was a man of sixty-seven who owned a small farm worth between $1,400 and $2,000. He was in good health, owed no debts, and had accumulated savings of some fifteen hundred dollars. From this modest hoard the local overseers of the poor attempted to extract the sum of $9.04, the cost of wood and other supplies furnished to Colebrook's needy daughter and her three young children several years earlier. Apparently Colebrook's income was negligible, so that any assessment would have required him to dip into his capital. The lower court approved such a levy, reasoning that the defendant's advanced age lessened the need of substantial savings for his future support. But Judge Samuel Dana Bell of the state supreme court strongly disagreed:

> [Such a view] tends to destroy one of the most powerful induce-ments to industry, prudence and economy in those who have the misfortune to have needy relations, the hope of improving their condition, and of leaving their children to commence life under better advantages; because it devotes all a man's net earnings, beyond a limited amount, to the support of his needy and, perhaps, undeserving relations. It is hard enough to say to a man, as the law, in effect, now says, All you have earned and laid aside, in the hope of fitting out your daughters respectably on their marriage, or of aiding your sons to buy their farms, or to procure the means of commencing business in their trades, must be devoted to main-taining your relations; especially where, as is too often the case, the misconduct of those relations has been a great obstacle to a man's own success in life, without adding that even the property which has been earned and saved to secure himself from the alms-house, must all be applied to the same purpose, so soon as, from the approach of age, it becomes more and more certain that it will not be required for his own support; so that when he dies he will have nothing to leave to his heirs, or to reward the kindness of those who have cared for him in his declining years.

In the future, Bell predicted, "when poverty and suffering become more common . . . as must unavoidably happen from a more crowded population," judges would be likely to interpret the support provisions of the poor laws in a still more liberal fashion. Wage earners might then anticipate no levies upon their income until they had managed to set aside sufficient capi-tal to assure a comfortable standard of living for themselves and their children.[75]

The support obligation, whether strictly or loosely enforced, remained an essential component in antebellum relief programs, especially in the older states. Yet judges found understandable difficulty on occasion in reconciling such statutory liability with the older common law of domestic relations. In state after state they wrestled with the same basic problem: Did the poor laws merely supplement existing common-law remedies for the pro-tection of wives and children, or did they create an exclusive family law of the poor, complete with its own bureaucracy and independent enforcement procedures? The issue arose most often in situations where the overseers, having relieved a destitute wife, sought to compel her husband to pay the cost of her maintenance. Since husbands were not mentioned in the poor laws, recovery was possible only if the courts agreed that poor law officials might sue the delinquent spouse at common law (or in a court of equity) for the breach of a nonstatutory duty to provide for his wife.

Most antebellum tribunals winked at any logical inconsistencies in such a tactic and refused to draw a sharp line between statutory and nonstatutory remedies. In a typical case decided by the Ohio Supreme Court in 1841, a wife had been physically abused by her husband, driven from his house, and reduced at last to pauperism. She appealed to the local overseers of the poor, who first assisted her, then secured a judgment against her husband to cover their expenses. The court, in holding the husband financially liable, did not distinguish between the overseers and any other third parties who might have supplied the woman with necessities, in reliance upon her husband's credit. "It was the legal and moral duty of the defendant to have paid this money," noted Judge Peter Hitchcock, "and being paid as it was by the township, it was paid to his use."[76]

But not all courts resolved the matter so simply. In New York the judiciary, after some vacillation, insisted upon the exclusiveness of the remedies and administrative techniques prescribed by the poor laws. The New York Supreme Court, in *Norton* v. *Rhodes* (1854), ruled that the superintendents of the poor had exceeded their statutory authority in assisting a destitute woman whose husband was financially able to support her. While agreeing that the superintendents were required by law to "take care of the poor," Judge Richard P. Marvin queried: "But who are paupers? Can the wife of a man who is bound by the law to support her, and who is abundantly able to do so, be regarded as a pauper?" Her case was not covered in the statutes, Marvin argued, because her rights were established and governed by common-law rules. In the event of nonsupport she might properly apply to the courts for a limited divorce or separation from her husband and secure a judicial order for her separate maintenance. But she could not qualify for aid under the poor laws, nor could relief administrators increase their statutory powers by relying upon common-law theories of liability: "The plaintiffs' [superintendents'] counsel invokes to his aid the common law principle obliging the husband to support his wife, and in case he neglects or refuses to do so, rendering him liable in an action at the suit of any one who furnishes her with necessaries. Those principles have no application to the present case, and in my judgment it would be extremely dangerous to confer upon the superintendents of the poor, in their official capacity, the right to interpose in cases of difficulties between husband and wife, and thus involve the county in the controversy, and array its power against one of the parties."[77] A concern for the privacy of family relationships, which had long guided the common law of domestic relations, thus reasserted itself against the threat of bureaucratic intrusiveness that the poor laws represented. If the courts of other states attempted to integrate, as far as possible, the two systems of family regulation, New York at least clung to the *Norton* rule of strict separation for the next thirty-eight years.[78]

Although, as the *Norton* case suggests, poor law officials could legally exercise only those powers granted to them by statute, in practice they enjoyed almost unlimited discretion in interpreting the vague provisions of state welfare acts. Trial courts hesitated to overturn administrative judgments, even in such sensitive areas as child apprenticeship, and few complaints of bureaucratic malfeasance ever reached the appellate bench. Two very different situations—one involving abandonment, the other apprenticeship—illustrate the lengths to which official zeal was sometimes carried, as well as the difficulties that poor families faced in attempting to secure redress through the courts.

In *Bowman* v. *Russ* (1826) local overseers erroneously reported that a man had abandoned his wife and children, leaving them a charge upon the town. They obtained a judicial order authorizing them to seize the absent householder's real and personal property and to manage it thereafter in the interest of his family. A short time later the man returned and proved that he had never abandoned his family or left them unprovided for. Despite such evidence, a lower court upheld the action of the overseers in taking possession of the man's estate. On appeal the New York Supreme Court ruled that such seizure had been illegal and found the defendant overseers guilty of trespass. "According to the point insisted on by the defendants," remarked Chief Justice John Savage, "the justices may proceed against any man, and take from his own possession the very property with which he is contributing to the support of his family."[79]

Fifteen years later the Supreme Court of Indiana rapped another set of poor law administrators over the knuckles for wrongful proceedings under the state's apprenticeship law. The statute in question authorized overseers to bind out as apprentices all poor children whose parents were dead or unable to maintain them. In *Stanton* v. *The State* (1841) an overseer arranged for the apprenticeship of three young children whose father, he charged, had "wickedly neglected" to support them over a long period of time. A probate court judge approved the overseer's action, but the state supreme court held otherwise, noting that parental neglect in itself did not subject a family to poor law controls:

> Overseers of the poor have no right to meddle with the children of living parents, unless they be found *unable* to maintain them. When such is the fact, and the parent objects to his child being apprenticed, the Probate Court has a right to act. In the complaint exhibited against *Stanton*, there is no allegation that he was not perfectly *able* to support his family. The charge is that he criminally *neglected* the wants of his children, and that they thereby became sufferers. Of this charge he was found guilty, and of none other. However reprehensible his conduct may have been, he did not, by mere neglect to perform his duty in providing for his family, subject the disposal of his children to the jurisdiction of the overseers of the poor, nor to that of the Probate Court. The law points out another mode of proceeding against those who neglect the wants of their families.[80]

The decision, although returning the children to their natural parent, reaffirmed the dual standard of responsibility that applied to poor and nonpoor families. It also reflected, perhaps, a dawning judicial mistrust of apprenticeship as a means of socializing youngsters and equipping them for life in a rapidly industrializing society. Indeed, by the 1840s a combination of factors—the emergence of the factory system, with its demand for cheap unskilled labor, the movement toward tax-supported public schools in the North and Midwest, and the growing number of foreign-born workers and their families—had robbed apprenticeship of much of its meaning. Instead of providing useful vocational training for the children of all classes, the apprenticeship system now functioned largely as a device for the recruitment and exploitation of young paupers. While masters were still required by law to educate their charges in the rudiments of reading, writing, and arithmetic, the obligation was often ignored in practice, and several states, including Kentucky, Missouri, and Indiana, specifically abolished any educational requirement for Negro apprentices.[81] The transformation of apprenticeship from a culturally enriching experience to a crude caretaker operation was especially notable in the Old South, where a majority of state legislatures passed compulsory guardianship laws that placed the children of free blacks under the control of white masters for security reasons, without regard to their parents' ability to support them.[82]

A similar trend toward greater repressiveness and regimentation affected other welfare programs in the antebellum years, as major changes occurred in the design and functioning of relief agencies of all kinds. If many judges and legislators managed to ignore the deficiencies of apprenticeship training for the poor, it was largely because they had learned to perceive the challenge of poverty and crime in a new light. Unlike their colonial forebears, Americans of the 1820s and 1830s considered the dependent and deviant classes as a genuine social problem, a threat to the very existence of a stable and orderly society. Aware of the momentous economic and demographic changes that were visibly transforming the world in which they lived, citizens in the early nineteenth century found scant comfort in theories of religious determinism or the fixity of social ranks that had satisfied earlier generations. Community cohesiveness, it appeared, was fast disintegrating under the stimulus of enhanced geographic and social mobility; the lower classes no longer deferred to their superiors; and religious appeals to Christian brotherhood made little impact upon a secularized age. Impelled by a sense of urgency, civic leaders across the nation agreed that Draconian measures were needed to control and reform those guilty of abnormal behavior. In time they worked out a containment policy that applied to the indigent and the deviant alike and involved what David Rothman has termed "the discovery of the asylum."

While, as we have seen, almshouses and jails were not

unknown in colonial America, they were few in number and used most often for the temporary confinement of individuals, who were not subjected to any distinctive institutional care or discipline. So long as men believed in a divinely appointed social order, they saw little need to remove paupers or invalids from the wholesome influence of family, friends, and church. But nineteenth-century reformers denied both the efficacy of divine planning and the soundness of basic community institutions. On the one hand, they rejected Calvinistic doctrines of innate depravity and held that men were morally responsible for their acts; yet they also blamed environmental factors—especially the malfunctioning of traditional agencies of social control—for the spread of poverty and crime. The breakdown of family discipline, they argued, encouraged juvenile delinquency; indiscriminate doles to the poor weakened their self-respect and hindered their chances of rehabilitation; and a debased neighborhood life, fostered by the presence of taverns, brothels, and gambling dens, made it doubly difficult for the lower classes to avoid a descent into penury, or worse. Convinced that individuals could be reformed through proper conditioning, penologists and welfare authorities demanded that the maladjusted be removed from their contaminated surroundings and placed in specially designed institutions where, isolated from the outside world, they might be taught through rigorous discipline to behave as responsible middle-class citizens. The nineteenth-century asylum, in all its manifestations—orphanages, prisons, mental hospitals, houses of refuge, poorhouses—thus represented a new concept, in theory and practice: the creation of a model environment in which social dropouts and misfits might be trained to accept conservative community values.[83]

For destitute families and orphan children, our principal subjects of concern, the shift to indoor relief and institutional care put an end to the informal, homelike treatment they had earlier received. The new asylums resembled factories rather than private dwellings and compelled inmates to conform to a factory-type regimen that included the ringing of bells for meals and work details, the assignment of prescribed tasks throughout the day, and the enforcement of a quasi-military discipline through appropriate punishments. Conditions varied with geography and administrative personnel: the repressive features of the new system were most apparent in the larger cities of the nation, while poorhouse managers everywhere found it difficult to design and execute rigorous programs for their charges. But few doubted the wisdom of confining the dependent in institutions that, for all their dehumanizing techniques, promised both rehabilitation and lower maintenance costs for those they serviced.

The enthusiasm displayed by the general public for the asylum experiment suffered only one minor setback in the antebellum years, and that related to the care of dependent children. By 1850 child abuse had grown so appalling in some almshouses and orphanages that a number of private agencies began to be founded with the avowed purpose of placing youngsters in foster homes as rapidly as possible. Out of this movement—involving "infants' hospitals," "foundling asylums," "maternity hospitals," and Children's Aid Societies—emerged the first comprehensive adoption statute passed by the Massachusetts legislature in 1851. The Massachusetts law, as previously mentioned, sought to secure for adopted children all of the legal rights enjoyed by natural children. In the next quarter century sixteen other states followed the Massachusetts example in framing their own adoption statutes, and if state courts often construed their provisions narrowly (as they had earlier done with the Married Women's Property Acts), such legislation did mark an important and innovative step in the protection of child welfare that cut across economic and class lines.[84]

Nevertheless, child placement efforts did not supplant institutionalization as the dominant response of American society to the plight of the orphaned and the destitute in the nineteenth century. Although poorhouses and other asylums gradually abandoned all serious attempts at social rehabilitation and degenerated into mere custodial agencies for the confinement of increasing numbers of foreign-born immigrants, reformers of the Gilded Age seldom questioned the propriety of an institutional solution to the problems of poverty and delinquency. Some structural reforms were made in the system: state control replaced local control of poorhouses, and certain categories of the "worthy poor"—the blind, children, the deaf and dumb, the epileptic—received special attention and improved facilities. But the family law of the poor continued, as before, to evolve independently of the libertarian movements that were transforming the common law of domestic relations. Women's rights and civil liberties still meant little to families on relief, whose status throughout American history has been cogently summarized by Lawrence Friedman:

> The root of the problem [of poverty] was not structural. It lay in society's indifference. The mass of the public feared and distrusted vagrants. Even men of good will were blinded by the fantasy of the able-bodied poor, unwilling to earn an honest living. Reform movements fed on a few noisome scandals, emphasized the failures of the old system, and called for fresh approaches. But reformers lacked the will to follow through, and no concrete interest group stood to gain from a thorough reform of public welfare. Thus, even when reform succeeded in changing formal law, the actual operation of the programs soon lapsed into their former evil habits. From poor laws to poor farms to AFDC is a continuous lesson, on the consequences of powerlessness in America.[85]

But I beg you to forbear (for you will be strongly tempted) from political life, until you have reaped the highest harvest of distinction in your profession. Depend upon it, the profession is the truest road to permanent character & fame, & when these are attained, public honors will flow in, so far as they are desirable, almost as of course.
Joseph Story to Timothy Walker,
April 1, 1832

5 Upgrading the Professional Image

In the folklore of American legal history the middle decades of the nineteenth century marked the collapse of an organized and socially responsible bar. While acknowledging the brilliant achievements of individual practitioners and judges during the years from 1830 to 1870, commentators from Charles Warren and Roscoe Pound to W. Raymond Blackard and Anton-Hermann Chroust have insisted upon a general decline in professional competence that allegedly accompanied the assaults of a militant democracy. The standard picture of professional development in the United States thus provides a study in dramatic contrasts. We begin with a golden age of jurisprudence in the early Republic, fostered by a self-regulating fraternity of educated judges and lawyers. Then come the barbarian invasions, as the semiliterate masses force their way into legal practice, aided by subservient state legislatures. Finally, after several decades of disorder and demoralization, an elite leadership arises to purge the profession of its populist standards of recruitment and performance, through the creation of the first modern bar associations in the 1870s. In its broad outlines this moral drama of light and shadow appeals strongly to the imagination, while offering at least a plausible account of the interplay between legal groups and the forces of social change. It even adds another link to the chain of causation leading to the Civil War, insofar as popular contempt for legal authority may have contributed to an ultimate recourse to armed violence.

On closer scrutiny, however, the argument tends to break down in several important ways. To begin with, it overemphasizes the role of formal organization as the appropriate yardstick by which to measure the strength of professionalism within the bar. This initial bias leads to a neglect of alternative methods for maintaining discipline and esprit de corps among practitioners, just as it imposes upon early bar associations attitudes and norms that properly belong only to the twentieth century. Lay criticism of lawyers, on the other hand, is magnified at key points into something approaching a coherent class movement that acts as a catalyst to force undesirable changes upon a disapproving, but largely defenseless, bar. The "degradation" of the nineteenth-century lawyer accordingly becomes a function of external pressures and interference rather than tensions within the legal profession itself.

Any thoroughgoing revisionist interpretation must, of course, rely for its persuasiveness upon detailed research into professional behavior on both state and local levels, and few studies of this kind, employing the latest social science techniques, exist at the present time. But there are sufficient data of a qualitative sort to support a working hypothesis that the crucial "middle period" of the nineteenth century represented no sharp break with the past so far as legal professionalism was concerned. Practitioners in Jacksonian America and the Civil War era were even more likely than their predecessors to cherish a narrow vocational outlook toward their work and to insist upon a technical competence that set them apart from their fellow men, as it enabled them to rationalize their elite status in American society on grounds that made some sense even to radical democrats.

While it is possible to write the social history of the American lawyer in terms of recurrent crises in public relations, the truth seems to be—as I have already noted in discussing the postrevolutionary public—that the American people have at all times distrusted attorneys.[1] The roots of popular suspicion perhaps inhere in the very structure of common-law justice, a system that places a premium upon aggressive individualism, pitting the self-interest of the client against that of his legal representative in matters of cost and efficiency. From Benjamin Austin's *Observations on the Pernicious Practice of the Law* (1786) to John W. Pitts's *Eleven Numbers against Lawyer Legislation and Fees at the Bar* (1843), antilawyer protest remains overwhelmingly a middle-class phenomenon that centers upon demands for cheaper and speedier justice.

Although attacks upon the antebellum bar were often accompanied by extremist rhetoric and flamboyant trappings, they represented, like earlier manifestations of popular unrest, little in the way of sans-culotte radicalism, but rather the insistence of an ever expanding bourgeoisie upon increased legal services and an updated recruitment program geared to changing population trends and the rise of marginal social groups to positions of status and power. The drive toward reduced educational qualifications for lawyers in the Jacksonian era thus paralleled and complemented the agitation by lower-middle-class constituencies for liberalized divorce laws and the efforts of small businessmen to secure general incorporation acts. In all three instances, moreover, public opinion was sharply divided, both inside and outside the bar, and reform-minded lawyers, who were fully as conscientious as their opponents, took the lead in promoting what they considered progressive legislation.

The integrity of most of these nineteenth-century legal crusaders needs to be emphasized because historians have tended all too often to dismiss them out of hand as unprincipled demagogues, ready to sell out their profession for a handful of votes. This was precisely the view taken by the conservative legal elite of the time, and our approach to the whole problem of law reform has long been colored by an appreciable Whiggish bias. We have accepted almost without question the jeremiads of Story, Kent, Hoffman, and Binney; if we speak of a "legal mind," it is their outlook that we consider normative; and if we engage in revisionism, we are far more likely to try to establish that Marshall and Story were really "liberals" than we are to re-examine the goals and attitudes of their allegedly "radical"

contemporaries. It is time to take a fresh look at the entire process of adjustment by which the bar was brought into line with
the aspirations of a fluid democratic society, and one essential
starting point must be a more open-minded inquiry into the
reasonableness of popular complaints against the early legal
establishment.

Although the bar in the pre-Jackson period has been generally
portrayed as a semiautonomous guild struggling to maintain
professional standards against the encroachments of anti-intel-
lectual legislative majorities, abundant evidence suggests that a
professional outlook, concerned with corporate power and
responsibilities, scarcely existed among the lawyers of that
time. Recent commentators have pointed to a crucial generation
gap within the legal community that accompanied the
Revolution, as one-fourth of all prewar practitioners joined the
Tory exodus.[2] The disappearance of this conservative group,
whose members were often bar leaders in their respective
colonies, may well have deflected any incipient drive toward
corporatism, for their replacements tended to be younger,
ill trained, and strongly individualistic in their attitudes. Even
in Massachusetts, where several county bar associations flourished in the postrevolutionary years, all efforts to establish a
statewide organization failed, and the eventual recognition in
1810 of the power of county bar groups to control local
admission standards was the work of sympathetic Massachusetts judges rather than lobbying lawyers.

Everywhere, in fact, it was the judiciary, not the bar, that did
most to establish the guidelines for legal practice, with the
acquiescence of state legislatures, and this pattern of joint
legislative-judicial regulation persisted through the middle
decades of the century. Outside New England early bar associations were virtually nonexistent, while an almost total absence
of organizational data makes it impossible to determine
whether most pioneer bar groups actually functioned as anything more than fraternal gatherings of practitioners attached to
a particular set of local courts. Gerard W. Gawalt, the most
careful student of the Massachusetts bar in its postrevolutionary development, has remarked that the major county bar
associations had been transformed into quasi-social clubs at least
as early as 1806—several years *before* they won what he terms
their "fifty-year struggle" for autonomy. And Gawalt further
concludes that the subsequent dissolution of these agencies in

the 1830s was due less to outside pressures than to apathy among the members themselves.[3]

Certainly far too much emphasis has been placed upon the closing of a few bar associations in the heyday of Jacksonian Democracy. In each instance one can point to the corresponding rise of new legal organizations at the same time—voluntary social groups, to be sure, but ones that, like the New York Law Association of the 1830s, often displayed a more intense professional consciousness than their earlier counterparts, along with a better understanding of the importance of good public relations. As William C. Russel of the New York group explained to Joseph Story in 1838,

> This Association was founded some eight years since and now numbers about three hundred members, consisting of Law students and the junior members of the profession. They meet every Saturday evening and are occupied on alternate evenings in hearing lectures and in legal argument. As a means of instruction the Association is most valuable and it promises to be very efficacious in the creation of an esprit de corps in the bar . . . The Lectures are public as we consider that the principles of legal science can gain only honour by being popularly known, while we entertain no fear of their being apprehended so easily as to diminish the respect which the Profession claims.[4]

Any attempt to assess the quality of the bar in a given era must, however, look beyond questions of formal organization and statutory criteria to the actual implementing of professional standards by courts and examining committees. While data of this kind are too meager to permit any sweeping generalizations about the lawyers of the Federalist and Jeffersonian epochs, we may note in passing that the Philadelphia bar—probably the most prestigious in the nation at the close of the eighteenth century—was by no means a model of self-policing. Horace Binney, who passed his qualifying examinations in March 1800, was frankly shocked at the laxity of admissions procedures. "No attention was paid at that time to the qualification of age, or, indeed, any other," Binney later recalled. "One of my examiners . . . did not know what was the general issue in an action of trover, and he knew about as much of law in general."[5] Counterstatements could doubtless be secured from other individuals, but if a systematic overview were feasible, the results might well support the comparison drawn by a law writer in 1840 between turn-of-the-century practitioners and those of his own day: "The labor of a lawyer was easy [then], compared with that of the present day. There were few books of authority to be examined and cited; there were no volumes of reports scattered as now, like the leaves of the sibyl, upon his path, and the standard of legal acquirement was moderate. A good voice, a fluid utterance, and a discussion of general principles answered every demand."[6]

From this perspective the kind of legislative interference that characterized the years after 1830 loses much of its shock impact. The scaling down of formal educational requirements, for example, which critics have so readily attributed to the anti-intellectualism of a raw democracy, may equally imply a reasoned assault upon the privileged position of upper-middle-class practitioners and their sons, while the popular election or short-term appointment of judges presupposes no necessary decline in the caliber of the bench. Isaac F. Redfield of Vermont is a case in point. Redfield, chief justice of the Vermont Supreme Court and a distinguished jurist, was reelected to his post annually for twenty-five years, from 1835 to his retirement in 1860, although he was a rather stiff-necked character who opposed the dominant political forces of his state. Except for his unusually long period of service, his career typified a general trend in Vermont, where judges were regularly returned to office from year to year during good behavior.

How representative was the Vermont pattern? Did the elective principle offer greater security of tenure to frontier judges than to their counterparts in more sophisticated urban environments? Such questions still await serious investigation, although a pathbreaking study of the performance of state supreme courts in the Old South vis-à-vis black litigants affirms the general competence and stability of the appellate judiciary, whether appointed during good behavior or elected for limited terms. Southern judges often got away with unpopular "liberal" decisions in the area of race, suggests A. E. Keir Nash, because the public recognized that the judicial role was inherently "non-gladiatorial" and hence applied a somewhat different set of standards in selecting judges than in choosing congressmen.[7] How well such reasoning might apply to the personnel of lower courts (who were presumably more vulnerable to community attitudes and pressures) remains an open question.

But, whatever the measurable effect of populist legislation enacted after 1830, conservative legal spokesmen did not remain passive in the face of what *they* at least considered a serious threat to their professional status. Instead, they set in motion an impressive public relations campaign that succeeded by the time of the Civil War in altering appreciably the lay image of the American lawyer—transforming him from a designing cryptopolitician into a benevolently neutral technocrat.

Legal periodicals played a vital role in this image-making process. These publications have been strangely neglected by historians, although in volume alone they form a striking feature of the post-1830 years, as the following chart attests:[8]

Date	New Law Magazines
Pre-1830	12
1830-1839	5
1840-1849	13
1850-1859	19
1860-1869	15

To be sure, these figures are somewhat misleading, since most fledgling journals failed to survive more than a few years. A tabulation of all law magazines in existence at the beginning of each decade reveals a more conservative picture:

Date	Law Magazines
1810	1
1820	1
1830	5
1840	2
1850	10
1860	9
1870	17

Nor should it be forgotten that magazine publishing in general experienced a boom during these years, owing to low postage rates, typographical innovations, and improved transportation and distribution facilities. Yet with due allowance for these caveats, the rate of growth for such specialized publications remains impressive and suggests that the law journal may have filled a peculiar need among American practitioners sensitive to popular distrust of more formal professional agencies.

The changing format of the law magazine itself supports this impression. Whereas earlier journals, of which Hall's *American Law Journal* (1808-1817) was both pioneer and prototype, tended to be speculative and treated many subjects of general interest to the educated community, the typical magazine of the years after 1830 conceived its function in rigorously utilitarian terms. Designed to serve the *"workingmen of the profession,"* such journals as the *Monthly Law Reporter* (1838-1866), the *New York Legal Observer* (1842-1854), the *Pennsylvania Law Journal* (1842-1848), and the *Western Law Journal* (1843-1853) disavowed all theorizing and offered their readers instead a "medium of communication concerning legal matters of fact useful and interesting to gentlemen of the bar."[9] The bulk of every issue was devoted to the bare reporting of recent court decisions, in advance of their appearance in official volumes of reports, with heavy emphasis upon law-as-it-is rather than law-as-it-ought-to-be.

Peleg W. Chandler, editor of the *Monthly Law Reporter*, spelled out the broader implications of this policy in a letter to a friend:

> It seems to me that the spirit of innovation is, in many respects, tearing away, in our profession, many of the most ancient and approved landmarks. There is a vast deal of theory—an immense longing for El Dorados in law. A great deal is said in particular cases, even in arguments to the court, about what the law ought to be or might well be, but precious little *of what it is.* Now it would seem that a good way to check this thing, as well as the political revolution founded in the same spirit, is to hold up before the profession and the public the decisions fresh from the court—to place before them the law as it comes from the dispensers of it—from those who are too far removed from the public to be easily affected by the changing fashions of the day . . . Noisy radicals are not men who have read intimately the reports and become acquainted with the intricate machinery, of which, if a part be disarranged, the whole may suffer . . . In conducting the L.R., I have been actuated by these feelings, and have striven to make it a *matter of fact* affair.[10]

Like the case material, the remaining contents—reviews of new law books, hints for the improvement of office habits or court-room strategy, summaries of recent state laws, and memoirs of practitioners living and dead—appealed to a narrow professional clientele. But behind a facade of objectivity and noncommittal exposition law writers busily pursued a further end: the creation of an effective counterimage to the popular stereotype of the lawyer as an enemy of the lower classes.[11]

In their quest for a usable symbolism the obituary notice took on an added importance. Perhaps, as Herbert Butterfield has suggested in regard to seventeenth-century science,[12] every great movement sooner or later enters a mythmaking phase, in which earlier achievements and personalities are reappraised and idealized as guides for the future. The traits of the departed pioneer then become an imaginary yardstick by which to measure the progress of his successors.

American law was clearly ripe for such a retrospective critique by 1830. A juristic revolution of sorts had taken place; new institutions and techniques were in successful operation; and the old actors were fast passing from the stage. For law writers sensitive to antiprofessional slurs necrology held both the seeds of corporate identity and a possible answer to the egalitarian challenge. A few simple themes recur from obituary to obituary, from journal to journal. The American lawyer was invariably a man of indomitable industry and perseverance. Lamenting the early death of a promising young Massachusetts attorney, his biographer struck a familiar chord when he informed his readers:

He was a born lawyer. His mind had a native affinity for the study of legal rules and principles . . . His taste for the law was natural and instinctive, and the study of it was a labor of love. He would have been a good lawyer with very little study, for the legal character of his mind would have supplied the deficiencies of book knowledge, and led him by a sort of *"rusticum judicium"* to the same results to which others had arrived by the laborious processes of study . . . Many men would have been contented with this original turn for the law, this legal mother-wit, and have preferred to solve the questions which came before them by a sort of Zerah Colburn process, rather than avail themselves of the borrowed aid of the learning of others. But his ambition was of a nobler and higher kind, and he studied the law as zealously and conscientiously as if his books had been his only guides and dependence. He had that invaluable property in a lawyer—one not often found in combination with a mind so rapid in its movements and powerful in its grasp as his—unwearied patience in legal investigation.[13]

The need for constant application scarcely diminished as one moved upward in the profession. The example of Reuben Saffold (1788-1847), chief justice of the Supreme Court of Alabama, could serve as a text for many another early jurist: "Endowed by nature with sound judgment and an accurate and discriminating mind, he never feared that laborious attention which enabled him to master the subjects he was to decide."[14]

A stress on the laborious pursuit of legal knowledge acquitted the lawyer of quackery but opened the door to a paradox. For if the path to success was indeed so arduous, how could the average man hope to achieve it? And was this not the chief complaint against the bar of the 1830s—that its members formed an exclusive clique sustained by esoteric rules which the masses could not understand? To reconcile the technicalities of the law with the demands of an open society required no little skill, but the publicists of the day measured up to the challenge. They were careful to dissociate the practice of their craft from mere dilettantism or an undue reliance on book learning. Since law was a rational science, they argued, its basic principles could be grasped by all men. Uncertainties arose only when one sought to apply these principles to varying fact situations. Success in this context depended upon common sense and a firsthand knowledge of everyday life, two qualities in which most early lawyers had excelled.

Plainspoken Oliver Ellsworth, chief justice of the United States (1796-1800), demonstrated the "active virtue" of an entire generation of legal types who solved their problems with rule-of-thumb practicality: "He satisfied or subdued the reason, with little endeavour either to excite the feelings or to gratify the fancy."[15] And a grass-roots realism characterized the successful practitioner of later days as well. When the brilliant Massachusetts jurist Lemuel Shaw died in 1861, his eulogists found that his most advantageous trait had been "good, sound, Anglo-Saxon common sense": "This it was which gave him such mastery over the rules and principles of the common law, that 'ample and boundless jurisprudence' which the experience and common sense of successive generations of men have gradually built up, and which came to us from our English ancestors, a precious inheritance of freedom and of the great principles of justice and right."[16]

As a paragon of industry, fortitude, and native intelligence, the American lawyer shared several of the qualities attributed to the self-made man by contemporary writers of success manuals and didactic novels. Nor does the analogy end here. Both ideals embodied the "work and win" formula of the Protestant ethic, according to which rewards invariably followed well-directed effort. "I have often thought that if other men could have been as diligent and assiduous as Mr. Webster, they might have equalled him in achievement," declared a member of the New York bar in a characteristic vein.[17] Success for the lawyer, as for the self-made man, did not necessarily imply large financial returns, however. The true measure of accomplishment lay in the moral satisfaction afforded by a life well spent in the service of others.

Striking in their parallelism, the two mythologies diverged in equally important ways that point up the limits within which law writers had to operate. As John G. Cawelti has shown, the self-help advocates of the antebellum period spoke in large part for a status-oriented, preindustrial America that no longer existed in fact. Most authors of juvenile guide books were Protestant clergymen who were anxious to preserve traditional ethical values in a time of unprecedented economic expansion and get-rich-quick opportunism. Fearful of disruptive social change, they continued to preach the gospel of improvement within one's God-given calling; hostile to big business and immigrant labor, they reaffirmed the standards of the independent craftsman as a guide to success in the age of the corporation. Self-made men, by their definition, were conservative Christians who aspired only to a modest respectability that posed no threat to established power structures.[18]

This formula did not meet the needs of law writers. Since the bar was already under attack for its alleged exclusiveness, any talk of stabilizing vocational lines would mean a gain for the enemy. Instead, publicists sought to show that the law had always been a wide open field, inviting ambitious men from other walks of life to abandon their previous pursuits in order to join the ranks of its leaders. This was a far cry from the static society envisaged by the self-help school; in its fully developed form it amounted to an endorsement of continuing social upheaval within the profession:

> It is as hard for a rich man's son to obtain the honors of the bar, as it is for the rich man himself to enter the kingdom of heaven. They come from the farm and the workshop, from that condition of life

to which the great majority belong. They are counted by the multitude as one of themselves, and they hail their elevation as a triumph of their own over all that looked like aristocracy. With enthusiastic pride they push them on from honor to honor, until a new generation arises that knew not their origin and see them only in their exaltation. They see them lifted above the common level; their jealousy is awakened; the order of aristocracy is scented in the atmosphere that surrounds them, and they receive no cordial support except for those august stations to which only advanced age and extensive renown can aspire. A new set is brought up from the same origin to run the same career. And thus it happens that the children of the cabins come up and occupy the palaces of the Republic.[19]

Such mobility received specific documentation in the obituary columns of the law journals. From a random sampling of forty-eight death notices carried in the *Monthly Law Reporter* (which made a point of listing obscure practitioners as well as celebrities), one gains a vivid impression of the diversity of family backgrounds from which the deceased came. Their fathers included three doctors, five merchants, eleven ministers, ten farmers, two mechanics, two soldiers, eleven lawyers, and four judges. The subjects of several eulogies were foreign-born, a further indication of the varied sources of legal recruitment. While spokesmen for the self-made man might draw invidious comparisons between the mores of the immigrant and the old-stock native, law writers could not ignore the contributions to their science made by men of the stamp of Peter S. DuPonceau of France, Thomas Addis Emmet of Ireland, and Francis Lieber of Germany.

Similarly, lawyers were more realistic in acknowledging pecuniary motives as a major factor in their choice of a career. If they insisted that the average practitioner "lived well and died poor," this was hardly a counsel of Christian moderation. A surplus of riches, in their view, enhanced one's legal reputation. "It is understood, that he was as eminently successful in the accumulation of wealth, as in the prosecution of his professional pursuits," observed the biographer of one minor figure, with obvious satisfaction.[20]

Having entered the law to improve their economic status, young men could not be expected to conform to the strict vocational restraints imposed by the self-help manuals. Law was accordingly defined as a primary, but not exclusive, pursuit. Since an attorney's practice so often revolved about business questions, a personal involvement in the world of affairs could prove beneficial both to his pocketbook and to his standing at the bar. He might safely engage in real estate ventures, railroad promotion, or banking so long as he continued to give his paramount allegiance to the law. For there was no way to move *up* from the legal profession, which alone offered a satisfying blend of material reward, intellectual challenge, and social utility. Attorneys who abandoned their practice to pursue other callings were like apostates from a true faith, and none received greater censure for their acts of heresy than lawyer-politicians.

The divorce of law from politics was the most significant contribution that publicists of the Jacksonian era made to legal mythology. Hitherto political service had always been regarded as a legitimate by-product of legal competence. Few of the practitioners whose deaths were recorded in the law journals of the 1840s had missed election to a state legislature or to Congress at some point in their careers. Collectively they established a pattern of public leadership which had answered well the needs of the early Republic. Biographers described their conduct in office as "fearless," "manly," and "independent" and paid tribute to their statesmanlike vision and grasp of sound principles.

Yet their example, however useful in the days of Washington, Adams, and the Virginia Dynasty, had—it now appeared —little relevance for a more democratic age. Latter-day lawyers were informed that they might learn more valuable lessons from studying the unworthy politicians of the past, such as the Maine legislator John Holmes, who "trimmed his sails to the prevailing wind of popular favor" during the first administration of James Madison:

> "The gladsome light of jurisprudence" was not bright and warm enough for him;—he loved law, but he loved politics more . . . In reviewing the life of such a man, we may perhaps derive a useful reflection upon the danger, not to say folly, of leaving the broad highway of an honorable and profitable profession, for the fitful and the exciting pursuits, and the unsubstantial rewards of the mere politician. That Mr. Holmes had as much of popular favor and its fruits, as falls to the lot of men, none will deny; that they furnished him the satisfaction and the rewards which he would have acquired in the quiet progress of his profession, we do not believe.[21]

Though Holmes's political opportunism, according to law writers, was exceptional for its time, they maintained that since 1830 the exception had become the rule. "It is well known," declared one commentator in reference to the latter period, "that men of the highest eminence in our profession are seldom members of legislative assemblies in this country, and, when they are, their influence is comparatively small."[22] Political posts now went to party men—third- or fourth-rate lawyers who acknowledged no higher principle than self-interest. To retain the support of a mass electorate, these legal turncoats placed themselves at the head of every popular movement, however unwise or dangerous its objectives. They even spearheaded legislative attacks upon the bar and the judiciary and encouraged a rash of other ill-considered measures that purportedly reflected an ever changing popular will. Under such circumstances politics no longer provided an attractive occupation for the responsible lawyer, who was advised by publicists to stick to his practice if he valued his self-respect.

Behind this warning lay no lament for the passing of the class-conscious "gentleman" in politics. Law writers of the 1830s denied that such a personage had ever existed, at least among lawyers, who had always been simple, hardworking, democratic types. It was not pride or fastidiousness that kept the best attorneys out of politics in the Jacksonian era, they argued, but the fact that politics had developed into a full-fledged profession with specialized rules of its own—several of which ran counter to deeply cherished legal attitudes and practices.

Representation, for example, no longer meant what it once did. When biographers praised the manly independence of an early legislator, they were reading political history through legal spectacles. A good politician, by their criteria, represented his constituents as an attorney represented his clients. That is, he acted to promote their best interests as he understood them, and in case of disagreement his judgment ultimately prevailed. This view of political responsibility could not be reconciled with the more democratic notion that a representative was bound in all cases to carry out the wishes of his constituents. While few successful lawmakers ever disregarded the majority will in practice, law writers continued to promote the theory of legal representation until the perfecting of party organization and party discipline in the 1830s demonstrated its obsolescence for all purposes save that of myth.

A similar conflict between legal attitudes and political realities occurred in connection with the problem of electioneering. Lawyers were trained to believe that the job must seek the man. A mass of literature stretching back to the Middle Ages condemned the improper solicitation of legal business and required that the lawyer wait patiently in his office for clients to appear (which they were certain to do, by a process of legal legerdemain, if the would-be practitioner had worked sufficiently hard to prepare himself for the duties of the profession). Publicists incorporated this trait into their image of the early American lawyer, who allegedly looked upon public office as a temporary employment, to be secured like any other retainer. Typical were the circumstances surrounding the election of Charles Marsh, a Vermont attorney, to the House of Representatives in 1814: "He was always averse to holding elective offices, and in this instance, was forced into Congress against his will."[23]

Twenty years later the reluctant candidate stood little chance of winning an election, even in fiction. Political campaigning had become an art in itself, demanding catchy slogans, colorful personalities, and a degree of ballyhoo foreign to the thinking of earlier generations. No lawyer could now be a successful politician, writers cautioned, unless he abandoned his professional integrity and became a hireling of the masses. Perhaps the insistent appeal to the tradition of the independent practitioner betrayed some uneasiness over current values within the profession itself, where many an attorney had already shown an unseemly willingness to exchange his independence for a secure job with a law firm or corporation.

From a tactical standpoint, of course, the separation of the "real" lawyer from politics offered several advantages to propagandists. It enabled them to class as unprincipled demagogues all members of the bar who spoke up for legislative reform of the law; it suggested that most statutes were either unwise or unnecessary additions to an existing body of basic principles; and it reaffirmed the image of the lawyer as a hardworking technician whose services were as necessary to society as those of any other skilled craftsman:

To the mass of practitioners, the law is not, except on some rare occasions, an intellectual pursuit. Truth compels us to own, with Wordsworth, that "the demands of life and action," with us, as with men of other pursuits, "but rarely correspond to the dignity and intensity of human desires." We are clever men of business, as a mass, and no more. It is our BUSINESS TALENTS, our PROMPT-NESS, ACCURACY, and DILIGENCE, that commands success, respect and influence.[24]

The defense of the bar in terms of its practical usefulness to society deserves special emphasis, since Perry Miller, in an important study of the legal mind in nineteenth-century America, has suggested that the antebellum lawyers were trying to establish themselves as an intellectual elite in the eyes of the public.[25] While this may have been the objective of certain scholarly jurists such as Kent, Story, and David Hoffman, a different view prevailed among the rank and file who patronized the law magazines. For them legal practice was a bread-and-butter concern, a daily business in which intellectual refinements found little place. "The most learned lawyer in the world would not get business, if he did not attend to it," warned Timothy Walker to the graduating class of the Cincinnati Law School in 1839. "The question with the client is, not who knows the most law, but who will manage a cause the best; and, all other things being equal, he will manage a cause the best, who devotes most attention to it."[26]

Practitioners could not afford to waste time on frivolous cultural pursuits when it took constant effort just to keep abreast of the increasing volume of new court decisions. If they turned to polite literature for occasional relaxation, they were likely to choose an established classic whose familiarity with the public could be put to good use in courtroom debate. The Bible and Shakespeare were particular favorites, for, as one commentator explained, quite apart from their aesthetic qualities, "they may also, sometimes, be quoted to great advantage; the former never but with reverence; the latter, never pedantically."[27] At a time when legal reputations still owed much to oratorical skills, an acquaintance with "good" literature could further aid an attorney to develop a graceful speaking style. On the death of Rufus Choate (1799-1859), perhaps the most cultivated orator of his time, an attempt was made to place the whole matter of nonlegal learning in proper perspective: "True, he laid his foundations deep and broad, by no means confined to legal acquirements, but embracing a rich classic culture, and what we believe aided him more than all, the devoted reading of the Bible: yet these other studies were only episodes, or rather recreations, renewing his professional energies."[28]

To picture the lawyer as detached from all interests that did not relate to his professional life suited the needs of the myth-makers, but they found it difficult to reconcile their antipolitical attitudes with the demands of public order. For if legislatures were corrupt and the laws they passed unwise, why should citizens obey? A mounting wave of lawlessness throughout the Union made the question far from academic, as journalists pointed with concern to lynchings in Mississippi, riots in Pennsylvania and Massachusetts, duels in Louisiana, and vigilante justice in the goldfields of California. Nor were these symptoms of social disintegration confined to the local level; even federal authorities met with popular resistance in their efforts to enforce fugitive slave laws. Some antislavery agitators openly professed adherence to a "higher law" than that found in the Constitution, making the individual conscience the determining guide to political, as well as religious, behavior. Such subjectivity impressed legal writers as the ultimate democratic heresy, and they denounced the use of moralistic arguments to justify the overthrow of existing institutions: 'It is among the strange signs of the times, that individuals are found saying and doing the most violent, unjust and dangerous things, without rebuke, *because they say and do them in the cause of anti-slavery.* Scarcely a voice is raised against these excesses, because, if raised, it would be answered with the charge of enmity to the slave. This should not be . . . If we would resist the extension of slavery, we must equally resist the spirit of rebellion against the constitution."[29]

But counsels of moderation and proposals to strengthen the police forces in major urban centers provided no adequate solution to the problem of bad laws. Acknowledging that the public had reason to distrust its legislators, spokesmen for the "workingmen of the profession" sought a technique by which the bar might assume responsibility for a reform program without becoming embroiled in partisan politics. Their strategy called for the creation of a governmental institution that did not materialize to any significant extent for another generation: the independent administrative commission.

In its most rudimentary form, the commission idea suggested to antebellum journalists a small body of skilled legal draftsmen appointed by the governor of a state to scrutinize the final version of all legislative measures. They would act primarily as stylistic critics, correcting the language of a law to make it more intelligible to the general public as well as consistent with professional norms. Some writers went further and argued for a true board of censors, with power to weed out in advance all doubtful bills, including any which contradicted previous enactments. Through such expert guidance, the argument ran, a haphazard mass of state legislation might in time be reduced to an orderly system of harmonious rules.

But it was as a potential planning agency that the commission made its strongest appeal to the legal imagination. Publicists dreamed of interstate boards of lawyers and jurists entrusted with the duty of framing national laws to cover such matters as commerce, land tenures, education, and crimes. Unlike "tinkering legislatures," these professional bodies would engage in comprehensive social planning, working from basic principles to their most far-reaching ramifications: "and this process seems to be most in harmony with the spirit of the time, which is inquiring, philosophical and theorizing . . . What would be said of the architect, who, to build his arch, should try, one after another, all possible shapes, till at last he hit the one which would stand, when he had a slate, and in his head principles, on which he could in a little while reckon just what must be built to form a true and perfect structure?"[30] For the first time since the early Republic, it appeared, the interests of the technician could fairly be reconciled with those of the statesman, as lawyers proposed to bury sectional differences within a network of uniform economic and cultural regulations coextensive with the Union.

Their visions remained unfulfilled, however, for reasons which should have been clear to every realistic member of the bar. Apart from their elitist pretensions, all of these schemes depended in greater or lesser degree upon the support of those very legislative bodies whose alleged irresponsibility had fostered the nation's lawless temper. Furthermore, the commission idea, for all its apolitical tone, pointed to the development of a fourth branch of the government—an administrative wing whose personnel would enjoy the substance of political power without its attendant risks. And it would take a Civil

War to demonstrate the merits of bureaucratic planning to a public still responsive to theories of laissez faire.

Meanwhile the idealism of the antebellum bar found a practical outlet closer to home. In 1849 the American Legal Association was established

> for the purpose of insuring safety and facility in the collection of claims and the transaction of legal business throughout the United States. Its design is to furnish professional and business men with the name of at least one prompt, efficient and trustworthy Lawyer in every shire-town and in each of the principal cities and villages in the Union, who will transact with despatch and for a reasonable compensation, such professional business as may be entrusted to him.[31]

Promoted largely through the efforts of John Livingston, a law writer and editor, the association was both broader and narrower than any previous legal organization in the nation's history. While it claimed members in every state of the Union (as well as two in England), its objectives were rigorously limited. As a lawyer referral service, it disclaimed all interest in politics, community welfare, or even the encouragement of a general spirit of fraternalism among practitioners. Instead, it appealed to the technician's desire for more rational procedures, as it focused attention upon the lawyer as a competitive businessman.

Every practicing attorney who subscribed five dollars and furnished "satisfactory evidence of professional integrity and capacity" could join the ALA on a two-year basis. He thereupon received an official manual, complete with constitution, bylaws, and a list of the names and addresses of all members (including one director in each state). The association undertook to distribute additional copies of the manual to the "business public" and also to place advertisements from time to time in major newspapers across the country. The advantages of such a centralized reference bureau were sufficiently alluring to keep the ALA in existence for some five years, after which it quietly expired.

As a stimulus to professional unity, the association served a useful purpose, but even more important was the work of its secretary, John Livingston. Drawing upon a voluminous legal correspondence, Livingston compiled in 1850 an authoritative list of the names and addresses of practicing lawyers and judges in the United States. His *United States Lawyer's Directory and Official Bulletin* incorporated data supplied by state and local officials down to the level of county sheriffs and formed the first accurate legal census ever taken in America. Its publication testified both to the coming-of-age of the American bar and to its growing preoccupation with intramural matters. Livingston revised his register annually until the collapse of the ALA in 1854; thereafter he continued to bring out new editions at irregular intervals through 1868.[32]

The approach of civil war did little to change the introspective bias of law magazines. Characteristically, most contributors tended to regard the slavery crisis as a contrivance of partisan politicians, useful in campaign years but of no real concern to the general public. As late as October 1860 one commentator predicted that if "these contending dogmas be pressed to the practical result of deranging trade, augmenting prices, and curtailing commerce, a spirit will be roused which will put an end to all further disturbance from this source."[33]

Even those who took a more somber view of the secessionist threat were often prone to accept the prospect of war with equanimity, since it promised to purify national politics and to elevate the country's natural leaders once more to positions of the highest public trust and responsibility. Only a "comparatively few minds" were capable of directing public sentiment toward constructive ends, remarked Alfred O. P. Nicholson in a representative speech before a group of honor students at the University of North Carolina. Disinterested professional men—and preeminently the nation's best-trained lawyers—constituted in his eyes a reserve force of immense talent, whose leadership potential was frequently ignored by the masses during periods of calm. But in an emergency, when the arts of the "mere" politician proved unavailing, such managerial types could be counted on to step forward and straighten things out, just as Clay, Webster, and Cass had saved the Union from imminent disruption in 1850: "When the danger comes again, who have we like this illustrious trio, to 'ride upon the whirlwind and direct the storm?' We cannot specify the individual names that will figure when the trial comes on; but we can confidently predict that in its dangers, its labors, its disasters or its glories, the lawyer will have his full share."[34]

The image of the altruistic technician, which dominated the law journals by 1860, may be traced as well through the earliest studies of state bars and the hortatory addresses of successful practitioners to antebellum law classes. Wilkins Updike's *Memoirs of the Rhode-Island Bar* (1842), the first important attempt at collective biography, is permeated with the idealism of disinterested public service and projects a strong antimajoritarian bias backward through time. "The best offices were worth nothing, and were mere worthless bones for worthless dogs to contend for," he wrote of state politics in the Confederation period. "It was all party—party—who can most avail us? Has he wealth or connections? How many votes can he bring to the polls? And was he honest—was he capable—was he faithful to the constitution? were requisites not called for."[35]

Updike's favorite subjects were self-made men who rose to prominence at the bar through their own efforts and were later elected to public office because of their acknowledged professional skills. The importance of legal training to a model politician could be seen most clearly in the careers of men like Rouse J. Helme (1743-1789): "Mr. Helme being an able lawyer, and a skilful draughtsman, his services were found to be so highly requisite in conducting the business of the legislature, that the dominant party, though politically opposed to him . . . elected him clerk of the House of Representatives, and testified their approbation of his ability by repeated re-elections."[36]

The same themes run through two companion works: Stephen F. Miller's *The Bench and Bar of Georgia* (1858) and John Belton O'Neall's *Biographical Sketches of the Bench and Bar of South Carolina* (1859). The southern publicists, however, tended to view the revolutionary and early national periods as a golden age in politics as in law and reserved their sharpest social criticism for their own degenerate times. When John MacPherson Berrien of Georgia was elected to the Senate in 1824, observed Miller, it was still an honor to represent the state there: "Unfortunately, the Senatorial robes do not confer as much reputation in these latter days, owing to causes easily understood. While something is lost on the score of dignity by the contrast, much is perhaps gained to *popular rights*, among which may be included the right of very moderate men to exercise high public trusts."[37] Similarly, the biographer of South Carolina's Theodore Gaillard commented upon his subject's active involvement in the political "revolution of 1800": "That conflict, my friends, was not the every day struggle of mere competitors for office . . . It was a mighty warfare for principles involving the very 'breath of life' of the national constitution."[38] A liberal use of classical allusions in both studies further contributed to the picture of an Olympian Establishment that had crumbled before the onslaughts of a graceless democracy.

All legal biographers conceded, of course, that there were *some* worthy lawyer-politicians left in the world, but only John Livingston offered to document their careers on a national scale. In compiling his amorphous *Biographical Sketches of Eminent American Lawyers Now Living* (1852), Livingston relied upon memoirs from many different hands, yet the finished product displayed a remarkable consistency of tone and interpretation. Regardless of specific authorship, every essay tended to treat its subject as a self-made (if not self-educated) man, businesslike and unpretentious, who still found in politics an opportunity for dedicated public service. Benjamin F. Wade of Ohio, for example, greets his election to the Senate in 1851 in characteristic fashion: "the news to him was unexpected, but not unacceptable. From principle, as well as from habits of modesty, he always avoided office-seeking . . . This [office] came unsought and unexpected, although during the winter his name had frequently been mentioned in connection with it. In his elevation to that position the bench and bar have lost an eminent jurist, but it simply transfers him to a field of more varied, and it is hoped, of more extended, usefulness."[39]

By adopting a more positive attitude toward the politics of their day, Livingston and his collaborators achieved the ultimate in wish fulfillment. Through their creative labors the model lawyer-statesman—who had virtually disappeared from law journals and legal histories—reemerged as a vital force in contemporary American life. The line between fact and fantasy breaks down almost completely in some of these sketches, and especially in the career profiles of such men as David Paul Brown of Philadelphia, "attorney for the poor and lowly," we are very close to the sentimentalized version of the antebellum lawyer endorsed by the writers of self-help fiction.

A romantic glow also surrounded the Supreme Court in the earliest attempts to place that institution and its personnel in historical perspective. That John Marshall, consummate politician though he was, should be depicted by Henry Flanders in his *Lives and Times of the Chief Justices of the Supreme Court of the United States* (1858) as a nonpartisan jurist who had always been totally devoted to his profession, is not very surprising. The legend of Marshall the Judicial Statesman had penetrated even the elementary schools as early as 1815, and throughout the antebellum years at least five popular textbooks for youngsters paid tribute to his farsighted nationalism and his "almost supernatural faculty for getting to the heart of the discussion" in his decisions.[40] But that Roger Taney, too, should be pronounced an exemplary public servant, despite the obvious partisanship he displayed during Andrew Jackson's Bank War, defies comprehension. (Taney's conduct as secretary of the treasury was irreproachable, explained the pioneer court historian George Van Santvoord to his readers in 1854. In ordering the removal of federal deposits from the Bank of the United States, Taney responded to no party directive but acted with "fearless independence," on the basis of his "previous judgment and convictions of duty," as well as his "disinterested friendship" for President Jackson.)[41] The hagiolatry of the high bench could be carried no further, and other law writers expressed a similar reverence for state courts, as they called for an "independent judiciary" to check the radicalism of legislative majorities.[42]

On a less exalted level, the law schools of the antebellum era promised to become an alternate source of conservative strength. Publicists who spoke before law classes accordingly tailored their message for a legal elite and modified the standard themes of the professional journals in several distinctive ways. Some, like Job R. Tyson, urged the need for more stringent self-policing by the educated members of the bar. Every attorney, Tyson argued, had a "stern duty" as *amicus curiae* to institute legal proceedings against "unworthy" fellow practitioners.[43] Implicit in this call to action was a reassertion of old-fashioned prerogative—a renewed consciousness of belonging to a professional noblesse—that received more extended treatment in the speeches of other men.

Since very few antebellum practitioners ever attended a law school, it was natural for commencement-day orators to hail the graduates of such institutions as a kind of natural aristocracy, the true "gentlemen" of the bar. "The sincere lover of his profession as a science; he who looks deeply into the framework

of society, and hopes by his forensic efforts to vindicate the
right and redress the wrong, must be, and ever will be, a gentleman," Bellamy Storer assured an audience of law students at the
University of Louisville, Kentucky, in 1856.[44] The revival of the
gentlemanly ideal for university-trained attorneys did not,
however, presuppose a continued insistence upon their absten-
tion from practical politics. Unlike the rank-and-file readership
of the law magazines, law school graduates were reminded that
they owed the electorate the benefit of their unique training and
that "great lawyers" could not long escape political preferment.
Indeed, speakers even encouraged their youthful auditors to
pursue certain nonlegal studies as a necessary prerequisite for
undertaking the inevitable duties of statecraft.

Chief among these valuable collateral subjects was history,
especially the circumstances surrounding the American Revolution and the framing of the Constitution. "It is upon such
studies as these," remarked a former governor of Tennessee in
1853,

> that we have to rely much for the arrest of that spirit of change and
> innovation which is one of the characteristics of the present period
> of our national existence. We are no enemy to real improvement in
> every thing: in law, jurisprudence, and in government. But we
> should advance with caution, and nothing but the surest convic-
> tions should tempt us to leave the beaten track of our ancestors.
> The founders of the republic attempted to raise barriers against this
> fondness for change, by the adoption of constitutions so difficult of
> amendment and alteration, that such could seldom be effected with-
> out a general concurrence of public sentiment. How long these bar-
> riers will prove sufficient, it is impossible to tell.[45]

But all commentators agreed that the educated lawyer-in-politics had a special duty to revive traditional moral and political
values and help build a "wall of defence" around "our happy
institutions."[46]

However appealing these Burkean counsels may have seemed
to legal neophytes, they understandably made little impression
on the public at large. The average citizen seldom attended a
law school function, any more than he subscribed to a legal
periodical. Yet the image of the new-style professional came in
time to captivate the popular imagination almost as much as it

influenced the legal mind. Two broader channels of communication facilitated an effective cultural interchange between lawyers and nonlawyers: the lecture platform and the world of escapist entertainment.

A whole subgenre of mid-nineteenth-century legal literature testifies to the importance that lawyers attached to lyceums, mechanics' institutes, and other agencies of popular education. As a substitute for partisan politics, speeches on grandiose moral themes—"The True Aims of American Ambition," "The Morals of Freedom," "The Duties and Responsibilities of the Rising Generation"—offered a unique opportunity to dispel popular myths about the bar while affirming the social utility of the lawyer's day-to-day services to the community. Stressing the interdependence between the professions and all other honest employments, lawyer-lecturers painted a glowing portrait of themselves as basically skilled workers who were as totally dedicated to the discipline of their craft as other workingmen.

The public had no reason to mistrust or envy lawyers because of any undemocratic class advantages they were supposed to possess, declared Emory Washburn of Massachusetts in a model address before the Worcester Lyceum:

> The truth is, the only thing like classification in society here, seems to be that of *employments*; and . . . there is nothing in this division of labor at all hostile to that equality of privileges, powers and immunities which are professedly guarantied by our constitution. There is nothing in the pursuit of one of these employments less honorable in itself than that of another. Some of them, it is true, furnish greater facilities for improving the mind and acquiring knowledge than others, and thus indirectly seem to possess peculiar privileges by means of the influence which the possession of intellectual powers always attaches to itself. But so far are what are called the learned professions from possessing superior claims, in the public mind, for offices of honor or places of emolument, that if any thing like the same degree of knowledge is acquired by those whose pursuits are not supposed to be favorable to such acquisition, they are generally rewarded with a share of public favor proportionate to the difficulties with which they have been supposed to contend . . . talents, rather than family, or profession, or employment, are regarded in those who are the objects of public confidence and favor.[47]

The diffusion of knowledge among all social classes in the United States had created a community of interest between them that was lacking in any European country, added Timothy Walker in a similar vein. Walker, one of the most sought-after public speakers of antebellum Cincinnati, delved into history for an explanation of the forces behind this mass enlightenment. It began with the Reformation, he contended, which opened religious knowledge to the masses and encouraged every man to study the Scriptures for himself. Then came the American Revolution, with its heavy reliance upon popular opinion and its irrevocable extension of the principle of self-dependence from religion to politics and society: "By this event, the unalienable right of every class and description of persons, not only to *power*, but *knowledge*, was finally and forever settled; and the settlement ratified by the sacrament of blood. And hence with us every possible obstruction to knowledge is removed."[48]

Material success and social advancement thus lay within the reach of any hardworking, intelligent American, for a republican system of government permitted no distinction of ranks, but only a "diversity of conditions." While insisting that every freeborn citizen must rise through his own efforts, however, Walker made it clear that "meritorious labor" encompassed mental as well as physical exertions: "I use the term [working-men] in its broadest signification. I would have it embrace all who employ their minds or their bodies for the good of society. The great end of their exertions is one and the same." Professional and nonprofessional pursuits were equally respectable, by this reasoning, because each contributed in a necessary way to the maintenance of the "social superstructure." Lyceums and other self-improvement organizations demonstrated this homely truth in practice by bringing together individuals from the most varied employments and social strata to exchange "useful information" on subjects of general interest. Through such voluntary discussion groups, Walker predicted, the average man would be disabused of "unnatural" class jealousies as he became better aware of the importance of his own vocational role within the community.[49]

Despite an insistence upon individual effort and its rewards, there was a curiously static and backward-looking quality about the public lectures of most antebellum lawyers that made their productions indistinguishable from the standard self-help oratory of the period. In contrast to the law magazines, for example, the typical lyceum talk did not encourage occupational mobility but reaffirmed the need for improvement within the limits of one's chosen calling. So, Robert T. Conrad told a Gettysburg, Pennsylvania, audience, the "true patriot" and "useful citizen" performs his duty to society in his proper sphere of activity, however humble, and is not seduced by a "false ambition" into politics or the already overcrowded professions.[50] And William Alexander Duer, stressing the influence that every well-informed man wields in a democracy based upon public opinion, ticked off a long list of worthy (and mutually exclusive) employments:

> The divine, who is necessarily restricted to his pastoral functions,— the lawyer, who eschews politics, and wisely confines himself to the practice of his profession,—the physician, who limits his intercourse to his patients and co-practitioners,—the merchant, whose walks extend no farther than from his dwelling to his counting-house, and thence to the Exchange,—the mechanic, whose industry has rendered him intelligent as well as independent,—and even the man of no visible occupation, if he be a man of information,—all these, each in his respective sphere, exert, through the medium of public opinion, an influence upon public affairs, as efficient, and often more beneficial than that exercised by those engaged in their administration.[51]

Other speakers called for a stronger infusion of traditional moral values into the educational process at every level to counteract the disruptive social effects of industrialism. Citing the habits of self-restraint and obedience to authority that had allegedly characterized the preindustrial culture of colonial America, they charged that latter-day educators were ignoring the conservative principles of the past. "The present age seems distinguished above all others in intellectual culture, as opposed to moral," complained Peleg W. Chandler in a representative statement. "To teach the people how to read and to write, is regarded as the most essential thing in our system. But I do not hesitate to say, that knowledge of itself is not a positive good . . . To educate a man's understanding, without at the same time strengthening his moral character, is only to give him greater power to injure society and himself."[52] Self-improvement, then, implied self-control and a heightened consciousness of one's personal limitations and dependence upon others—the sort of training that, in the words of another platform orator, separated the pious and public-spirited merchant from the "mere capitalist or trader."[53]

Admittedly, there was no way to turn back the clock, or to halt the momentum of a developing technology. With all their concern for the preservation of order and balance in society, legal spokesmen professed to welcome those scientific and industrial advances that were transforming the material environment from day to day. But they drew a sharp line between the physical sciences, with their reliance upon experimentation, inductive reasoning, and the exploitation of natural resources, and those moral and behavioral sciences, such as law and theology, that were based upon "historic and traditionary" truths of permanent validity. As Daniel Lord explained in a lecture *On the Extra-Professional Influence of the Pulpit and the Bar,* "The principles of law are not open for discoveries: this is a continent not open to colonization . . . The interests of man, his passions, their deranging as well as their compensating effects on the general welfare and on private right are and will continue the same as they have ever been. No new traits of human nature remain to be discovered."[54]

The layman was thus assured that the virtues of a simpler agrarian past—thrift, hard work, moderation, humility—were still relevant to meaningful achievement in the complex world of the nineteenth century. To apply the lesson to the conditions of legal practice with maximum dramatic effect, an increasing number of lawyers turned to fiction after 1830, recounting for a national audience the forensic exploits of a generation of youthful idealists.

The lawyer had figured prominently as a character in American prose literature ever since the first native novelists began to appear toward the end of the eighteenth century, but he seldom received a fair hearing, according to professional spokesmen. "How many despicable rogues, in the garb of attorneys, have novelists depicted?" grumbled one irate publicist in 1851. "Be it tragedy, comedy, or farce, if a lawyer be introduced, he is the villain or dupe of the piece."[55] The complaint was common enough at the time and may be readily documented by appealing to the masters of antebellum fiction, many of whom exploited legal themes with a layman's zest for muckraking. Who does not recall the pharisaical Judge Jaffrey Pyncheon of Hawthorne's *House of the Seven Gables*, or the oppressive law office atmosphere that Melville created in his memorable tale "Bartleby the Scrivener," or the furious attack that Cooper launched against New York juries and "Code pleaders" in *The Ways of the Hour*?

Still—putting aside the tantalizing question of how many people actually read the "best" books, as opposed to more ephemeral productions (including the literary offerings of newspapers and magazines)—it seems clear that the fictional view of the nineteenth-century lawyer was by no means so one-sided as commentators have suggested. There was, to be sure, a continuing tradition of antilawyer protest handed down from colonial times that helped, as we have seen, to shape popular attitudes toward the bar during the troubled years that followed the American Revolution.[56] But, to balance this legacy of suspicion and ill will, there developed in the nineteenth century a rival body of literature that celebrated the constructive aspects of legal practice and transformed the ambitious attorney from a public enemy into a folk hero. The rehabilitation of the lawyer-in-literature was the work of many hands and proceeded by fits and starts until writers discovered in the idealized traits of the antebellum practitioner a subject of unfailing interest to lay readers.

Attempts to "sell" the lawyer through fiction began with judges and attorneys who were alarmed at the democratic tendencies of their time. Imbued with strong elitist feelings, these talented littérateurs weakened their case by emphasizing unduly the immense gap that separated the trained professional from the average man. In common with all other creative writers in the young Republic, they approached their material from a narrowly didactic perspective: they sought to instruct their readers rather than to entertain them. Hence they made little effort to personalize their characters, most of which remained mere abstractions—wooden mannikins to be moved about in arbitrary fashion pursuant to some preconceived intellectual design. The first fictional lawyers thus resembled allegorical types that embodied some idée fixe of their creators, and little else. Background details, distinguishing character traits, and realistic motivation were alike neglected as unworthy of a reader's attention and apt to distract him from the edifying political or philosophical thesis which the novelist was most concerned to expound.

The results of this literary utilitarianism are apparent in such works as Hugh Henry Brackenridge's *Modern Chivalry* (1792-1815), William Littell's *Epistle . . . to the People of the Realm of Kentucky* (1806), and George Watterston's *The Lawyer; or, Man as He Ought Not to Be* (1808). Despite obvious differences of tone and polemical purpose, all three books depict the lawyer as an embattled intellectual whose professional acquirements have somehow isolated him from the rest of society. The alienation theme is not developed in dramatic terms, however. Instead of showing through concrete details why some men hated lawyers, the authors ignore individual considerations in favor of a more abstract analysis, elevating the tensions between community and bar into an epic struggle of opposing principles: law vs. anarchy, reason vs. passion, republicanism vs. democracy. Such a formulation precludes any sympathy for the misguided masses and gives even the best legal fiction of the pre-Jackson years the aspect of a hard-hitting partisan brief.

Brackenridge's *Modern Chivalry* offers perhaps the most striking illustration of the limits of legal apologetics. Published in instalments over a period of twenty-three years, this interminable satire stands without peer as the most exhaustive treatment of the early American lawyer in fiction. Brackenridge—a frontier journalist, legal practitioner, and politician before his appointment at the age of fifty-one to the Supreme Court of Pennsylvania—was an incisive critic of grass-roots democracy who pleaded for a vocationally stratified society in which public offices would be reserved for men with professional skills and a broad educational background. "A ditcher," he remarked, "is a respectable character, with his over-alls on, and a spade in his hand; but put the same man to those offices which require the head whereas he has been accustomed to impress with his foot, and there appears a contrast between the individual and the occupation."[57] Much of his disdain for the demagogic vote getter stemmed from bitter personal experience: his own political career, begun in 1786, ended abruptly the following year, when he suffered a resounding defeat at the hands of one William Findley, a rabble-rousing ex-weaver.

But if in *Modern Chivalry* the political process is depicted in terms of a continuing class struggle—a "perpetual war" of the "aristocrats" against the "multitude"—Brackenridge hammered home the idea that middle-class lawyers stood apart from the conflict and could be relied on to defend the popular interest in government more effectively than self-seeking opportunists from lower-income groups:

> There is a natural alliance between liberty and letters. Men of letters are seldom men of wealth, and these naturally ally themselves with the *democratic interest* in a commonwealth. These form a balance with the bulk of the people, against power, springing from family interest and large estates . . . They are a safe auxiliary; for all they want is, to have the praise of giving information. The study of political law and municipal jurisprudence qualifies to inform, and hence at the commencement of the American revolution, lawyers were the first to give the alarm and assert the rights of the people. Shall we forget the recent services of lawyers in framing the federal and state constitutions? The name of lawyer ought not to be hunted down, because there are characters, unworthy of the profession, with whom the love of money is inordinate and insatiable.[58]

Despite the didacticism of such passages, a spirit of good-humored raillery generally informed the early volumes of *Modern Chivalry* as Brackenridge attacked pomposity and philistinism wherever he found them—not excepting the legal profession. One of his most memorable creations was counselor Grab, a mordant portrait of the Philadelphia "black-letter lawyer" whose grasp of procedural niceties enables him to extort unconscionable fees from his clients by prolonging at will the progress of legal actions. But in exposing such "cattle" as Grab, Brackenridge aimed only at the reform of abuses which his own experience had convinced him were real enough. He had no idea of encouraging a popular revolt against legal principles or institutions as such. So, with all his Jeffersonian sympathies—and he *had* helped to found the Republican party in western Pennsylvania—he strongly opposed any partisan campaign to uproot the common law and its Federalist interpreters within the state. As public clamor against his legal colleagues became a live political issue around the turn of the century, his writings quickly lost the comic élan that had earlier sustained them and degenerated into a series of ill-tempered diatribes against the excesses of an unrestrained democracy.

The last three volumes of *Modern Chivalry* (1804-1815) focus almost exclusively upon the contest between the lawyers and the masses in Pennsylvania and contain endless digressions on all manner of abstract legal topics: the nature and historical development of the common law, the merits of arbitration, the utility of the legal profession, libel laws and press censorship, the qualifications and duties of judges, the nature of political representation, the importance of balanced governments and stable constitutions. Swallowed up in polemic, the satirical episodes reveal little originality or inventiveness; they merely provide additional illustrations of the iniquity of popular politics—a theme that in Brackenridge's hands admits of no qualifications or surprises. As one who found himself by 1804 directly threatened with a loss of income, status, and profession, the aging jurist could not laugh off the foibles of the "multitude" any longer.

Accordingly, he took up the cudgels in defense of law and lawyers with a vengeance in these later pages. Ignoring the very existence of unworthy practitioners, he idealized the entire profession through a single symbolic figure: a blind old village lawyer who pits his forensic skill and ripe wisdom against the fury of the mob. This virtuous public servant, after a lifetime of hard work, has accumulated so little material wealth that he is forced to earn his livelihood by giving public lectures, accompanied by a blind fiddler, with whom he divides his receipts. Scarcely a creature of flesh and blood, the disabled advocate mirrors the rational perfection of the common law, and Brackenridge points up his universality by denying to him alone, among the major characters of his satire, a proper name.

As the champion of orderly social progress, achieved through legal forms, the fictitious attorney speaks for his creator, and defines the common law in terms that anticipate by three quarters of a century the pragmatism of Oliver Wendell Holmes, Jr.: "For it is experience that has made that law; dictated by the wants of men successively brought to view . . . We read the decisions in such cases, because the reason of those who have gone before, is a help to those that follow . . . It is the construction of the judge that makes the law."[59] To discard established legal principles and tribunals, one would have to turn his back upon centuries of painfully acquired collective knowledge and tested procedures for the adjustment of social problems. The only free government, Brackenridge warned, was a government of laws, under which every citizen might claim evenhanded justice:

> It seems to me that a poor man is safer in a country of laws, than one without laws. "For wealth maketh many friends;" and I do not hear any complaints that the rich are favoured in the courts. But, that may be owing to the mode of trial, which is in the face of the world, and where lawyers are suffered to make as free with the character and conduct of a rich rogue in a cause, as with one of a more circumscribed estate . . . I have no idea that anything can hurt the profession, but the overthrow of liberty. Council to advise, and an advocate to speak, will be always wanted where *the laws govern and not men*. Rules of property and contract in civil cases, and the principles of law in matters of life, liberty, and reputation, will always call for the assistance of the head, and the powers of speech, in a republic.[60]

Significantly, the arguments of the blind lawyer fail to persuade his listeners. Convinced of their superior wisdom, the masses resolve to take direct control of law and government themselves. A reign of violence ensues, as bench and bar are made to feel the power of majoritarian misrule. At one point an irate mob seizes a local lawyer, noted for his long-winded speeches, and thrusts a large piece of wood between his jaws, in which gagged condition he is paraded triumphantly through the village streets; elsewhere a crowd sets out after an unpopular judge, hoping to string him up to the nearest tree. Excess follows upon excess, until Brackenridge reduces the antiestablishment argument to its ultimate absurdity by describing a frontier settlement of "madcap democrats" whose egalitarian zeal leads them to permit even brute animals to vote and to practice law. The latter conceit—already somewhat threadbare by the late eighteenth century—inspires a host of comic images satirizing the layman's anti-intellectualism and belief in natural justice. Readers are treated in turn to a monkey acting as clerk of court, a buffalo-judge, two beagles snarling at each other from the benches of opposing counsel, a forensic contest between a wolf and a fox, and the courtroom antics of squirrels and pigs. The laboriousness of the demonstration more than redeemed the judge's pledge to explain himself to "all grades of intellect."

Yet in the end he persuaded himself that his prolonged efforts at adult education had helped materially to raise the level of public discourse in Pennsylvania. The device of the fictional lawyer was pivotal to this campaign, for he came increasingly to typify the man of reason, a benevolent father-figure against whose mature judgment and broad knowledge the delusions of the masses might be weighed. Deprived by vulgar prejudice of that political influence to which his intellect entitled him, the attorney-in-literature thus found his proper vocation as gadfly to the community, or keeper of the popular conscience. He became, in Brackenridge's words, "a thorn in the flesh to buffet the people"—a task that he likewise performed in the work of the eminent Kentucky jurist, William Littell (1768-1825).

Littell was a scholarly reformer who championed a variety of projects in the early nineteenth century: a liberal divorce law for women, a state bank and state-financed internal improvements, the publication of state laws. Public indifference or hostility drove him to write his burlesque *Epistle*, in which he assumed the guise of an Old Testament prophet to chronicle the wickedness of his countrymen. Not properly a novel, Littell's *Epistle* contains a wealth of vivid social commentary, punctuated by the author's luckless encounters with the "*Wise men* and the chiefs of the people," who oppose every constructive suggestion he makes: "Thou, O Lord, knowest that they have often gone astray and done that which was an abomination in thy sight, but it was never by the advice of thy servant." Ignored by the community but assured of his own righteousness, the prophet William finally consigns the whole population of Kentucky to hell for its pigheadedness: "O foolish Kentuckians! . . . the anger of the Lord has been kindled against you, and unless ye repent suddenly, he will cause your cities to be wasted, without inhabitants, your houses without men, and the land to be utterly desolate."[61]

Both Littell and Brackenridge emphasized the creative power of the legal mind when enlisted in the service of society. It was the lawyer's superior intelligence, they asserted, that elevated him above the common herd and enabled him to act as an American philosophe, a wise and trustworthy counselor to the masses. But what if that same rational faculty were turned to selfish ends? Then, warned George Watterston in a sensational account of early shysterism, the average layman could do little to defend himself against machinations carried out under legal forms and sanctions.

Watterston, a Maryland attorney, was well qualified to muckrake the profession, having practiced law for several years with growing dissatisfaction. (He subsequently abandoned the bar to become the first librarian of Congress.) And he did not mince words in describing to his readers the corrupting tendencies of the adversary system:

> The practice of the law, it is said, tends to brutalize the feelings, to subvert the judgment, and to annihilate every virtuous principle of the human heart. I had not been long at the bar before I discovered the truth of this declaration; indeed it cannot possibly have any other tendency. A lawyer, from the first moment he enters into business, becomes habituated to scenes of injustice and oppression; from which, if he possess the smallest particle of sensibility, he turns at first with disgust and abhorrence; but custom soon renders them familiar, and in process of time, he can view them with the utmost coolness and indifference. This lamentable consequence is the frequent result of the practice of the law. For, it is evident, that a perpetual fellowship with dishonesty, and a constant intercourse with villainy, will in time destroy every tender emotion and sap by degrees the foundation of the most rigid virtue.[62]

Unfortunately, Watterston did not substantiate his charges with anything much in the way of specific incidents, so that, as a dramatization of the seamier side of professional life, *The Lawyer* fails conspicuously to deliver what it promises. Morcell, the protagonist, is a moral monster with no redeeming traits, but he is irrevocably launched on a career of evil long before he takes his bar examination. His legal training in fact merely reinforces the conditioning he has already received at the hands of a grasping, dissolute father and an equally vicious tutor. Few fictional characters have had the deck so stacked against them from the start, for Watterston was a firm believer in the behavioral psychology of Locke and Rousseau and insisted upon the irreversible effects of a person's childhood experiences. Morcell's depravity therefore is predetermined by his early environment, regardless of all else, and the fact that he later becomes an attorney has nothing whatever to do with most of his crimes (which run the gamut from drunkenness and gambling to rape and attempted murder).

Only twice is criminality linked to the conditions of legal practice. On one occasion Morcell loses a lawsuit (in which he represents a deserving widow and her six small children) through gross negligence, then seizes all of his client's meager possessions to satisfy his fee, while in a second case he accepts a bribe from the defendant—a rich landlord —to betray the cause of his working-class client. The suggestion of class bias in the American legal system, which might have been developed into a significant theme, receives no elaboration, however, and elsewhere Watterston makes it clear that no restructuring of the bench or bar will be necessary to alleviate the abuses he has described. Poor boys would be just as likely to succumb to the temptations of professional life as rich ones, he maintained, for the problem of shysterism boiled down in the end to a simple matter of individual ethics. A virtuous man, such as Maryland judge John Buchanan (to whom *The Lawyer* was dedicated), might practice law for many years "with honour and reputation," in the same institutional setting that permitted the Morcells of the bar to flourish.

The public apparently took little interest in Watterston's work, and with good reason. Thanks to his creator's psychological determinism, Morcell is surely one of the dullest characters in all fiction. He carries out his dastardly deeds in an unbelievably mechanical fashion, and with an air of weary resignation that soon communicates itself to the reader. To make matters worse, he indulges in philosophical afterthoughts that point up still more his moral helplessness: "I saw the beauty and loved the fascinating charms of virtue, but had not power to abandon the course of iniquity which I had so long pursued, and to which, from the earliest dawn of reason, I had been accustomed. We may attempt to change or erase the indelible impressions of youth; we may endeavour to destroy the pernicious influence of habit, but will ultimately find our efforts ineffectual, and our firmest resolutions yield to the resistless force of early education."[63]

Even a shyster deserves better treatment than that! But if *The Lawyer* fails to deal convincingly with the realities of legal practice, it does reaffirm the social and intellectual pretensions of the early bar. Like the exemplary old jurist of *Modern Chivalry*, Morcell the monster displays a conscious pride of intellect—a technician's awareness of his superiority to the laymen who employ him—that dominates the portrayal of the legal personality by the first generation of novelists: "I had always conceived and was ever taught to believe, that I was infinitely superior to all the young men of the neighbourhood. I was indeed, the only one acquainted with law. I could point out the distinction between a trespass on the case and a trespass *vi et armis*, as accurately as any county court lawyer in the state; but was wholly ignorant of the fundamental principles of justice, and the genuine effusions of philanthropy."[64]

All head, and no heart: the dichotomy was central to the public's case against the fictional lawyer. So long as writers chose, for whatever reason, to focus upon the intellectual preeminence of the bar and to make their characters little more than disembodied intelligences, they could not hope to wring much sympathy or enthusiasm from their flesh-and-blood readers. And especially was this true in the half century following the American Revolution, when the bare mention of a professional career was apt to conjure up for the average man negative images of elitism and social snobbery, such as Charles Brockden Brown conveyed so well in a sketch that he published in 1798. Brown, the most gifted of the pioneer novelists, began his career as a disgruntled law student in Philadelphia, and perhaps drew upon personal experience in describing the reactions of a would-be attorney to some workingmen who lived in the same boardinghouse:

> I often ask myself why I despise these people? In what respect am I entitled to look down upon them? It is true, they are less knowing; they have read, written, and reflected less than I have; but this is not the cause of my scorn. I imagine that I see the full extent of their ignorance; but it offers itself merely as a subject of compassion. I see how it was that they became thus illiterate and gross: I regard their condition, in this respect, not as a crime but as a misfortune. What kind of inferiority, then, is it that awakens my contempt? It lies in their profession. An usher! a clerk! a taylor! Whenever these images occur, some emotion of contempt is sure to bear them company. I analyze these thoughts: I exclaim, What is there in these professions worthy of contempt? Is it dishonourable to labour for our own subsistence? Who am I that dare to plume myself upon my rank? My father had just enough to enable him to live comfortably without labour: I have not enough for this purpose but my destiny has given me a *liberal* profession. I am a student of law, whereas they are servile *mechanics*.[65]

Until writers found some way to reconcile the aristocratic

ideal of the gentleman practitioner with a democratic faith in the omnicompetence of the common man, they stood little chance of "selling" the legal profession to the public at large. But the task of reshaping the fictional image of the bar to suit the romantic temper of antebellum America proved less difficult in practice than might have been anticipated. In the transition decades of the early nineteenth century, as the Age of Reason and its literary symbols waned, one man did more than any other to rehabilitate the law in the eyes of the young and the aspiring poor. He was William Wirt, who was almost as famous for his literary accomplishments as for his courtroom battles. Wirt succeeded so well in smashing the stereotype of the over-educated and passionless technician that later writers to the time of the Civil War did little but flesh out the contours of the new-style practitioner that he had been the first to envision.

In *The Letters of the British Spy* (1803), his earliest attempt at fiction, Wirt moved tentatively toward a redefinition of the lawyer's place in a democratic society. While paying due obeisance to the "exalted intellect" of the postrevolutionary bar in Virginia, he suggested that professional success depended far more upon native intelligence than upon formal education or class advantages. Too much respect for classical models of elo-quence could prove a positive handicap in oral argument, observes his narrator, an "English gentleman of rank," for in a republic the successful pleader must be simple, direct, forceful, and, above all, natural. He must be able to stir the feelings of a socially mixed audience—a qualification that presupposed the ability to transcend class and status differences in the name of a common humanity. Did it also imply an open door policy in the matter of legal recruitment from the lower classes, since commoners might be presumed to understand "the people" even better than a sympathetic elite? Wirt did not push his intuition-ist argument that far, but he did call in more general terms for social mobility and broad employment opportunities. One of his most memorable passages celebrated the emergence of talented "new men" in Virginia since the Revolution: a "groupe of *novi homines*, as the Romans called them; men, who, from the lowest depths of obscurity and want, and without even the influence of a patron, have risen to the first honors of their country, and founded their own families anew."[66]

The theme of self-help and rugged individualism among

American lawyers—which was only hinted at in the *British Spy* —received definitive elaboration a decade later in the most popular book that Wirt wrote, his *Sketches of the Life and Character of Patrick Henry* (1817). Less a biography than a romance, the work interpreted Henry's career as a dramatic rags-to-riches story, a case study in the evolution of a representative "new man" of the American bar. Contrasting the artificial "civilization" of tidewater Virginia with the experiential life of the frontier, Wirt pictured his hero as an untutored genius, a yeoman farmer who spent his youth roaming the forests like an Indian until he embodied the very essence of an untamed Nature. Coarse, lazy, and undisciplined, Henry seemed to his contemporaries to be devoid of brains and ambition alike, but his unsuspected powers were merely slumbering, Wirt asserted, in the absence of a challenge sufficiently important to call them into play. When the revolutionary crisis provided such a challenge, Henry promptly threw off the clown's mask and displayed charismatic qualities of leadership that carried him to the forefront in both law and politics.

Wirt made his most distinctive contribution to legal mythmaking by emphasizing the spontaneous and impassioned character of Henry's oratory. Instead of relying upon laborious research and erudite argument to win his cases, the empathic backwoodsman appealed directly to the heart "with a force that almost petrified it." Spectators reported that his performances sometimes "made their blood run cold, and their hair rise on end," that he seemed to "worm his way through the whole body, and to insinuate his influence into every mind."[67] Such inspired pleading ran counter to all established canons of courtroom propriety, but its very effectiveness signaled its importance for coming generations of American practitioners. Wirt himself assured the "young men of Virginia"—to whom he dedicated his book—that they could find no better model of professional success than Henry, the "natural aristocrat." Ignoring his subject's reputed lust for money and power, Wirt attributed his rise solely to a combination of altruistic motives and raw talent. Here at last, he implied, was a culture hero worthy of a democratic people: not the highly trained scholar-statesman that Jefferson had envisaged, but a romantic solitary, an uncultivated "genius" who learned his lessons directly from the book of nature.

Over the protests of Jefferson and others who had known the

real Henry, Wirt's *Life* became an immediate best-seller that
went through twenty-five editions by 1871. Even critics were
forced to concede that the book contained some powerful
passages and that it marked a new departure in historical
writing. But such considerations only damned it the more in the
eyes of conservative legal reviewers, who predicted chaos for
the profession if Wirt's populist views caught on with the general
public. Three decades after the work's initial appearance, some
lawyers were still complaining that their local bars were being
inundated with would-be Patrick Henrys, who had nothing but
naiveté to recommend them.

"Inexperienced men" were forever trying to cut corners, protested a committee of bar examiners in Bloomington, Iowa, in
1847:

> Some short road to wealth, some "royal road to knowledge," is
> always sought with avidity, and when the imbecile but ambitious
> mind is taught by the polished pen of a Wirt, that a good lawyer
> was once made without human labor from rather coarse and forbid-
> ding material, it is fired with a kind of puerile ambition for distinc-
> tion in the same way. The undersigned are of opinion that Wirt's
> *Life of Patrick Henry* has done more towards the destruction of the
> usefulness of young men in the United States by throwing them out
> of their proper sphere, than any other one cause to which loafism
> can be traced.[68]

Nor did Wirt's pernicious influence end there, for, following
his death in 1834, he quickly became a legendary figure in his
own right: another self-made man whose mythical success story
rivaled Henry's in popularity. It could scarcely have been otherwise, since all of the essential ingredients from which Wirt had
constructed his idealized portrait of Henry were present in his
own background as well. The son of a Maryland tavern keeper
who had emigrated to America as an indentured servant, Wirt
was orphaned at an early age; received little formal education
of any kind; loved nature and was regarded as somewhat "wild"
in his younger days; entered upon a legal career with little prior
preparation; and rose to become attorney general of the United
States and the acknowledged peer of such forensic giants as
Webster and Pinkney. Small wonder, then, that his biographer,
John Pendleton Kennedy, chose to cast him in the Henry mold,
minimizing his frailties and bowdlerizing his letters in order to
present him as a paragon of self-help, a model for all young men

"who seek for guidance to an honorable fame."[69] By 1850 the writers of success manuals took up the same theme and made Wirt the hero of an inexpensive little book, *Success in Life: The Lawyer*, which was designed for nationwide circulation.

In the face of such evident public interest, legal novelists, too, hastened to incorporate the Henry-Wirt mythology into their works. The idea of the natural "genius" combined readily with other manifestations of the Romantic movement in literature and encouraged writers to depict a society made up of potentially interchangeable parts, in which anyone might be called on to play multiple roles. Legal characters as a result ceased to be mere projections of professional intelligence and took on a three-dimensional aspect, as authors portrayed them for the first time in a variety of nonprofessional relationships: as frontiersmen, planters, statesmen, husbands, lovers, friends. The static quality that had characterized earlier presentations of life at the bar—where the success of the erudite practitioner was assumed in advance—gave way to exciting courtroom confrontations and the day-to-day struggles of ambitious young tyros to unseat their elders. In the progress of the resolute law clerk, readers applauded the rise of Everyman, but behind his fictitious attributes might be discerned, more often than not, the shadowy features of Wirt or Henry.

The most representative account of the antebellum practitioner occurs in Frederick W. Thomas's engaging novel *Clinton Bradshaw; or, The Adventures of a Lawyer* (1835). Based in part upon Thomas's own experiences as a young Baltimore attorney, the story traces the career of its hero from his student days through a successful law practice to his eventual involvement in state and national politics. A wealth of circumstantial detail adds plausibility to the narrative and marks the change in outlook that separates romantic fiction from earlier satires and allegories. Even Bradshaw's personal appearance is minutely described, in a passage that offers a composite profile of all the brave young courtroom crusaders of nineteenth-century romance:

> He was rather below the middle size, and of slender and graceful proportions; his head was finely shaped; the hair thick and wavy, and worn carelessly, without any regard to the fashion, though it had been cut fashionably; the forehead was rather broad and perpendicular, than high; and his eye was dark and deeply set, with a

quick and searching glance. It was capable of every variety of expression, and no one could look upon it, for a moment, without being struck by its expression. His nose was straight and finely formed, and the mouth chiselled, with compressed lips, for one so young, but which relaxed into a winning or scornful smile in an instant. There was, in him, that undefinable interest which some men create in the bosoms even of their most familiar acquaintances, and which strikes the most casual observer, and makes him anxious to know more of the character before him.[70]

All of the major themes discussed in the antebellum law magazines reappear in Thomas's story, although with some adjustments to accommodate the conventions of self-help fiction. There is, for example, no reference to the existence of Irish, French, German, or other non-English practitioners. Bradshaw and his acquaintances are old-stock, white Anglo-Saxon Protestants, and if Clinton, the son of a yeoman farmer, is poor in terms of material wealth, he can trace his pedigree back to Plymouth Rock and boast that the "proud imperial purple of the 'commonwealth of kings,' the Pilgrims," flows through his veins. His genetic inheritance reinforces a uniquely attractive personality, making him a "gentleman" by birth as well as temperament and a symbol of the continuing efficacy of traditional moral values.

In highlighting the elitist aspects of his hero's background, Thomas was careful, however, to distinguish between family pride and undemocratic family influence. Despite his impressive ancestry, Bradshaw enjoys no privileged social status or competitive advantages in Jacksonian America. He is rather looked down on by the new mercantile aristocracy, which gauges a man's worth solely by the size of his pocketbook. As one foppish young parvenu remarks of Clinton in his impoverished student days: "His father, I believe, is an old farmer-ploughman who sells his own turnips in the market, and has, I suspect, hard times to raise the wind to support my gentleman in the study of the law. Really, Mr. Bates, the professions are becoming quite common!"[71] Such criticism, which appears early in the book, effectively identifies Clinton as a man of the people and further directs the reader's attention to the sociological function of the bar as an avenue of upward mobility for poor but ambitious youngsters who have only their intelligence to recommend them.

In his study habits and general behavior Bradshaw emulates his favorite professional model, Patrick Henry. Like Henry, he is moody and passionate, a child of nature who vows to "read the hearts of mankind." Scornful of mere book learning, he is yet a deeply reflective thinker whose reputation for idleness is wholly undeserved. But, unlike Henry, he refuses to wait upon some stroke of destiny to reveal his talent to an astonished world. Instead, he sets out in the most methodical way to impress the public with his usefulness, employing all of the preferred strategies for self-advancement to be found in the law magazines of the 1830s. Even before his admission to the bar he regularly attends political and cultural gatherings, delivers addresses before the literary societies of the city, and writes a series of articles on politics for the newspapers. He also helps to found a city-wide debating society which he insists must be open to all young men of talent, regardless of their social origins or occupation. "Genius is of no country, and . . . of no profession, either," he argues, echoing the sentiments of Emory Washburn and other proponents of the lyceum movement. "No, sirs, I am for having every young man join, who is respectable, be he who he may, or what he may. Let us have our society upon republican principles." Elsewhere he equates intellectual effort with manual labor, in the style of Timothy Walker: "The stern necessity is on me to labour—to do head work—and if the sweat of the brain is like other sweat, a plebeian offering to the goddess industry, may be I may pluck, in my rough road, a certain leaf or two, and hide the sweltering stain upon my brow, as Caesar hid his baldness."[72]

Sympathetic to the plight of the urban poor in their brushes with the law, Bradshaw chooses to begin his practice in the city's criminal court, where he soon develops into a first-rate public defender: "He defended every one who applied to him, from a petty larceny through all the grades of crime."[73] While stressing the substantial pro bono nature of his hero's practice, Thomas stops short of indicting the legal system as such for unjust discrimination against lower-class litigants. Like Watterston before him, he views the problem of the indigent defendant from an individual, rather than an institutional, perspective, and is content to balance Bradshaw's volunteer public interest work against the unscrupulous activities of the pettifogger Scrags, who viciously exploits his vulnerable clients. But if Thomas offers no new prescription for the deficiencies of criminal justice, he does explore the environmental roots of urban violence more thoroughly than any previous writer had done. A pioneer realist in his treatment of slum conditions, he describes in vivid detail the squalor of Baltimore's shantytown district, with its impotent (and often venal) police and its ever present threat of mob risings. Few antebellum novelists buttressed their work with such impressive sociological documentation.

Bradshaw's championship of the underprivileged brings him inevitably to the attention of local politicians, and against his will he is nominated for the state legislature by the working-class wards of the city. Thomas thus raises in fictional form the key issue concurrently under discussion in the law journals: Does the paramount duty of a lawyer to his profession preclude his active involvement in partisan politics? For Bradshaw, the dilemma is resolved only after some intensive soul-searching, in which he appeals for advice to a trusted colleague, the brilliant but cynical Glassman.

A lawyer of the "old school," Glassman is an English-trained practitioner, a proud relic of a dying generation, whose own aversion to politics is more a matter of temperament than conviction: "I always preferred the even tenor of my profession. This ducking of the head to every plebeian dog you may meet, I never could, nor would do, for his vote—there is personal debasement in the thought." Nevertheless, after rehearsing all of the standard arguments against a political career, Glassman concludes that they do not apply in Clinton's case:

> You are not compelled to tread the road, in becoming a politician, that others tread—if I have read you right, your nature will not let you. A man of your character and talents, (I speak to you as a friend—I use no flattery,) cannot avoid becoming a politician. You have every requisite for making a statesman; no ambition can be loftier than that of a successful and patriotic one—and, as you will sooner or later enter the arena, be your resolutions now what they may, I do not know but what you had better commence now: you can thus test the soundness of your partiality for political life, and if you think yourself unfitted for it, which, if you do justice to yourself, I believe you will not, you can quit it at once, and much easier than if you were to commence politician after you had acquired an extensive legal reputation: *then* you would be more anxious to succeed even than you are now, because you would be aware, more would be expected from you, and ambition grows; yet, to tell the

truth, your capability might be less, for the fact is, few lawyers, who commence politicians late in life, do succeed. The law, as Burke says, is the "Chinese shoe of the mind,"—and, to make a pun, if you put the shoe on early, and wear it perpetually, you must expect to have a narrow *understanding*.[74]

Reassured by his friend's reasoning, Bradshaw launches an energetic vote-getting campaign that involves almost nightly appearances at ward rallies, where he makes "speeches and friends." His platform (as Thomas vaguely describes it) denounces privilege and corruption in government, and his grass-roots strategy pays off in a resounding victory over his opponent Talbot, a young man with strong family connections but an upper-class disdain for electioneering. Instead of making personal appeals to the electorate, Talbot loiters at the springs and lets his chief supporters canvass for him (much as the celebrated South Carolina lawyer, Hugh S. Legaré, did in real life, with equally disastrous results, in his unsuccessful bid for reelection to Congress in 1838).

The high drama of the electoral contest is not matched by any corresponding exposure of political infighting at the state capitol; of Clinton's legislative experience we learn absolutely nothing. Unwilling to link his hero to any existing party or concrete public issue, Thomas merely comments that the legislature contained no "marked individual talent—there's rather a democracy of it—it's pretty nearly equally distributed."[75] From such prosaic surroundings Clinton is, in any case, promptly delivered, through another gratuitous public draft that speeds him onward and upward. This time "a very large meeting" nominates him in absentia to the House of Representatives to contest the reelection of the Honorable Samuel Carlton, a shrewd machine politician and the father of the girl Bradshaw loves.

The ensuing race brings the story to an exciting climax and enables Thomas to juxtapose two contrasting views of the lawyer-in-politics. Carlton, on the one hand, is a professional renegade, the bugbear of the antebellum law journals: a selfish demagogue, he early abandoned the labors of the bar in return for wealth and political power. To Clinton, however, politics represents simply an extension of his public interest work, and he manages to maintain an active practice even in the midst of a campaign of slanderous abuse from his opponents. He relies upon the good sense of the electorate to counteract these efforts at character assassination, and seeks support in particular from low-income groups and independent voters. Defending the integrity of his previous record, he asserts his complete freedom from all entangling political alliances: "No, my fellow-citizens, I am under no man's patronage or pupilage—I am one of the poor ones who go to the great free-school of liberty." He also steals a march on his wily competitor by approaching prospective voters informally, and well in advance of any scheduled public appearances: "Long before the usual time for calling the meetings, at which the candidates addressed the voters from the stump, Bradshaw again and again visited his political friends in town and country. He frankly told them why he was so anxious; that he felt it a personal as well as political matter. But he made no noise in his operations."[76]

Eventually, after a hotly contested election, Clinton wins with a plurality of three hundred votes from his home district. In the process he vindicates his good name, woos his opponent's daughter, and gallops off at last in a euphoric haze: " 'Clinton Bradshaw,' he exclaimed, rising in his stirrups, and speaking to his horse, that at the word sprang forward at full speed; 'Clinton Bradshaw, you will win your way in this broad world. 'Tis a good omen to be the elected of your lady love, and your countrymen, on the same day.' "[77]

Thomas could suggest that politics, like marriage, opened the door to a blissful future for his hero, because he studiously overlooked the grubby details of legislative maneuvering and the conformist pressures that political life might bring to bear on a novice like Bradshaw. The strength of party organization, the ambiguities of major public issues, the factionalism and shifting legislative alignments that may produce unforeseeable results—these considerations found no place in Thomas's work. But other lawyer-novelists dealt with them at length, to reach less sanguine conclusions about the compatibility of legal and political careers. In William Price's anti-Jackson narrative, *Clement Falconer; or, The Memoirs of a Young Whig* (1838), as in Ralph Ingersoll Lockwood's *The Insurgents* (1835), a fictional account of Shays's Rebellion, the idealistic heroes withdraw from political life in disgust after a close acquaintance with the degrading aspects of party rule.

Thomas's nonpolitical themes, too, were modified and enlarged by rival lawyer-littérateurs until virtually every facet

of antebellum legal practice found its way into print. George
Lunt in *Eastford* (1855) sentimentalized the labors of a country
lawyer in Massachusetts, while Cornelius Mathews and
Augustus B. Longstreet poked fun at his counterparts in rural
Connecticut and New York and in backwoods Georgia.[78] The
life of a slaveholding practitioner in the Old South received
sympathetic treatment from John Pendleton Kennedy in
Swallow Barn (1832) but provoked Richard Hildreth to fierce
denunciation in *The Slave; or, Memoirs of Archy Moore*
(1836). Several writers, caught up in the frontier experience,
explored from various angles the impact of law and lawyers in a
wilderness setting: Joseph G. Baldwin recorded for posterity the
exhilarating conditions of practice in the Old Southwest in *The
Flush Times of Alabama and Mississippi* (1853); Alfred W.
Arrington's *The Rangers and Regulators of the Tanaha; or, Life
among the Lawless* (1856) described from firsthand knowledge
the operation of lynch law in Texas; Judge James Hall celebrated the civilizing influence of the midwestern practitioner in
his *Legends of the West* (1832); and Leonard Kip in *The
Volcano Diggings* (1851) exposed the workings of a kangaroo
court in the California gold fields. Finally, on the urban scene,
such figures as Theodore Sedgwick II (*Hints to My Countrymen*, 1826), Theodore S. Fay (*Norman Leslie: A Tale of the
Present Times*, 1835), and John Treat Irving (*The Attorney: or,
The Correspondence of John Quod*, 1842) further scrutinized
the administration of criminal justice in relation to America's
class structure, while Richard B. Kimball introduced his readers
to the specialized practice of the Wall Street attorney in *Under-
currents of Wall-Street* (1862).

Together, such works—which represent only a small part of
the total fiction produced by legally trained authors in the
antebellum years—add up to a richly diversified portrait gallery
of distinctive legal types. Ranging from humor to pathos, from
romance to satire, with a corresponding variety of styles and
viewpoints, these fictional perspectives cannot be neatly
absorbed into some overriding interpretive synthesis. They do
nevertheless reflect certain common preconceptions that link
them unmistakably to the larger body of antebellum legal
writing. There is, first of all, the matter of gentility. With few
exceptions the lawyer-novelists tended to choose for their
heroes young men of good breeding, "natural aristocrats" who
owe their courage and sense of fair play to generations of vir-

tuous American—and often Puritan—ancestors. To their
genetic endowments they add an iron will, an enormous
capacity for work, and a thirst for intellectual preeminence.
Knowledge, not wealth, is the mark of the professional elect,
and writers do not hide their disdain for "mere" money-making
and the ostentatious life-style of parvenu businessmen. An
equally censorious tone is apparent in their treatment of many
backwoods practitioners, whose boorish antics they describe
with the relish of urban sophisticates. Yet, even as they justified
the existence of social stratification within the bar, most writers
acknowledged the pull of a contrary open-door policy. The
clash of competing values is distinctly audible, for example, in a
novel like George Lunt's *Eastford*.

Lunt's story, set in a small New England town, focuses upon
the legal training and early practice of George Atherton, scion
of a proud old family of clergymen and doctors whose Puritan
roots stretch far back into the seventeenth century. While
studying law in the office of a local practitioner, George
encounters another clerk, Mr. Cobstalk, a loutish farm boy
who inspires some predictably negative reflections: "This
person had enjoyed those advantages of early education, which
are obtained in the common schools, and, much to his worthy
father's dissatisfaction, had determined to devote his somewhat
crude abilities to the pursuit of a profession, which demands
sound training and thorough cultivation of the mind, for its
successful and honorable practice . . . There could be no doubt
he was of nature's coarser grain,—rough, rude, loud,—and that
nothing could avail to give him any essential polish."[79] A closer
acquaintance merely confirms these impressions, although
George concedes that his office mate does possess a few redeeming traits: native shrewdness ("well calculated to serve him in
some parts of legal practice"), abundant energy, and unyielding
determination. In the end such qualities prove decisive in over-
coming the deficiencies of birth and formal schooling, for Cobstalk, having dropped out of sight through much of the
narrative, resurfaces in the final pages as a successful practitioner in a neighboring town, a "man of good sense," whose
very manners are undergoing steady improvement since his
prudent marriage to an heiress. The unpromising bumpkin thus
develops, through self-discipline and the rigors of legal
apprenticeship, into a pillar of the local establishment,
and—what is more important—his new status is acknowledged

by the Brahmins of the bar. The entire sequence underscores both the elitism and the genuine democratic sympathies that alike characterized the antebellum legal profession.

Nonlawyers also contributed in significant ways to the literary vogue of the antebellum practitioner. Novelists such as Thomas H. Shreve, the author of *Drayton: A Story of American Life* (1851), emphasized the rags-to-riches mobility associated with a successful career at the bar; magazines like the popular *New York Mirror* published a variety of articles and stories—such as the anonymous "Labours and Love of Walter Austin" (1840)—that celebrated the advent of a new generation of Patrick Henry types;[80] while the playwright Joseph S. Jones scored one of his greatest hits with *The People's Lawyer* (1839), a comedy of social justice whose hero, a young attorney of independent means, devotes his full time to the service of the poor. On yet another plane, some writers sought to improve the profession's standing in the previously neglected area of children's literature.

The cultivation of the child mind certainly deserved serious attention from legal apologists, since many youngsters were regularly indoctrinated with antilawyer sentiments in the course of their early schooling. Throughout the nineteenth century a majority of textbook writers, while professing unqualified admiration for the Constitution, republican government, and a few select "legal statesmen" of the Marshall stripe, denounced the average practitioner for his alleged venality, parasitism, and subservience to monied interests. In the antebellum years alone, nine textbooks widely used in elementary schools referred to a game called "The Colonists," which pretended to rank every occupation according to its social value. Farming stood at the head of the list, followed by a variety of other "useful" trades and callings. Lawyers, however, were not represented at all, since they posed a standing threat to the welfare of any community. Or, as fifth-grade students learned to chant:

> To fit up a village with tackle for tillage
>   Jack Carter he took to the saw.
> To pluck and to pillage the same little village
>   Tim Gordon he took to the law.[81]

This negative stereotype remained virtually unchallenged

until the 1840s, when no less a personage than Jacob Abbott helped to swing the balance in favor of the profession. Abbott, the author of more than two hundred books, was the undisputed master of juvenile fiction in his day, and he owed his transatlantic reputation in large part to the strong "educational" flavor of his works, which contained much accurate information about places, institutions, and mores. Like all the others, *Marco Paul's Adventures in Pursuit of Knowledge* (1843) purported to tell the "strict and exact truth" about its several subjects, including the bar—a pledge that Abbott redeemed by restating for his youthful readers the utilitarian arguments then being advanced in defense of the profession by law writers and lecturers.

The coincidence of views is especially notable at one point, where young Marco is introduced to the life of a small Vermont village by his friend and tutor John Forester. In explaining the origins of the community, Forester expounds the familiar thesis that every occupational group is dependent upon some other for necessary services and that wants multiply in proportion to population. Although farmers alone may be the first to settle an area, he points out, they will soon be followed by a miller, a blacksmith, a storekeeper, a carpenter, a mason, and in time by professional types as well: "a physician . . . to heal them when they are sick, and a lawyer to prevent disputes."

"To *prevent* disputes!" said Marco. Marco had not much idea of the nature of a lawyer's business, but he had a sort of undefined and vague notion, that lawyers *made* disputes among men, and lived by them.

"Why, I know," said Forester, laughing, "that lawyers have not the credit, generally, of preventing many disputes, but I believe they do. Perhaps it is because I am going to be a lawyer myself. But I really believe that lawyers prevent ten disputes, where they occasion one."

"How do they do it?" asked Marco.

"Why, they make contracts, and draw up writings, and teach men to be clear and distinct in their engagements and bargains. Then, besides, when men will not pay their debts, they compel them to do it, by legal process. And there are a vast many debts which are paid, for fear of this legal process, which would not have been paid without it. Thus, knowing that the lawyers are always ready to apply the laws, men are much more careful not to break them, than they otherwise would be. So that it is no doubt vastly for the benefit of a community, not only to have efficient laws, but efficient lawyers to aid in the execution of them."[82]

Marco's Adventures succeeded well enough with the public to justify four reprintings later in the nineteenth century. And Abbott further popularized the workings of the legal system in two other books: *Jonas a Judge; or, Law among the Boys* (1840) and *Judge Justin; or, The Little Court of Morningdale* (1857).[83]

For a more specialized audience of young people—those who attended Sunday school classes—such respected female authors as Harriet Burn McKeever added a reverential touch by making their legal characters models of Christian piety. Thus Roland Bruce, the lawyer hero of Miss McKeever's *Woodcliff* (1864), is not only a conscientious practitioner and a self-made man but also a "gentleman" of deep religious convictions, who regulates his every action according to scriptural norms. The bare hint of selfish political aspirations is enough to make Roland wince. "Madeline," he tells his sweetheart, "I have but one ambition,—to serve my God faithfully in whatever station he appoints, and to walk hand in hand with one of the purest and loveliest of God's creatures in the path that leads us home to Heaven." Even his family tree seems somewhat overburdened with righteousness: "All I can boast, in the way of pedigree, is that my ancestors, as far back as I can trace them, were a hardy race of plain Scotch farmers, shepherds, and mountaineers, among whom were always found faithful, earnest ministers of the Lord Jesus; their greatness consisting only in heroic deeds of calm and patient endurance in the cause of truth and holiness."[84]

These Sunday school themes—the identification of law with Christian ethics and the consequent apotheosis of the dedicated practitioner—reached their culmination in a work that appealed to young and old alike: Mrs. Emma D. E. N. Southworth's gargantuan Civil War novel, *Ishmael*. Based loosely upon the career of William Wirt, *Ishmael* first appeared as a serial in Robert Bonner's famous story paper, the *New York Ledger*, but its immediate popularity led the author to reissue it in an expanded hardcover edition of two volumes: *Ishmael; or, In the Depths* and *Self-Raised; or, From the Depths* (1864). Each volume sold more than two million copies, making the story one of the top ten best-sellers of the nineteenth century.

The labyrinthine plot chronicles the rise to legal fame of high-minded Ishmael Worth, who represents for Mrs. Southworth the perfect male. An illegitimate child whose mother dies soon after his birth, Ishmael is reared in abject poverty and forced to struggle unaided against the ingrained class prejudices of Maryland society in the early nineteenth century. Nevertheless, this soft-spoken "peasant youth," through a combination of intellect and will, triumphs over all obstacles and wins the respect of imperious Judge Randolph Merlin, who becomes his friend and patron. Once admitted to the bar Ishmael predictably champions the cause of the deserving poor, but, more than Clinton Bradshaw or any other fictional practitioner, he becomes the special defender of oppressed womanhood. For Mrs. Southworth, who understood only too well the tribulations of working mothers, had no qualms about making her hero a spokesman for women's liberation:

> He spoke noble words in behalf not only of his client, but of woman —woman, loving, feeble and oppressed from the beginning of time—woman, hardly dealt with by *nature* in the first place, and by the laws, made by her natural lover and protector, *man*, in the second place. Perhaps it was because he knew himself to be the *son of a woman only*, even as his Master had been before him, that he poured so much of awakening, convicting and condemning fire, force and weight into this part of his discourse. He uttered thoughts and feelings upon this subject, original and startling at that time, but which have since been quoted, both in the Old and the New World, and have had power to modify those cruel laws which at that period made woman, despite her understanding intellect, an idiot, and despite her loving heart, a chattel—*in the law*.[85]

As Ishmael self-consciously dedicates his professional labors to God, so his piety in other respects intrudes upon the reader at every turn. The only "bad" thing he ever does is to drink a little brandy under circumstances of extreme provocation—a moral lapse that torments him long afterward, as he confesses to his sweetheart, Beatrice Middleton: "Dearest girl, only this once will I pain you by alluding to that sorrowful and degrading hour. You found me—I will not shrink from uttering the word, though it will scorch my lips to speak it, and burn your ears to hear it—you found me—intoxicated." The offense, needless to say, is not repeated ("Never, no, never, even as a medicine, will I place the fatal poison to my lips again!"). Small wonder, then, that Ishmael's wastrel father, in seeking to account for his son's extraordinary personality at the close of the book, finds it necessary to invoke comparisons with the Deity:

> His birth, in its utter destitution, reminds me (I speak it with the deepest reverence) of that other birth in the manger of Bethlehem. His infancy was a struggle for the very breath of life; his childhood for bread; his youth for education; and nobly, nobly has he sustained this struggle and gloriously has he succeeded . . . I believe it was intended from the first that Ishmael should "owe no man anything," for life, or bread, or education, or profession; but all to God and God's blessing on his own efforts. He is self-made. I know no other man in history to whom the term can be so perfectly well applied.[86]

Helen W. Papashvily, a modern critic, once happily remarked that Ishmael shared "another attribute of the heavenly beings, neuter gender."[87] Her comment is only too apt, and from a twentieth-century perspective it is difficult to comprehend the influence that Mrs. Southworth's tale allegedly wielded over scores of impressionable young men. But we are not left to guesswork alone, since there does exist at least one testimonial from an unimpeachable source. Roujet D. Marshall, an otherwise stolid attorney who represented Wisconsin lumber interests for many years before his elevation to the state supreme court in 1895, never forgot the crucial role that *Ishmael* had played in determining his choice of a legal career:

> While I was laboring in the state of uncertainty indicated, without any one at home or otherwise to advise with me as to choosing a vocation, the story of "Self Made or Out of the Depths," by Mrs. Southworth, came to my notice. The fact that the leading character created by the author was a lawyer who, wholly by his own efforts, rose from a humble origin to be an associate of Webster and Chief Justice John Marshall, and participate in the Dartmouth College Case, the impeachment trial of Aaron Burr, and many other of the most noted cases reported in the books, and was for many years the head of the legal department of our government, made the story of special interest to me. It was written in such a true-to-life way that one circumstanced as I was could not proceed far after reaching the border line of the struggle to become a lawyer without losing sight of the fact that it was only the creation of the author's imagination. It was so in my case. I became possessed of the idea that attainment of the object of one's highest ambition is within the competency of

one who, barring sickness or accident—mere possibilities, which should not deter a man of courage from effort in the line of his laudable desire—will tirelessly and persistently work with the single purpose of possessing such object, to win the prize sought.[88]

Fired with enthusiasm, the nineteen-year-old Marshall next turned to a biography of William Wirt, whose real-life background, he soon discovered, bore little relation to the fabulous incidents of Mrs. Southworth's narrative. Yet in one important respect—the treatment of professional idealism—Wirt's biographer fully corroborated the message of *Ishmael*: "the key to [Wirt's] success was [his] conception of a lofty ideal of what a lawyer should be, individual attention to the performance of his professional duties—devotion to his profession as his single vocation—careful preparation in respect to every detail of matters to be presented to court and presentation thereof according to his convictions as to the law and the facts and with clearness of statement and logical, convincing reasoning and without apparent attempt to embellish or move by florid style."[89] Thereafter, with Wirt as his guide, Marshall entered upon the study of law.

The episode is revealing, for it indicates that—whatever we may think of Ishmael today—to readers of the Gilded Age he figured as a genuine folk hero, in whom the myth of the self-made man was fused with the legal profession's own preferred vision of its role in American society.

How strongly did these antebellum attitudes influence the actual behavior of practitioners? No satisfactory answer can be given to such a question, although it is safe to say that their practical repercussions were not confined by any political, geographical, or generational lines. We can readily discern their impact upon the careers of such men as William Cabell Rives of Virginia, Peleg W. Chandler of Massachusetts, Hugh S. Legaré of South Carolina, Timothy Walker of Ohio, William Pitt Ballinger of Texas, and Roujet D. Marshall of Wisconsin. The ideal of a depoliticized profession emerges from the correspondence of Manning F. Force, a young Harvard Law School graduate trying to establish a practice in the Midwest during the 1850s, as it underlies the admonitions of Albert Gallatin Riddle to one of the early graduating classes of Howard Law School in the period following the Civil War.[90] Even in the midst of that terrible conflict, a law professor like Emory Washburn could exult in the impending triumph of technical expertise over politics, and point to unparalleled leadership opportunities for his Harvard students once the fighting stopped:

> You have only to wait a brief time, when the business of reorganization must be resumed; and the people will look to the aid and counsel of others than the mad or selfish politicians, whose evil counsels or rash judgments first involved them in the disastrous consequences of alienated affections and civil discord. Such a violence has been done to our institutions, such a strain has been made upon the strength of the common bond that bound us together as a nation, that it will require the wisest counsel, the calmest judgment, and the most devoted patriotism to restore the government again to anything like harmonious action. And these, I repeat, are not to be found in the political leaders who caused the mischief to begin with. Nor is it to the mere man of business that we are to look, nor to the scholar, or man of letters, however speculative he may have shown himself in his study into causes which be hid beyond the reach of his unpractised vision. In the restoration of peace to our distracted country under the dominion of well administered law, such as she had enjoyed for three quarters of a century, I am sure that our profession are to take a most important part.[91]

In the postwar world of regulatory commissions and attempted scientific planning, the elitist dreams of the antebellum bar did find a substantial measure of realization for the first time. Apolitical practitioners, who had perhaps rendered their first important public service for some wartime agency like the United States Sanitary Commission, now gravitated toward Mugwump politics, Civil Service reform, and the movement for independent regulatory boards. But the growth of administrative government, far from disarming lay criticism, merely opened a new chapter in the troubled history of lawyer-community relations.

When will this carnage cease?
When will the hounds of thrice-damned Rome
Be surfeited with blood?
. . . . .
Americans will not stand by and see
The untamed renegades of other climes
Do murder on the natives of the soil.
We are proscribers, persecutors, all.
*Six Months Ago; or, The Eventful Friday and
its Consequences* (1844)

6   Riot Control in Philadelphia

The tendency toward increasing
specialization and withdrawal from public life that divided the
antebellum bar affected other leadership groups in American
society as well. Cities in particular experienced a sharp decline
in the quality of municipal governing bodies at the very time
when industrialism and its attendant social dislocations most
demanded bold and innovative action. A philosophy of privatism inherited from a simpler preindustrial age continued to
define the effective limits of community power, despite changing circumstances. Saddled with hopelessly inadequate administrative agencies, city officials found themselves threatened by
recurring waves of lawless violence in the three decades preceding the Civil War. Out of these successive confrontations
between bureaucrats and mobs—between eighteenth-century
political norms and nineteenth-century economic impera-
tives—emerged the modern municipal corporation. The process
was virtually complete by the time of the Civil War, which in a

sense projected the basic issue into national politics, as a dynamic industrial technology collided with the traditionalism of the Washington political establishment.

Of all the major antebellum cities, Philadelphia suffered most severely from outbreaks of mob fury in the crucial transition years of the thirties and forties. Her experience highlights with special clarity both the magnitude of the urban dilemma and the changing role of the lawyer in municipal affairs.

When Andrew Jackson became President of the United States, Philadelphia was a booming commercial port which yet retained much of the appearance and life-style of an English provincial town. A relatively homogeneous citizenry—drawn in large part from the British Isles—carried on the skilled trades and small businesses of earlier generations in surroundings that had changed little since the days of William Penn. Political life was still dominated by a small merchant elite who believed that government should interfere as little as possible in the affairs of individuals, most of whom were busily exploiting the avenues to wealth afforded by a fluid competitive society. The prosperity of old Philadelphia rested upon private initiative and the willingness of the mercantile class to assume burdensome civic responsibilities. So long as the city remained merely a center for local trade her traditions of voluntarism and skeleton government worked well enough. But by 1830 Philadelphians found themselves on the threshold of an industrial revolution that in three decades transformed their old-fashioned town into something new to America and to the world—the modern big city. The process of adjustment would have been a trying one under any circumstances; given the meager machinery of social control and accompanying popular attitudes, it proved almost catastrophic for the City of Brotherly Love.

Industrialization at first meant less the introduction of new large-scale enterprises—such as the Baldwin and Norris locomotive works, with its six hundred employees—than the rearrangement of work patterns and personnel in established businesses. The old general merchant gave way to wholesale or manufacturing specialists who served a regional market; skilled artisans, accustomed to working independently in their own homes, found themselves required to commute to textile mills or factories, where machines made a mockery of their skills and forced them to compete with untrained, newly arrived immigrants. The shift to mechanization varied from trade to trade: hand loom weavers continued to flourish in some branches of the textile field, while furniture and cigar manufacturers were not directly affected by new production techniques at all. Yet artisans as a class feared for their future livelihood, as they resented their diminishing chances of moving up to the status of master workman or small shopkeeper. Their frustrations found a legitimate outlet in the trade union movement that flowered briefly in the mid-thirties, before the Panic of 1837 wiped out all wage-and-hour gains and ushered in six years of unprecedented economic distress. While businesses, both large and small, struggled to survive the crisis, Irish and German immigrants poured into Philadelphia in ever larger numbers to compete with old-stock laborers and declassed artisans for the lowest-paying jobs available.

Unlike their counterparts in the late nineteenth century, the newcomers were not shunted into working-class ghettos. Apart from a small Negro quarter, no such segregated slums existed in antebellum Philadelphia, whose physical expansion had been too rapid and indiscriminate to create any large tracts of run-down housing. Instead, foreign-born laborers settled in the midst of native Americans—either in back-alley, two-room flats in the city's wards or in mixed neighborhoods in the industrial suburbs on the North and South Sides. Wherever they went, the immigrants found no municipal agencies waiting to welcome them on behalf of the larger community. City life began and ended with the neighborhood, and each neighborhood formed a separate melting pot with its own built-in tensions and hostilities. Deprived of substantial public outlets for collective action and group loyalties, urban residents turned to private associations of all kinds to assuage their sense of loneliness and insecurity. Many of their clubs—fraternal benefit associations, lyceums, mechanics' institutes, and the like—performed a useful socializing function, but some served chiefly to perpetuate Old World feuds and factions. Volunteer fire companies, organized along ethnic lines, spent much of their time battling rival firemen, while the Ancient Order of Hibernians and the Loyal Orange Institution stood ever ready to restage the Battle of the Boyne on the shores of the Schuylkill.[1]

In the presence of so much combustible material, the task of peacekeeping in Philadelphia would have been a formidable one for even the best-run police system. But few persons claimed that the local police were well directed. As fragmentation characterized the city's social life, so her political authority was diffused and contested through many contrary channels. The county of Philadelphia in the early 1840s resembled nothing so much as a medieval fiefdom, parceled out as it was among twenty-nine separate and competing jurisdictions. In ascending order of importance, these included: thirteen townships, six boroughs, nine districts, and the city proper. Large tracts of open country separated some of these divisions, and communications were poor with outlying areas. But even adjoining districts maintained with their neighbors a formal protocol better suited to European principalities than to American suburbs. Each unit was self-governing, and each jealously guarded its prerogatives against outside intereference. Boundary streets became in effect so many Chinese walls—a fact much appreciated by the roving criminal gangs of the period, who knew that they had only to cross Cedar or Vine streets to elude further pursuit by city police.

Nor was the average criminal likely to be deterred by any fear of prompt arrest at the scene of the crime. By the late thirties the inefficiency of the Philadelphia police had become proverbial. Law enforcement machinery followed a common pattern in both city and suburbs: a modified version of the old constable-and-watch system. The city proper boasted a total force of 177 men, including 12 day policemen, 27 night policemen, 126 watchmen, 1 captain of night police, 4 captains of the watch, 4 high constables, and a 3-man detective bureau. These lawmen served a population of some 325,000 souls, making a ratio of one enforcement officer for every 1,800 inhabitants—a force much smaller than the one New York provided at the time for her citizens.[2]

But numbers alone do not tell the whole story, for effective training and deployment might have remedied any deficiencies of that kind. Unfortunately, Philadelphia's police received no formal training and operated for the most part with a minimum of supervision. During the daylight hours only a skeleton force was maintained; no beats were patrolled until dusk, when the watchmen came on duty. Throughout the night these watchmen walked the city's streets armed with a short stick and a rattle, with which they signaled the discovery of fire or other disorder.

As fire wardens they performed a useful service; as a preventive police they had been a standing joke since colonial days, when adventuresome teenagers had amused themselves by overturning their watch boxes and otherwise making their lives miserable.

Any serious public disturbance revealed both the physical weakness of the rank-and-file patrolmen and the absence of any unified direction from their superiors. Although in theory the mayor retained control of the entire unwieldy police establishment, in practice his authority was undercut from a number of different directions as one moved down the chain of command. Distrust of a strong executive had been a hallmark of Pennsylvania politics since the Revolution; in municipal affairs it took the form of creating rival power centers to accomplish a unitary task. Constables, for example, took orders from the mayor, the recorder, and individual aldermen. Half of the constables were appointed by the mayor, half by the recorder, while the clerk of police owed his position to the city councils. To cap the jurisdictional muddle, the day and night forces were organized along totally independent lines. Each had its separate cadre which acknowledged no round-the-clock responsibility for preserving the city's peace.[3]

The absurdity of the situation was self-evident, and every year grand juries and citizen groups loudly demanded reform. But every attempt at major reorganization—including a very promising effort in the early thirties—foundered on one of two obstacles: economics or ideology. From the taxpayer's standpoint, continued police inefficiency appeared preferable to further increases in the already high rate of municipal assessments. Middle- and upper-class property owners balked at financing basic structural changes in the system and supported only minor adjustments, such as an increase in the number of watchmen or an enlargement of the constable's powers. This shortsighted policy proved doubly unfortunate in its results. While the quality of law enforcement steadily declined, the normal operating costs of a bumbling police administration mounted from year to year: $50,402.12 in 1839, $77,989.23 in 1842, and $88,860.51 in 1844, according to official reports.[4]

Behind the reluctance of propertied groups to endorse a professional police lay other considerations of a more general nature, which permeated every stratum of the community. In the national mythology, as we have seen, America figured as a

uniquely virtuous land whose citizens, schooled in self-govern-
ment, had no need of repressive agencies of social control such
as characterized the regimes of the Old World. Republican
institutions presupposed a responsible electorate and eliminated
by definition the most potent source of public disorder—a
permanently depressed underclass. "We venture to assert there
can be no mob proper, in any part of this roomy land of ours,"
observed a Philadelphia pamphleteer in 1844. "*Mob* is the offspring of a starved, ignorant, over-numerous, and ill used
population. They have a mob in Europe . . . where the unhappy
people . . . are, by the very structure of communities, a complaining and perilous party of the body politic—an ache, a sore,
a disease." In free America, on the other hand, where the
avenues to wealth and status remained open to all, there was
little danger that the mob spirit would ever become institutionalized. It might display itself on extraordinary occasions,
but then it could be dealt with on an ad hoc basis, without
resort to an official gendarmerie.[5]

The very idea of a professional police inevitably suggested
European analogues: military bearing, distinctive uniforms,
deadly weapons, arbitrary authority—all those features that
filled American tourists with a vague unease when they traveled
on the Continent. Professionalization meant police tyranny,
journalists warned, but to many Americans it implied even
more. The policeman abroad was a visible symbol of Old
World corruption; he marked the absence of virtue and reason
in society. To admit his type to America would be an open confession that somehow even here the democratic dream had gone
sour.[6]

Hence, in the face of increasing urban lawlessness, Philadelphians clung to the self-help techniques bequeathed to them by
their revolutionary forefathers. When serious public disturbances arose, they turned from their amateur constabulary to a
still more quixotic peacekeeping force: the sheriff's posse. Introduced into the American colonies at a time when it was already
dying out as an enforcement mechanism in the mother country,
the *posse comitatus* proved admirably suited to the needs of a
sparsely settled frontier. But urban sophistication and a declin-
ing community spirit gradually robbed it of all but a symbolic
value. By law, to be sure, the sheriff was empowered to
mobilize the manpower of his county for the suppression of

dangerous tumults and riots. At the head of an aroused citizenry he might march to the scene of disorder, command a crowd to disperse, and arrest the most obvious troublemakers. The procedure was in keeping with the finest traditions of American voluntarism. It presupposed a willingness on the part of the average citizen to put aside his private interests for the duration of a public emergency. The urban posse in fact represented less a demonstration of physical than of moral force: armed only with a constable's mace, the citizen-lawman sought to impress upon wrongdoers the collective strength of community norms and democratic self-policing. Unfortunately, large-size mobs seldom took the lesson to heart, and sheriffs learned that moral intimidation could be a two-edged weapon. From year to year the number of volunteers who responded to the tolling of the State House bell dwindled, until only a handful could be counted on for any service outside their immediate ward. Yet in 1842 the Select Council of Philadelphia, after carefully investigating the causes and prevention of riots, recommended an even greater reliance upon ad hoc citizen groups to put down future mobs. In addition to the regular police force, the council's published report called for the creation of two back-up organizations: an emergency riot squad of two hundred Minute Men, appointed by the mayor equally from each ward and paid $1.50 a day when called into active duty, and, most important, a force of at least one thousand unpaid householders enrolled in "volunteer ward associations for the preservation of the peace." The latter group would be supplied by the city with appropriate badges and means of defense as occasion required, and "it shall be *their* duty, as it is their interest, at all times to aid, with their physical as well as their moral force, in the suppression of all riots and disturbances; to furnish patrols whenever called upon by the Mayor, and to superintend the peace and good order of their wards."[7] In the City of Brotherly Love the myth of the citizen-hero died hard.

While the council's suggested reforms never took effect, their intended scale tells much about the extent of the problem confronting municipal authorities. Since 1834 Philadelphia had been racked by successive riots which became almost an anticipated annual occurrence in some part of the county. These outbursts flared up for a variety of reasons, from race to politics. They included railroad construction disputes, election-

day brawls, weavers' strikes, and assaults on the South Side
Negro ghetto. From the beginning they followed a pattern of
escalating violence, abetted in some instances by halfhearted
expressions of sympathy from respected community figures.
Negroes, for example, were marked as legitimate targets for
violence in 1835 after Robert T. Conrad and other civic leaders
publicly denounced the abolitionist program and its adherents.
Thereafter an air of ambivalence characterized the city's efforts
to protect the lives and property of its black population, for
both rioters and authorities were aware of divided community
sentiment. A similar situation prevailed in nonracial contexts as
well, so that, as Sam Bass Warner, Jr., has acutely observed,
most of Philadelphia's riots boiled down to "brutal street plays,
in which gangs of toughs . . . acted out the fears and enmities of
the ordinary citizens by attacking their scapegoats."[8] Each new
disturbance tended to become a bit more boisterous than its
predecessors, and crowds of people who had been content to
remain indoors during the earliest demonstrations regularly
poured out into the streets in later years to savor the action.

By the 1840s the Irish were fast replacing Negroes as prime
targets for mob fury. There had long been friction between Irish
Catholics and Protestant Orangemen in the Philadelphia area,
but the community at large stood apart from their inveterate
broils until a peculiar convergence of circumstances made further neutrality impossible and set the stage for the bloodiest
street fighting the city had ever known.

Religious bigotry did much to lower the level of community
tolerance by reinforcing a negative stereotype of the priest-
ridden Irish immigrant. Sensational exposés of priestly corruption and the horrors of convent life—such as The Awful
Disclosures of Maria Monk (1836)—appealed chiefly to the
lower classes, but the New York school controversy of 1841
provided a rallying point for all shades of Protestant opinion.
Middle-class churchgoers in particular were incensed at Bishop
John Hughes's alleged efforts to banish the King James Bible
from the public schools of the state, and when Hughes unwisely
sponsored a Catholic ticket for the fall elections in New York
City, fears of papist domination multiplied. At stake, it seemed,
was nothing less than the preservation of "American" values in
education, for the anti-Catholic press was not slow in establishing a connection between nationalism and the Protestant
tradition:

The Union and the Bible!
Oh, in what mystic ties
These sacred things are woven with
Our future destinies . . .
Shall Rome dictate to us a rule
To Educate our youth;
And banish from the Common School
The word of light and truth?[9]

In Philadelphia, Bishop Francis Kenrick's demands that Douay Bibles be furnished to Catholic students attending public schools sparked the formation of many neighborhood clubs to combat "Popery." This grass-roots resistance soon found its most effective outlet in the American Protestant Association (1842), a loose alliance of some hundred ministers from various denominations who delivered weekly lectures on the Catholic menace to large and enthusiastic audiences. The hysterical preaching of the APA fell little short of a "war-cry for Protestants to take the field against Catholics," noted one unsympathetic contemporary. Tense listeners were told

> that there was not a Catholic Church that had not underneath it, prepared cells for Protestant heretics; that every priest was a Jesuit in disguise,—that the Pope was coming to this country with an army of cassocked followers, and that each would be trebly armed with weapons, concealed under the folds of "Babylonish robes." Never did Titus Oates detail more horrible conspiracies, in virtue of his station as informer general, than did these clerical sentinels; and all that was wanting was the power, and such a judge as Jeffries, to make every Roman Catholic expiate his "abominable heresy" upon the scaffold, or amid the flames.[10]

While religious zealots preached no compromise with a corrupt Catholic hierarchy, politicians took the same line against their allegedly slavish followers. In December 1843 the American Republican party arose in Philadelphia to contest the influence of the foreign-born in American politics. The platform of the new group was unequivocal: a naturalization period of twenty-one years for all immigrants; the restriction of public office to citizens born in the United States; and the exclusive use of the Protestant version of the Bible in the public schools. Three party newspapers—the *Native Eagle*, the *Native American*, and the *Daily Sun*—carried the nativist message to Philadelphia residents and complemented the attacks launched by the sectarian press. Through these media the outlines of a massive alien conspiracy were firmly implanted in the popular mind, until even the most neutral observer could no longer deny the existence of an "Irish problem."

In its final form the case against the Irish shrewdly exploited the half-suppressed fears of every social class in greater Philadelphia. To artisans and semiskilled workers the Irish peasant symbolized hard times and unfair competition. Against him was directed all the frustration and bitterness that would otherwise have vented itself against employer groups and their newfangled machinery. The middle class, on the other hand, took a special interest in moral issues. Fearful of a decline in national character, the bourgeoisie deplored the drinking habits of the Irish, their reputed sexual prowess and high birth rate, and their disturbing impact upon public education. Worse still was the threat to democratic institutions posed by the prospect of hordes of illiterate voters marching to the polls in blind obedience to corrupt political bosses and their clerical allies. The political issue aroused even the city's elite, who glimpsed the eclipse of old family leadership beneath the weight of a manipulated mass electorate. For the time being, city politics remained safely in conservative Whig hands, but in some suburbs a new breed of professional vote getter already prevailed—the first big-city bosses, like Democrat Joel Barlow Sutherland, who abandoned old-style gentility in favor of direct appeals to lower-class ethnic voting blocs. Such specialized leadership was the inevitable counterpart to an increasingly complex and rationalized industrial system, but its inevitability made it no more palatable to Main Line Philadelphians. They sought a more personal reason for their waning political fortunes and found it in the mindless regimentation of Irish voters, who held the balance of power in the local Democratic party organization. As these foreigners increased in numbers, embattled conservatives feared that their collective influence would subvert the social order at home and plunge the nation into a reckless adventurism in foreign affairs. The diplomatic bogey—an interventionist foreign policy dictated by the Vatican—brought the nightmare full circle and grounded it in an unchallengeable religious mystique. For while rational apprehensions might be countered by rational arguments, certain phenomena evaded logical analysis to impose themselves willy-nilly on a more primitive emotional plane. Such was the brute fact of Roman Catholicism, which suffused all aspects of the Irish question and justified the use of measures otherwise questionable; much as the fact of color served as the ultimate unanswerable rationale for attacks upon Negroes.[11]

Of course, nativists and sectarians, for all the violence of their rhetoric, had little intention of inciting actual riots. But their inflammatory harangues demonstrated serious cleavages within the community and helped to reduce the risks attendant upon a resort to force. Would-be rioters knew in advance that they could count on some sympathy in high quarters; they also appreciated the weakness of the law in dealing with large crowds. Previous riots had established a reliable scenario of actions and responses: first, desultory street fights, building up to a full-scale engagement, accompanied by arson and murder; next, the tardy intervention of the police and the sheriff; finally, the summoning of armed militia companies, after which hostilities quickly terminated. Thus far the militia had never fired on the crowd, and many doubted that the volunteers would obey an order to shoot down their fellow citizens.

If unlucky enough to be arrested by the police or the military, a rioter could look forward to nothing worse than a light jail sentence at most. A special board set up by the city to collect riot data reported in September 1843 that during two years of major disturbances eighty-three persons had been arrested for rioting. Grand juries had indicted sixty-eight of them, but only six were ultimately convicted. Of these, three went to jail for ninety days, while the remaining three received sentences of ten days.[12] Crowded court dockets and lax administrative procedures partially explain this result, but it also owed something to the attitudes of bench, bar, and jury. Edward King, for example, who presided over Philadelphia's court of common pleas, came from a lower-class background and shared much of the outlook of the old-stock workingman, while his colleague Judge James Campbell, son of an Irish shopkeeper, was a prominent figure in Catholic political circles.[13] The complex crosscurrents of judicial administration, no less than a weak police and a partisan press, helped to maintain a condition of instability in urban affairs, in which even a minor incident could provoke a chain reaction of accelerating violence.

At six o'clock on Friday evening, May 3, 1844, about one hundred American Republicans (or Native Americans, as they were now beginning to call themselves), assembled on a vacant lot in the suburb of Kensington for a political rally. Their plans had been announced well in advance and had aroused threats of retaliation from Irish Catholic residents. Violence was no stranger to the district, which had witnessed serious industrial disturbances for several years. As a fast-growing textile center Kensington boasted the largest concentration of native artisans and unskilled Irish laborers in the entire Philadelphia area. Despite previous clashes between these groups, no police were on hand to monitor the Nativist meeting, which soon degenerated into a predictable Donnybrook. Irish hecklers, both men and boys, shouted down the speakers from the edge of the crowd until fighting broke out in several quarters, and an Irish drayman became the man of the hour by charging pell-mell into the speakers' stand with his dirt-filled wagon.

Disgruntled, the Natives withdrew to a nearby temperance hall, but resolved to return in force the following Monday to vindicate their rights as American citizens. Over the weekend the city's newspapers reported the occurrence and Nativist handbills appeared in prominent places urging a mass turnout in support of American constitutional principles:

NATIVE AMERICANS.

The American Republicans of the city and county of Philadelphia, who are determined to support the NATIVE AMERICANS in their Constitutional Rights of peaceably assembling to express their opinions on any questions of Public Policy, and to

SUSTAIN THEM AGAINST THE ASSAULTS
OF ALIENS AND FOREIGNERS

Are requested to assemble on MONDAY AFTERNOON, May 6th, 1844 at 4 o'clock, at the corner of Master and Second street, Kensington, to express their indignation at the outrage on Friday evening last, which was perpetrated by the Irish Catholics, in tearing and trampling under their feet the American Flag, [and] to take the necessary steps to prevent a repetition of it.[14]

In response to this appeal a substantially larger crowd, drawn from all parts of the city, attended the second Kensington meeting, which got under way peaceably enough. Two speakers had already completed their remarks when a sudden thunderstorm ruled out further proceedings and sent the audience scurrying for cover to the nearest public structure—a local landmark one block away known as the Nannygoat Market. Here, after the initial confusion had died down, an attempt was made to carry on the program, but at this point a scuffle began in the rear of the crowd and several pistol shots rang out. Screams, oaths, and general pandemonium followed. Those closest to the assailants pursued them into the street, where Irish reinforcements from the surrounding neighborhood met them with a shower of stones and bricks. A pitched battle ensued, punctuated by sporadic gunfire from the windows of the Hibernia Hose Company and from sundry rooftops and fence holes.

The Irish first had the advantage, in terms of weapons, but the Nativists quickly secured their own stock of firearms, and the contest waxed hot and heavy for over an hour. A kind of skirmish line extended from the market house, stronghold of the Native Americans, up Master Street into the Irish territory. Irish gangs charged down the street and the Natives drove them back, stopping at several houses to break windows and smash furniture. As darkness fell, the Irish at last succeeded in routing their opponents.

Reported casualties were light. Fourteen persons were listed as seriously injured; most of them were Native Americans, as was the sole fatality, an eighteen-year-old apprentice named George Shiffler. Shiffler's death gave the Nativist cause its first martyr. He died, announced the party press, while defending the American flag from papist desecration. In the days and weeks that followed, the Shiffler legend, backed up by an authentic tattered flag, did much to keep alive an intense anti-Catholic feeling among the working classes of Philadelphia.[15]

When the worst of the fighting had ended, Sheriff Morton McMichael arrived on the scene with a fifty-man posse to preserve the peace. The habitual poor timing of the authorities was due in this instance less to official vacillation than to the inherent defects of the posse arrangement. Since it was called into being only as the result of an emergency, the posse seldom functioned well as a preventive police but rather resembled a mopping-up force designed to restore the status quo. Sheriff McMichael, a conscientious Whig journalist-politician, had worked harder than any of his predecessors to improve its effectiveness. Six months earlier McMichael had proposed the creation of a permanent posse to replace the slapdash arrangement then in use. Fifty-four prominent Philadelphians obligingly attended a series of meetings at the sheriff's home on

Liberty Street and passed resolutions setting up a "voluntary posse" of unpaid "good Citizens . . . to serve at the shortest notice, in any and every emergency which in the opinion of the Sheriff may render their aid necessary." By December 4 recruitment was complete, and McMichael had in his hands a detailed organizational chart showing six fully staffed companies of twenty-five men each, on which he might draw in future emergencies.[16] The picture was most impressive on paper, but when the May troubles started the shadow posse never quite materialized. Despite all his prior planning, McMichael found himself still dependent for aid in emergencies on such bystanders as he could find in the area of the State House. Even so, the belated presence of the sheriff's men in Kensington helped to ease tensions for a time. During the rest of the night no other major engagements occurred, although armed gangs of Irishmen and Natives prowled the streets until after midnight.

Dawn brought another sultry day, hot and humid, with temperatures climbing toward eighty degrees. Residents of downtown Philadelphia awoke to find placards posted throughout the city calling upon all Catholics—in the name of their bishop, Francis P. Kenrick—to humble themselves before God, to avoid any further bloodshed, and to cultivate a spirit of charity toward those whom Kenrick termed the "party of persecution." Nativist spokesmen, equally sensitive to the rising tide of public excitement, eschewed forbearance in favor of a mass protest rally to take place in Independence Square at 3:30 P.M. "Let Every Man Come Prepared to Defend Himself," handbills urged. Alarmed at the prospect of renewed large-scale rioting, Sheriff McMichael contacted military authorities early in the day, and General George Cadwalader ordered units of the First Brigade of the Pennsylvania Militia to go on standby alert at 4:30 P.M.[17]

A crowd estimated at between four and six thousand persons assembled for the mid-afternoon meeting to hear speeches from a slate of Nativist politicians and Protestant ministers. The events of the previous day were dramatically recounted and coupled with urgent pleas for political action to stop "aggression by foreigners." By the time the speeches were over popular feeling was running high, and when a motion was made to adjourn, someone in the audience shouted: "Adjourn to Second and Master streets." Others at once took up the cry, and soon a majority of those present were marching north toward Kensington, picking up additional supporters as they moved up Second Street through the intervening Northern Liberties district. The mob reached the Nannygoat Market about five o'clock, planted an American flag, and began an extemporaneous memorial service in honor of George Shiffler. Firing promptly broke out from nearby houses, to inaugurate a new round of rioting. Angry Nativists stormed the Hibernia Hose House, from whose upper windows a handful of snipers fired down on them, as on the previous day. This time the Irishmen were dislodged and their hiding place burned to the ground. Flames soon spread to adjoining houses on the north, threatening a general conflagration. No firemen dared enter the area, and for more than an hour the blaze continued unchecked.

Meanwhile street fighting raged along now familiar lines: gangs of men and boys launched intermittent attacks against houses or rushed headlong toward the sound of gunfire. Young boys in particular were much in evidence, shooting off guns at random as they did on the Fourth of July. "They were seen among the crowds shooting at the people," noted the lawyer-scholar Sidney George Fisher, "several of whom were killed by little fellows scarce able to carry a musket, who laughed and hurra[h]ed when shots were directed at themselves without effect. Women, too, were busy, as in the French Revolution, cheering on the men & carrying weapons to them. These are strange things for Philadelphia. We have never had anything like it before."[18]

The sheriff, after protracted efforts to control the situation, confessed himself beaten and sent for the military. Sometime in the early evening General Cadwalader's brigade arrived but took little direct action against the rioters. Most of the troops were employed to form a cordon around the fire-ravaged neighborhood—"looking passively on," as one eyewitness put it, "and endeavoring to keep the people from rushing forward."[19] Hundreds of curious spectators from other districts made policing more difficult, but under the protection of the military, firemen at last made strenuous efforts to bring the blaze under control. The last fires smouldered until midnight, by which time more than thirty homes had been destroyed, along with the fire station and the neighborhood market. Small military patrols scoured the surrounding streets at intervals to break up any remaining fights, and an artillery corps was detailed to guard

St. Michael's Church, which was rumored to be a major target of Nativist incendiaries. As in the past the military did not use their weapons, although many of their opponents were fully armed. The tactics of forbearance led to a slow reduction in the level of violence, for every attempted arrest of a rioter required a new show of strength from the troops. The streets were not finally cleared until the early morning hours, when peace again descended upon Kensington and all but a few military units were disbanded.

The role of the militia in suppressing Philadelphia's Great Riots has long been a subject of controversy. Critics then and later charged that the volunteers were reluctant to perform their duty, that they secretly sympathized with the rioters, and that their halfhearted efforts at riot control tended, if anything, to encourage the continuance of disorder. Modern sociologists have pointed out that both rioters and militia came from the same socioeconomic background: they were laborers, clerks, artisans, and shopkeepers who shared a common set of class values and assumptions. Every riot situation thus arguably provoked an identity crisis within the ranks of the military; divided counsels and hesitant behavior followed; and in the later stages of the Kensington Riots, some units refused to serve at all.[20]

Without disputing the validity of sociological insights, it is clear that more fundamental factors of an institutional nature were also at work. The commanding officer of the rebellious First Artillery Regiment alluded to them in an official report to his superiors.

> I will merely mention [wrote Colonel A. J. Pleasanton to General Cadwalader] that the discontent in my Regiment at having been kept in a state of inactivity on Tuesday night the 7th instant at Kensington, while they were fired upon from neighboring houses with musketry, and were surrounded by a large assembly of excited men, with arms in their hands, whom they were not directed to disarm or disperse, and while some thirty Buildings were burning before them, and no effort was made to extinguish the fire, or prevent its extension, was so obvious, that I was convinced their Services on any future occasion would not be rendered, unless their officers should take a decided stand for the preservation of their Character and lives.

Pleasanton accordingly refused to order his men into action on

May 8 and 9 to aid the civil authorities, who, he claimed, deprived the troops of their basic right to self-defense by withholding from them the use of deadly force against the rioters. "I was willing to sacrifice myself as an officer, to save the Character and lives of my Command, which I thought to be in jeopardy," he concluded. "A stern and pressing necessity for such conduct, if it does not palliate the military disobedience, is the only reason that I can offer for it."[21]

The episode, a classic instance of civil-military conflict, points up anew the thorny legal issues surrounding early efforts at urban riot control. Technically, when the militia was called out for riot duty, it acted as part of the sheriff's posse and was subject to the overriding authority of the sheriff or mayor. For any acts unauthorized by the civil authorities, soldiers were liable to prosecution in the civil courts. The limits of military power were thus spelled out in clear-cut fashion, but it was far otherwise with the hapless magistrates.

Unlike their English cousins, Americans had no Riot Act or other statute defining the authority of the sheriff to put down riots. (Even here McMichael had tried to fill the gap. In the winter of 1844 he went before the Pennsylvania Assembly to urge the passage of effective riot control legislation, but the lawmakers declined to act.)[22] Under the common law, of course, it was arguable that peace officers already had all the power they could possibly want—and then some. Judges had long recognized that a magistrate might lawfully employ all "necessary force" to suppress public disturbances. But this deceptively simple formula opened up a Pandora's box of difficulties in practice. It left everything to the unguided discretion of the magistrate, who alone had to determine the proper degree of force that each situation called for. As elected officeholders neither the sheriff nor the mayor relished such intuitive decision making. Both were painfully aware of the consequences that might flow from a wrong guess, but whichever way they turned abysses yawned. Theirs was a "most delicate position," commented Sidney Fisher in 1844:

> If a mob occurs & is successful in its attempts, [the magistrate] is blamed by all. If he resists by military force & life is sacrificed, he is sure of encountering the most furious persecution from the party of rioters, their friends and adherents. His conduct is also certain to be seized upon for the purpose of electioneering influence & to be

grossly misrepresented. He will be made the object of incessant, unsparing, cruel abuse in newspapers and mob speeches, and may think himself very lucky if he escape indictment in a criminal court & punishment, for a jury are sure to sympathize with the mob & a Governor always takes the popular side.[23]

Faced with such unsavory prospects, most officials tried to walk a perilous tightrope between appeasement and repression. The vacillating policy pursued by municipal authorities added to the uncertainties of mob action and smoothed the way for the vicious church burnings that climaxed the third, and final, day of the Kensington Riots.

That day—Wednesday, May 8—began quietly enough. Militia detachments still policed the strife-torn suburb and assisted the sheriff in a house-to-house search for firearms. Toward noon crowds again gathered in the streets, including many mere curiosity seekers, as on the previous day. Anti-Irish threats were renewed, and the troops were kept busy answering distress calls—false alarms, for the most part, although a few scattered fires were set. By the early afternoon hundreds of Irish Catholics, fearful of their safety, were evacuating the district. "We observed," reported one Nativist source, "women and children piled high upon furniture cars upon their goods, apparently delighted to escape the scenes of turmoil and bloodshed which presented themselves to their eyes, for the last three days." Nativist householders took their own precautions against an anticipated renewal of mob action. Some displayed the American flag for protection; others scrawled the words "Native American" on their doors with charcoal, or posted the latest issue of the "Native American" newspaper.[24]

Around 2:30 P.M. the militia guarding St. Michael's Church moved out to investigate a reported disturbance several blocks away, and during their absence incendiaries set fire to the building. There had been unfounded rumors of a large arms cache in the church, and for its greater protection the pastor had left it in the exclusive care of the military. Thousands of impassive spectators reportedly watched the rapid spread of the flames. By three o'clock St. Michael's was a smoking ruin, its spire and cross collapsing last, to the accompaniment of scattered cheers from the crowd. "To hell with the Pope and O'Connell!" some shouted, while others struck up the "Boyne

Water," the favorite battle song of the Irish Orangemen.[25] There was no fighting on this occasion, however, and firemen were permitted to go about their work unmolested. Apparently no effort was made to save the church or the adjoining rectory, but most of the surrounding buildings were spared. During the rest of the afternoon both militia and firemen had to contend with repeated fire alarms, and several other buildings in scattered locations, including a Catholic convent, burned to the ground before help arrived.

News of the destruction of St. Michael's reached downtown Philadelphia in short order, along with the rumor that plans were afoot to burn St. Augustine's and other city churches later in the day. The prospect of an impending invasion from Kensington created a sensation, especially among the lower classes. Catholic residents in the immediate vicinity of St. Augustine's hastily packed up their belongings and fled the area. In the city's factories and shops workers refused to continue at their jobs, and all manufacturing establishments closed their doors at 4:30 P.M., an hour and a half ahead of the normal quitting time. This had the effect of pouring into the streets some of the most troublesome members of the urban underclass and giving them a head start in harassment.

Before dusk crowds began to gather in front of St. Augustine's Church, at Fourth and Vine streets. They were not a very fearsome lot at the outset, to judge from the account of a Catholic eyewitness:

> These were not the men who had burned St. Michael's; they, although they had cried—"to St. Augustine's"—"to St. Joseph's"— "to St. Mary's,"—had gone home to get their supper,—to have their wounds dressed,—to rest from their (thank God!) unusual labors. These were, at first, principally men and boys, hobble-de-hoys, drawn together by curiosity. A more pitiable, cowardly set it would be hard to find. "Look out, I see an Irishman's head," in shrill voice of a ragged urchin, would send them to Third, to Race, to Vine Street, to return again to be again startled and started by an old woman from the bonny braes, crying out: "O'ch! Jemmy, I'm blest if I didn't see a big man wid a musket looking a'out that windy in the cupoly."[26]

Prompt action by the authorities—employing only a small force of regular police—might have dispersed the crowd easily

at any time prior to seven o'clock, when substantial reinforcements arrived from Kensington. But Mayor John Morin Scott,
the city's primary law enforcement officer, did not act. Fussily
presiding over a birthday celebration for his youngest daughter,
Scott ignored the gradual buildup of mob strength for almost
two hours. Only after all the streets leading to the church had
become jammed with spectators did he call out a strong force of
police and proceed in person to the scene.

He arrived around eight o'clock in a hansom cab, the mob
making way for him when he shouted his name. A dense mass
of people surrounded the church, which was filled with armed
Irishmen who threatened to shoot any attackers. Scott climbed
to the top of his cab and addressed the crowd briefly, ordering
them to go home and let the proper authorities handle the situation. He then entered the church to confer with its defenders. At
his urging the Catholics agreed to lay down their weapons and
move out, leaving the mayor and his police to protect the
church property in the name of the city. Scott accepted the keys
of the church, locked the front door, and opened a new dialogue with the mob.

While his police stationed themselves in a skirmish line behind
him, the mayor reasoned with crowd leaders, showed them the
keys, answered their questions. Neither threats nor entreaties
produced much effect, however. In time sullen mutterings all
but drowned out Scott's remarks as some members of his audience, tired of further negotiation, began to hurl bricks and
stones at the church windows. The First City Troop of Cavalry,
summoned in haste by the sheriff, begged for permission to
arrest or shoot the rioters, but the mayor refused to give the
orders. The troopers accordingly did no more than gallop down
the street at intervals, their erratic forays tending rather to
encourage the general excitement.[27] A stalemate prevailed
between mayor and mob for about twenty minutes, until a
resourceful teenager managed to sneak into the church through
a side window and set fire to the curtains. At the sight of the
blaze a shout went up and the crowd redoubled its rock
throwing, driving the mayor and his police from the ground in a
shower of missiles.

The flames from the burning building attracted attention for
miles. A young West Pointer, who watched the blaze from the
rooftop of a friend's house, noted: "the conflagration lighted up
the Delaware river and adjacent shores, and the Shipping, the

Factories at Gloucester Point could be distinctly seen. It was truly a magnificent sight." Northeast of the church the heat was so intense during the height of the fire that spectators several blocks away declared they could hardly bear to look at it; the brilliance of the light, they said, dimmed even the gas lamps.[28]

Firemen were again permitted to play their hoses on neighboring buildings, but the entire church property—including an adjacent school and monastery—went up in flames. Particularly disheartening to ecclesiastical authorities was the loss of St. Augustine's valuable theological library, a collection of five thousand volumes, many of which were irreplaceable. Threats were made against other city churches, but the military were alerted and stationed strong detachments of men at each location to forestall further violence.

At 11:30 P.M. a dispirited mayor called the city councils into emergency session to map out a crisis strategy. The meeting continued through the rest of the night, but beyond appropriating $20,000 for additional police expenses the group made little headway. Dawn found them still unable to agree on a common plan of action, until, weary and worried, they did what Philadelphia's leaders had long been accustomed to do in times of trouble: they sent for Horace Binney.

Binney, at sixty-four, was a living legend in his hometown. Residents proudly pointed him out to visitors as one of the city's stellar attractions, worthy to be mentioned in the same breath with the Fairmount Waterworks and Wonderly Butter. Handsome and austere, with courtly ways and a commanding presence, Binney exuded a spirit of eighteenth-century certitude that younger men found irresistible. As a boy he had grown up on the same block where Washington and Hamilton lived, and something of their imperious style clung to him ever after. He early established his reputation as a brilliant lawyer serving the commercial and maritime interests of the city and condescended, after much urging by his friends, to sit for a term in the state legislature and later in the House of Representatives. But politics in the larger sense held few charms for Binney, compared to the satisfaction he derived from professional service on the municipal level. Unlike the younger generation of merchants and lawyers, who begrudged time given to civic projects, Binney immersed himself in urban affairs with zest. To him the law still meant noblesse oblige—a stern duty to superintend the less favored nonlawyers of mankind—and from that duty he never shrank. While he retired from active practice at the age of fifty, he continued to devote his best energies to the betterment of the city that he loved: a city that had already supplied him with a tidy fortune of half a million dollars. He served as elder statesman to every city administration, sat on numerous municipal boards, headed the subscription lists for all important charities and cultural enterprises—became, in short, the acknowledged grand old man of Philadelphia, as truly the father of his city as George Washington was reputed to be the father of the nation.

Summoned early on May 9 to advise the municipal authorities about riot control, Binney found City Hall in a state of near panic. "I shall never forget the appearance of the Council chamber when I entered it," he later remarked.

There were perhaps five and twenty in the Council chamber. Mr. Meredith, the president of the Select Council, was there, the Attorney-General, Mr. Josiah Randall, and some others. I never saw a body of more unresolved men. One or two of them had countenances a little below this. They looked as if they were excessively puzzled. I believe there was no formal organization of the meeting, but I started some irregular talk by asking whether any person had anything to suggest or to say in regard to the occasion of the meeting. The Attorney General and one or two others said a word or two, which looked to getting assistance elsewhere, and to the responsibility of meeting the violence of the mob in the only way effectually. I replied that assistance from other quarters might be very useful, but that if we did not mean to be unworthy of it we must assist ourselves immediately; and that as to the responsibility of resisting a mob in the very degree, however severe and extreme, which their designs and violence made necessary, I had as little hesitation about encountering it as I had [doubt] of the ability of the citizens with their own hands to make the resistance effectual. It was immediately moved by some one to appoint a committee to prepare resolutions to be submitted to a town meeting, which I then for the first time heard was to meet in the State-House [yard] at ten o'clock, it being now about half-after nine. The committee was appointed, myself as chairman, and we immediately retired to a committee room, two or three of my friends, as I passed along, saying that the meeting would agree to anything I would propose. The resolutions which I drew up were short and plain; they did not ask for any help but from ourselves; they recommended the immediate enrolling of the citizens in each ward under the command of the civil authority of the ward; and they asserted the legal right, for the protection of property and life, to resist and to defeat the mob by the use of any degree of force that was necessary for this purpose.[29]

An estimated audience of ten thousand persons cheered Binney's resolutions at the mid-morning meeting, and volunteers hastened to enroll in the new companies of Peace Police being organized by the aldermen of each ward. Every recruit wore a badge of white cloth wrapped around his hat and carried a musket supplied by the state arsenal. The Peace Police patrolled the streets of their respective wards nightly for almost a week, until all threats of further mob attacks had subsided. As civilian adjuncts of the militia, these local vigilantes more than satisfied Binney's desire for a respectable home guard—especially since it was widely understood that they would not hesitate to shoot down the first rioters they encountered.

But even the regular forces of law and order were now prepared for bloodshed, according to reliable spokesmen. Once Binney's Olympian dictum on force had cleared the air, state and local officials went even further in endorsing the principle of legalized violence. Attorney General Ovid Johnson advised the mayor and the sheriff that they might henceforth treat all rioters as "open public enemies or pirates," and Governor David R. Porter adopted an equally tough line when he arrived in the city to take personal charge of antiriot operations. Taking the lives of offenders was preferable to a continuance of such "disgraceful outrages," the governor declared, in ordering the immediate mobilization of the entire First Division of the Pennsylvania Militia. "Relying upon the patriotism of the citizen soldier, who is thus called upon in the hour of peril to protect the institutions of his country from assault, the Commander in Chief is confident that no soldier will under any circumstances, fail to discharge his whole duty, and to preserve his own and his country's honor untarnished."[30]

Porter and Major General Robert Patterson set up their headquarters in the Girard Bank, and for several days volunteer companies from the country poured in to swell the ranks of the militia, turning Philadelphia into a garrison town. The massive buildup of armed strength, coupled with a strict nine o'clock curfew, brought a prompt, if uneasy, calm to the city. Only Catholic residents continued to feel woefully insecure as anonymous threats against churches and individuals persisted. Most of the clergy had fled or gone into hiding, and on Friday Bishop Kenrick, fearful of more trouble, ordered the temporary suspension of all public worship in the Catholic churches of the area. Kenrick's cautious stance, though criticized by many well-wishers, probably helped to win additional public support for the cause of peaceful coexistence. Over the weekend tensions visibly declined, and on Sunday the riot sites were thronged with no more dangerous types than ordinary sightseers. "It is estimated that at least ten thousand persons were on the ground [at St. Augustine's]," reported one journalist, "drawn there from motives of curiosity. Numbers with their families have visited the spot in cabs and private carriages."[31]

So far as the general community was concerned, the May riots did little to alter preexisting attitudes. Although citizens and soldiers joined forces at last to put down the mob, they acted rather to protect imperiled property interests than to vindicate the constitutional rights of an unpopular minority. Binney, for instance, took little notice of the riots until he saw the smoke of St. Augustine's from his own door a few blocks away. The church burnings themselves were universally condemned in the public prints, but privately many civic leaders continued to voice strong Nativist sentiments. The Quaker owner of the largest dry goods store in Philadelphia, a prominent exponent of religious toleration, remarked, in the hearing of a clerk: "The Papists deserve all this and much more . . . It were well if every Popish church in the world were levelled with the ground."[32]

To the lower classes George Shiffler remained a potent symbol. Workingmen in large numbers attended Shiffler's final rites and viewed the now historic tattered flag that draped his coffin. Concerts were given for the benefit of the surviving Shiffler family; a ship built exclusively by American labor was dedicated to George and the other Nativist dead; and, to crown all other demonstrations, the newly formed Shiffler Hose Company perpetuated his memory with a vengeance at every fire in Kensington.

More subtle influences, too, threatened the future peace of the city. Binney's Peace Police introduced the elite classes to the positive attractions of violence, and they did not forget the lesson easily. Although no actual encounters took place between rioters and peace patrols, alarms were frequent, and the heady sensations of the night watch left even the most blasé participants with a vague longing for more. "I began rather to like the excitement," confessed one young man who had joined a special company of lawyers to avoid the "many low people" in the ward associations. "It was an interruption to the usual dull monotony of life here, and produced emotions which varied the blank of Philadelphia existence. The mind easily adapts itself to new scenes & changes of condition, and I believe in a little while the life of a soldier would seem very natural & pleasant."[33] Such thinking permeated upper-class circles in the aftermath of the riots, tinged with regret that the municipal authorities had not forced a showdown with the mob, whatever the cost in lives.

Official inquiries into the causes of the late disturbances began immediately and merely confirmed the prevailing views of the community. A grand jury convened in regular session on May 6 undertook the most elaborate investigation. For thirty-six days the panel heard testimony from a parade of witnesses, almost all of whom were Nativist in their sympathies. The result was an ex parte document filed in mid-June that placed the blame for recent occurrences squarely on the Catholic party. The riots had their origin in the school question, according to the report, which scored "the efforts of a portion of the community to exclude the Bible from our Public Schools." Out of this controversy had emerged the Native American party, whose protest meeting in Kensington provoked a wanton attack by "a band of lawless irresponsible men, some of whom had resided in our country only a short period." The initial act of Irish aggression opened the door to all subsequent violence. While the grand jury went on to condemn everyone who had participated to any degree in the riots, the main thrust of its argument was reassuring to old-stock Americans: the basic guilt, it appeared, lay with foreign-born agitators.[34]

Judge John R. Jones expounded the same thesis with even greater vehemence a few weeks later at one of the early trials of accused rioters. The ultimate sources of urban unrest, he told a common pleas jury, were idle vagabonds, criminals, and foreigners: "Foreigners especially, used at home to a military police, taught by long oppression to regard all laws as tyranny, and all officers of the law as enemies, and feeling none of the American interest of self government, are a constant element of disorder." While there were good individuals among the foreign-born, the judge declared, in the mass they were an unruly lot.[35]

Such statements go far to explain the meager record of convictions for crimes growing out of the Kensington Riots. Although the grand jury brought indictments against seventy-two persons, all but a handful were eventually acquitted. Of the nine or ten who did face prison terms, most bore Irish names. Sheriff McMichael and the police magistrate of Kensington faced negligence charges for their handling of the riot situation, but a trial court promptly exonerated them.[36]

The Irish had their own version of the May troubles, of course, and they were not backward in bringing it to public attention. On June 20 a group of Catholic laymen headed by U.S. District Judge Archibald Randall launched a vigorous counterblast to the grand jury probe. Claiming to speak for a local community of sixty thousand coreligionists, Randall's committee denounced the grand jury's presentment for its alleged bias and innuendo. In a carefully documented pamphlet of twelve pages, the Catholic partisans sought to prove that the Church had never tried to exclude the Bible from the schools but only to place a Catholic version in the hands of Catholic students. Moreover, they asserted, there was no Catholic voting bloc; priests exercised no influence over their congregations in nonreligious matters; and the Kensington Irish had not been the aggressors in the early fighting. The real issue was a constitutional one: the protection of minority rights against the demands of an intolerant majority. As Americans and Philadelphians, Catholics claimed for themselves the full guarantees of religious freedom contained in the Pennsylvania Constitution: "We are willing that the principle [of majority rule] should be applied to all things wherein public interest and order are concerned, saving always those principles and rights which the Constitution holds to be inviolable. We are the minority; and for us, therefore, does the Constitution exist . . . UNDER NO CIRCUMSTANCES IS CONSCIENCE AT THE DISPOSAL OF A MAJORITY."[37] An eloquent plea, which conveniently ignored the grand jury's equally impassioned defense of the right of peaceable assembly.

Between these two extreme positions individual pamphleteers carried on their own idiosyncratic warfare, borrowing now from one side, now from the other. The most interesting of these middle-of-the-road efforts was contained in a lengthy anonymous publication titled *The Truth Unveiled*. The author identified himself as a third-generation Philadelphian, a Protestant, and the scion of a family long prominent in public affairs. Through an ingenious bit of analysis he managed to balance a commendable sympathy for the Irish against a deeply felt need to assuage the guilt feelings of the respectable urban middle classes. While he did not minimize the incidence of Irish aggression, he argued that Catholics were driven to violent tactics by the vehemence of the Protestant crusade and the daily slanders of the Nativist press. Furthermore, he charged, the Nativist leaders were themselves "foreign-born" agitators: "an immigration of adventurers from other States, and particularly from the Eastern." These non-Philadelphians had forced their views upon the old-stock natives and succeeded at last in corrupting the Quaker tradition of tolerance. The thesis gave a novel twist to Nativist clichés, but few were prepared to heed its humane message.[38]

Through the month of June the battle of words rumbled on, keeping up a cold war that some observers feared might grow hot again at any moment. Bishop Kenrick—ever the Cassandra —warned the laity on June 27 to hold no more public meetings and to be particularly circumspect in their behavior over the Fourth of July holiday. "I am convinced that the enemies of our faith have not given up the idea of attack and given the occasion they will try to destroy us and our faith," Kenrick wrote to his brother. "It is sad to think of these things for we have no safety in the law or in the magistrates who administer the law."[39]

But even as he fretted one magistrate was taking positive precautions of his own to guarantee the public peace. On June 28 Sheriff McMichael went back to his paper work and came up with a new plan for augmenting the strength of his posse. In a confidential circular letter the sheriff instructed the aldermen of each ward to sign up "reliable citizens" to serve as Civic Police in case of an emergency. The recruitment must be managed quietly, he cautioned; there was no need to alarm the general public, but he feared some disturbance over the holiday weekend from "the present excited state of popular feeling."[40]

Thus, as the anniversary of national independence approached, both civic and religious authorities braced themselves for a possible storm. As matters turned out, they were not disappointed.

The Native Americans predictably chose the Fourth of July to stage a massive demonstration of strength. In the afternoon a parade of forty-five hundred men and boys representing every ward association moved slowly out Chestnut Street with flags and banners flying. The most eye-catching display depicted the Catholic church in the guise of a huge serpent coiled menacingly around the American flag. George Shiffler and the other Kensington martyrs were also prominently represented, the inevitable tattered flag was much in evidence, and Nativists wounded in the May riots occupied a special place of honor atop a float. The procession culminated at Fisher's Woods north of the city, where a giant rally and picnic were held. Despite the intense partisan excitement generated by the occasion the entire affair came off without incident.

In the early hours of the following morning, however, a cleanup crew that had slept on the ground overnight was attacked and beaten by a gang of hoodlums. Rumor promptly credited the Irish with the assault, but this minor affray was soon overshadowed in Nativist eyes by a more flagrant example of popish aggressiveness: the stockpiling of arms in a South Side church in broad daylight. Eyewitnesses in suburban Southwark reported they had seen a load of muskets being carried into the church of St. Philip de Neri, and for once the tale proved accurate. Like its Kensington counterparts St. Philip's was located in a working-class neighborhood, close to docks, mills, and factories. Here, too, a large Irish population rubbed elbows uneasily with numbers of old-stock Americans. The church, although established only in 1841, had become a local storm center through the bombastic preaching of its pastor, Father John Patrick Dunn, whose anti-Protestant tirades were more than a match for the APA. Dunn had been threatened during the May riots, and his brother had secured permission from the governor to organize a company of armed volunteers for the defense of the church. The Philadelphia Arsenal supplied the Irishmen with a stock of little-used firearms, a dozen of which proved so defective that they had to be sent out at once for repairs. By a fatal mischance the job was not completed until Friday, July 5, when the delivery of the weapons to the church basement gave rise to talk of a new papist conspiracy. (Ironically, the fear of armed aggression at the time was even stronger on the Catholic side. A female parishioner of St. Philip's claimed to have overheard a Protestant arson plot, and one hundred fifty anxious men camped in the church throughout the night of July 4 waiting for an attack that never came.)[41]

As news of a Catholic arms cache spread through the neighborhood small knots of men and boys began to gather in front of St. Philip's. By nightfall a sizable crowd had collected, and the local police magistrate sent an urgent call for help to the sheriff. McMichael hurried to the scene, pausing en route at General Patterson's house to alert the military. An angry mob confronted the sheriff on his arrival and threatened to demolish the church unless every weapon was removed immediately. Taking with him the two aldermen of the district, McMichael conducted an impromptu official search that turned up the twelve unloaded muskets delivered earlier in the day. These he confiscated and showed to the crowd before depositing them for safekeeping in the Southwark Commissioners Hall. But the mob remained unappeased, insisting that many more weapons were still concealed on the premises. Reluctant to make a further search that night, McMichael deputized twenty men from the neighborhood to guard the building and reassure local residents that nothing would be tampered with until a full investigation could be launched the following day.

This cooling-down tactic was unhappily sabotaged by the posse itself. After listening to an inflammatory harangue from Wright Ardis, one of the leading Kensington rioters, the twenty deputies resolved to make an independent search of their own, over the sheriff's objections. This time the church was thoroughly ransacked and the suspected hoard unearthed: fifty-three muskets, ten pistols, a keg of powder, and a box of cartridges. Making the best of a bad situation, McMichael armed his posse with twenty of the muskets and ordered the rest of the cache taken to Commissioners Hall. The crowd now began to disperse; a militia company arrived to take possession of the church; and by midnight quiet returned to Southwark.

Rumors of additional undiscovered arms started up the next morning, however, and combined with the continued presence of the military to spark fresh troubles. General Cadwalader, on a mid-afternoon reconnaissance in the vicinity of St. Philip's, encountered numbers of sullen loiterers who greeted him with shouts of "Irish Cadwalader!" and "Bloody Cadwalader!" when he ordered them to move along. Street activity increased from hour to hour as nervous householders for several blocks either abandoned their homes or hung American flags in their windows for protection.

At dusk the sheriff arrived from the city with a posse of 115 men—the saving remnant from the 600 Civic Police he had notified earlier in the day. Backed up by five additional militia companies, the posse moved to clear the streets adjacent to the church, acting as a buffer force between the soldiers and the populace. The strategy worked well enough for a time. Queen Street, on which St. Philip's fronted, was slowly cleared, as were the intersections at Second and Third Streets. A cannon was placed at each of these locations to guard the main approaches to the church. Then the military took over, charging the densely packed throngs on Second and Third with platoons of mounted men. The crowd on Second Street broke and ran, but those on Third stood their ground and hurled a barrage of stones at their attackers. Goaded to fury, General Cadwalader threatened to turn the cannon on them, but, he reported, "they cried out, 'fire and be d--d,' and continued throwing stones at us."[42]

At this critical juncture, after preliminary firing orders had been given, ex-Congressman Charles Naylor, one of the sheriff's posse, stepped melodramatically before the cannon's mouth and protested that the general had no authority to fire on the crowd. Promptly arrested, Naylor was whisked off to the church, where all prisoners taken during the evening were being held under military guard. His last-minute interference gave both sides a breathing spell and forestalled a decisive showdown between the militia and the mob. Unwilling to test Cadwalader a second time, the crowd gradually broke up, vowing to return and tear the church apart if Naylor were not released the following day. Around 2:00 A.M. a definite lull set in, but it was not until four o'clock that the sheriff decided it was at last safe to return home for a few hours' rest. Three militia companies—including the Hibernia Greens, an Irish unit—remained to guard the church and its prisoners.

By 8:00 A.M. Sunday the streets were again astir with people. George Roberts of Northern Liberties visited the area along with other sightseers and recorded some vivid impressions of a mob in the making:

I approached the place by Third Street; large crowds at all the corners of the adjacent streets; those crowds somewhat remote from the building composed of decenter material—but those near. the church composed of the worst class of mankind, the very dregs of the canaille of a large city, a great number of boys . . . this was the same class [that rioted in Kensington in May]; men drunk with liquor and devilishness, boys of 16 to 21, of the most insubordinate and lawless character, insane almost with love of devastation, and others looking respectable, but entirely passive . . . Great discussion of law, rights, liberty, &c., in relation to the arrests that had been made the night before, with a large display of ignorance, malice, with every species of denunciation and avowal of revenge directed against certain persons who were in the church and holding certain persons in custody; whether they were military or civil I could not know, and could get no information.[43]

Around mid-morning, as Naylor was still detained in the church, a group of some forty men and boys dragged a dusty four-pound cannon up to the front door and prepared to fire. Wet priming prevented the charge from igniting, but another group then seized a beam and broke open a side door. The militia handed over their prisoners without resistance, and Naylor was carried off by a cheering crowd to his home in the city.

Afterward the victorious mob returned with two more cannon. These they loaded with large pieces of iron and fired in desultory fashion at the rear of the church. The intermittent bombardment terrified the neighborhood but did little damage to the building. Meanwhile, in front of St. Philip's, editor Lewis Levin and other Native American leaders tried to calm the crowd and prevent further violence. At length an agreement was reached: if the Hibernia Greens moved out at once, the mob would spare the church. A few minutes later the front doors opened and the Irish volunteers, flanked by one of the two remaining militia companies, marched out into the crowd.

There was immediate pushing and shoving from all sides as the Greens were alternately heckled and pelted with stones and bricks. After two and a half blocks of such harassment several Irishmen lost their nerve completely. Convinced that they would never leave Southwark alive, they snatched up their muskets (which were supposed to be unloaded) and fired wildly into the crowd. A general hubbub ensued, with militiamen scattering in all directions and the mob in hot pursuit. Most of the soldiers escaped with minor injuries; only one (an Irishman) was severely beaten by his pursuers, and even he went on to live to a ripe old age.

The rout of the Hibernia Greens played into the hands of

militant rioters and led to a fresh attack upon St. Philip's. Over the objections of Levin and other moderates the mob battered down a part of the side wall and brushed past the few remaining defenders. For several hours large crowds milled about inside, searching every nook and cranny, breaking up furniture, and setting small fires, which Levin and his friends managed to extinguish. By five o'clock the moderates had largely succeeded in regaining control of the situation. They emptied the church of all but a few stragglers and set up a Committee of Forty to protect the building from any further intruders. At that point it seemed the worst was over; even the crowd outside showed definite signs of breaking up.[44] But hopes for peace dimmed abruptly when news arrived from the city that a large force of militia was marching on Southwark to restore order. The dispatch of the military, it is clear in retrospect, acted as a lever to impel the drama forward to its bloody denouement.

The authorities in Philadelphia, unfortunately, had little inkling of the true state of affairs in Southwark. All sorts of conflicting rumors circulated throughout the day, but by mid-afternoon several things at least were certain: the rioters were armed; they had forcibly removed a number of prisoners from military custody; and they had driven three militia companies from the church they were ordered to defend. To civil and military leaders alike these developments spelled mob rule. "The City and County of Philadelphia are at present in a state of insurgency," Sheriff McMichael informed the governor after drafting two proclamations for immediate release to the public. The first called upon every able-bodied citizen to report at once to the sheriff for posse duty; the second declared that since the Southwark rioters had resorted to firearms they must now be considered "in open rebellion to the laws, and will be dealt with as traitors and insurgents." McMichael had learned his lesson in the May disturbances. If public opinion demanded a tough line from law officers, he would not be found wanting a second time.[45]

But as usual mobilizing a posse proved no easy task. ("The weather was extremely hot," recalled one resident, and "the solemn sound of the tolling bell had a most melancholy effect" on the nerves.)[46] Only six or eight men answered the summons, but by late afternoon the sheriff managed through personal exertions to impress about sixty bystanders into service. When some protested that they would not face an armed foe with no other weapon than a night stick, McMichael hurriedly requisitioned a supply of fifty muskets and sent a majority of his posse off to join General Cadwalader, who was preparing to move out with a force of 165 militiamen.

Around 6:00 P.M., when marching orders had already been given, one of the Southwark committee arrived with an urgent plea to the sheriff to call off the expedition. A group of responsible Nativists was now in possession of St. Philip's, he explained, and would guarantee its future security. "They wanted to stipulate with me that the church should be left to them, and that the military should not go down," McMichael later testified to a grand jury, adding, "the military were then in motion."[47]

Had the sheriff listened to his anxious informant, much violence might have been averted. But in fact the chances of a peaceful settlement had been foreclosed several hours earlier, when McMichael, Attorney General Ovid Johnson, and military leaders all agreed that this time the mob must be taught a lesson. The combined civil-military force that moved on Southwark in the early twilight accordingly resembled an avenging army, bent on reprisals. Its nominal objective was simply the retaking of St. Philip's Church from the lawless elements (that is, the Committee of Forty) that still occupied it, but in the event of forcible resistance those in charge made it clear that this time there would be no nonsense about the use of counterforce. Commanding General Robert Patterson expressly instructed his subordinate officers to open fire on the rioters at the first signs of trouble.[48]

And trouble there was—almost as soon as the troops had reached their destination. The Committee of Forty gave up the church to Cadwalader without protest, but the street crowds were far less obliging. They stubbornly resisted all efforts by the military to drive them back down Queen Street, and a lively scuffle broke out at the Second Street intersection between rock-throwing rioters and a detachment of City Guards. During the fracas Captain Hill, the commanding officer, was disarmed and knocked to the ground, where a rioter attacked him with his own sword. At that point his lieutenant gave the order to fire. The crowd broke, screaming, in all directions, leaving seven men dead and others wounded. Several of the casualties, it turned out, were passive onlookers who had taken no part in the actual fighting. The Guards fired two more volleys—one up and one down Second Street—before falling back to form a skirmish line that sealed off the east end of Queen. Another platoon stretched across the Third Street intersection, barring access to the church from the west. Then a temporary lull set in while the troops waited uneasily for the mob to make the next move.

When it came, it was spectacular. At about nine o'clock, under cover of darkness, a gang of sailors and dockworkers pushed a cannon stealthily up Sixth Street from the wharf. Their approach was unsuspected: the cannon wheels were muffled, the gas lights in the immediate vicinity extinguished in advance. At the Queen Street corner one man lit a slow-burning fuse; then the others ran the piece round into position and discharged it straight at the line of soldiers who stood clearly silhouetted under the lamps. The first salvo killed two men (the only militia fatalities of the evening) and wounded several others. Before the stunned troops could retaliate the rioters had seized the dragropes and pulled their piece back into the darkness, to be reloaded with another miscellaneous charge of nails, iron scraps, knives, chains, broken bottles, and any other projectiles that came to hand. The maneuver was repeated intermittently for the next three or four hours, the mob making use of three different cannon and firing from widely scattered locations.

Meanwhile other rioters broke into the Commissioners Hall and seized the muskets taken earlier from St. Philip's. Armed snipers then positioned themselves in alleyways and atop surrounding buildings, from which they carried on a nagging (if largely ineffectual) guerrilla warfare. In some instances women and children joined them on the rooftops, hurling stones and hot water on the exposed militiamen below. For more than an hour the military made little headway against their hit-and-run assailants. When cavalry units tried to charge the darkened byways, horses tripped over unseen ropes and their fallen riders were pelted with rocks and other missiles. Substantial reinforcements, including two new field pieces, arrived about 10:00 P.M., however, and from then on the tide began to turn in favor of the embattled militia. In the early hours of the morning the troops seized the last of the mob's cannon; the sporadic sniping died out; and the exhausted militiamen stretched themselves on the pavement for a few hours' rest.

Military losses, considering the duration and intensity of the engagement, were surprisingly light: two dead and nineteen wounded, according to General Cadwalader's official count.[49] Much more damaging to troop morale was the unexpected backlash in public opinion that accompanied a full disclosure of the night's operations. As reports of the slaughter of inoffensive civilians circulated through the city, Philadelphians of all classes joined in condemning the militia for overreacting to the riot situation and for using deadly force against rock-throwing opponents. Popular indignation at alleged military brutality was further whetted by sensational journalistic accounts that described in lurid detail the scene of the conflict: "All along Queen Street, above and below the church for some distance, presented a truly warlike appearance. Window shutters, doors, fronts of houses, trees, tree-boxes, awning posts, lamp posts, pumps, watchboxes, and signs, are all pierced with balls and shot; and the pavements, gutters, streets, steps, and doorjambs stained with blood. In some places it flowed down the gutters."[50]

The abrupt withdrawal of public confidence left Cadwalader's forces stranded in St. Philip's Church like a garrison under siege. On Monday morning General Patterson found that he could secure no relief troops locally. The volunteer companies of the area uniformly refused to turn out for duty in Southwark, and the sheriff was no more successful in mustering a civilian relief group. Urgent appeals were dispatched to President Tyler and Governor Porter for outside military aid, but meanwhile alarming rumors spread that the mob was rapidly gaining in strength and would likely launch a new offensive before any sizable reinforcements could arrive.

While city authorities fretted with uncertainty a mass meeting took place at Southwark's Wharton Market, the control center for mob operations during the previous evening. Angry resolutions were passed demanding the immediate removal of all militia from the district but once again moderate Nativists volunteered to try for a last-minute settlement. Acting in the name of the meeting, a delegation approached Sheriff McMichael with an offer: if the troops were removed, the Nativists themselves would guarantee to keep the peace in Southwark. True to form, the sheriff refused even to consider the proposition, coming as it did from so tainted a source.

But Southwark officials, caught in the eye of the storm, took a different view. In the early afternoon a committee of district commissioners met with McMichael and General Patterson to report that the *civil authorities* were now prepared to maintain order without further military assistance. The subterfuge was transparent enough: once again the sheriff and the general were being invited to capitulate to the Southwark masses. But this time at least the pill was sugarcoated, and in the absence of needed reinforcements the two commanders gratefully gulped it down. After a show of grave deliberation they yielded to official entreaty and ordered the militia back to Philadelphia.

General Cadwalader and his men left St. Philip's for the last time around 4:00 P.M., with what must have been considerable feelings of relief. "They had gone thro a severe contest, in intensely hot weather, & had been without food or drink for 24 hours," noted a sympathetic observer. "If again attacked, they would probably have been massacred, as they had not even the strength to make good a retreat."[51] No incident, however, marred their orderly evacuation from Southwark, which signaled the end of violence in the district.

Although no fresh disturbances broke out thereafter, a crisis mentality prevailed in Philadelphia for several weeks. Governor Porter arrived in the city on Monday afternoon to announce that he had sent for militia units from seven neighboring counties. Again the streets bristled with bayonets, as a force of nearly five thousand men assembled to do battle with a nonexistent enemy. Porter's unqualified defense of military tactics—the use of force in riot situations, he declared, "becomes as much an act of patriotism as of duty"[52]—left no doubt of his response to further disorders. But accompanying the threat of stepped-up military operations went another shift in public opinion that robbed potential rioters of the moral support they had temporarily received from the community. For this psychological volte-face—which brought citizens and soldiers together once more in a solid defense of the established order—Horace Binney's forensic talents were largely responsible.

"The citizens seemed to be getting all wrong upon the question [of riot control]," Binney grumbled to his diary in the aftermath of the July bloodshed, "and had they gone completely over, neither the men nor the Churches would have been safe. No one would have perilled his life again to suppress such rioters, if the first who devoted themselves were permitted to fall a sacrifice."[53] Many of Philadelphia's elite shared similar apprehensions. In response a group of business and professional men gathered at Evans' Hotel on July 10 to voice approval of the measures that had been taken to put down the recent riots. Binney's lawyer son, Horace, Jr., chaired the meeting, which voted to present a testimonial address to the governor. At the request of those present, the elder Binney agreed to draw up a strong statement of "correct principles" to be submitted to the general public for signatures. Two hours later he reported back with a lengthy document that all agreed was admirably calculated to rally the "friends of order and law."

Binney's argument—a hard-hitting brief in defense of the militia—was classic in its simplicity. Ignoring all questions of underlying causation, he focused upon one stark fact: the lives and property of the community had been jeopardized by the assaults of lawless men. In such circumstances the first duty of every citizen was to uphold established authority. "Obedience," Binney declaimed—"implicit, unhesitating, and unquestioning obedience"—was due to the law and its administrators. Pursuant to this basic obligation, the volunteers had risked life and limb in the public service. Acting under civilian control, they had done only what any man must have done in their place: they had used "the lawful force which unlawful force made necessary." Yet their casualties went unregarded while public sympathy was extended to their enemies. As to the mere spectators who fell in the fighting, Binney minced no words:

> Every person standing in the ranks of the mob, adds to its apparent force, and to its actual violence. The duty of every one is either to resist the rioters or to retire. Deeply as such calamities are lamented by us, and none the less notwithstanding repeated public cautions to all persons to retire from the scene of riot and disorder, we deem it our bounden duty to declare that such wounds and deaths are in law and in conscience, in legal responsibility and in moral, before man and in the light of Heaven, wounds and deaths caused by the rioters and insurgents, and by them only. Theirs is the whole guilt, and theirs should be the whole responsibility.

Behind every urban disorder, he concluded, lay a hard core of criminal types who succeeded in their designs only through the passivity or acquiescence of respectable citizens. A sound public opinion must therefore reckon every future bystander as an accessory to riot.[54]

Two hundred copies of Binney's address were printed for immediate circulation, and several newspapers published the text in full. By the time it was formally presented to the governor the following day, at least ten thousand persons had signed it. The propertied classes breathed a collective sigh of relief. "This meeting was of immense service," commented Sidney Fisher, echoing Binney's own feelings. "It gave a start & direction to public opinion & fixed many who were wavering." One of the first by-products of renewed civil-military cordiality was a subscription list for disabled volunteers. By the end of July Philadelphians had collected more than ten thousand dollars for the relief of wounded militiamen and the families of those killed in the Southwark rioting.[55]

The grand jury of Philadelphia, which completed its official investigation of the riots on August 3, heaped fresh praise on the heads of the citizen soldiers, but otherwise its report added little to what had already been said at the Kensington inquest. The panel found merely that the arming of St. Philip de Neri Church had furnished a "plausible pretext" for the resumption of hostilities begun in May with the "murderous attack" upon the Kensington Natives. Evidence indicated that a criminal underclass on both sides sought to provoke violence, but the jurors made it clear that they considered Irish firebrands the most dangerous of all. Still, they remarked, with a burst of optimism, "We rejoice with the peaceable portion of our fellow citizens, that we are safe from any further tumult, since the rioters know that the forfeit of life must be the penalty of such offences in future."[56]

On that mildly encouraging note the Great Riots of 1844 sputtered to a close in the daily prints as the community settled back to take stock of its losses. A final tally revealed fourteen dead and fifty-odd wounded, a slightly larger number of casualties than those reported for the May disturbances. Total property damage (plus the city's share of militia costs) amounted to more than a quarter of a million dollars by the most conservative estimates. No roundup of Southwark mob leaders or troublemakers followed the restoration of order; as in May, only those persons arrested by the police or militia during the riots faced court charges. Grand jury records indicate that nineteen men were indicted by late October for offenses growing out of the July troubles, but only three or four were ever convicted.

Property owners who suffered from mob violence did secure an eventual measure of justice through the courts, however. A statute of 1841 imposed liability on the county for all property damage occasioned by riots or mobs, and John Bannister Gibson, chief justice of the Pennsylvania Supreme Court, interpreted the indemnity measure in liberal terms to open the door to substantial awards. Despite resistance from such lower-court judges as Edward King, Irish litigants recovered in time impressive damages. Juries awarded $27,090.02 to St. Michael's Church; $47,433.87 to St. Augustine's Church; and $6,468.98 to St. Michael's Convent in Kensington. (The actual damage done to St. Philip de Neri Church proved slight. Authorities returned the building to Bishop Kenrick on July 10, and it was in active use again for public worship the following Sunday.) Even individual householders such as James Lavery, whose Kensington home had been burned by rioters on May 9, recovered compensation for their losses.[57]

The public funds expended for the relief of riot victims may have helped to discourage further Nativist outbreaks in Pennsylvania, as some historians believe;[58] but the lasting importance of the Philadelphia experience must be sought in other directions. The events of 1844 threw into sharp relief the institutional weaknesses of old-fashioned city government and set in motion a process of modernization that brought legal and political structures at last abreast of urban growth.

The most obvious lesson that the Southwark violence brought home to the average Philadelphian was the need for specific riot control legislation. Civil and military authorities, grand juries, and concerned citizens alike clamored for a tactical blueprint that would make a repetition of such scenes impossible in the future. Their demands were met by an omnibus police bill that Philadelphia assemblymen introduced into the Pennsylvania legislature early in 1845. The more important sections dealt exclusively with problems of riot control and were the handiwork of the indomitable Binney.

Binney outlined a step-by-step procedure for putting down riots that made maximum use of both civil and military resources. Stage one occurred when a sheriff was first summoned to the scene of a disturbance. At that point he was empowered only to call upon the rioters (defined as "any twelve or more persons") to disperse in peace. But if they refused or forcibly prevented him from making his proclamation, he was obliged at once to "use all necessary force" to suppress them. Despite the hackneyed phraseology, this was in reality a latitudinarian grant of power, for Binney followed it up with a blanket indemnity clause that relieved the sheriff and his posse of all liability for the "killing, maiming, or hurting" of any persons in the crowd. If the full weight of civil authority proved unable to restore order, one final step remained: an appeal to the militia.

Since recent events had underscored the friction likely to develop between militiamen and magistrates in riot situations, Binney's proposed law made the military posse an independent force. When called out for riot duty, the volunteers, acting "under due military command and subordination," were directed to proceed against the mob just as they would in case of war or public insurrection. The sheriff could no longer claim any control over military operations; his role was limited to the sending of official notices that activated or discharged the troops. As Binney thus greatly expanded the range of power available to the authorities, he imposed added disabilities upon all rioters. Any persons who resisted the sheriff, or merely remained on the ground after being ordered to disperse, committed a felony, for which they became liable to a prison term of three months to three years at hard labor in the state penitentiary. During their imprisonment they would further be treated in all respects as convicted arsonists. The rigor of the sentence reflected Binney's view that everyone who contributed to the strength of a mob was equally guilty of riot. From now on there would be no more innocent bystanders, at least in the eyes of the law, to complicate the work of crowd control.[59]

The draft Act for the Prevention and Suppression of Riots occasioned sharp controversy when it came before the house of representatives in mid-February. James Bayard, its principal sponsor, summarized the leading opposition arguments in a letter to Philadelphia's new mayor, Peter McCall:

We have had a hard battle . . . on the Riot-Act—and have at last carried it through second reading with a restriction confining it to the City & County of Philad[a]. It was opposed by the County members as unnecessary for their constituents and when restricted to the

City & County it was strenuously opposed by the County members
. . . as a slur upon their constituents and a bloody bill introduced to
our country from the worst pages of the British statute book.[60]

Anglophobes pointed with glee to the ponderous phrasing of
the sheriff's proclamation, which concluded with "God save the
Commonwealth!" and antimilitarists protested the strengthening of an already dangerous military establishment.

After three days of acrimonious debate, however, a majority
of house members agreed that the Philadelphia area deserved
strong-arm police methods and passed the bill with its major
features intact. Binney's stylized proclamation was struck
down, and the riot penalties were reduced to suit the more
modest capabilities of local penal institutions. Rioters now
faced only a misdemeanor charge, with the prospect of
spending one month to two years in solitary confinement at
labor in the county prison. The senate made no further changes
in the measure, which became law on April 12, 1845.[61]

While the Riot Act gave municipal authorities broad powers
for use in emergency situations, it did little to establish an
adequate day-to-day police. Instead of providing for major
structural reform, it added more men to another makeshift
organization. This time the city of Philadelphia was linked to
five adjoining suburbs in a loose federation, each unit of which
was required to maintain one able-bodied policeman for every
150 taxable inhabitants. The new quota system led to the
following results:

	Population	Police
Philadelphia	21,946	146
Northern Liberties	8,842	59
Kensington	5,919	40
Spring Garden	8,074	54
Moyamensing	3,456	23
Southwark	6,778	45
Total	55,015	367

Since the city proper already maintained a force of 177 men, the
measure was clearly aimed at suburban weakness—a considera-

tion that helps to explain much of the resentment that county members expressed during the debates in the state legislature.

The sheriff of Philadelphia was empowered to take command of all suburban units in emergencies, but otherwise they continued to function as independent agencies, subject only to the control of local superintendents. The absence of centralized administration hampered the emergence of an effective metropolitan police for another decade, until city and suburbs were consolidated into a single governmental entity.[62]

Although the Great Riots had made apparent the need for a county-wide preventive police, many considerations other than law enforcement complicated the progress of urban consolidation. Conservative city leaders, such as Horace Binney and others of the Whig elite, opposed any plan that might upset the existing political balance by adding a mass of Democratic votes to future municipal elections. On the economic side, owners of city bonds and real estate feared that the value of their investments would be jeopardized as municipal funds were reallocated to support suburban improvement projects. "The city in short would be governed by the mob of the districts and its own mob combined," declared Sidney Fisher with his usual incisiveness; "its property would be applied to the improvement of the districts, its patronage & revenue be placed in the hands of demagogues & partisans of the lowest stamp. The whole [consolidation] scheme is one of plunder."[63] Vested interest groups in the suburbs similarly objected to changes that threatened to disrupt established patterns of political or economic control.

So, despite public meetings and continued propaganda, the cause of consolidation languished from year to year, while gang warfare increased and occasional mob violence flared up on a lesser scale. In 1848 the city took one essential step toward the modernization of *its* police, as a municipal ordinance abolished the night watch and set up for the first time a coherent, round-the-clock force, under the exclusive control of the mayor. Improved record-keeping procedures, the introduction of uniforms, and the publication of recruitment criteria further laid the foundations for an efficient metropolitan department. All that was lacking was the extension of the new system to the suburbs—a process that came about in the end through political realignments that were almost as startling in their implications as the spiraling crime rate itself.[64]

Most historians who have looked into the Philadelphia riots have concluded with some satisfaction that they heralded the downfall of the Native American party in local and national politics. Church burnings and smear tactics, we are told, alienated the mass of American voters, who repented that they had ever heeded the siren song of Nativism. Comforting as the moral may be, it is unfortunately not borne out by the record in Philadelphia. The Natives there outran both major parties in the county during the fall elections of 1844 and combined with the Whigs to control two-thirds of the city vote as well. Philadelphians sent three out of four Nativist candidates to Congress on the heels of the Southwark riots; they consistently reelected Lewis C. Levin to the House of Representatives for the next six years; and they saw to it that other Nativists continued to obtain choice municipal offices. (Irish Catholics, on the other hand, were barred for generations from resuming the prominent role they had earlier played in the city's cultural life.)[65] While the Native American party did decline in strength appreciably after 1846, its local losses were due less to moral factors than to the adoption of Nativist issues by the two major parties.

Here lay the real impact of the Great Riots on Philadelphia voters: by the early fifties traditional city vs. county, mechanic vs. merchant divisions had given way to a new-style politics based upon racial and religious stereotypes. The Democrats of Philadelphia now represented proslavery, proimmigrant, and Catholic interests, while the Whigs and Nativists were identified as old-stock Protestant and pro-Abolitionist. The shift to ethnic politics helped to create a whole new class of neighborhood leaders, to multiply small-scale ties and loyalties, and to institutionalize the expression of conflicts that formerly found their only effective outlet in violent street fighting. Political appeals to race and religion also produced a county-wide balance of party strength that facilitated the passage of a long-delayed Consolidation Bill through the Pennsylvania legislature. On February 2, 1854, the city and its twenty-nine suburbs became at last one great metropolis, patrolled in all its parts by the mayor's police.[66]

So ended a turbulent period in Philadelphia's history, and with it the patrician leadership of men like Horace Binney, who claimed to stand above the hurly-burly of popular passions. There would be little place for such elitism in the cities of the future, conservatives sighed, as they mourned the passing of an era:

Everything here and in Europe [wrote Sidney Fisher in December 1844] indicates that the old order of things is passing away, that the present civilization is to be destroyed, that the period of change has arrived. The masses are everywhere rising and claiming to govern society, to alter not only its political constitution but its organization, its relations, its life. What new forms will grow out of the chaos is a question which concerns a distant future. We, our generation & our time, have unhappily to suffer all the troubles & griefs of the process of change, a fiery ordeal, of which the present foretaste is bitter enough.[67]

My heart sickens at the profligacy of public
men, the low state of public morals—& the
utter indifference of the people to all elevated
virtue & even self-respect—They are not only
the willing Victims but the Devotees of Demagogues—I had a letter a few days ago from
Chancellor Kent, in which he utters language
of entire despondency. Is not the *Theory* of
our govt. a total failure?
Joseph Story to John McLean,
August 16, 1844

7   Frederick Grimké and the Dynamics
of Social Change

To many political analysts the
upsurge of mob violence in American life after 1830 appeared
symptomatic of a deeper social malaise that was slowly but
surely eroding the national character. Men who burned con-
vents or carried out backwoods lynchings scarcely constituted a
model electorate, yet in an age of universal manhood suffrage
their political influence could not be discounted. The virtuous
Republic of the Founding Fathers had, it seemed, been superseded by an irresponsible democracy, and if the masses were
sunk in ignorance and gross materialism, what chance had
popular institutions for survival?

Tocqueville's dark forebodings of majoritarian misrule
assumed an aspect of heightened urgency in the forties and
fifties, especially among American jurists, who were keenly
alive to the crisis of confidence in representative government.
Compelled day after day to apply legal rules to social behavior,
antebellum judges (like their counterparts in every age) could

not avoid a personal assessment of the prevailing Zeitgeist and its related problems: the accommodation of law to changing mores and the limits of judicial accountability to the public in a democratic system. Conservatives like Justice Story insisted that the law must always lag behind social change and that the judiciary should act as a brake upon the rash demands of the multitude. More populist-minded judges disagreed. But only one member of the legal community ventured beyond conventional clichés to a systematic reappraisal of the democratic process in action. The work of Frederick Grimké, which has been long neglected by scholars, rivals that of Tocqueville for acute sociological insights into the nature of "free institutions." It also anticipates the iconoclasm of twentieth-century legal realists in its candid analysis of judicial behavior.[1]

The Grimké family occupied a modest but secure position in the aristocratic society of colonial Charleston. John Faucheraud Grimké, growing to manhood on the eve of the Revolution, could look back upon three generations of Carolina ancestors—low-country planters of mixed German and French stock who had worked hard, lived frugally, and advanced themselves in the social scale through a succession of prudent marriages. A strong Calvinist drive furnished a spiritual sanction for their upward mobility, although in later years they regularly attended services in the Church of England, the only acceptable religious establishment for the "gentlemen" of the province.

Like other sons of the planter class, John Faucheraud was early sent to England for his education. After completing his public school courses at Westminster, he attended Trinity College, Cambridge, and in 1769 was admitted to the Middle Temple of the Inns of Court for such legal training as those moribund institutions still claimed to provide. Five years later he was one of eight American law students who signed a petition to King George III protesting the Boston Port Bill. On his return to Charleston soon afterward he obtained a license to practice before the South Carolina courts, but the outbreak of war cut short his prospective career.

From 1776 to 1782 Grimké served with distinction in the revolutionary army, rising in rank from captain to lieutenant-colonel and taking part in such major engagements as the battle of Eutaw Springs and the climactic Yorktown campaign. The habits of military command and strategic planning carried over

to civilian life thereafter to secure for him in short order a string
of responsible state offices that culminated by the end of the
century in a place on the Supreme Court of South Carolina.
Meanwhile he added new luster to the family name in Charleston social circles through his marriage in 1784 to Mary Smith,
daughter of "Banker Smith of Broad Street," one of the
wealthiest and most respected businessmen of the state. The
Smiths were direct descendants of old Thomas Smith, proprietary governor and landgrave of South Carolina in the previous
century—a circumstance that might be shrugged off elsewhere
but that carried portentous implications in a structured society
still greatly influenced by colonial mores.

The Grimké-Smith union, a mingling of Huguenot and
Puritan strains, produced in due course fourteen children. Of
these the brightest—Thomas Smith, Frederick, Sarah, and
Angelina—all displayed remarkable qualities of self-determination and moral courage, along with more than a trace of
instability and neuroticism. Frederick, born in 1791, grew up
somewhat in the shadow of his multitalented older brother
Thomas, who was five years his senior, and with whom he
enjoyed a closer relationship than with any of his other siblings.
The plantation system shaped the outer contours of family life
during his boyhood by bending human nature to the implacable
demands of the seasons. From November to mid-May the
Grimkés lived on their Beaufort plantation, traveling to
Charleston only in February for the traditional pre-Lenten
festivities of "race week." But to remain in the country during
the summer in close proximity to acres of swampy rice lands
that were breeding grounds for malaria, "country fever," and
like ills was considered suicidal, at least for whites; so every
spring the whole family trekked cityward, over sandy roads
and corduroy causeways, to spend six months in their handsome town house on Church Street. This alternating pattern of
rural-urban living gave a unique flavor to Charleston society
and, as Henry Adams once remarked, tended to make Charlestonians more urbanized in their outlook than most southerners.

To the Grimké children, however, a trip to town promised
nothing very exciting in the way of fun and games. Although
the straitlaced decorum of prewar Charleston was fast disappearing beneath the pressure of new wealth and a more
relaxed moral code (so that there was even a "pleasure garden"
operating in Friend Street by the end of the nineties), no com-

parable transformation was visible in the regimen of the Grimké household. Indeed, as John Faucheraud Grimké grew older and more deeply involved in business ventures of all kinds, from banking to land development, he clung the more tenaciously to the simple certitudes of the Mosaic law and hardened his heart against the wickedness of squatters and other scoundrels. "Starke holds and Grimké skins," commented a backwoods bumpkin in describing the judge's deft disposition of a batch of criminal defendants at one session, and the stern old jurist protected his personal interests with equal zeal, dragging friends and neighbors into court for the most trifling matters until public indignation almost caused his impeachment. Even then he did not flinch but wrapped himself in scornful silence as he took comfort from searching out and transcribing the opinions of various authors on his favorite subject: moral discipline. (Years later his son Frederick, an equally austere recluse, amused himself with a similar project, but Frederick's reflections were original and took the form of mordant maxims on human nature that resembled those of La Rochefoucauld more than the church fathers.)

Such impieties from the younger generation Judge Grimké never countenanced during his lifetime. Each Sunday, under his watchful eye, the whole family (servants included) trooped off in carriages and on foot to attend Episcopal services at St. Philip's Church, and only sickness could excuse anyone from participating in the daily morning prayers that he conducted at home. He also took personal charge of his children's general education, drilling his sons in the rudiments of logic and English composition and pitting them against one another in family debates, over which he presided as umpire and critic. To his role of tutor he brought intellectual gifts of no mean order, for he was a legal publicist of unquestioned ability whose several treatises—along with his monumental compilation of the *Public Laws of the State of South Carolina*—remained standard professional tools for decades. But his pedagogical insights, while profound, were also narrow, and under his guidance the Grimké children came to view education as a relentlessly *purposeful* process that justified itself only when directed toward some constructive social end. "The true use of learning is to shed light upon our own times," Frederick later wrote, echoing his father's insistence upon applied knowledge—the sort of knowledge, incidentally, that was so discernible in judicial opinions, where data from old law cases were used to settle disputes in the present.[2]

That the judge was consciously grooming his older boys for legal careers became apparent in retrospect, and their early immersion in systematic study and utilitarian precepts paid off during their college years. Both Thomas and Frederick achieved brilliant records at Yale, where Frederick became prominent in the debating society, was elected to Phi Beta Kappa, and delivered the senior oration at the graduating exercises of the class of 1810. On his return to Charleston he dutifully studied law, was admitted to the bar in 1813, and practiced for five years before turning his back forever on his birthplace and moving to the Midwest.

His departure was characteristically low-key, unmarked by the emotional soul searching that accompanied the later exodus of his antislavery sisters Sarah and Angelina. Like other facets of his personal life, the episode offers little to a would-be biographer beyond tantalizing hints—a penumbra of suggestive intimations, no one of which can be satisfactorily pinned down. One solid explanation for his behavior has nevertheless been advanced: a story that almost rises to the dignity of a folk myth in some quarters contends that a blighted romance was the cause of it all, as, "maddened by the desertion of his promised wife, he shook the dust of his native place from his feet, and wandered forth a despiser of the fair sex, a woman-hater as he was known, to the time of his death."[3] Unhappily, there is not the slightest proof that Grimké was ever the victim of such a *grande passion*. His extant correspondence reveals him as a born bachelor, a man who really enjoyed (if the term is not too strong to describe his emotional capabilities) hotel living and one who was interested in women only for their intellectual qualities. (Hugh S. Legaré, another perennial bachelor, at least regaled his female correspondents with gossipy tidbits and sighed for the joys of home life; whereas Grimké in his letters seldom descended below the intellectual level of Kant's *Critique of Pure Reason* and thought nothing of including in a personal letter a detailed précis of Comte's *Politique positive*.)

More than likely it was sibling rivalry rather than puppy love that drove him westward. His older brother Thomas, admitted to practice four years before him, was fast becoming one of the most prominent lawyers in South Carolina. While Frederick still looked up to him with admiration he must have felt somewhat stunted in the presence of Thomas's sunny sociability —"saintliness," some called it—and his evident professional success. Perhaps, too, the mere physical conditions of life in a large household, with its inevitable factionalism and infighting, came to grate upon the nerves of one who cherished his privacy. There is more than a suggestion of autobiography, at any rate, in the discussion of family mores that Grimké later incorporated into his *Free Institutions*:

> Domestic society in all its relations, if its secrets were not happily concealed from public observation, would as often exhibit mischiefs of the same character [as the ill treatment of slaves]. Perhaps it may be asserted that every new country has to a great extent been peopled by young persons who at home were surrounded by influences of one kind of another with which they were not satisfied. There is always a limit at which the most downright and headlong philanthropy is fain to halt and that stopping place is the inmost chamber of domestic life, although there it is that the foundation of all the virtues and vices of our race is laid. It would not do to lift the veil here, else it might show us how little genuine virtue exists.[4]

Whatever family problems he may have encountered, however, the Grimké name aided him materially in his move to Ohio. Prominent Charlestonians who had known his father were quick to provide him with letters of introduction to Governor Thomas Worthington and other midwestern notables, and with these to cushion the shock of his uprooting he set out in 1818 for Columbus and "the rising Empire of the West."

"Mr. Frederick Grimké . . . has been in the state about eighteen months, and has received the distinguished appointment of President Judge of the Court of C[ommon] Pleas," wrote a young Ohio lawyer from the state capital in January 1820. "He is a man of fine talents."[5] While the twenty-eight-year-old jurist doubtless owed his sudden eminence more to political connections than to demonstrated abilities, his interim judicial post brought him to the attention of lawyers across the state and helped him to decide upon a permanent location for his future practice. When he completed his brief term on the bench, he settled in Chillicothe, forty-five miles south of Columbus, where an equable climate and a half-southern society promised something extra in the way of fringe benefits.

Located in the rich bottomlands of the Scioto Valley, this

former capital of Ohio had been largely settled by emigrants from Virginia and Kentucky, who were later joined by numbers of Yankees and others, including a sprinkling of ex-Charlestonians, most of whom Grimké already knew. With its wide, tree-lined streets laid out neatly at right angles, its advantageous trade position at the confluence of two streams (the Scioto River and Paint Creek), and its handful of impressive mansions in the Greek revival or southern colonial styles, the town resembled Philadelphia in the eyes of its inhabitants. But in its past history and future prospects it was more akin to Charleston. Just a quarter of a century before Frederick arrived the whole area was a wilderness presided over by hostile Shawnees, who drove away the first group of settlers in 1795. Then followed an accelerated cycle of urban growth and prosperity, as overnight the tiny hamlet mushroomed into the state's first capital, complete with imposing public buildings of stone and a bustling, adventuresome population drawn from all parts of the Union. The bonanza years were as short-lived as they were brilliant, however, for the decision to transfer the seat of government in 1816 to more centrally situated Columbus sapped the vitality of her southern neighbor and made Chillicothe in time a sleepy backwater.

But her deterioration was little apparent to observers in the 1820s (which was true as well of Charleston, whose comparable decline set in about the same time, although for vastly different reasons). When Grimké became a full-time resident Chillicothe was still the second largest city in the state. It contained a branch of the Bank of the United States, the office of the U.S. surveyor general, and more than twenty mercantile establishments that served the needs of a population of some three thousand persons. As a river town and (after 1832) a canal port as well, Chillicothe did a thriving trade in grain, flour, produce, and merchandise for another generation, and Grimké was most impressed in his early years by the evidence of material "civilization" that he saw all around him—the creature comforts and aspiring middle-class life-style that seemed to exist at all social levels, side by side with the most glaring incongruities of individual personality and behavior.[6]

These polar tensions between cultural conformity and self-determination were also apparent within the Ross County bar, whose members, despite their uniform grounding in common-law principles, displayed all the vagaries of character and conduct incident to the larger life of a frontier community. William Creighton, the leading trial lawyer of Chillicothe in the 1820s, was an urbane Virginian who delighted in gourmet dinners and gentle courtroom humor; Richard Douglas, a flamboyant ex-sailor from Connecticut, interspersed his pleadings with nautical terms, snatches of old hymns, and dramatic monologues from Shakespeare and Ben Jonson; while the scholarly recluse Benjamin Greene Leonard moved his law office farther into the woods each time he heard the sound of a carpenter's hatchet and read Sophocles' plays in the original Greek to refresh his spirits after a hard day of circuit work. All of the Chillicothe lawyers spent much of their time traveling around the Sixth District (which included Ross and several adjoining counties) to provide legal services for scattered backwoods settlers. Generally they were employed on a catch-as-catch-can basis and had to work up their cases for trial with only one or two days' notice. The schedule was as grueling physically as mentally, to judge from one contemporary account:

> It was the custom to follow the courts in their terms, for the several counties of their circuit; so that, substantially, the same Bar would be in attendance, at courts distant from others fifty to one hundred miles. We traveled on horseback, over very bad roads, sometimes mid-leg deep of mud, or underlaid with the traditional "corduroy bridge." Our personal riding gear, the saddlebags stuffed with a few changes of lighter apparel, often our law books; our legs protected by "spatter-dashes," more commonly called "leggins," and our whole persons covered with a camlet, or Scotch plaid cloak; we were prepared to meet whatever weather befell us.[7]

Grimké, who suffered from chronic ill health and recurrent bouts of indigestion, seems nevertheless to have adjusted pretty well to the rigors of circuit riding and the equally intensive demands of a masculine and highly competitive professional environment. It is almost impossible to reconstruct the details of his practice in the lower courts, apart from the evidence provided by his correspondence that, like almost every other young practitioner, he engaged in debt collection and transacted some long-distance business of this kind for clients living in Charleston.[8] But on the appellate level published reports provide a clearer picture. Charles Hammond, the first official court reporter in Ohio, was authorized by the state legislature to compile and publish the decisions of the Ohio Supreme Court beginning in 1821, and Hammond's *Reports*, though far from complete, include six cases that Grimké argued before the high court during the 1820s.

All of these were chancery cases, and several went off on narrow procedural grounds. On one occasion Grimké success-fully represented the interests of the Bank of the United States; while in *Adm'rs. of Hough* v. *Hunt* (1826) he obtained the rescission of an unconscionable contract extorted from his client by a moneylender. But *McCoy* v. *Corporation of Chillicothe* (1828) best reveals the tenor of his early legal thinking, since it reprints much of his brief, along with the opinion of the court. (This practice was quite common, especially during Ham-mond's eighteen years, 1821-1839, as reporter. Until 1831 even the supreme court judges in Ohio were not required to prepare a written copy of their decisions, which often tended to be summary résumés of the arguments of counsel. A reporter therefore found it expedient to quote at length from the written briefs in cases that he deemed of particular interest—a criterion that doubtless explains the substantial number of Hammond's own learned arguments that fill the pages of his *Reports*.) In the *McCoy* case Grimké sought to enjoin the collection of a city tax that had been levied upon the stock of a retail merchant who imported most of his goods from other states. Traditionally an equity court would intervene in such circumstances only to pre-vent an anticipated flood of litigation from disgruntled taxpayers, but Grimké argued that the principle should be broadened to grant relief to a single individual who otherwise would be forced into a "multiplicity of lawsuits" to protect himself against the repeated assaults of the tax collector. In his brief he urged the importance of changing social conditions as a factor to be weighed in determining the applicability of estab-lished legal rules: "Indeed, he who looks for an exact precedent in every case, must be very little aware to what an infinite extent the affairs of men are ramified by experience, and by the ever-varying exigencies of society."[9] The hint was tentative and the court disregarded it, pointing out that the tax in question was minimal and that for every alleged trespass upon his rights Grimké's client had a full and adequate remedy at law. But the sociological thrust of the brief well reflected its author's growing interest in the informal mechanics of change within a democracy—the general norms that governed the evolution of a people quite apart from, and sometimes in spite of, statutes and court decisions.

He had ample opportunity to pursue such philosophical inquiries since the volume of his legal business was only moderate. As he remarked to his friend William Greene, a young Cincinnati lawyer:

> Sir Jas. McIntosh in his first lecture on the law of nations . . . declares that the professional business which he then had (1802) was not sufficient to occupy him thoroughly and to keep his mind in full training, and that he had therefore resorted to a course of lectures on an interesting branch of science. I may say the same. If Sir James had not business enough in the city of London, it can hardly be expected that a lawyer of ordinary ambition and mental vigor should have sufficient in Chillicothe.[10]

To fill up the idle hours Grimké read voraciously in the leading modern writers of Europe and America, paying particular attention to social theorists such as Adam Smith and David Hume. He also wrote a number of original newspaper pieces that explored the distinctive aspects of the American experience since the Revolution. Nine of these early essays appeared between 1826 and 1828 in the pages of the *Scioto Gazette* of Chillicothe and the *Ohio State Journal* of Columbus. At the time they won for their pseudonymous author a minor literary reputation in Ohio, but they are chiefly important today for the light they shed on his more impressive later work. It is scarcely an exaggeration to say that in these few pages Grimké touched upon all the major themes that were to preoccupy him for the rest of his life and to receive extended treatment two decades later in his monumental study of free institutions.

"An Essay on the Ancients and the Moderns," his most popular effort, provides a useful perspective from which to view his other writings. Here Grimké predictably asserted the superiority of modern literature over the classics of Greece and Rome. But what begins as an inquiry into the merits of individual writers soon expands into an analysis of comparative civilizations. In the end nineteenth-century culture stands vindicated less for the achievements of its great men—although

Grimké pays due tribute to Scott, Byron, and others—than for the diffusion of learning and "habits of reflection" through all social classes. Stressing the importance of "practical" as well as theoretical knowledge, Grimké carried his argument to its logical conclusion by insisting that the relative lack of an American literature should be taken as a positive sign that citizens were directing their intellectual energies toward other ends, on a scale undreamed of by the aristocratic elites of past ages:

> The literature of the United States, although exceedingly under-rated, has yet never been commensurate with the mind of the country; and this I attribute chiefly to the extraordinary prosperity of the nation since the revolutionary war. The thoughts of every one have been perpetually occupied with the animating and ever shifting scene without, and the mind has been rendered unwilling, and consequently unable, to give itself up to an pursuit which demanded the intense concentration of its faculties . . . Until all the active pursuits of life are overflowing, we cannot expect the separate existence of a very splendid literature . . . In ELIZABETH'S and even ANNE'S reign the institutions of the country did not require the one thousandth part of the talent which is in perpetual and active exercise in this country; and for that reason, posterity has been informed of nearly all which did exist. But if the condition of society in this country, had existed in ELIZABETH'S reign: and that golden age of literature, as it has been termed, were realised here: we should say that the human species had retrograded more fearfully than during any period of which history gives an account.[11]

Several companion pieces rang variations on this theme as Grimké moved beyond literature to show the determining influence of social forces upon a nation's politics and laws. In the United States, he maintained, the bulk of the population consisted of "comparatively independent" property owners who were accustomed to manage their own affairs and to wield political power from an early age. Their extensive freedom of action in all matters of self-improvement made them thoughtful as well as highly individualistic, unlike the slavish masses in European countries, whose character was molded solely by external circumstances—climate, geography, paternalistic government—rather than inner-directing "moral causes."

The middle-class mores of the American electorate thus accounted for the unique consensus features of American politics and offered the only security for democratic institutions: "Where men's private affairs constitute the absorbing interest of life, and public affairs become a consideration of secondary importance, political institutions must stand firm upon their basis, and must indeed endure until that state of things is reversed."[12] Even the violent partisanship that flared up during election campaigns posed no serious threat to the pervasive bourgeois ethos but rather served as a release for private frustrations of all kinds: "a vast electrical conductor, by which discontent of all sorts, and not merely political discontent, is easily carried off and dissipated."[13]

In a society so committed to a philosophy of privatism, there was little occasion for the vigorous exercise of governmental power. State legislatures, Grimké remarked, might appropriately establish free public schools for all children and promote the construction of roads, canals, and other works of broad cultural utility. But he pointed with approval to the innumerable checks and balances that were built into the federal system to safeguard the rights of individuals against officious or arbitrary governmental action.[14] Courts in particular were entrusted with the delicate task of reconciling even the most personal differences between man and man—a peacekeeping function of peculiar importance to a society in which private feuds generated far more passion than public issues:

> Courts of justice may well be described as an institution framed for the express purpose of putting an end to the practice of private war. The legislature is well fitted to make general rules for the government of the people and the executive to keep watch over the public safety. But without the instrumentality of the judicial tribunals which act in detail and not merely in the gross, society would be a prey to perpetual civil dissensions. Disputes between private individuals are occurrences of every day. The manifold relations which men have to each other in a thriving and cultivated society multiply them greatly. These disputes have relation to the most valuable interests of society: life, liberty, and property. And to have devised a mode by which they may be quietly appeased is one of the greatest achievements of modern civilization.[15]

How well the judiciary performed its mediating role was another question, but one that Grimké could answer on the basis of personal experience after 1830. In that year a vacancy occurred on the common pleas bench in his district, and the General Assembly elected him to the post of president judge. For more than a decade thereafter he struggled with the legal implications of his theories as he sought in specific cases to effect some meaningful adjustment between abstract rules and the perversities of human behavior.

The courts of common pleas as set up by the Ohio Constitution of 1802 were emphatically the "people's courts." Only the president judge was required to be a lawyer; the two or three associate judges appointed by the legislature from each of the several counties that made up a particular judicial district tended from the start to be laymen (leading one legal wag to remark that every court seemed to be composed of one hundred men: "one Judge and two ciphers"). Most of Grimké's colleagues on the bench were local businessmen whose principal duty was to assist the president judge when he arrived from time to time to conduct the regular sessions of the court. (The president judge did all the circuit traveling; the associate judges were rooted in their respective counties.) Despite these folksy trappings, the common pleas courts generally functioned with a high degree of efficiency in dealing with a heavy work load of important cases. As the only judicial tribunals of consequence below the Ohio Supreme Court, they handled a wide variety of civil and criminal causes, including probate matters and equity suits. Much of this same litigation ultimately found its way to the supreme court, which was given unusually broad powers of review by the constitution; hence there was some truth in William Greene's observation that a post like Grimké's, on an important circuit, differed in name only from a place on the high bench.[16] At least it seems to have kept him fully occupied, for his correspondence and publications alike peter out in the early thirties, leaving a hiatus for the six years (1830-1836) that he spent as a common pleas judge.

There can be little doubt, however, that he owed his appointment to the Ohio Supreme Court in February 1836 primarily to the excellence of his previous judicial record. The Democrats, who controlled the legislature at the time, commanded his intellectual assent but little else, for if Grimké adhered to most Democratic tenets on principle, he was anything but an active or influential party man. His supreme court nomination, which he had not solicited, came to him as an unexpected boon that pleased him greatly, as he admitted to one well-wisher: "To be elected to an office which is surrounded with some honor, is always a matter of gratification."[17]

The other three judges whom he joined on the high court continued to serve through most of his tenure and contributed to a collective image of solid learning and ability. Ebenezer Lane, the chief judge, was a native of Connecticut, a well-trained Harvard graduate two years younger than Grimké, an omnivorous reader of literature, and by all accounts one of the finest jurists who ever graced the Ohio bench. (Even the fastidious Frederick was somewhat impressed by his colleague's intellectual gifts, noting in private that Lane was "quick, sagacious, and sufficiently learned," although "by no means a . . . mind of the *ruling order*.")[18] The remaining associate judges were also transplanted New Englanders, with bluff Peter Hitchcock much the senior in point of talent as well as age. A Connecticut Yankee and Yale alumnus, Hitchcock had already served two seven-year terms (1819-1833) on the supreme court and was reelected for the fourth time in later years to set an unbreakable record of judicial longevity that was as much a tribute to his legal competence as to his personal popularity with Ohioans. Only the final member of the court, Reuben Wood, failed to measure up to the high standards set by his colleagues. A physical giant from the backwoods of Vermont, Wood was an archetypal self-made man who aspired to political rather than legal eminence and eventually became governor of Ohio. (Posterity remembers him best for his unsuccessful bid to capture the Democratic Presidential nomination in 1852 as the Cuyahoga Chief.) Each judge received an annual salary of $1,200 when Grimké came to the court; in 1837 the figure was raised to $1,500—a record high for the antebellum period but scarcely a windfall considering what had to be done to earn it.

One might expect, for example, that the burdens of circuit duty would diminish perceptibly at the top rungs of the judicial ladder, but in Ohio the case was just the reverse. The state constitution, which had been drafted when most of the area was still an unsettled frontier, required the supreme court judges to hold court once a year in every county. By the late thirties this meant an annual trek to seventy-six different locations, or a statewide circuit of more than 2,250 miles, according to one jurist's calculations. To keep from spending all of their spare time in transit, the judges divided themselves into two-man teams, each of which canvassed one-half of the appointed territory. Such an arrangement contributed to physical survival but brought with it obvious difficulties of another kind, since half the court never knew what the other half was doing, and similar cases arising in different parts of the state might be decided quite differently during the same term of the Supreme Court on Circuit. As a result all of the judges were forced to return to the state capital each December for a special session of the Court in Bank. During three or four weeks of hectic activity the full bench resolved any inconsistencies in recent circuit opinions and heard other important cases that fell within its original jurisdiction. The decisions rendered at this time were, with few exceptions, the only ones that were later published, and any evaluation of their merits must take some account of the circumstances in which they were delivered. For every member of the court they represented a final flurry of judicial activity that was superimposed upon an already intolerable work schedule— one that included some fifteen hundred circuit cases a year by the time of Grimké's appointment.

Timothy Walker, who claimed to be "a great admirer of Judge Grimké's style as an essayist," could find little to praise in the latter's performance on the Ohio Supreme Court. "In that position, he did little to enhance his reputation," Walker commented in the *Western Law Journal*. "His charges to the jury were sometimes singularly involved and confused; and his written opinions, though abounding in law learning, were very far from being models of perspicuity and condensation."[19] The criticism was just, although Grimké's discursiveness, which was all too evident in his nonlegal writings as well, often conveyed shrewd insights into the nature and creative potentialities of the judicial function. Much of the extreme technicality that characterized his decisions sprang from the kind of cases that were regularly assigned to him. A majority of the 73 published opinions that he wrote during his six years on the supreme court (representing 22 percent of the 335 decisions reported) dealt with intricate conflict of laws problems, the niceties of equity procedure, or the fine print in a contract, will, or deed. The pressure of deadlines drove him on many occasions to discuss only the narrow legal principles involved, abstracted from their social context, but at other times he revealed a keen awareness of the educative value of a judge's work and went out of his way to explain himself to the general public and to point up the social realities that lay back of a particular decision.

In one of his earliest reported cases he stated his judicial credo:

> I shall always give a preference to the American over the English cases, other things being equal; for I do not believe that a judge is bound to deal only with abstract principles of law. It is his duty also to understand the habits and condition of the people among whom he lives, and this he will be best able to do, by studying the adjudications which have been made in his own country . . . The law is intended to be a help to morality; it is intended to set an example to the community, with how much ease the great principles of justice may be maintained and dispensed, and of how great importance it is to the welfare of individuals, that they should be inviolably preserved. But if a loose morality should begin here, and a loose administration of the law is nothing more or less than a loose morality, it will be impossible for parties to feel that degree of confidence in our courts which they are entitled to feel. And however the technical forms in which our law is wrapped up, may contribute to blunt our feelings as men, yet it is impossible for an upright tribunal not to desire both to do justice and to inspire confidence.[20]

Applying these notions of social accountability to specific situations, Grimké upheld an established business practice by which an insurance company served notice on the public that its liability to policyholders would not commence until the first premium had been paid in cash; gave effect to informal (and legally defective) language in wills or private agreements, where the surrounding circumstances clearly indicated the intention of the parties; held sureties liable on the bonds of public officers, although these bonds suffered from procedural irregularities that made them technically invalid; and construed liberally, in accordance with legislative intent, statutes that sought to protect the rights of married women.[21] The test in all cases, he maintained, was functional. Behavior had to be judged in terms of its probable consequences within an evolving social order and not in relation to a priori labels: "Human interests are not like mathematical abstractions . . . Rules are necessarily made very broad and general in the early history of jurisprudence; but afterwards limitations to them are found to be as indispensable as the rules themselves; and hence the good sense of the maxim, that there is no general rule without its exceptions."[22]

Where deviation from a familiar rule or practice might lead to unnecessary confusion in social relations, of course, the logic of Grimké's position dictated a continued adherence to precedent. In a variety of situations he yielded to the weight of authority even when he doubted the wisdom of some time-honored principle. "That which is of the greatest importance, is that the law should be definitively settled," he noted on one occasion; "parties can then accommodate their conduct and agreements in conformity with it, and in no event can they reasonably complain that they have been deceived."[23] In *Moore* v. *Brown* (1840) he demanded strict compliance with the rules governing notice in appellate cases, fearing that any other course might prejudice the interests of the opposing party. He also defended the jurisdictional autonomy of probate and equity courts, arguing that they represented a healthy division of labor and that their specialized procedures brought added "order, regularity, and precision" to the administration of justice.[24]

A marked strain of Jacksonian idealism ran through much of his jurisprudence and displayed itself most tellingly in several important decisions relating to corporate power and federal-state relations. *Rosebaugh* v. *Saffin* (1840) involved a municipal ordinance that empowered the marshal of Cincinnati to impound and sell any stray livestock he found on the city streets without giving the owners a hearing. Such a summary procedure, Grimké declared, violated the individual's right to due process and was unauthorized by any express provision of the city charter. Moreover, he added, in words that might have been written by Roger Taney,

> If the construction of the clause in the charter were only doubtful, such construction ought to be put upon it as is most favorable to the rights of the citizens . . . the maxim, that the safety and well being of the people are the supreme law, sometimes persuades those who are invested with authority that they may be permitted to pursue so noble an end, by any means short of tyrannical. It is a great improvement in legislation to pursue the good of the majority, but the true end at which American institutions aim, is to consult the rights and interests of all conditions of men.[25]

The absence of a proper judicial proceeding in this instance ran counter not only to the spirit of the charter but to the "general genius" of American institutions.

State of Ohio v. *Washington Social Library Company* (1841) raised anew the question of implied powers, this time in relation to a private corporation. Here a company formed for the sole purpose of managing a library had begun to engage in banking operations as well. In ordering the immediate termination of such unauthorized activities, Grimké remarked that judicial recognition of powers not expressly granted in a corporate charter would produce "great inconvenience" under any circumstances; but if the defendant company were permitted to exercise the banking powers it claimed, it would escape the specific restrictions imposed upon other banks through their charters and would enjoy an unfair competitive advantage over every other banking institution in the state.[26]

The preservation of a competitive balance on a much larger scale engaged the court's attention in *Perry* v. *Torrence* (1838), in which a state tax levied against the owners of the steamboat *Adriatic* was challenged as an unlawful attempt to regulate interstate commerce—a power specifically granted to Congress by the United States Constitution. The ship in question was one of the largest of those "floating palaces" that transported passengers and freight up and down the Mississippi on a regular schedule, stopping only occasionally at the port of Cincinnati, where the owners resided. In an opinion that commanded the assent of the full court, Grimké first considered the nature of the tax and its applicability, from a conflict of laws standpoint, to the *Adriatic*. The guiding principle behind all lawful taxation, he observed, was to make the property of every citizen contribute as equally as possible to the "public burdens," and the Ohio legislature had measured up to this standard by enacting a general revenue bill aimed at stock ownership of all kinds. Despite its extensive out-of-state business, the *Adriatic* was properly taxable under this law because—quite apart from any abstract rules about the situs of personal property—a boat navigated beyond the boundary of any one state could not, "in the nature of things," be located for tax purposes at any place other than the town where her owners resided. Having thus dismissed the possibility of multiple state taxation, Grimké moved on to the most serious substantive question raised by the case: the effect of the interstate commerce clause upon a state's power to act in these circumstances.

"It must necessarily be difficult, in a government so complex as ours, composed of one government within another, or perhaps more properly, of two jurisdictions standing side by side of each other, to prevent all interference of their respective powers," he asserted, in announcing a theory of concurrent jurisdiction much akin to that held by Taney himself. State health laws, wreck laws, harbor regulations, and internal improvements measures had all been upheld in the past, although they interfered indirectly with the acknowledged power of Congress to regulate interstate commerce. By analogy a nondiscriminatory state tax upon the capital investments of its citizens was likewise constitutional, since it, too, formed part of that "class of powers . . . which is of the very essence of state legislation, and which can not be denied to the states, without impairing the very constitution whose integrity is intended to be preserved."

In keeping with his broader vision of the creative tensions in American life, Grimké further insisted that occasional overlaps between state and federal activities were essential to the workings of the political system, for they provided a "salutary control" upon the powers claimed and exercised by each jurisdiction. He cited with approval the recent decision in *New York v. Miln* (1837), in which the Taney Court sustained a New York statute that required the masters of incoming ships to make a detailed report on every passenger they brought to the state. Such recognition of state authority by the highest tribunal in the land offered added proof, if any were needed, that a vast field of social action had been reserved to the states by the Constitution: "The happiness and welfare of the people are as much, if not more, wrapped up in their administration than in that of the federal government, inasmuch as the sphere of legislation which is prescribed to them comprehends a greater variety of vital interests."[27]

One such "vital interest"—the control of internal improvements—formed the basis of two related cases that came up together for decision in 1839. A number of merchants and shippers who owned warehouses and other facilities along the Cuyahoga River near Cleveland sought to enjoin the construction of a drawbridge that would connect the city with a neighboring town on the opposite shore. The bridge company's promoters had already obtained permission to build from the county commissioners, and the proposed site had been approved by the Ohio legislature. But, the complainants alleged, if this structure were erected it would seriously impede the navigation of the river and drive down the value of waterfront property, in direct violation of the Northwest Ordinance and its guarantee that such streams should be "forever free" to navigation by the people of the territory and surrounding states.

Grimké met this challenge to state power with an elaborate inquiry into the meaning of the "free navigation" clause of the ordinance. It was intended to guard against two kinds of legislation, he argued. Congress might not pass any navigation act adversely affecting the rights of the territorial population, and the new states to be carved out of the Northwest Territory might not discriminate in their trade regulations against sister states. But all nondiscriminatory state measures relating to internal trade or navigation were constitutional, since the ordinance also provided that the new states should be admitted to the Union on terms of complete equality with the older ones. If any other interpretation were permissible, "then it might become a question whether such a provision was not, *ipso facto*, abrogated by the constitution of the United States; for the people of a state have not even the right to cede to the government of the Union any of those powers which appertain to its domestic jurisdiction, and which go to make up the idea of a distinct state. It would not only subvert the authority of the state, but would also disturb the necessary balance between the federal and local governments."

On the narrower issue of whether the proposed bridge would in fact constitute a nuisance whose abatement might be ordered by an equity court, the evidence was contradictory and inconclusive, Grimké ruled. But he did not doubt that a court was the proper agency to resolve such a dispute, whatever the political or legislative aspects of its deliberations might be (for example, determining the acceptable height of a bridge). Where Taney and others had counseled judicial self-restraint in similar circumstances, Grimké endorsed an activist policy that envisioned the judiciary as Socratic participants in a continuing dialectical process that was coextensive with society itself. Although individuals by their very nature tended to perceive things differently, he wrote, their conflicting viewpoints were amenable to high-level synthesis through judicial decisions. Once a case had been decided, "things are seen in a different light from what they were before, which alone occasioned such a difference of judgment; and the parties frequently find that their interests, which were believed to be absolutely contradictory, are not only reconcilable, but acquire strength from their alliance . . .

Minds which before saw things differently, now see them alike."[28]

The incongruities of American life, which he glimpsed only fitfully from the bench, continued to fascinate him as they had done ever since he first began to practice at the Ross County bar. In 1840 he yielded at last to inclination and began work on a comprehensive study of the national experience. Despite painfully slow progress his enthusiasm for the project mounted, and two years later he resigned from the court to devote his full time to research and composition. His hotel rooms in Chillicothe became his workshop where, surrounded by books and papers, he settled down for a long siege. "If the work should only terminate in making me better acquainted with American institutions, in giving me a better insight into the new world in which the human mind seems to be born, it will not be without use," he told a friend. "If it should be of no further service, I can burn the manuscript."[29]

The first draft of the book was not completed until August 1846, more than four years after his retirement. In part the delay was attributable to physical factors: each spring and summer Grimké experienced a severe loss of appetite and other symptoms of debility that left him unfit for sustained composition. But his plodding pace was a matter of design as well, since he had resolved from the outset to make a distinctive contribution to political philosophy that should depend in no way upon the observations of previous commentators such as Tocqueville. "A work without originality, is like a man without a soul," he insisted,[30] and he subjected the entire manuscript to a careful revision before turning it over at last to a publisher. In 1848 the Cincinnati firm of H. W. Derby brought out the amended version in a sturdy volume of 544 pages, whose appearance on booksellers' shelves virtually coincided with the outbreak of revolution on a massive scale throughout Europe. The timing could not have been better, Grimké mused, for the reception of his theories: "The minds of men are [every] where intensely engaged in pondering upon the great problem of free institutions. I could not well have fallen upon a more interesting period."[31]

True to his intention, the book—Considerations upon the Nature and Tendency of Free Institutions—approached its subject from a broad-gauged cultural perspective that found no real parallel in American writing until the publication of Max Lerner's *America as a Civilization* in 1957. Like Lerner, Grimké rejected the idea that any single organizing principle could adequately explain the contradictory pressures that operated within American society at any given moment. To understand why Americans actually behaved as they did, one had to discard simplistic formulas in favor of a close examination of what Lerner termed the "total civilization pattern": that cluster of basic attitudes and values that determined the identity of a people and imposed discernible limits upon their freedom of action. Such a multicausal analysis ruled out in advance any smooth-flowing linear argument, but in Grimké's case the difficulties of exposition were compounded by his refusal to patronize his audience in any way. Employing a dry, spare style whose monotonous lucidity was calculated to try the patience of the most sympathetic reader, he seemed bent upon further illustrating the power of cultural paradox through lengthy chapters that managed to be both dense and diffuse at the same time.

As a starting point for his inquiry into the cultural determinants of the American character, he examined the nature of "civilization" itself. By definition, the term imported "that state in which the higher part of nature is made to predominate over the lower, and the qualities which fit men for society obtain an ascendancy over their selfish and anti-social propensities."[32] Western man had already progressed through several inferior stages of development, from primitive hunting and pastoral societies to the complex nineteenth-century world of trade and consumerism. He had about reached the top of the ladder, Grimké implied, with nothing to do now but await the full flowering of bourgeois culture. The identification of "civilized" values with middle-class mores made possible the ranking of non-Western societies on a descending scale, from the semicivilized Chinese and Hindus to the "savage" Africans and North American Indians. Such a classification also placed the United States in the vanguard of progress, since the middle class predominated there as nowhere else in the world. The reasons for this middle-class ascendancy Grimké traced to the objective conditions of colonial settlement, linking the scattered insights of his early essays to more recent reading in Comte, Buckle, Guizot, Sismondi, and other students of European civilization.

The structure of American society had developed naturally

out of the nation's colonial experience, he noted. Early settlers had encountered a virgin wilderness, ill defended by a sparse native population. The conquest of the Indian had been easy, and his weakness contributed to his rapid disappearance from areas of colonial settlement, leaving the white man master of the field. Problems of inequality arising from the presence of a large subject race living side by side with its conquerors—a phenomenon familiar to every European state—never troubled the American pioneer. Here the "whole field of enterprise" lay open to the whites, who soon developed common traits of industry and self-reliance in their efforts to exploit the limitless expanses of vacant land that beckoned them onward.

"The leading fact in the history of American civilization undoubtedly consists in the very equal distribution of the landed property of the country," Grimké asserted.[33] Any attempt to fasten feudal tenures upon a backwoods wilderness was bound to fail. Instead, the New World environment tended to produce a single large class of farm owners, free of the tensions that embittered European proprietor and renter groups. As budding capitalists in their own right, the farmers of America further shared the interests and attitudes of urban businessmen. Conflicts between city and country, which so often disturbed the internal security of stratified societies, found little to feed on in such a pervasive bourgeois atmosphere.

On the political level, written constitutions reflected the prevailing uniformity of popular thought, as they withdrew from partisan debate the agreed-on essentials of the middle-class ethos:

A written constitution, framed by representatives of the people, locks up, and forever withdraws from the field of party strife, almost all those questions which have been the fruitful source of discord among other communities. For almost all the civil commotions which have occurred in the European states, have been caused by a disagreement about questions which are no longer open to debate in America. The constitution, with the approbation of men of all parties, has placed them beyond the reach of the government. The authority appertaining to the political departments is also strictly limited; and thus, a large class of powers which other governments have been in the habit of dealing with, without any control, cannot be exercised at all. In the same way as religion is withdrawn from the political world, and has given rise to religious toleration, the fundamentals of government are also withdrawn from all interference with by party; and all men agree to think and act alike with regard to them.[34]

A sound public opinion, operating outside formal political structures, provided the ultimate guarantee of stability to the American system. Unlike European regimes, which were regulated solely by internal check-and-balance mechanisms, American democracy relied upon continuing control from without by the people as constituent power. Political parties in the United States, representing no privileged interests apart from the community, served to balance competing forces in society as in government. Minorities of all kinds were thus encouraged to participate actively in the electoral process. By way of example Grimké cited the importance of young people and their involvement in public affairs.

Each new generation offered fresh insights into major political questions, he observed, and so-called "revolutions" in public opinion, such as America had experienced in 1776, 1801, and 1829, invariably coincided with generational changes within the population. To assimilate these new viewpoints in an orderly way, Americans elected young men to public office as a matter of course. In legislative assemblies their presence balanced the influence of older politicians, broadened the area of consensus on pending issues, and insured against violent demonstrations or other forms of youthful alienation. (There was violence enough in the routine deliberations of many a western state house, to be sure, but the frequent fistfights and name-calling represented personal quarrels, not class conflicts, and made no impact upon society at large.)

Even if popular majorities tended to be broadly based and responsive to minority pressures, however, what could be said of the *quality* of a mass electorate? Political parties in a republic might act as sounding boards for new ideas, as Grimké maintained; but what chance had any enlightened policy to win the approval of the average voter? Even with the aid of a public school system, innumerable individuals seemed destined to go through life with the bare rudiments of an education. The ignorant outnumbered the wise in every country of the world, but only in America did mere numbers generate power. While democratic theory demanded that all voters be well informed, democratic practice placed the future of free institutions in the hands of those least qualified to comprehend their operation. From this dilemma no escape seemed possible without undermining the foundations of popular rule.

Grimké himself had no illusions about the virtues of a mass electorate. "The great majority of persons I met," he confessed, "appeared to know nothing beyond the narrow circle of their daily occupations." Like the Founding Fathers he believed that human nature was unchanging and that every man was a potential troublemaker whose selfish drives outweighed his nobler impulses. To prevent a dangerous accumulation of power in some narrow clique it was therefore necessary to diffuse political authority broadly through the population. But where the old-line Federalists had made property ownership the test of a "safe" citizen, the Democratic jurist of the Jackson era argued for universal manhood suffrage: "The lowest class have a stake in the commonwealth as well as any other class; they are the most defenseless portion of the population; and the sense of independence which the enjoyment of political rights inspires, in innumerable instances acts as a stimulus to the acquisition of property."[35]

The ballot box itself, he urged, could be an educational force of uncalculated importance in shaping the manners of a democratic people. Through its unrestricted use bourgeois values might be disseminated among the entire population. Propertyless voters given a chance to participate in politics would soon feel the attraction of a legal system designed to enable all comers to acquire property on an equal basis. Spurred by envy and a desire for self-improvement, the lower classes were likely to become the most active supporters of the democratic state. Nor would their educational deficiencies make them any less responsible in their voting behavior than other citizens, since a knowledge of political affairs, like other kinds of learning, was partly intuitive. Did a munitions manufacturer have to understand the philosophy of chemistry, or a laborer the nature of the mechanical power he used, in order to do a competent job? Politics involved basic moral issues which simple natures often perceived more clearly than sophisticated ones. Even by failing at times to comprehend the exaggerated importance that demagogic leaders attached to certain pet measures, the masses might help to "moderate the ultra views of politicians of all parties."[36]

Grimké thus denied that any irrepressible conflict between numbers and intelligence lay ahead for America. The lower

classes in his view were more jealous of each other than of
their intellectual superiors, to whose opinions they generally
deferred. If unscrupulous demagogues succeeded on occasion
in winning mass support, they tended in the end to become
unwitting agents of public improvement. Speaking the language
of the people, they brought the leading issues of the day within
the ken of Everyman and stirred the masses to greater reflection
and inquiry. Since honest politicians in such circumstances were
soon able to regain their preeminence, the abuses of the electoral process found a natural corrective in the same robust
democracy that had invited them.

By 1848 it was scarcely shocking to suggest that all men were
entitled to vote for candidates to the legislature, but when
Grimké went on to apply the elective principle to the judiciary
he more than established his credentials as an iconoclast. A
reviewer in the *Western Law Journal* singled out his chapter on
"The Judicial Power" as an example of "extreme radicalism,"[37]
and it still is the most provocative segment of his study—a
devastating assault upon the mythology of judicial behavior.

After some twelve years of practical experience on the bench
he was only too aware of the fallibility of the judicial character.
"Sometimes on peeping into our courts, and seeing who pre-
side there," he wrote to Greene in 1846, "I am reminded of the
expression of Shakespeare, 'Handy dandy, where is the judge,
where the thief.' "[38] But at least Ohio limited her judges to a
seven-year term, while in half of the American states they continued to enjoy tenure for life.

The privileged status of the judiciary in an otherwise representative system could be traced, Grimké thought, to mistaken
assumptions about judicial "independence." Properly understood, the term meant simply that judges must not be subjected
to invidious *private* influences of any kind. In England, for
example, where they were appointed by a hereditary monarch
whom public opinion could not control, it was necessary to
make them irremovable so that they might be better able to
carry out their responsibilities to the people. But in the United
States the appointing power was exercised by the people, either
directly or through elected officials, and any insistence upon
judicial "independence" in the English sense could only elevate
the bench above community surveillance and encourage in time
a dangerous gap between judicial doctrines and evolving social

needs: "A public officer may be wonderfully skilled in all the mysteries of his profession and yet lag miserably behind the age in which he lives. It is a great mistake to suppose that because the judges are called to expound the principles of an abstruse science that they should be insensible to the general movement of the age and country in which they are born."[39]

Most Americans, while recognizing the importance of making governors and legislators accountable to the public for their actions, clung to the idea that judges were apolitical types who needed no policing because of the circumscribed and essentially derivative nature of their work. Nothing could be further from the truth, Grimké warned. Not only were courts called upon to decide many cases of political interest, but every tribunal in its workaday operations necessarily made law as surely as did any legislative body. Jurisprudence itself, contrary to popular belief, in no way resembled an exact deductive science in which a mass of subordinate principles flowed inexorably from a few elementary truths. The law was rather an "experimental science . . . which does not deal with abstract propositions simply, but with a state of facts where the question is perpetually recurring—what does human experience prove to be the wisest rule which can be adopted? or what does it prove to be the wisest construction of a rule already in existence?"[40] In almost every case precedents were both plentiful and conflicting, since they represented subtle variations in the rules applied to a multitude of similar, but never identical, controversies. Judicial discretion therefore determined the choice of one approach over another in any given situation, and the more evenly balanced two rival principles might be, the greater was the lawmaking power exercised by the court. What often tipped the balance was no more than a judge's personal predilections or even "prejudices . . . unperceived by himself," but the risk of his yielding unreservedly to individual idiosyncrasy could be lessened by subjecting him more closely to public scrutiny and the "healthful influence" of public opinion.

Ideally, Grimké argued, judges should be elected to office for a sufficient number of years to enable them to demonstrate their competence without losing their sense of dependence upon the community. He favored a maximum term of ten years for all incumbents and expressed the hope that the practice of legislative selection would soon give way everywhere to the direct election of judges by the people, as New York had provided in her new constitution of 1846. While most of his remarks were directed at state judges, he indicated that even the Supreme Court would be improved if its members were appointed only for a term of years. They would then be less disposed to ignore the prima facie constitutionality of state and federal legislation or to uphold erroneous judgments out of that "pride of opinion which makes [a court] desire on all occasions to give an example of consistency with itself, even at the expense of inconsistency with the rule of right."[41] Such a cogent critique of judicial policymaking was little appreciated in antebellum America. As a legal realist Grimké was several generations ahead of his time.

The stabilizing force of public opinion, which according to Grimké's argument kept the government on an even keel, could be seen at work in the private sector of American life as well. There a society of middle-class consumers successfully resisted extremist tendencies through an unrestrained power of patronage. Newspapers, for example, might disseminate the most radical views without hindrance since they were certain to be counteracted by the "voluntary censorship" of competing organs; religious sects had to vie for public support in the absence of government sponsorship—a condition that led to majority rule in church affairs and prevented the growth of a priestly caste; and professional groups, which were widely dispersed through the population, enjoyed no special privileges or centralized organization to set them apart from the untrained majority. Wherever one turned, the free interplay of selfish interests seemed to be contributing to social harmony, in the approved style of Adam Smith. The only threat to bourgeois complacency lay in the disruptive potential of two imponderables: working-class radicalism and Negro slavery.

Grimké paid little attention to the urban working class in the first edition of his *Considerations*. He assumed that any prospective danger from that quarter would be offset by the mobility of American society and the more humane outlook imparted to the workingman through a common-school education. But the revolutions of 1848, which raised the specter of class war throughout Europe, caused him to qualify his earlier optimism. In a revised version of his work published in 1856 he pondered the possible emergence of a rural as well as an urban proletariat. Still pinning his hopes on the continued prevalence of middle-class ideology at all social levels, he nevertheless predicted that "if the time ever arrives, when the danger to the institutions becomes imminent, from the banding together of the lowest class, the right of suffrage will be limited. The maxim of equality is a great regulative, but not a constitutive principle, of society; a distinction of great importance in the political world: when it ceases to perform the first function, it ceases to be a principle in the construction of the government."[42] There could be no clearer indication of his leitmotif: American democracy was a function of middle-class rule. To extend the egalitarian principle beyond the limits set by bourgeois practice would be to destroy democracy. In the name of "free institutions," then, one might as a last resort deny to disaffected voting blocs—such as socialists or communists—the power to undermine the proper goals of representative government.

But the threat of radical subversion appeared pleasantly remote in antebellum America. Of more pressing concern was the slavery issue and its political repercussions. True to his southern heritage, Grimké believed that the Negro was racially inferior to the white man and could never measure up to the responsibilities of middle-class democracy. In one of his earliest essays he had defended the right of a state to deny entrance to all free persons of color, remarking: "While they continue their wretched habits, consuming without producing, . . . we have no motive of policy, interest or humanity, to open wide our gates to them."[43] And he never tired of drawing invidious comparisons between the slovenly appearance of Negro settlements in Ohio (where "sloth, idleness and vice constantly meet the eye") and the neatness of the slave quarters on southern plantations. The emancipation of the slave, he contended, would create a debased black electorate to poison the very source of democratic institutions, for any hope of a mass exodus of freedmen to Liberia amounted to a philanthropic pipe dream. Under these conditions slaveholders had little choice but to maintain the plantation system handed down by their fathers, a way of life in which the hand of a benevolent paternalism was apparent: "The institution of slavery, when it is imposed upon the African race, may simply import, that inasmuch as the period of infancy and youth is in their case protracted through the whole of life, it may be eminently advantageous to them, if a guardianship is created to watch over and take care of them."[44] (Ironically, Grimké's dim view of the Negro's capacity for "civilization" was belied by two notable instances of black achievement within the ranks of his own family. His brother Henry had sired three mulatto sons by a slave on his Cane Acre plantation, and two of them—Frederick's nephews—moved north to carve out brilliant careers for themselves in the years following the Civil War. Archibald Henry Grimké went to Harvard Law School, practiced law in Boston, wrote biographies of William Lloyd Garrison and Charles Sumner, and championed the cause of Negro rights in Massachusetts politics; Francis J. Grimké, a graduate of Princeton Theological Seminary, became pastor of the Fifteenth Street Presbyterian Church in Washington, D.C., and a trustee of Howard University.)

Although Grimké felt assured that a majority of whites, North and South, shared his racial outlook, he noted that slavery was becoming a more explosive political issue every year. Misguided fanatics on both sides were partly to blame for the situation, but its exaggerated repercussions he traced to the emergence of a new breed of politicians in the nonslaveholding states. "We cannot hide our eyes to the fact," he wrote in 1850, "that the radical, the abolition party in the free states, are in reality fighting *their own fellow citizens*, through the men of the South."[45] Six years later he spelled out this thesis even more clearly, in regard to the rapidly growing Republican party.

The Republicans represented in his eyes "an array of one class of society against another." Their leaders, he charged, were second-rate politicians who saw in the manifold aspects of the slavery question a lever by which to dislodge more responsible old-line statesmen. In Boston, for example, "new men" of the stamp of Wendell Phillips, Josiah Quincy, and William Lloyd Garrison had long chafed under the sway of a conservative elite led by Daniel Webster. Now, with the death of Webster and other nationalist-minded politicians of the old school, these parvenus were busily constructing their own party on narrow sectional lines. Similar groups were at work throughout the North and West, paying no heed to the effect which their local feuds might have on the future peace of the Union.[46]

The outcome of any major sectional crisis depended, of course, in large part upon the mechanics of federal politics, and here, as elsewhere in the American system, Grimké thought he discerned a built-in safety valve. He compared the Union to a private association in which each member, having freely joined, became bound by the joint will of the group in carrying out the purposes of the club. No individual could set up his own program against that of the majority any more than a single state could veto a federal law. For, Taylor and Calhoun notwithstanding, each state by its entrance into the Union had alienated part of its sovereignty to the whole body of states that together created a central government. This joint procedure placed federal power forever beyond the control of the separate states and insured that in national affairs the will of the majority must prevail. But just as in private life a disgruntled individual might always resign from his club, so a state inveterately opposed to federal policies enjoyed one ultimate recourse: the right of secession.

Unlike the veto, secession did not involve an assertion of state power, but a confession of weakness in the face of a prevailing national consensus:

> Instead of forcible resistance to the federal head, instead of unlawful attempts to annul the laws of the Union, while the member is within it, that member is at liberty quietly to depart, while others retain their position in the confederacy. This is one of the most important attributes of a federal government. Secession is the instrument happily substituted in the place of open hostility to the laws. So that in the confederate form of government, the law itself provides against those great emergencies which in other countries are said to make laws for themselves.[47]

The secession argument appealed the more strongly to Grimké because he was convinced that the nation was bound to divide naturally into three or four independent confederacies at some future date. Cultural ties would then supersede narrower political loyalties, with studies such as his helping to link the several republics in a nexus of common institutions, manners, and ideas. "It is the maintenance of one civilization, not the maintenance of one union, which we are most deeply interested in," he declared, underscoring the broader implications of his work.[48]

On its first appearance in 1848 his book aroused little general interest. A few western reviewers praised it; those in the East tended to be cool. While he had never expected to attract a wide popular audience, he expressed disappointment at what he considered the provincialism of East Coast critics. "I verily believe if the work had appeared as from the pen of Webster or Calhoun, it would have had an unlimited circulation," he complained. "Its being written in a *small town*, in the heart of a *western* State, sheds a damper over the minds of the dull; and they are *Legion*, and an author has no more chance of justice, than an angel would have in Pandemonium."[49]

Still, the noted political scientist Francis Lieber regarded the book with unqualified admiration; it was adopted by the University of Virginia as a basic text for a course called "The Progress of Society" (along with works by Guizot and Tocqueville); and as late as 1854 Grimké reported "constantly receiving testimonials" from readers, some of whom found his *Considerations* superior even to Tocqueville's classic study of American democracy.[50] Encouraged by these marks of favor and by the gradual disappearance of the 1,100 copies already printed, the judge brought out a "corrected and enlarged" edition in 1856, though by that time the state of popular opinion in many parts of the country scarcely justified his reiterated faith in the moderation of middle-class Americans.

Man has always been disposed to frustrate the expectations of behavioral theorists; and in the wake of Bleeding Kansas and other outbursts of mass violence Grimké wondered at times what had become of that safe and sane society he had so painstakingly delineated. "I think our country is now passing through a more trying and critical period than has occurred since the foundation of the government," he admitted to Greene in September 1856.

> The Union may be dissevered, and if it is, feuds and animosities will as certainly grow up in the parts dismembered. They may disclose themselves very gradually at first, but in the end, they will be equally violent. An extensive country is favorable to reflexion, and is one of the cures for those intestine animosities, which will always exist, but which burn more fiercely the narrower the bounds within which they are confined. Let us keep together, until nature points to a separation.[51]

He seldom gave way to such gloomy thoughts, however, because he continued to draw a line between government and society. Whatever the defects of public men, he argued, the "condition of the population" was fundamentally sound, and the American people would not be pushed into civil war as the English had been in the seventeenth century. Even the raid on

Harper's Ferry and the support John Brown received from many middle-class spokesmen did not destroy his confidence in the underlying pacifism of the bourgeois character. As late as January 1861 he could still predict to his sister Sarah that the political crisis would be settled by a "moral force, and not by the arbitrament of the sword."[52]

His inveterate optimism did not spring from any Pollyanna-like refusal to face facts or from that species of intellectual pride that sometimes afflicts the worthiest exponents of philosophical systems. Grimké was the last person in the world to make a fetish of consistency, and he regarded it as axiomatic that every hypothesis must be tempered by the realities of daily experience. What kept him from grasping the full import of sectional differences was a basic misreading of human psychology. Lacking passion himself, he failed to appreciate its strength in others.

His psychological theories were spelled out in several essays on "The Nature of the Will" and related subjects that he wrote in the late forties and fifties. Here he developed his own version of the familiar faculty psychology of the time, emphasizing the predominant role of one master faculty that he termed "reflex consciousness." "Man is the only being in the whole range of the animal creation, who is endowed with this distinguishing faculty," he explained to Sarah, "and the consequences are obvious on the slightest examination. The materials of nearly all his knowledge are drawn from within, those of the animals are derived from without; and what an infinitely wider acquaintance has he even with the external world, in consequence of this important accompaniment of his senses."[53]

While he was somewhat vague in describing the actual operation of this all-important agency, it is clear that he regarded it as the prime regulator of individual behavior, analogous in its effects to the impact of public opinion upon society. And it was a *rational* mechanism par excellence, in no way subservient to the senses, for every feeling possessed an intellectual component that accompanied it to the brain and checked in advance any precipitate gratification of animal urges. Man therefore never acted upon blind impulse, but only after reflection. Or, as Grimké put it in another context: "I consider the brain as the immediate and exclusive organ of that immaterial principle we call the mind, and all our affective and intellectual acts, as manifestations of that organ. The consequence is, that instead of acts of intellection being transformed sensations, all our sensations, together with the rest of the affective part of our nature, are transformed intellections."[54]

To one who placed such a high value upon human rationality, the outbreak of war came as a particular shock. At first Grimké was inclined to treat the event as a monstrous aberration, to be explained only by the temporary ascendancy of a factitious public opinion that had been manufactured by party leaders. But he soon decided that invincible social forces had combined to produce the catastrophe, regardless of the actions of individuals. (In this respect his cultural determinism placed him in the same boat with nineteenth-century Marxist intellectuals, who found it equally convenient to appeal to "objective conditions" as a mode of exorcizing undesirable revolutions.)

He embodied his latest views in a series of "reflections" on current events that he published from time to time in the local papers. "My intention," he told Greene, "is, when they are completed, to incorporate them with my work on Free Institutions: the one containing the principles which lie at the foundation of our government and the other serving as a *commentary* upon the whole, by unfolding in concrete, if I may say so, the structure of American society in the nineteenth century."[55] Besides reiterating the major themes of his masterwork and drawing additional analogies (for example, comparing the Republicans to the Italian Carbonari and the French Socialists), he continued in these essays to plead the cause of peaceful secession. But his most incisive writing occurred in those numbers in which he examined the constitutional issues raised by the war and denounced the wholesale violations of civil liberties that characterized the Lincoln administration's treatment of suspected civilian traitors. To those who protested his lack of patriotism, he replied that "every one is bound, under all circumstances, to investigate the motives and conduct of public men: and the more perilous the times, the more imperious is the duty: otherwise, there might be no end to the most unjust war, and no meaning in the constitutional provision which guarantees freedom of opinion, and of the press."[56]

Long before his death Grimké's hermitlike existence in various Chillicothe hotels had earned for him an undisputed position as the town's leading eccentric. For years Miss Baskerville, the local schoolteacher, held him out as an awesome example to her young charges. "What would Judge Grimké think?" she would demand of them at each fresh hint of juvenile depravity. The students, for their part, were convinced that much of the judge's perfection lay in the eye of the beholder, and that Miss Baskerville—despite her predilection for Elizabethan ruffs and close clustering curls that gave her an uncanny resemblance to her favorite female model, the "Virgin Queen" Elizabeth I—cherished in secret a hopeless passion for the dry little man who never gave her a second look. In any event the Grimké mystique so impressed one susceptible schoolgirl that she was able years later to draw up an affectionate portrait of the old judge as he appeared to her in her youth:

> an elderly gentleman, of stiff and stately mien, his immobile face most granite and sphinx-like, striding along, looking neither to the right nor to the left, taking no apparent pleasure in the stroll, but since he had elected to walk, walking solemnly and slowly, until the proper amount of exercise had been taken. His nearly white hair was brushed smoothly back around his head; his face, long, thin, and sallow, with pronounced features and eyes that looked always straight ahead, was clean shaven. A stiff, white neckcloth encircled his throat in voluminous folds, the ends tied in a precise little bow. The swallow-tailed coat, the gloved hands held stiffly straight to his sides, the strapped pantaloons were guiltless of crease or wrinkles, and his whole appearance was so stiff, so mechanical, so wooden, as to resemble one of those figures whose jerky motions are governed by machinery.[57]

Such was the man who could philosophize dispassionately about the most bitter fratricidal conflict in American history. Even in his final illness, which began in the winter of 1863, he continued to dream of an impending reconciliation between the warring confederacies, as the heritage of middle-class solidarity reasserted itself above the din of the battlefield. His mental powers remained unimpaired to the last, and his lifelong attention to the minutiae of human experience never flagged. According to local legend he summoned a servant to his bedside a few minutes before the end to point out a particular suit of black clothes in which he wished to be buried; then he added, "I want you to see to it that they are well aired before you put me in them!"[58] With that final detail taken care of, he composed himself for a long night's sleep and quietly expired.

In his will he set aside the sum of $2,000 to defray the expenses of a final edition of his work (including the wartime essays), and he further directed that a complimentary copy should be distributed to every state library, to the principal college in each state, and to the congressional libraries of the United States and of the Confederate States. It was an appropriate gesture from one who believed so strongly in the cultural unity of white America.

The romantic racialism that informed Grimké's treatment of nonwhite cultures had its counterpart in the writings of most other antebellum intellectuals. Like them he believed that his inferences were based upon sound "scientific" evidence. If he had lived into the postwar era he would surely have responded to the biological determinism of Herbert Spencer and John Fiske. Hence it is doubly ironic that his political theories should have attained their greatest influence (and their only real popularity) in Venezuela, a nation that he would have classified as semicivilized at best. For this phenomenon the enthusiasm of one Latin American admirer was primarily responsible. Florentino González, a prominent political scientist and law teacher, translated Grimké's *Free Institutions* into Spanish as early as 1869 and thereafter publicized the judge's views so well that they were still being studied and quoted in the 1920s.[59] One wonders what Grimké would have said to such a surprising development—he who had once termed the Mexican people "one of the most pestiferous populations on the globe"[60] and who thought little better of their neighbors to the south. Probably, instead of turning over in his grave, he would have reflected that somewhere in his massive corpus there must be a principle to account for this contingency, as for all others— some secondary law of societal development under which to range a fresh illustration of the ineluctable progress of civilization.

Thos. Harrison wrote me that the children of
those not in the front of the present secessionists wd. be ashamed of their fathers. I am
willing to bide the test of time on that subject
. . . Secession is Revolution—I submit to it in
preference to Civil War—and shall do the part
of a loyal citizen to the State—But my line of
duty more than ever is in a strict & diligent
devotion to my profession.
Diary of William Pitt Ballinger,
December 31, 1860

8   William Pitt Ballinger, Confederate Lawyer

The collapse of consensus politics
in the 1850s weighed with peculiar force upon the western portions of the Cotton Kingdom. Areas like the Texas Gulf Coast,
standing on the threshold of a boom period of cotton production, clung to the defense of slave labor with even more desperation than the older producing regions to the east. Yet the
typical southwesterner remained also acutely conscious of the
benefits of continued union. He clamored for national railroads
and expanded water connections with the Atlantic Coast and
acknowledged a dependence on the Northeast for capital and
culture. Well-traveled lawyers who transacted much local
business for northern clients found it difficult to take seriously
the secessionist threats of the fire-eaters. Only belatedly were
many practitioners caught up in a ground swell of political
emotionalism that forced them at last to choose between the
South and the Union. The experience of William Pitt Ballinger
(1825-1888), apart from its unique personal features, testifies to

the underlying economic unity of the sections as well as to the incalculable strength of that phenomenon known as the southern way of life.

Farming, piety, and a taste for military adventure vied with legal skills to shape the outlook of three generations of Ballinger men. Joseph Ballinger, patriarch of the clan, was a Virginian who successfully combined tobacco planting and the supervision of twenty slaves with his duties as an occasional Baptist preacher. His son, Colonel Dick, moved to Kentucky in the late eighteenth century, fought Indians under Arthur St. Clair, and survived to become the first clerk of the courts of Knox County. In due time he relinquished this office to his son James, who had early shown a tendency to follow closely in the paternal footsteps by enlisting in the War of 1812 at the age of seventeen. Tall and powerfully built, James Ballinger won the confidence of the Kentucky mountaineers as much by his legendary feats of strength in country games as by his legal talents. With a wide circle of friends but few profitable causes, he derived his major income from the fees incident to his official duties at Barbourville, the county seat. Here he raised a family of two daughters and three sons, the eldest of whom he named after the celebrated English statesman William Pitt.[1]

The grandiloquence of the name was in keeping with the cultural pretensions of the town of Barbourville. Although it numbered less than two hundred inhabitants in the 1830s and 1840s, Barbourville boasted a vigorous intellectual atmosphere that led some later historians to dub it the Athens of the Kentucky Highlands. Situated in the hills of southeastern Kentucky on the turnpike leading down from Cumberland Gap into the bluegrass country, it lay athwart one of the great paths of emigration to the Ohio Valley—an outpost of empire, where continental concerns came as naturally as breathing to the informed citizen. When, for example, the Barbourville Debating Society was organized in 1837, its members wasted little time at their weekly meetings in discussing conventional or esoteric topics. Instead, they attacked such problems as: "Would it be to the interest of the United States to declare war against Great Brittain if she refuses to give possession of the disputed territory?" and "Should congress refuse the reception of abolition documents as contended by the Southern delegation?"[2] The final answers were seldom in doubt, for Knox County was overwhelmingly Whig in its politics and (with less than seven hundred slaves out of a population of seven thousand inhabitants) largely antislavery as well. Few important public questions remained unexplored by the debaters, however, and for spectators like young Will Ballinger the evening speeches at the courthouse brought the excitement of the great world into the routine life of a mountain hamlet.

Reared in a staunchly Whig household, Ballinger filled his early notebooks with voting statistics, culminating in the electoral results of the great Log Cabin campaign of 1840. Years later, when the party of Clay and Webster had passed into history, he reassessed the long-range implications of his youthful exposure to Whiggish principles and concluded that the Unionism so extolled by his father's political generation had been a deeply ambivalent thing:

Education & association made me a Whig—a Unionist—a "Native American" in politics . . . I was raised up to consider the Whig party the party of gentlemen, the Democrats that of rowdies . . . I thought Satan not more the Archfiend of wickedness, the foe to peace, harmony, & good order in Heaven, than was Jno. C. Calhoun on earth . . . For the principle of Union, of order, of stability, I had a sincere, a religious veneration. But for the Government—for any Department of it, such was not the case. I can look back now, and understand that my father and his friends—the old Whig elite of Kentucky—had the very lowest amount of respect for or confidence in the govt. —not in the original structure, but in its practical workings to secure the blessings for which it was designed. They didn't believe that Jackson, or Van Buren, or Tyler, or Polk, or any Democratic Congress, had any more real respect for or was more bound by the Constitution of the United States in their administration of the Govt. than if no such cons. had been in existence. They believed the Supreme Court of the U.S. as much a mere political machine as the President's Cabinet. In short, I can reflect, now, that in every circumstance which can constitute the failure of a govt. to secure the ends of its creation, they considered the govt. of the U.S. a *Failure*. True, they attributed it all to Democratic ascendency— but it is not less true that they considered it an existing fact.[3]

After attending local schools and completing two years (1840-41) of advanced studies at nearby St. Mary's College, Ballinger went to work for his father as deputy clerk. Soon he was meticulously extracting from Blackstone's *Commentaries* and familiarizing himself at first hand with the routine business of the courts. James Ballinger proved an able teacher, at least in his son's eyes: "He was no doubt the best Clerk in Kentucky— Knew the form of every judg^t & order known to common Law and Equity Practice."[4] In the natural course of things William would probably have followed family precedent and spent the better part of his life dealing in writs and warrants. But chance, in the form of a spate of ill health, decreed otherwise. Hoping to benefit from a change of climate, the fledgling lawyer accepted an invitation to continue his training in the office of his uncle James Love, who had moved to the republic of Texas in 1837. "Uncle Jimmy" was a man of many talents, not all of which found an outlet in his legal practice. A successful planter with large holdings on the Brazos River, he was also an intensely partisan politician whose hospitable Galveston home served as a rallying point for the opponents of Sam Houston. There he welcomed his eighteen-year-old nephew in the fall of 1843, and there for more than two years William Ballinger learned many things not found in Kent and Story.

He had almost completed his apprenticeship when the outbreak of the Mexican War stirred his romantic spirit and moved him to defend the cause of Anglo-Saxon progress. Enlisting as a private in the First Regiment of Texas Foot Volunteers, he took part in the storming of Monterey and returned in the fall of 1846 with the rank of first lieutenant. By that time the legal system of Texas had been restructured to meet the requirements of a new constitution adopted in 1845, when the republic became part of the United States. An act of May 12, 1846, regulated admission to the bar through the state courts, and *Judge* James Love (one of the framers of the late constitution) now presided over the business of the First Judicial District. To him Ballinger promptly applied to take the qualifying bar examinations. On November 12 a committee of three practicing attorneys, after examining the applicant in open court, pronounced him "possessed of sufficient skill and learning in the science of Law" to entitle him to a license, which was issued the following day by his uncle, "with a scrawl for a seal, there being no seal of Court furnished."[5]

A strong local tradition maintains that Ballinger's license was the first ever granted by the state of Texas. Certainly an impromptu, makeshift flavor attaches to the event, while the antidueling stipulations in the attorney's oath point to the continuance of a raw frontier society. In fact, however, the local Wild West was fast shedding its ferociousness, and the legislative outcry against dueling (which dated back to 1840) connoted the extinction, not the upsurge, of that violent practice. When Ballinger first began to plead in the Texas courts, the lusty, lawless days of the young republic were fading into memory, as business and professional leaders collaborated with increasing success to impose form and rationality upon the disordered fragments of a heroic age.[6]

Texas guidebooks described Galveston in the mid-nineteenth century as the Queen City on the gulf. Blessed with a superb natural harbor, the island community served as the chief port of entry and commercial entrepôt for the rest of the state. Its heterogeneous population of nine thousand persons gave it first rank among Texas cities and contributed to the support of an unusually large contingent of about fifty attorneys. The ablest of these practitioners, together with a sprinkling of native American merchants, bankers, planters, shippers, physicians, and clergymen, comprised the ruling elite of the island. Linked by marriage, friendship, and business associations, the first families saw eye to eye on most issues, meeting on their broad verandahs to plan for the day when Galveston, through its privileged trade position, should become the Manhattan of the Southwest.[7]

In a society where personal contacts and initiatives counted for much, Ballinger was fortunate in his family connections. At the outset of his career the influence of Judge Love helped him to secure a junior partnership in the leading firm of Jones and Butler, and his prospects brightened still more with his marriage in 1850 to Hally Jack, "the belle of the Brazos." Besides a well-deserved reputation for beauty, Hally brought to her ambitious young husband the support of one of the most extensive and powerful families in the state. The Jacks had played a conspicuous role in Texas public life since the days of Mexican rule. Patriots, politicans, jurists, entrepreneurs—their deeds were legendary in the Waco area, and, in conjunction with their numerous Harrison kin, they represented a network of politico-economic interests that stretched from central Texas to Mississippi and Alabama. Welcomed as an equal to the family circle, Ballinger soon broadened the base of his practice and discovered the added delights of land speculation. "Uncle Tommy

[Harrison] . . . has made sale of all *our* lands below Waco—at a profit of a little over $7000 on the purchase—to be divided between three of us," he reported in March 1854. "The news made me feel *almost rich*, as it will be the first money I have ever made, outside of my profession. I trust, though, when I get a little more to operate with, as our town is improving rapidly, that it will not be the last."[8]

Several months later he severed his connection with Jones and Butler and formed a new partnership with his brother-in-law Thomas M. Jack, a recent Yale graduate who had been reading law under his direction. The combination of the dashing, high-spirited Jack and the careful, scholarly Ballinger proved highly rewarding. Although the two men seldom agreed in their politics (especially in the early years, when Tom Jack was a secessionist Democrat), they remained close friends as well as legal associates until Jack's death in 1880, by which time their firm enjoyed an enviable reputation throughout the South.

In the formative antebellum years of his practice, Ballinger handled everything from assault cases and the defense of "cow-stealers" to divorce suits and probate matters. But most of his cases touched at some point upon land claims, for the continuing validity of Spanish and Mexican grants, coupled with the intricacies of community property concepts, created a mare's nest of legal problems for businessmen, legatees, and the general public. Debt collection provided an important secondary source of revenue, although in this field Galveston attorneys encountered stiff competition from local commission merchants, who processed a substantial volume of routine claims, especially for out-of-state creditors.

To secure a larger share of this interstate business, Ballinger made an ambitious promotional trip to the East in the summer of 1854. Over a two-month period he visited scores of businessmen in Boston, New York, and Philadelphia, offering to handle all of their Texas accounts for a small commission and, in some cases, supplying lists of prospective customers in the Southwest. The variety of firms he approached attests to the burgeoning trade that passed through the port of Galveston in those palmy days before the construction of the great railroad systems. Besides ironmongers, ship suppliers, and dry goods merchants, Ballinger interviewed saddlers, liquor dealers, clothiers, shoemakers, grocers, soap manufacturers, booksellers and stationers, dealers in agricultural implements, hardware, and crockery, tea merchants, druggists, and perfumers.

The results were not always encouraging. Some firms did little or no business in Texas, and other preferred to retain the existing pattern of merchant collections. A few individuals responded with open hostility, as did S. Cochran of S. Cochran & Co., who maintained that "Texas lawyers charge too much— Don't like lawyers—rather keep out of their hands." On the whole, however, Ballinger concluded that his campaign had been successful. In a small diary he recorded the name and address of every contact he had made, together with pertinent comments for future reference. Letters of introduction from Texas politicians and businessmen paved the way for meetings with such notable figures as Alexander T. Stewart, who conducted his appreciative young visitor on a personal tour of his dry goods emporium before turning over several valuable claims for collection. Equally responsive was the "great abolition house" of Bowen McNamee & Co., while elderly soap manufacturer Samuel Colgate provided, in addition to encouragement, a free cake of soap and a lengthy lecture on the more esoteric passages of Scripture. "Sebastopol & Armageddon are the same," he confided. (Ballinger's comment: "Very kind.")[9]

The terms of employment varied from company to company, but a representative offer was that made to Wolfe & Gillespie, a New York hardware firm: "I told [Mr. Wolfe] I w^d collect at maturity for 1% and do his gen^l collections by suit for 5."[10] Whether he struck a bargain with a prospective client or not, Ballinger was careful to leave one or more business cards on the premises as a standing reminder of his availability. He also advertised in the newspapers of each city he visited, a practice which he continued on his homeward journey through Mobile and New Orleans. This thoroughness soon paid off in increased firm receipts from out-of-state sources. The records of Ballinger & Jack for the sample year 1858 reveal an impressive volume of interstate business, the full extent of which may be gleaned from an official report that Ballinger compiled for Confederate authorities in July 1862. At that time, in compliance with a Sequestration Law which required disclosure of all debts owing to "alien enemies," he reported that his firm represented seventy-nine business concerns located in New York, thirty-eight in Philadelphia, and fifteen in Boston.

Local entrepreneurs likewise figured more prominently among his clients by the late fifties, heralding the transformation of his miscellaneous practice into one increasingly preoccupied with corporate problems—a trend that would in time make Ballinger a recognized authority on receivership proceedings. In 1858 he pleaded the first of the "Flats cases" for the Galveston Wharf Company, a semipublic corporation whose monopolistic control of the Galveston waterfront was sanctioned by the courts a decade later; in 1859 he successfully vindicated the right of the powerful mercantile firm of R. & D. G. Mills to engage in banking activities, despite the express prohibitions of the Texas Constitution; and on the eve of the Civil War he was actively engaged in a suit to set aside a special state tax imposed on the Wharton Railroad. Each spring and fall he traveled several hundred miles to attend the sessions of the district court at Brazoria and Matagorda, as well as the sittings of the Texas Supreme Court in Austin. While he sometimes had to swim swollen rivers and put up with substandard accommodations, he was in no sense a circuit-riding frontiersman. Texas still had plenty of them, to be sure: footloose country lawyers who accompanied a judge from one small community to another, picking up clients wherever they could. But Ballinger's practice from the start had been urban-based, and his trips represented no dragnet attempt to attract new cases but a logical extension of his dominant Galveston business.

By 1860 he estimated his annual income at between six and ten thousand dollars, only part of which he received in cash. Typical of the settlements he made with clients was one that he recorded in 1859 after winning a controversial inheritance suit: "The property was valued at $21,000—our part being one third —$7,000—We took Martin & Beall's indebtedness $3700; and the 1/2 block north of Atchisons for which Potter is offered $3150—and $150 to be made up otherwise—That will do for a good fee."[11] The ultimate amount of compensation depended in most cases upon Ballinger's ability to secure a favorable judgment from the court, for, like other Texas attorneys of the time, he preferred to negotiate on a contingent fee basis. The terms that were accepted by the Galveston Wharf Company for his services in 1860 thus included "$2000 certain"—to be paid in four instalments over an eighteen-month period—"and $4000 contingent on success."[12] In part an institutionalizing of the frontier passion for gambling, the contingent fee offered rich premiums to the most persuasive courtroom personalities.

Immersed in an expanding law practice and in regular touch

with northern businessmen, Ballinger's economic interests, like his political Whiggism, pushed him toward a vigorous support of the Union. But in the crisis of 1860 one added factor—the slavery issue—overrode all other considerations, to confound his logic and to reassert the claims of his southern heritage.

"Every people in the course of their history collects their ideal of independence and sovereignty around some one of their institutions, or some feature of their government, usually that which has met with the most opposition and cost them the greatest sacrifices to establish. Slavery is the institution fulfilling those conditions with us." Ballinger made the observation in a propagandist editorial written toward the close of the war,[13] but it summarized a long-standing faith in the necessity and benevolence of southern slave labor.

As a lawyer's son he had early been taught to appreciate the strength of institutional ties, whether political, religious, or social. Like his favorite philosopher, Edmund Burke, he regarded law as subservient to popular custom and relied upon glacial shifts in public opinion to bring about meaningful social change. Any other course he feared might destroy traditional behavior patterns and lead to the violence and anarchy that had characterized the French Revolution of 1789. Although not a professing Christian himself, he strongly supported churches as agencies of social control: "they are *organizations* for virtue. They put one publicly before the world on his responsibilities of a strict line of conduct, & by associations institutions &c they continually aid to hold him to the course of duty, & stimulate his growth in grace. Men need all the restraint and assistance possible to their acts."[14]

Such views when applied to the "peculiar institution" left little scope for reform efforts, save at the purely personal level, where Ballinger's involvement in the system was slight. He owned only a handful of slaves—eight, according to the tax records for 1861—some of whom he retained as household servants while others were hired out to local businessmen or to plantation overseers on the mainland. Whatever their ultimate disposition, Ballinger maintained a continuing interest in their welfare, as he scrupulously protected the rights of other slaves who came under his control through the liquidation of estates. Probate matters served as the connecting link between his law practice and slavery and sometimes brought him into violent collision with community prejudices. His most celebrated ante-bellum case involved Betsy Webster, a slave whose deceased master had left a will in which he not only set her free but bequeathed to her the bulk of his large estate. Certain heirs living in New York raised an immediate outcry, as did a number of prominent Galvestonians. In the face of stiff popular opposition, Ballinger undertook to carry out the testator's wishes, and by a powerful courtroom argument won for Betsy both her freedom and her legacy.[15] From time to time he also intervened to defend free Negroes who had fallen into the clutches of ship-master Thomas Chubb and his Galveston-based kidnapping ring.

These token gestures—the responses of a humane man to immediate circumstances—implied no indictment of slavery itself as a legal or ethical system. Ballinger stood ready at all times to enforce the generous whims of individual masters, but he served the hard-line taskmasters with equal zeal. "I think slavery has its evils," he acknowledged on the eve of secession,

> & I am not prepared to say that I consider the best social state of slavery preferable to the best social state of free institutions—But it has also its blessings—its "ennobling" influences to use Mr. Mason's well considered expression on the White case—& is far better for the slave. It is in fact the only relation that can exist where the African is in any considerable numbers, and it seems to me if the hand of Providence be visible in any thing in this world it is in the American slavery—necessary, I believe, in the first place to the development of this country—"elevating" to the African race & promising their redemption hereafter.[16]

This roseate outlook may have owed something to the peculiar attributes that slavery displayed in its local context. As one careful study has shown, the fifteen hundred island slaves enjoyed a privileged position that was not shared by their counterparts in the interior of the state. Large numbers of Gal-veston "city Negroes" found employment in the households of merchants and professional men who vied with one another to maintain them in a style befitting the dignity of their masters. Since local custom frowned upon any direct display of one's wealth in public, the best families indulged their taste for conspicuous consumption by showering their slaves with cast-off finery of a cut slightly better than that of the neighbors next door. On Sundays and holidays a gala carnival atmosphere accordingly prevailed among the blacks, to the amazement of uninitiated observers. James A. Fremantle, a British colonel who visited the island in 1863, was but one of a long line of travelers who could not get over seeing "innumerable Negroes and Negresses parading about the streets in the most outrageously grand costumes—silks, satins, crinolines, hats with feathers, lace mantles, &c., forming an absurd contrast to the simple dresses of their mistresses. Many were driving about in their master's carriages, or riding on horses which are often lent to them on Sunday afternoons. All seemed intensely happy and satisfied with themselves."[17] Ballinger's most intimate impressions of slavery grew out of his daily contact with this elite group of "merchant-employed" slaves, whose counterfeit image of the white man's ways may well have buttressed his faith in the "civilizing" influences of the system.

In any event, he identified with the slaveholding classes to a degree that cannot be explained in purely economic terms or by reference to the simple loyalties of the attorney-client relationship. Like the empire-building planters of the 1850s, he too fretted over the absence of an adequate supply of cheap black labor to open up the rich bottom lands of the Sabine and Brazos rivers to massive cotton production. And even more than most plantation owners he cherished a paternalistic ethic that he did not doubt could survive the most pragmatic of all wartime tests: the arming of slaves for military service.

As early as August 1863 he pressed such a radical proposal upon the civilian and military leaders of the Confederacy. Let the southern slaves be equipped with muskets, he pleaded, and sent to the battlefields to defend a way of life that was as beneficial for them as for their masters. (Characteristically, he thought it would not be necessary to pay the blacks for their services.) Although the authorities rejected the idea as too risky, Ballinger continued to agitate for Negro troops down to the closing days of the war. "We have blundered in this matter," he told readers of Houston's influential *Tri-Weekly Telegraph* in a final editorial plea of March 29, 1865: "If slavery is what we believe it to be—the best form of society—it is not only fitted for peace, but for the extreme exigencies of war. It is capable of fighting for the defence of society, and not alone for its destruction . . . We have not shown sufficient faith and trust in the institution."

For all his commitment to the slaveholding mystique, however, Ballinger never became a secessionist in his prewar politics. True to form he viewed the mounting crisis in North-South relations as a constitutional problem, to be worked out within the framework of the existing Union. When the old party of Whig nationalists collapsed as a viable force in the early fifties, he drifted into other "America first" groups: the Know-Nothings, then the Constitutional Unionists. A belated acquaintance with the writings of John C. Calhoun convinced him that sectional interests were ill protected against the excesses of majority rule, and he called for constitutional amendments to put into effect Calhoun's plan of "concurrent Executives," one of whom should represent the South as a distinct geographical entity. But he refused to follow the "South Carolina metaphysician" to the end of his argument, for in Ballinger's view (which he once described as "Whiggish even unto federalism") no state had a "right" to secede from the Union or to interpose its authority to nullify an act of Congress.[18]

Every disunionist was in fact a revolutionary, he protested, and revolution was the most dangerous of all expedients, to be pursued only after every legal remedy had failed. As the crucial election of 1860 approached, Ballinger threw off his customary reserve and took to the hustings locally to campaign in defense of his party's platform: "the Constitution, the Union and the Enforcement of the Laws." With legalistic thoroughness he prepared his case against the southern Democrats and argued it before the public in his best courtroom manner. "Let us not err here," he warned on August 23, 1860, in a major speech delivered under the auspices of the Bell-Everett Club of Galveston. "We should be satisfied beyond reasonable doubt that our ills are owing to the Union—that they are of such magnitude as to justify Disunion—and that Disunion will be their remedy."

On all three counts, he charged, the secessionists within the Democratic party had failed to establish their claims. Like the "designing reckless politicians" so prominent in Republican circles, the southern fire-eaters had exaggerated sectional grievances and made extremist principles a test of party loyalty. Their rise to power Ballinger attributed in large part to the misguided organizational techniques employed by American political parties—particularly the introduction and widespread acceptance of authoritative party platforms. The framers of these campaign documents, by substituting emotion-laden abstractions for sober facts, knew only too well how to impose illusory alternatives—"Honor v. Degradation—Union or Disunion"—upon the voting public.

Why is it that the world has been desolated by religious wars upon the most trivial & absurd points, except that they have been embodied in creeds or religious platforms, & therefore made essential instead of the broad charities & toleration of the Bible? Why is it that the Whig party & the American party & now the Democratic party have all broken down upon the construction of platforms; and that Democrats who yesterday stood as brethren are, with the same opinions, today reviling each other as enemies to good govt, and have split upon points of no present practical utility . . . except for that innovation in party machinery which is substituting party conventions & platforms in the place of the forms of the Constitution and of the abilities & consciences of able & honest men?

Preoccupied with imaginary perils, the secessionists had lost faith in the American people, Ballinger told his listeners. An "elect few" controlled the destinies of the southern democracy and now sought to force a proslavery program upon the rest of the nation. In the event of failure at the polls, these "hot enthusiasts" were resolved to sever all connection with the Union, as if political allegiance implied no more than an ordinary business relationship, "just the same in legal effect as between a planter & his commission merchant, between a client and his lawyer."

But what of the ties of race and history? What of the deeply felt emotions that stirred within the average man whenever his thoughts turned to the government of his fathers? Subconscious loyalties formed an invincible bond between the masses, North and South, Ballinger maintained: a bedrock of reality that would not yield to the sophistries of politicians. Even if Lincoln were elected, the southern people were not likely to be stampeded into revolution. Mindful of their responsibilities to a national heritage, they would demand and secure from their northern brothers those constitutional amendments that alone promised lasting protection to the institution of slavery.[19]

These remarks carried more conviction than the usual campaign oratory. At the time Ballinger genuinely believed that if secession ever became an immediate danger the "people" would rise up and repudiate their leaders "in a whirlwind of public wrath."[20] But events soon undeceived him. News of Lincoln's election reached Galveston on November 8, producing a "deep sensation" in the city. Within a week local militants issued a call for an emergency meeting to mobilize public support for a Secession Convention. Ballinger attended the gathering, held November 14, and found it the largest assemblage he had ever seen on the island. From the start the secessionists had things their own way; several moderates made speeches, but it was clear that the crowd was not with them. At one point Ballinger pushed toward the platform, intending to make one final plea for the Union, but the press of people and their hostile temper discouraged him, and he gave up the attempt.

That night he could not sleep. Doubts and forebodings devoured him, and in the weeks that followed he fell prey to an ill-defined sense of guilt.

Sadder, gloomier days—of deeper, truer reflection and self-communing than those, I have never passed [he wrote to a friend]. The prospect of the destruction of our National Government caused me an anguish that no event has ever done, or I supposed could do . . . Oh, for one quiet hour for men to have reasoned & felt, truthfully, why are we on the brink of Revolution—to have searched not for the immediate occasions thereof, but for the original, organic causes —to have searched for a remedy, not in patching & healing for the day, or assuming that force was to decide; but in providing a full sense of security not only for the apprehensions of the minority then, but of future minorities.[21]

The more he reviewed the situation, however, the more convinced he became that the time for compromise and conciliation had passed. One simple fact impressed him above all others: a "very large portion" of the southern people distrusted and feared the national government to such an extent that they were willing to risk the uncertainties of war rather than submit to the incoming administration. Despite constitutional restraints and guarantees, they had lost all confidence that their rights as slaveholders would be protected at the hands of the Black Republicans. No simplistic explanation, Ballinger reasoned, could account for such widespread popular disaffection. One could not attribute it to the influence of a single individual like Calhoun; or rely upon the alleged instability of the southern character; or even derive much comfort from blaming the wicked designs of politicians. (Too many of Ballinger's closest friends and relatives were enrolled among the secessionists to make a devil theory in any form credible to him.)

The true cause of the present crisis, he concluded, was institutional. It lay, as he had long suspected, in the breakdown of those mechanical checks devised by the Founding Fathers to protect slave property. Only if the American people acknowledged the defects of their Constitution and began major structural reforms might they preserve the Union. But, ironically, neither side would admit the need for constitutional change: "The doctrine of the perfection of the American Constitution is almost a superstition—& certainly an Absurdity. It was a mere experiment . . . And yet every one North & South, cries out, 'the Constitution is perfect—Only give us the Constitution.' " Such blind adherence to outmoded forms made disunion inevitable, Ballinger thought, as it also insured that the secessionists would not be allowed to leave in peace.[22]

Yet the use of force to maintain the Union struck him as so repugnant to "the spirit of our Govt." that he branded it a worse folly than secession itself. In the end he resolved to share the fate of his neighbors, even though that might prove to be a state of "degradation worse than that of any people of the globe":

> The Union can never be what it is. The silver cord is loosed—the golden bowl broken . . . The national govt may be reestablished— The political union may be perpetuated—but if so, it will be by force and we will be practically a conquered vassal people—Men may become involved in an error—but in that may be embarked all their manliness—all their honor, all their virtue—and then to be chastised & whipped back crushes out their spirit forever.[23]

With such grim reflections—and with the nagging premonition that the secession movement was earmarked for disaster—Ballinger pledged his considerable talents to the cause of southern independence.

To a former Unionist, support of the South's war effort implied no belated endorsement of the principle of state rights. "If the Union must be broken up I am for the largest confederacy that can be formed," Ballinger declared at the commencement of hostilities,[24] and throughout the war he consistently upheld the Richmond authorities against the attacks of state politicians, including some within his own family circle.

He was early introduced to the Confederate high command and to the logistical difficulties that hampered their strategy from the start. In late July 1861, in company with two other Texans, Ballinger undertook a special mission to Richmond to procure cannon and shells for the defense of Galveston.[25] He met with vexing delays at the War Department, where the secretary seemed "polite" but *didn't understand and wd. be technical*"; but bureaucratic bumbling proved minor compared to the technological hazards of the homeward trip. Despite assurances by the military that his cargo would be shipped straight through to New Orleans, it took almost a week to transport the guns by rail from Richmond to Bristol, on the Virginia-Tennessee border. Engines had a way of disappearing from lonely sidings without making scheduled connections; the trains did not move at night; and Ballinger heard numerous reports of derailments and collisions during daylight runs. The journey from Bristol to New Orleans consumed another twelve days and marked the end of rail travel, for no lines ran west to the Texas border.

It was now September, and the rainy season was fast setting in. Gun carriages, unavailable in Richmond, had yet to be secured from New Orleans manufacturers. A delay of several more weeks appeared inevitable, and blockading federal gunboats ruled out the possibility of expediting delivery of the guns by water. In desperation Ballinger resolved to push on overland, taking part of the matériel with him in wagons and leaving his fellow agent, Henry N. Potter, to follow with the rest as soon as the carriages were ready. The drive to Alexandria proceeded smoothly enough, but thereafter Ballinger faced increasing difficulties as he tried to cross the marshy bayou country of southwestern Louisiana. Torrential downpours slowed his progress from day to day, and he managed to reach his projected rendezvous point—Niblett's Bluff on the Sabine River—only with considerable help from the local population. (The entire citizen body of one small hamlet turned out to help him construct a makeshift bridge across a neighboring creek.) Potter fared less well, sending word on October 10 that his cannon were hopelessly mired in the mud sixty miles away. Since further land movement was out of the question, Ballinger had to appeal to military authorities in Galveston for men and transports to convey the guns down river on the last lap of what was beginning to seem an interminable journey.

The experience at least taught him one enduring lesson: in his subsequent reflections on the war he seldom lost sight of the South's economic and technological disadvantages.

> Our supplies . . . I fear will prove our real difficulty [he noted in his diary]. The Nos. of the enemy are so superior—their advantages of every kind so much greater that if their endurance will only continue it would seem that they must crush us by their greater bulk. Napoleon sd., speaking of invading England—that the French were 40 millions, the English 15 & if he could only bring them body to body he must conquer—His difficulty was he was never able to bring them "body to body," but with their facilities by water & railroad, the U.S. are able to do this—and I can not but fear for the result.[26]

He kept his qualms to himself, however, reasoning that only the most single-minded collective effort could save the southern people from subjugation. Through the worst days of the war he never wavered in his public support of Confederate policies, finding some encouragement in the idea that Southerners were fighting the same kind of struggle for national self-determination that the Greek patriots of the 1820s had successfully waged against the overwhelming forces of the Ottoman Empire.

With his romantic temperament and his earlier zest for military adventure, one might have expected Ballinger to seek an army commission, but, significantly, he chose to play out his wartime role well behind the lines. "The glory I leave to others," he announced, ignoring the example of relatives and friends who hastened to answer the call for volunteers. (Even Uncle Jimmy Love enlisted, at the age of sixty-six, and saw active duty with Terry's Texas Rangers.) Ballinger served the Confederacy in much less dramatic fashion by accepting an appointment as receiver of alien enemy property in October 1861.

The post was an important one, although its recipients were not likely to win any popularity prizes. On August 30 the Confederate Congress had passed a Sequestration Act, aimed at confiscating all enemy-held property within the South. Such a measure had long been under consideration, but the fortuitous passage of similar legislation by the United States Congress during the previous month enabled southern lawmakers to justify their work as an act of reprisal, adopted to "indemnify our own citizens for their losses, and restrain the wanton excesses of our enemies." Proceeds from the sale of sequestered property were to be paid into a special Treasury fund, which enthusiasts predicted would eventually total $250 million. Enforcement of the program centered in the Confederate district courts, whose judges were empowered to appoint receivers to ferret out and secure all locally held enemy assets. The law required every citizen to report such property on pain of fine and imprisonment, and receivers could count on obtaining additional information through private denunciations and grand jury probes. Thereafter a comprehensive battery of legal controls lay at their disposal: writs of garnishment to be served on uncooperative suspects; ex parte sequestration judgments; and the sale by court order of perishable goods and other impounded property.[27]

"I am afraid there will be odium attached to the office," Ballinger mused, but he could not resist the guaranteed stipend of $5,000 a year—"a God send during war times."[28] On October 28 he took the oath as receiver for the First District of East Texas, embracing the counties of Galveston, Liberty, Harris, and Chambers. In a circular letter prepared the next day he reminded all citizens of their duties under the law and pledged that he would enforce its provisions with justice and moderation. Merchants in particular were assured that any disclosure of their private business affairs would be kept strictly confidential. The public's response to his plea for cooperation was both immediate and heartening. "Real busy all day," he reported on November 14. "Quite a no. of calls—Parties seem genly employed in making up Statements." Items of movable property poured in upon him from week to week, ranging from cattle and slaves to railroad iron, sawmill machinery, and the fire engine Lone Star, complete with twenty-five feet of hose. By mid-December he found it necessary to rent a "large warehouse" in Houston for the storage and sale of these acquisitions, most of which brought a fair price at auction.

The most promising source of revenue lay in quite another direction, of course: confiscation of the immense indebtedness owed by Southerners to "alien enemies" in the North. But any move toward this objective raised loud outcries from businessmen, some of whom shrank from the mere reporting of their northern debts. Alternatively, a few shrewd types offered to reconcile patriotism with self-interest by setting their own terms for compliance with official directives. "I am indebted to and have in my possession some property of persons residing within the United States," advised C. F. Duer of Rose Hill Post Office in Harris County. "Not wishing to appear upon the records of the Court as having voluntarily informed against my northern creditors but at the same time cordially approving of the confiscation act passed by Congress I request that a writ of garnishment be served upon me. And I would beg that my evidence be taken before Jacob Chill a Notary Public of Harris Co. as my business is such that I cannot well leave home to attend at court."[29]

Although the Sequestration Act did contemplate the active collection of prewar debts, merchant protest soon led to an official change of policy. An amendment of February 15, 1862, exempted from collection the principal of debts owing to alien enemies until twelve months after peace should be declared. This moratorium on principal remained in effect till the end of the war, leaving only interest payments to be made in the meantime, as they fell due. While the new policy cut drastically into anticipated Treasury receipts, it also brought Confederate regulations into line with the liberal stay laws enacted by individual states for the benefit of their local debtors.[30] And it relieved the anxieties of many district judges who had been reluctant to enforce the rigorous provisions of the original act. Ballinger's friend William P. Hill was one such jurist, who had early informed the business community of Galveston that he would require only the payment of interest on confiscated debts. But Hill's financial conservatism did not stop there; he also opposed the sale of most sequestered property except for an occasional lot of movable goods.

To Ballinger such moderation, in the face of wartime needs, appeared incomprehensible. The more he learned of the receiver's business, the more persuaded he became that the entire confiscation program needed some massive rethinking. "My opinion has always been that the Sequestration Laws were impolitic," he observed in the fall of 1863.

Practically, they will do us no good in carrying on the war. The funds derived are a mere drop in the bucket. If, by peace, the northern merchts. could recover their debts no doubt they wd. be for peace, & it wd. be a most powerful & probably controlling influence—Now, the merchants look to the subjugation of the South as their only chance of recovering their debts—If there were no such laws, they wd. look to peace as re-establishing their rights. The money influence on Legislation is notorious at the North. A line of steamships, or Railroad can carry any project. What, then, cd. not the mercantile influence—interested in the hundreds of millions of Southern debt accomplish? .

But the sympathies of the northern business community had already been alienated, and no amount of wishful thinking could undo the ill effects of the Sequestration Laws in that quarter. Only one vital question now remained: How should those laws be administered to secure for the Confederacy the maximum support of her own business and mercantile classes? On this point Ballinger's ideas were clear and specific. He called for the prompt payment out of Sequestration Funds of all debts owed by alien enemies to Confederate citizens, and the sale of all sequestered property, including real estate, to southern purchasers. "Merchts. & purchasers [ought to be] made interested in the success of our govt.," he urged. "This wd. increase the liberality of many, & make *Patriots*, otherwise indifferent."[31]

Ballinger embodied his Hamiltonian proposals in a bill that Peter W. Gray, a representative from Texas, tried unsuccessfully to push through the Confederate Congress in 1863. (Although a majority of the house judiciary committee approved the measure, it was eventually voted down.) The rebuff from Richmond was offset, however, by a modest victory on the local front. Under Ballinger's prodding, Judge Hill agreed in October 1863 to permit the sale of sequestered lands whenever his receivers deemed it advisable. A flurry of petitions soon followed. By the end of November Ballinger noted with satisfaction a decided upswing in court activity as he and two other receivers obtained orders of sale for several tracts of land and began collecting "a good deal of money."

Historians have been unable to determine with certainty the total amount of funds paid into the Confederate Treasury under the Sequestration Laws. Until 1863 Treasury reports did not separate sequestration items from miscellaneous receipts, and no figures were published for the half year between September 30, 1864, and the evacuation of Richmond. During the intervening seven quarters (from January 1, 1863, to September 30, 1864), Treasury officials reported net receipts of $7,468,083.28 from confiscated property. The period of reliable accounting covers only half the lifetime of the Sequestration Laws; from start to finish the program, with all its deficiencies, probably brought in well over $12 million.[32] Ballinger estimated in June 1864 that some $2 million had passed through his hands since he began his work as receiver. There is little reason to doubt the figure, which includes not merely his own collections but those of the other four receivers from the Eastern District of Texas, for whom he acted as depository. The scattered receipts that he kept among his papers testify to the substantial sums which he transmitted at irregular intervals to James Sorley, chief depository for the state of Texas—payments that did not cease until the spring of 1865.

During the war years Ballinger's legal practice was virtually confined to his duties under the Sequestration Laws; his official position provided by far the major part of his income. (In addition to his regular salary as receiver, he was paid a commission of several hundred dollars each year for his services as depository.) Although the total amount of his earnings reached an impressive level on paper, the depreciation of Confederate currency, combined with mounting family expenses, soon made most of his balance-sheet gains illusory. By 1864 he complained that only his "private means" enabled him to get along, and he constantly looked for ways to improve his financial situation. The war itself brought him a little new business, as it accounted for most of the cases on the active docket of the Confederate district court. From time to time he found himself involved in habeas corpus proceedings, to secure the discharge of a client from military service; or arguing novel questions of salvage rights and prize law; or defending an army officer accused of taking bribes. He also acted as defense counsel at several courts-martial, where his clients were accused of such crimes as mutiny, desertion, and assaulting a superior officer. Sometimes he obtained a good fee for his services, but the occasions were rare, while the opportunity of pleading any type of case before the state courts seldom materialized.

The docket books of Ballinger & Jack, for example, reveal that the firm appeared before the Galveston district court in 116 cases during the June term of 1857. By the spring of 1861 the number of cases had fallen to 32, and most of these were continued indefinitely as a result of the wartime situation. Ballinger thus found himself in much the same position as that described by his friend William Webb, an attorney of La Grange, Texas, who reported in January 1864: "I regularly attended Columbus

Court before the war, but since that time I have not been there once. The attys & parties of all the cases civil & criminal I have there are nearly all in the army and the cases by common consent are to lie over till the war ends: hence I should have no other business to call me to Court." Similar conditions prevailed in all parts of the state judicial system, including the Texas Supreme Court. Toward the end of the war Ballinger hopefully inquired about the disposition of certain appellate cases long pending before that tribunal. "They are very pleasantly sleeping on the Court Docket," responded an Austin practitioner. "Nothing has occurred to disturb their repose. When their resurrection will take place I cannot really tell."[33]

Some matters of a routine nature continued to claim Ballinger's attention despite the war, of course. He was retained in several probate actions and debt proceedings initiated before the state tribunals; he also did a certain amount of office counseling and drew up title deeds and other legal documents. These activities added comparatively little to his income. The largest wartime counseling fee he charged was $200, for which he prepared a "full written opinion" covering the major points in a complex case that involved the sale of valuable crops. This occurred in 1863; a year later he was happy to receive for comparable services "a dozen nice stockings for the children—a good fee these times!"[34]

Professional duties and government service still left him with much free time, which he put to use in writing for the press. Journalism had always interested him, and he fully agreed with those friends who assured him that in becoming a lawyer he had "spoiled a good editor." Before the war he had contributed an occasional article on political or cultural matters to Willard Richardson of the Galveston *News,* although usually with some feelings of guilt for having strayed beyond the narrow limits of legal professionalism. Now the wartime crisis relieved his scruples and enabled him to reconcile private taste with public duty. As a community leader who abjured involvement in politics, he found the role of propagandist eminently suited to his sense of noblesse oblige. In the beginning he wrote without pay for the two foremost journals of the Texas Gulf Coast—the Galveston *News* and the Houston *Telegraph.* Eighteen of his pieces had been published by the fall of 1864, when his worsening financial situation led him to seek a less altruistic arrangement. On September 29 Edward H. Cushing, editor of the *Telegraph,* agreed to pay him $12.50 per week in specie for regular editorial contributions. Thereafter Ballinger supplied the Houston paper with three lengthy editorials each week, down to the closing days of the war.

His propaganda efforts, while scarcely brilliant, did not lack either verve or credibility. With a rambling yet dramatic style—the product of extensive reading in Scott, Cooper, and other romantic authors—Ballinger was able to cajole his readers through an often tedious argument by pausing at judicious intervals to assault their emotions. The formula was not fool-proof, but with him it generally succeeded because his innate respect for facts kept him from going too far. "I shall endeavor to tell the truth," he promised himself,[35] and if he touched up a few details here and there, he never ignored underlying realities, however disagreeable they might be—unlike editor Cushing, who sometimes indulged in wishful thinking and pounced upon every wild rumor that promised success to southern arms. Thoughtful readers valued Ballinger's sober pronouncements and encouraged him to persevere in the task of giving "a proper direction" to the public mind. "The influence of a journal of considerable circulation is tremendous," wrote the lawyer-politician Fletcher S. Stockdale in January 1865, "not only upon the opinions and moral tone of the country, but also upon the action of the government . . . If I were competent and could get the position I should deem my duty in this struggle fully per-formed if I faithfully exerted my faculties in and devoted my time to such pursuit."[36]

Ballinger directed his own journalistic talents to the defense of Confederate policy at all levels—from the suspension of the writ of habeas corpus by Congress down to the imposition of unpopular economic controls by local military commanders. The difficulties of his task increased considerably after the election of Governor Pendleton Murrah in 1863. A state rights advocate, Murrah soon began to interfere openly with the financial and military programs of the Confederacy in Texas. To raise needed state funds, the governor set up his own organ-ization to compete with the Confederate Cotton Bureau for the acquisition of that valuable commodity, upon whose sale depended the provisioning of Confederate forces. Murrah also claimed a concurrent jurisdiction over all Texas conscripts and refused to turn them over to Confederate authorities for service outside the state. Rumors of an impending Yankee invasion from the coast or through the Indian territory strengthened his hand and brought strong support for his Lone Star policy from many of Ballinger's friends, including his irascible brother-in-law Guy M. Bryan.[37]

"I am convinced that the Govr. is undertaking to vindicate State rights or state might, rather, in a perilous manner for these times," Ballinger commented after a personal meeting with Murrah in the winter of 1864. He devoted most of his articles for the next few months to a sustained attack upon the governor's program and succeeded by June in converting both the *News* and the *Telegraph* into strong antiadministration sheets. He also bombarded Murrah with "frank" letters denouncing his course, to which the governor replied with bland politeness. ("He says if all intelligent citizens wd. deal with equal candor it wd. be better for the public interests," Ballinger reported on one occasion.)[38] Within his own family circle, however, the candid approach produced less happy results, as quarrels over state rights led to a personal secession crisis of sorts. According to Ballinger's diary, it took him the whole of one wintry night— until three or four o'clock in the morning—to placate Guy Bryan, who proved to be not only "rabid about Texas influence" but neurotically convinced that his brother-in-law had never treated him as an "equal member" of the family.[39] Both conflicts were resolved in time, the more important one being settled through the firmness of Edmund Kirby Smith, commanding general of the Confederate forces in the Trans-Mississippi District.

After July 1864 Governor Murrah abandoned all further attempts to pursue a separate Texas policy and cooperated with Confederate authorities until the end of the war. The climax of the struggle was fast approaching, as every week brought news of fresh military reverses in the East. "We are over-matched —and not skillfully commanded," Ballinger mourned. "God help us—All looks dark." But he continued to write spirited patriotic broadsides, "deducing all the comfort & encouragement I could."[40] The surrender of Lee's army in early April, followed swiftly by the assassination of Abraham Lincoln, left him with a sense of exaltation, as if the two events were somehow linked in a vast cosmic design that might yet spawn a miracle to save the southern cause. In an emotion-packed, two-column editorial he elaborated his reflections upon the

President's death, inviting readers to share the fierce and unfamiliar joy that now possessed him.

Lincoln, he acknowledged, had been a man of rare abilities. A born leader, his personal charm and organizational genius had enabled him to build up a strong political following and to heal the rifts within his party. But his very virtues, when enlisted in the service of northern fanaticism, made him a more dangerous monster than even Robespierre had been:

> Abraham Lincoln had as fell a purpose as ever existed in the bosom of despotism, that the Southern people should be bereft of their liberties, subjugated to a government hateful to their inmost souls, and ruled forever, not by their own free will, but by the bayonets and the votes of the more populous North. He was the instrument of the North to effect upon us and our children this destructive, ruinous object . . . Not a soldier, nor a woman, an old man nor a limping child with true heart to this Southern land but feels the thrill electric, divine, at this sudden fall in his own blood of the chief of our oppressors. Monomaniac, assassin, villain, may have been the hand. We approve it not. Open, fair, and honorable shall be all our own acts, and those we shall ever advise or uphold. But we stand still before the Providences of God. And with that deep, ineffaceable, eternal feeling which led the great-souled patriots of noble old Virginia to inscribe as her motto upon her shield, "Sic Semper Tyrannis," so say we a thousand and a thousand times, Sic Semper Tyrannis. Not in fair fight merely, not on the field of honorable battle, not by the law's formal sentence, but every where and by all means, Sic Semper Tyrannis. Whoever would impose the fate of servitude and slavery on these Confederate States, whatever fatal Providence of God shall lay him low, we say, and say it gladly, God's will be done. These are feelings for which we are ready to stand at His judgment bar. Our prayer to Him, like that of the great French patriot is, "whoever may perish, may our country be free."[41]

But the time for heroic countermeasures had already passed, and with it the dream of an independent South. Even as Ballinger wrote, the remaining Confederate armies east of the Mississippi were laying down their arms, leaving only the westerners under Kirby Smith to oppose the triumphant progress of the Yankee conquerors.

Ballinger had long distrusted the capacity of the southern people to endure the hardships of a protracted and ruinous war.

The *"mass of the people* without property" had no sufficient stake in the contest to ensure their continued loyalty, he noted in 1863. Once the tide of battle turned sharply against the South, the lower classes were likely to rise up in "a reaction against the leaders of the Revolution & the Slaveholders."[42] Subsequent events had failed to confirm his suspicions, but in the spring of 1865 they still occupied a central place in his thinking.

By mid-May he was convinced that further military resistance would be both futile and dangerous. The Texas troops were thoroughly demoralized; some units, it was reported, were already disbanding, as officers and men daily drifted away, taking their guns and other military property along with them in lieu of back pay. To attempt a new campaign under such conditions would inflict "useless sufferings" on soldiers and civilians alike, while the long-term psychological effects might be even more appalling. Most Texans, Ballinger believed, were "now attached to the revolution, & wish it success. Some member of almost every family has been lost in it or rendered honorable service which associates perhaps their fondest recollections and their strongest sense of patriotism with the Revolution. They will remain *Southern* in their sympathies and feelings, notwithstanding its failure unless their sense of justice and right are outraged by its future conduct." The lesson to him seemed clear: policymakers should seek an immediate termination of hostilities to forestall an enemy invasion and retain the support of the masses.[43]

Governor Murrah and other top state officials had reached much the same conclusion in their own deliberations. On May 17 the governor sent for Ballinger to discuss the advisability of appointing a special civilian peace mission to negotiate with federal commanders in New Orleans. Ballinger approved the plan although he warned that the Texas commissioners could not expect to win any political terms from the generals. Federal authorities recognized the Confederate military organization as a fact and were empowered to treat for its disbandment, but they acknowledged no legitimate secession governments with whose agents nonmilitary matters might be resolved. "Their demand is inflexible," Ballinger pointed out; "lay down arms, return to the Union, come under the constitution—submit to the laws. We have to take the laws present & future with all their contingencies. If unconstitutional we test that by the courts. If consl. they must be obeyed." Nevertheless, an impromptu attempt at mediation he thought might do some good, if only by convincing the generals of the good will of the civilian population. The commissioners might at least hope to secure a military stipulation that the state would not be invaded, and if they were particularly persuasive they might even be able to prevent the establishment of a postwar military regime in Texas.[44] Impressed by these considerations, Murrah urged Ballinger to become one of the commissioners himself, and after some initial hesitation he agreed. A week later he and Ashbel Smith, the veteran Texas diplomat—carrying letters of authorization from Governor Murrah and Confederate General John B. Magruder—sailed for New Orleans aboard the U.S. gunboat *Antona*.

Even before they arrived at the Crescent City the signs of a new order became apparent. "I notice that Ft. Jackson is occupied altogether by negro troops," Ballinger scribbled in his diary. "They look well dressed & seem to move well. There are a good many negro sailors aboard this ship."[45] Other changes, of a far-reaching political nature, threatened to wreck in advance the prospects of the peace mission. By the time the *Antona* docked on May 29, Kirby Smith had already surrendered the Trans-Mississippi District, leaving Ballinger and his associate with little to say to their federal hosts.

Nonetheless they persevered, in a valiant effort to demonstrate that a military occupation of Texas would now be unnecessary. Let the normal legal process take its course, Ballinger pleaded. Regular elections were scheduled to take place in August, pursuant to state law. The procedure was automatic, and required no action by any secessionist officeholder. "Proper tests of allegiance & fidelity" might be administered to the voters to ensure that only those who had remained loyal to the Union participated in the election. They would choose a governor and legislature pledged to enforce the policy of the United States government and fully able to do so, since the machinery of civil rule, if undisturbed, was more than adequate for the preservation of public order.

Generals Edward Canby and Phil Sheridan listened politely but turned down all such proposals. In the end the commissioners secured only one minor concession: to prevent the failure of the current cotton crop, the army would do its best to keep the Negroes from leaving their plantations. "There might be commotion a little while," said Canby, "but they wd not be permitted to follow the army or be idle." With this modest assurance to crown two weeks of confidential talks, Ballinger and Smith gave up and returned to Texas.[46]

The Seventy-sixth Illinois Regiment was soon camped along the northern fence line of the ex-commissioner's Galveston property, over which venturesome troopers daily scampered to pilfer chickens and "distract" the ladies. Indoors another minicrisis was brewing, as several former slaves declined further household employment, even for wages. But Ballinger resolutely ignored these temporary inconveniences of the postwar scene to devote his full energies to the securing of pardons for himself and his friends. His record as an antebellum Unionist served him well and enabled him to obtain a prompt review of his case from the new provisional governor, Andrew J. Hamilton, a Johnson appointee. In late July the governor recommended amnesty for him "in strong terms," and a group of local businessmen at once retained him to carry their petitions, along with his own, to the nation's capital for final action by the President. "I have the greatest solicitude for promptness & success in the business," Ballinger observed on the eve of his departure from Galveston. "I feel that I had no rights & was not my own master until I get my own pardon. Success for the others will enable me to realize something considerable—& most acceptable at this low ebb in my fortunes."[47]

Thanks to the ramifications of a prolific family, he could count on some influential support in Washington. His uncle Green Adams, a prominent Kentucky Unionist, was already on the scene, hoping to land a lucrative government post as a reward for his wartime services. Uncle Green knew his way around the government offices, had a personal acquaintance with the President, and was more than willing to earn some ready cash by pulling what strings he could to aid his nephew. Ballinger relied heavily on Adams's connections to push through the petitions of his clients, but he owed his own speedy pardon to the good will of another relative: his brother-in-law Samuel F. Miller, associate justice of the United States.

Miller, a staunch Republican appointed to the Supreme Court by Abraham Lincoln, had been a close friend of Ballinger since the latter's boyhood days in Kentucky. Despite their political differences (which they frankly acknowledged), the two men had maintained a steady and affectionate correspondence that lapsed only for a time during the war years. Thereafter, at Ballinger's request, the judge provided him with strong letters of introduction to President Johnson and William Henry Seward, secretary of state. "I have known [Ballinger] since he was ten years old intimately," Miller avowed, "and I have never known a man on whose integrity I would rely more confidently."[48]

These assurances worked wonders in the Executive Department. The day after he called upon Secretary Seward, Ballinger read in the newspapers that his pardon had been granted. (At Seward's personal request, whispered his uncle.) The President might have been a bit less compliant had he been aware of the opinion Ballinger expressed of him four months earlier in the pages of the Houston *Telegraph:* "Of all partisans, Andrew Johnson has ever been the most unscrupulous, the most extreme, and the most vindictive . . . He is known of all men to lack integrity, to lack justice, to lack honor, to lack humanity . . . it is our sincere belief, that no man is less fitted to bind together, to sustain and to guide."[49] But circumstances alter cases, as every lawyer knows. With his pardon in hand, Ballinger took a fresh look at the President and found him surprisingly salvageable. He was, after all, "rather a good looking man," with "a good deal of dignity of person"—sufficiently prepossessing, in fact, to make his erstwhile critic now privately resolve to "sustain" him against the more radical elements of the Republican party.[50]

The immediate success that attended Ballinger's efforts in his own behalf proved impossible to duplicate for his clients. By the time he reached Washington in mid-August 1865 pardon peddling had become an open scandal. A special Executive Bureau was being organized to screen all incoming applications, and the volume of pardons granted had dropped to a bare minimum—about two a day, he reported glumly. His own pardon was signed on August 19, but it took an additional two months to process the petitions of his friends. Personal interviews with Johnson and Seward failed to speed things up, although Ballinger labored manfully to convince them that geographical and economic factors justified special treatment for his clients. They were businessmen, he argued,

not criminated in secession—useful to the community in the restoration of business—that in a commercial town for its business men to be under disability prevented the restoration of prosperity . . . the repairing of railroads &c.—that travel had not been opened from Texas—none but Govt vessels were running—the Govr had suggested to me to come on & knew I wd bring on the petitions he had recommended—that pardons had been granted in other states—& if Texas far off & behind hand as she was could not get a little special attention to her cases, it wd operate very unfairly.[51]

His contentions were plausible and evoked expressions of sympathy from his listeners, but the President's docket was so cluttered and chaotic, he was told, that it was simply impossible to assign priorities at present. Yet some applications were receiving prompt attention, Ballinger knew: like those which Colonel Carter, a fellow Texan, was handling. Carter, it was rumored, had found a useful ally in the attorney general's cousin, who was willing to expedite his cases on cut-rate terms: ten pardons for $150. "This is disgraceful and shabby," Ballinger snorted.[52]

His own operation, although slower and more decorous, was also a good deal more profitable for all concerned. On October 27 Green Adams finally delivered twenty pardons, for which Ballinger paid him $3,000 and promised an additional $500 after making further collections in Galveston. Ballinger's own net receipts totaled approximately $5,000, exclusive of the payment to Adams, and he obtained further fees of $2,500 on his return home. Despite four years of ruinous war, he remained in comfortable economic circumstances, with real and personal property valued at $12,000 for tax purposes in 1865. (At the outset of the struggle he had been worth $29,200 in the eyes of the assessors, but this figure included an investment of $6,000 in Negro slaves and reflected a scale of general valuation that had plummeted sharply downward as the fighting continued.) The return of peace, moreover, brought renewed opportunities for professional enrichment.

While in Washington Ballinger ascertained that six of his important prewar cases were still pending on the docket of the Supreme Court. He took immediate steps to reactivate them, and he moved with like promptness in Texas to reinstate those northern claims that had been surrendered to him as receiver. By the early months of 1866 Ballinger & Jack was employed in 192 suits on the district court level alone. "We take lunch in a basket, and do not come home to dinner," Ballinger remarked.

"Our business prospects seem to be excellent."[53] Defeat, it appeared, held few terrors for those skilled in the techniques of adjustment.

In later years Ballinger moved from one professional triumph to another. Reputed by the mid-seventies to be one of the most brilliant corporation lawyers in the country, he narrowly missed a seat on the Supreme Court during the administration of Rutherford B. Hayes. His large face, with its seamed and craggy features, and his gangling physique were a familiar sight at every important social or civic function held on Galveston Island, and friends commented (with unconscious irony) that "the Judge" in his old age was getting to look more and more like Abraham Lincoln. The war, which accelerated technological change in many parts of the South, did little to alter preexisting patterns of societal thought and behavior. The "peculiar institution" had gone by the board, to be sure, and Ballinger sometimes had to plead before black jurors, much to his distaste. But behind the appearances of legal change the old relation of master and man continually reasserted itself, as did the paternalistic spirit of the elite classes. (Before the war Ballinger had housed slaves in his own home; now he rented low-cost cabins to black freedmen.) The Federalist tradition, shared by Northerners and Southerners alike, sanctioned in the end the right of local agencies to deal with the "local" problem of race. How conscientiously the lawyers of postwar Galveston resumed the "white man's burden" may be inferred from the fact that the first black attorney did not appear in their city until 1895[54]—some seven years after William Pitt Ballinger, "the Nestor of the Texas bar," had been summoned to his final judgment.

The Negro steps up in the presence of the white American lawmakers, statesmen and politicians and the masses of the people, and demands none other than absolute and complete equality before American law.
John Mercer Langston, speaking before the Radical Union Club of St. Joseph, Mo. (1866)

9   John Mercer Langston and the Training of Black Lawyers

American legal history, like other facets of the national experience, has too long been viewed merely as a white man's story. Biographers from the nineteenth century to the present have tended to concentrate upon the exploits of a few celebrated "bar leaders" whose careers (usually impinging upon politics, journalism, business operations, or other fields apart from legal practice) have been assumed to mirror the opportunities and achievements available to the profession in general. Secondary figures—even within the Anglo-Saxon community—have been largely neglected, as have country lawyers and those serving the needs of smaller towns and cities, while the distinctive contributions made by various ethnic groups to the liberalizing of American law have yet to be explored in a systematic way by researchers.

In part the elitist orientation of legal scholars may be traced to the pull of a conservative tradition handed down by the

American Bar Association since its founding in 1878, but non-
ideological factors have been equally at work to discourage
interest in the populist side of the profession. The problem of
source materials alone presents formidable difficulties for those
trained to think in terms of the primacy of unpublished manuscripts. Even an eminent antebellum personality like Horace
Binney left little private correspondence, and less famous
practitioners were apt to be even more indifferent to the
demands of posthumous research.

On the other hand, court records, city directories, and census
reports all contain invaluable data on professional mobility and
the changing patterns of bar leadership and operation within
particular localities. Utilization of this kind of evidence in
future group studies is indispensable if one would reconstruct
the experience of immigrant, black, or women lawyers who
were seeking a place within the profession in the late nineteenth
century. With all the attention currently being directed toward
black history, it is most surprising that this perspective should
continue to be neglected by scholars, since many pioneer Negro
lawyers played an honorable and constructive part in the
advancement of legal reform—constituting, in effect, a "lost
generation" of civil rights activists.

Their task was similar in many ways to that faced by Sampson and the legal staff of the United Irishmen almost a century
earlier. Both groups were fighting a vicious caste system and
using the legal doctrines of the Establishment to force changes in
the social order. Both, too, were required at times to place their
lives as well as their legal skills on the line. But there was one
important difference: the Irish liberals could draw strength from
a national tradition that gave them a sense of common identity
and pride, while the Negro lawyers of America, with no such
vital nationalist ideology to fall back upon, were forced to
define themselves by reference to the very value system that
denied them full status as men or citizens. Under these conditions legal training for the American Negro had to provide more
than a technical preparation for courtroom debate; it had to
build racial character and confidence as well, so that black
attorneys might compete effectively in a white man's world.
Such was the vision behind the founding of Howard Law
School, from which more than four hundred graduates emerged
by the end of the century to serve black communities across the
nation.

The plantation of Ralph Quarles lay deep in the heart of Louisa County, Virginia, about fifty miles northwest of Richmond. A revolutionary war veteran and the son of a well-to-do landowner, Quarles had used part of his paternal inheritance to buy a substantial tract of land—some twenty-five hundred acres in all—along the banks of Hickory and Gold Mine creeks, in the thinly populated interior of the state. Here he raised tobacco, wheat, corn, and livestock, with the aid of a sizable work force of slaves. In its essential features his experience paralleled that of other white planters of moderate means: blacks supervised the work of other blacks on the Quarles plantation; there was no overseer, and Captain Ralph was the only white man on the place. But he became a social pariah in the neighborhood through his romantic involvement with one of his slaves, Lucy Langston—a slim, dark-eyed beauty whom he had acquired in settlement of a debt. Defying public opinion, Quarles installed the girl in his home as housekeeper and mistress and lived with her openly until his death almost thirty years later.

Lucy's mother, a full-blooded Indian, claimed distant kinship with Pocahontas, while her father, whose history remains more obscure, was of Negro blood. Quarles made generous provision for all of his mistress's close relatives, bringing the old Indian mother-in-law to live with them in the "big house" and emancipating Lucy's three children by a previous slave marriage. Then, in April 1806, soon after the birth of his daughter, Maria, he formally emancipated both mother and child through public court proceedings. The three sons who followed—Gideon (1809), Charles Henry (1817), and John Mercer (1829)—bore their mother's surname, since the law did not recognize the legitimacy of their parents' relationship. But, as the status of a slave child followed that of its mother, each of Captain Ralph's boys came into the world a free person, according to the law.

Looking back at his childhood half a century later, John Langston described it in idyllic terms. As the spoiled younger son of fond and aging parents, he apparently enjoyed a privileged position in the plantation hierarchy comparable to that of any white "massa" of the same age. Too young to be called upon to do any of the chores that fell to the lot of his older brothers, he remembered his Virginia birthplace primarily as a vast playground, a natural wonderland of Edenic beauty. Whether such recollections reflected more of wish fulfillment than reality is debatable, since Langston was not quite five years old when both of his parents died, bringing the plantation idyll to an abrupt and sorrowful close.[1]

Scarcely had the captain and his Lucy been laid to rest side by side in the plantation burial plot than the surviving family was broken up and dispersed to separate locations. By the terms of his will Quarles left each of his sons a substantial legacy, consisting of a one-third interest in all of his lands and other plantation assets, along with some Virginia bank stock. He further directed that all of them should emigrate to the free state of Ohio, where they might pursue careers of their own choosing. A special arrangement had been worked out for young John Mercer: he was to be brought up in the family of Colonel William D. Gooch of Chillicothe, a transplanted Virginian and personal friend of Quarles, who had already agreed to act as the boy's guardian.

In October 1834 the brothers loaded their possessions into a wagon and carryall and began their westward journey. The trip to Ohio, over dirt roads that were almost impassable at times, took all of three weeks. En route the travelers were joined by their half-brother, William Langston, the oldest of Lucy's seven children, who since his emancipation had established himself as a carpenter in Chillicothe. By prior agreement William took personal charge of John and saw him safely to his final destination.

Chillicothe at the time was enjoying an economic boom, thanks to its favorable location on the Ohio Canal. The town claimed more than three thousand permanent residents, one-tenth of whom were black. It was this Negro community that supplied Frederick Grimké with most of his data on the shiftlessness and incompetence of free blacks, and the judge was perhaps jotting down occasional notes even then, for he still presided over Chillicothe's court of common pleas.

But John Langston was scarcely aware of the town, much less its racial tensions, during the next few years. His guardian, Colonel Gooch, lived on the "old Carlisle Place," a hundred-acre farm he had purchased about a mile below Chillicothe, on the banks of the canal. There the boy was raised in a rural setting that made adjustment easier, and there he spent the happiest days of his youth as a member of the Gooch family. The colonel was an American-style Micawber, a warmhearted but somewhat improvident old gentleman who never quite succeeded at anything but was always ready to try again somewhere else. He had a wife and three daughters, who welcomed Langston with such warmth that he came in time to think of them as genuine blood relations. The youngest girl, Virginia, for whom he developed a boyish infatuation, tutored him in reading and writing until he reached the age of eight, at which time he was enrolled in a private school whose sessions were held in the gallery of the local Methodist church. The seats were long wooden benches without backs; the classes met for six hours a day; and the discipline was strict. Accustomed to having his own way and dependent upon the approval and indulgence of his elders, Langston promptly rebelled against these innovations but was at last cajoled into continuing his studies, in which he gradually displayed considerable proficiency.

By 1839, however, changes of a more traumatic kind were in the making. As land values in the Scioto Valley rose until realty was selling anywhere from ten to fifteen dollars an acre, the colonel, ever alert to the possibilities of speculation, succumbed to the "Western fever" and resolved to sell his Ohio holdings and move on to the Missouri area. Invited to join the family exodus, John readily agreed, but just as they were setting out by canal boat on the first stage of their journey, William Langston rode up with the sheriff and a summons that ordered Gooch to appear at once before the common pleas court to answer abduction charges.

The colonel and his ward returned to town, where a trial judge, after hearing the evidence, ruled that Gooch had exceeded his authority in attempting arbitrarily to remove the boy and his property beyond the jurisdiction of the court. John was therefore released from his old friend's further control and placed temporarily in the custody of Richard Long, the new proprietor of the Gooch farm. The settlement was a friendly one on both sides; only the boy protested bitterly. With little understanding of the legal or moral issues involved, John knew only that he was losing a close and valued friend. Again a strong emotional tie was being severed, and he faced anew the prospect of disorientation and an uncertain future among strangers.

Richard Long, his new guardian, was a New England abolitionist; admirable enough in his fashion, but a complete contrast to the garrulous old colonel. A reserved, taciturn man, he carried the world's weight on his shoulders and never forgot that he was a deacon in the Presbyterian church. Under his guidance Langston learned mainly how to do additional farm chores and to recite lengthy passages from the Bible. Consequently, when his brother Gideon, now a barber in Cincinnati, suggested that he come there to further his education, he responded with enthusiasm. Had he anticipated, as he prepared for his departure in 1840, the full range of lessons that the Queen City held in store for him, he might have been less eager. Hitherto his experience has been exclusively rural and he had been sheltered from the uglier facts of life by the watchfulness of his white guardians. Now he was to discover at first hand what the color line really meant in Ohio.

A well-known Negro song of the antebellum years complained:

> Ohio's not the place for me;
> For I was much surprised
> So many of her sons to see
> In garments of disguise.
> Her name has gone out through the world,
> Free labor—soil—and man—
> But slaves had better far be hurled
> Into the lion's den.
> Farewell, Ohio!
> I cannot stop in thee;
> I'll travel on to Canada,
> Where colored men are free.[2]

Free blacks as well as fugitive slaves could take the lyrics to heart, for their situation, too, remained precarious within the state. While anti-Negro legislation was commonplace throughout the North, Ohio's Black Laws were peculiarly oppressive in their scope and implementation. As early as 1804 the legislature had sought to obstruct the immigration of free blacks by requiring, as a condition of residence, that they furnish "freedom papers" from a federal court and post a bond of five hundred dollars to guarantee their future good conduct. Further restrictions were added in later years, until—by the 1830s—Negroes were denied the right to vote, to sit on juries or to testify against white litigants, to serve in the militia, to attend public schools, or to enter any poorhouse, asylum, or other charitable institution within the state.[3]

Enforcement of these discriminatory measures was especially vigorous in Cincinnati, where three-fourths of all Ohio blacks resided and where the presence of a boisterous slaveholding population across the river in Kentucky provided an added stimulus to extremist action. Segregation in the Queen City of the West extended even to her cemeteries, and it took considerable courage for white reformers to cross the color line in defiance of popular opinion. Nevertheless some did, including Messrs. Goodwin and Denham, who conducted a notable school for Negroes in the basement of the Baker Street Baptist Church of Cincinnati.

It was to this institution—the best of its kind in southern Ohio—that eleven-year-old John Langston came to pursue his education. For two years he attended classes regularly five days a week, studying such subjects as ancient history, advanced arithmetic, grammar, and rhetoric, for the last of which he showed a special aptitude. His brother Gideon arranged living quarters for him, first with the family of John Woodson, a carpenter and joiner, and then in the home of William Watson, the city's best-known barber. With characteristic snobbery, Langston later noted that his "associations while in Cincinnati were with the best colored families, their children and intimates" and that if "anything like an aristocratic class . . . has ever existed in any colored community of the United States, it was found in Cincinnati at the time."[4] Perhaps the very absence of strong family roots during his formative years dictated this lifelong insistence upon his impeccable social connections. Lacking the assurance of status that could be verified by external circumstances, he early constructed for himself an exceptional character that enabled him to transcend his environment, ennobling even the bootblack chores that he performed every Saturday at Watson's barbershop and bathhouse.

In the fall of 1841, while he was still living in Cincinnati, racial tensions erupted into open violence in one of the worst riots the city had ever known. The outspoken abolitionist editorials of Dr. Gamaliel Bailey—publisher of the *Philanthropist*, a local newspaper—sparked the outbreak, but race relations had been worsening for some time, and little incentive was needed for mob action. Trouble began one Friday night, when a gang of Kentuckians joined forces with city laborers (mainly Irishmen) to storm the Negro quarter. The mob gained possession of a cannon from the militia and turned it on the nearest houses, but the blacks, after a period of initial confusion, rallied their forces for a desperate counterattack, and heavy fighting continued for hours. On Saturday morning the city authorities took advantage of a lull in hostilities to call out large numbers of volunteer police, who were ordered to arrest every male Negro they could find and place him in "protective custody" in the city jail. About three hundred blacks were rounded up in this way, while the rioters continued their terrorism, attacking the offices of the *Philanthropist* and smashing Bailey's press, which they later threw into the river.[5]

Fearful for the safety of themselves and their families, the remaining Negro men went into hiding to avoid arrest. John saw Woodson, with whom he was boarding, conceal himself in the chimney of his house; then the badly frightened boy ran off to find his brother. The streets were filled with white patrols, and he narrowly missed capture when several policemen noticed him and gave chase. By the time he reached Gideon's barbershop, after a frantic dash of more than a mile, he was breathless and almost hysterical. But his knocks were quickly answered, and he joined his brother and five other men in the darkened shop, where they sat out the rest of the disturbance behind barred doors and windows.

> The Sabbath following these occurrences was one of the greatest beauty and loveliness [he recalled long afterward in his autobiography]. The quiet of the city was truly impressive; and but for the hundreds of horsemen, the mounted constabulary forces found necessary to parade the streets and maintain the good order of the city, while protecting the lives of its people, it would have been a day fit for the calm and peaceful worship of our Heavenly Father in a civilized and Christian community. As it was, however, the horrid sight of the vast company of such policemen, the solemn, awful tread and tramp of their march, with the recollection of the sad, dire events of the preceding nights and days, drove every feeling of love and veneration out of the hearts of those who had thus been outraged and terrified.[6]

He was shortly recalled to Chillicothe on business connected with the settlement of his father's estate and a change of guardians. (At his request his half-brother William now assumed the responsibility of looking after his welfare.) A removal to quieter surroundings did not erase his memories of racial injustice, however, and his dawning sense of an emotional kinship with other blacks was soon strengthened by an acquaintance with several dedicated young reformers.

During the winter months of 1842 and 1843 he was tutored successively by George B. Vashon and William Cuthbert White-horn, two Negro students at Oberlin College who were actively engaged in efforts to improve the condition of Ohio's black population. From them and from his idealistic older brother Charles (who had spent two years at Oberlin) he learned how rewarding a career of public service might be, and the vision of a lifetime of practical activity in behalf of the less fortunate members of his race gradually supplanted the vague chivalric fantasies of his boyhood. Encouraged by his teachers, he prevailed upon William Langston in the spring of 1844 to allow him to continue his studies at Oberlin.

Vashon was then returning to the campus for the final quarter of his senior year, and John accompanied him to the small Ohio village that rose from a level plain ten miles south of Lake Erie. They arrived on a Sunday morning in early March, just in time to hear Charles Grandison Finney, the famed revivalist (and one of the pillars of the college faculty), deliver a stirring sermon to an overflow crowd in the Presbyterian church. It was an impressive introduction to college life for the adolescent visitor, who drank in the music and eloquence with feelings akin to rapture. The next day he enrolled in the preparatory department of the college, and a year later, after completing several basic courses and passing a required entrance examination, he was formally admitted to the class of 1849.

Oberlin, one of the most controversial educational institutions of its time, had been founded a decade earlier as a stronghold of the western antislavery movement. It was one of only four colleges in the nation to admit Negro students, and its tolerance extended to women as well. (During Langston's sophomore year 36 percent of the student body was female.) The spirit of muscular Christianity that enabled school authorities to challenge prevailing mores in their admissions policy also influenced the curriculum, so that undergraduates received a classical education strongly laced with ethics and evangelism. Under the guidance of President Asa Mahan, a moral philosopher and antislavery activist, and his coadjutor Finney, young Langston was introduced to fervently held beliefs about the vast improvability of man and the personal duty of every individual to work for social betterment.[7]

Predictably he cultivated his earlier predilection for literature and public speaking and joined the newly formed Union Literary Society during his freshman year. His first effort before the group proved a complete fiasco, however. Assigned to debate the question "whether the teachings of phrenology interfere with man's free moral agency," he froze when his turn came to speak and had to beg off. Thereafter, like many another famous orator, he resolved to conquer his timidity once and for all by force of will. At the next opportunity he delivered a speech that won enthusiastic applause from his audience and foreshadowed his development into one of the most forceful and articulate polemicists of nineteenth-century America.

By the summer of 1849 he had completed all of his required courses and was graduated with honors. The achievement was both impressive and a little disquieting from the standpoint of his role as a potential race leader. He had proved, to be sure, that he could compete on equal terms with whites, and gained much in knowledge and self-esteem. But his very success bound him the more narrowly to the white man's set of values and led him to think of black improvement as dependent upon the Negro's assimilation of middle-class mores. Despite his occasional pose of romantic independence and self-sufficiency, Langston remained from his college years onward vulnerable to white patronage, and grateful for the friendly interest that teachers and other representatives of Anglo-Saxon culture displayed toward him from time to time. One of his few extant letters to an Oberlin classmate is especially revealing in this regard:

You certainly remember [our first meeting]. It was a beautiful Sabbath morning, just before the commencement of the spring term. You invited me to your room on the fourth floor of Tappan Hall. I accepted your invitation, and we spent the time in reading Latin and playing checkers. Colored boy as I was, and one too who had never before had a young white friend who was willing to treat me as his peer, I was somewhat astonished at your conduct. I felt much as Topsy felt when Eva spoke a word of kindness and love to her. You nor I can not begin to tell how much your conduct at that [time] did towards making me what I am. It led me to feel that after all there might be something in me. This is the feeling that begets effort—this is the feeling that brings success to effort.[8]

Did he believe, even as an undergraduate, that his mulatto

origins gave him some special insights into the race problem—insights that were denied to those less cultivated blacks
who knew only the brutalities of slavery? It is at least clear that
by the time of his graduation he possessed a well-developed
sense of racial mission and a firm faith in his own leadership
potential. In a speech before the Union Society on May 23,
1848, he reminded his listeners that they were living in a revolutionary age in which kings were abandoning their thrones and
authority everywhere was under siege. The moment was at
hand, he declared, for the emergence of new leaders: "The
prospect is before us—the field is large & capacious—the
portals are thrown wide open—men must act and first they
must be prepared . . . The great advantage which we derive
from a proper performance of the duties of the society is this
power of expressing our thoughts & ideas in an intelligible and
accurate manner, while we learn to think—to develop originality and make great intellectual acquisitions."[9] He had
already decided, at the age of eighteen, how he personally
would answer the challenge of the times. He had made up his
mind to become a lawyer.

Few Negroes could be found in any of the professions in antebellum America, for obvious reasons. Apart from educational
deficiencies and the lack of opportunity for proper training,
there was no prospective clientele to take advantage of their
professional skills. In the law, for example, since free blacks
were excluded from the jury box in most northern states, they
saw little to be gained from hiring a Negro attorney to plead for
them in an otherwise lily-white setting, while, at the other end
of the scale, few white litigants were prepared to entrust their
claims to practitioners whose inferior abilities were taken for
granted by the general public. Of the handful of Negro lawyers
who managed to survive in the 1850s, most were clustered in
the great metropolitan centers of the Northeast, especially the
Boston area, where such figures as Macon B. Allen, Robert
Morris, and Aaron A. Bradley enjoyed the active patronage of
Ellis Gray Loring and other antislavery practitioners and
judges. Beyond the eastern seaboard (and the uniquely favorable cosmopolitan environment of New Orleans), black
attorneys were virtually nonexistent, save for an occasional
pioneer like Vashon, Langston's former tutor, who became a
member of the bar of Syracuse, New York.[10]

As an ambitious young college graduate, Langston at first discounted the obstacles in the way of his successful pursuit of a professional career. His record at Oberlin had been excellent, and he counted on his academic credentials to gain him entrance to some reputable law school. In this hope he was soon disappointed. When he applied for admission to the Cincinnati Law School, the great training ground for practitioners throughout the Mississippi Valley, Timothy Walker promptly turned him down, noting that the "students would not feel at home with him, and he would not feel at home with them."[11]

A similar rebuff came from James W. Fowler's small school in Ballston Spa, New York—a recently established institution that was still trying to build a reputation and to attract students. One of Langston's Oberlin classmates was already enrolled there, and for a time John's prospects seemed fairly bright. Although Fowler reported some strong opposition from faculty and trustees, he encouraged the applicant to come for a personal interview. Langston did so, arriving in time for the commencement exercises of 1850, but again his efforts proved fruitless. John C. Calhoun had visited the school during the previous year, Fowler told him, and had agreed to recruit some promising students from South Carolina; the institution could not take the risk of alienating them at the outset by ignoring the color line in his case. At the same time the learned professor outlined certain alternative strategies, whose comic overtones are richly developed in Langston's autobiographical account of the incident:

"You have my sympathy," he said, "and I would be pleased to do something to help you on in your studies. I will tell you what I will do. I will let you edge your way into my school. Or, if you will consent to pass as a Frenchman or a Spaniard hailing from the West Indian Islands, Central or South America, I will take you into the school." When he had finished his statement, Mr. Langston asked, "What, Mr. Fowler, do you mean by your words 'Edge your way into the school?' " He answered, "Come into the recitation-room; take your seat off and apart from the class; ask no questions; behave yourself quietly; and if after a time no one says anything against, but all seem well inclined toward you, you may move up nearer the class; and so continue to do till you are taken and considered in due time as in full and regular membership."[12]

Langston understandably found the proposition somewhat less

than appealing and tried clerking for a Cleveland attorney instead, only to find at the end of a year that he knew little more law than before.

In desperation he sought advice from some of his old professors, who suggested that he enter the theological school of Oberlin as a way of continuing his preparation for the bar while waiting for better law office opportunities to materialize. The composition and delivery of sermons, he was told, would be good practice for the later task of drawing up briefs and presenting oral arguments in court; didactic theology, like law, was an intellectual discipline in which exegesis played a fundamental role, and the moral issues encountered in theology classes would have a carry-over value for legal studies as well. Convinced, the would-be lawyer enrolled at once as a graduate student in theology, becoming the first Negro in the nation to do so. Three years later he completed the program successfully and received several invitations to fill permanent pastoral positions. Even Finney encouraged him to remain in the ministry, but, as his granddaughter later remarked, "A minister could not dabble in politics. He wanted rather to express himself in worldly affairs."[13] Accordingly, he chose to complete his legal training in another law office, this time accepting an offer from Philemon Bliss, a white newspaper editor and antislavery advocate, to read law with him in the neighboring town of Elyria.

Under Bliss's direction Langston soon gained a good working knowledge of courtroom procedure and the major doctrines of American jurisprudence. Although "the judge" was too busy to give his clerk much special attention, he saw to it that Langston regularly accompanied him to court for on-the-spot illustrations of legal tactics and the variability of precedents. Afterward he elaborated on the day's proceedings in lengthy discussions at the Bliss home, where Langston lived during his apprenticeship. At the end of a year Bliss pronounced his pupil ready for the bar examiners, after crediting him with sufficient previous study to satisfy the statutory bar requirements. A committee of three local lawyers (two Democrats and one Whig) examined the candidate at the fall term of the Ohio District Court in 1854 and reported favorably on his qualifications. The Democratic members noted, however, that his race might prove a stumbling block to his final certification by the court.

Langston had feared such an eventuality, although his mentor had scoffed at the idea. On the one hand, no statute specifically excluded blacks from the legal profession in Ohio, yet no black had ever been admitted to the state bar. Conceivably an ill-disposed court, relying upon custom and certain implications that might be drawn by analogy from those legal disabilities that *were* spelled out in the Black Laws, might reject a Negro applicant regardless of his acceptability in all other respects. In Langston's case the matter was happily resolved through a resort to that time-honored device available to judges who desire to sidestep unpalatable dilemmas: the legal fiction.

When he appeared before the five-man court that controlled his professional destiny and reference was again made to his race, Bliss rose at once to protest that under Ohio law his clerk must be regarded as a white man. At this a scene worthy of nineteenth-century melodrama unfolded. The chief justice, a member of the Ohio Supreme Court known for his anti-Negro views, called out, with manifest irritation, "Where is Mr. Langston?" and ordered him to stand up. Langston rose from his seat within the bar, and after scrutinizing him in silence for several seconds the old jurist directed him to step forward and take the attorney's oath. Later he learned that a line of judicial decisions in Ohio had established the principle that the term "white man" included all persons having more white than Negro blood.[14] Visual examination satisfied this criterion with respect to him, and he was promptly granted his license, dated September 13, 1854. Then began the task of attracting clients.

In his legal practice, as in so many other aspects of his early career, Langston benefited from a remarkable run of good luck. He first settled in Brownhelm Township, an outlying hamlet close by Lake Erie and some two hours' drive from Oberlin. Here he had previously purchased a fifty-acre farm (complete with a two-story frame house and several outbuildings) that he leased to a white tenant and his family under a sharecropping arrangement. The exploitive features that so often characterized such agreements were visible in this one as well, for Langston drove a hard bargain. In return for the use of the premises, the tenant had to supply half of the seed he planted and to divide with his landlord one-half of everything produced on the farm; he also had to see to the upkeep of the place, provide free board and lodging for Langston (and later his wife), and wash and mend his clothes.[15] From the start, then, the new lawyer presented himself to the community as a property owner of substance and respectability.

In most parts of the Western Reserve, where New England ancestry offered no guarantee against widely held racial prejudices, such assertions of status from a Negro would have been accounted pretentious at best; but Brownhelm was a special case. The village prided itself upon its progressive outlook and catered to a local elite of reform-minded Yankees, who supplied Langston with much the same support in the backwoods that other black practitioners received in eastern cities. Grandison Fairchild, the town's leading citizen, was a strong antislavery man who was more than willing to patronize a black college graduate of independent means and courtly manner, particularly since he was the sole Negro in the area and therefore something of a special advertisement for the abolitionist cause.

Within a month of his arrival Langston was invited by Hamilton Perry, a white attorney of the neighborhood, to assist in the defense of a landowner involved in a property dispute of some notoriety. The trial took place in a barn, where a sizable audience had gathered to witness the proceedings. Midway in the case Perry introduced his cocounsel, who took over the final questioning and summed up the evidence for the jury. The defendant was acquitted, and the following day Langston received a visit from his first clients: several white liquor dealers who were charged with violating the state's temperance laws.

Criminal cases accounted for a large part (and certainly the most lucrative part) of his practice thereafter. For several years the active enforcement of temperance legislation in Lorain and adjoining counties threw much defense business his way, and he later recalled with some complacency that most of his early clients had been white Democrats: "Such persons did not seem however to fear Mr. Langston's color, nor on account of it to question his ability and skill. They sought him and his services as if they had the largest respect for him personally and full confidence in his learning, ingenuity, and fidelity." He always got them off, too, he added, with characteristic modesty.[16]

The law of supply and demand, which seemed so incontestable in his case, had its limitations, but these he brushed aside. He did not tell his readers, for example, that if criminal litigation offered a road to wealth for black attorneys, it was also likely to prove a dead-end street. Ethnic minorities had traditionally gained a foothold in the profession through their involvement in criminal cases, and in the early nineteenth century, when the greatest lawyers in the land did not scruple to appear in criminal trials, the ambitious immigrant could often use his reputation as a successful defense lawyer to secure a wider and more challenging practice. But conditions were changing by the 1850s, as law business grew more specialized and well-connected practitioners—restricting themselves more and more to corporate clients and those from upper-income groups—tended to abandon the criminal field to the young, the foreign-born, and the nonwhite.

Langston's own experience illustrated the trend: to the end of his first period of active practice in the mid-sixties, he remained primarily a run-of-the-mill criminal lawyer, with no real chance of diversifying his business. Although he once described his trial work as "exciting," there is little reason to think that it would have appeared so to anyone else. One commentator, indeed, has conjectured that he may have turned his legal skills to the defense of those charged with violating the provisions of the Fugitive Slave Law,[17] but there is no evidence to support this assumption. Even Langston, with his considerable talent for self-advertisement, fails to mention any incidents of this kind in his autobiography. He does talk at some length about his most famous case, however, which occurred in 1863, when he successfully defended Mary Edmonia Lewis, a black student at Oberlin, who was accused of poisoning a white classmate.

But any profile of his early practice would be incomplete without some reference to the ubiquitous element of debt collection. For local businessmen and other creditors Langston undertook to enforce payment on a multitude of minor obligations, some of them infinitesimally small. A representative list of accounts left with him for collection in January 1860 included 123 separate items, totaling $569.56. The largest debt on this list amounted only to $43.25; the smallest was nine cents! While his records are admittedly scanty, it seems probable that few of the claims entrusted to him amounted to as much as two hundred dollars.[18]

One other source of minor legal business grew out of his involvement in municipal politics, beginning in 1855. In that year Charles Fairchild nominated him for the post of town clerk, to which he was elected on the Liberty party ticket by an all-white vote. (His victory made him the first of his race ever to hold an elective office in the United States, as he likewise claimed to be the first black admitted to the bar in the West.) Since the town clerk was ex officio attorney for the township, the new incumbent found his modest practice enlarged by a number of routine legal chores. A year later he moved to Oberlin in search of broader opportunities, and was promptly elected clerk of Russia Township and acting school superintendent. By 1860 he had risen to a place on the Oberlin City Council as well as the board of education.

Gratifying as these marks of public favor were, they did not satisfy his ambition or assuage the bitterness he sometimes felt at the real or fancied slights inflicted upon him by white acquaintances. Even in his legal practice he was forced on occasion to resort to blows as the only sufficient answer to the provocative racial slurs directed at him by opposing counsel in the course of a trial. In the notes for a political speech that he drafted in 1853, he referred to his "caged up desires" and to the humiliation he suffered "from being looked down upon as if of no account amongst men."[19] Convinced that his own elevation was inextricably linked to that of his race, he early distinguished himself as a leader of black protest groups in Ohio, and was well on his way to becoming a national celebrity in the antislavery movement when he married Caroline Wall, an Oberlin student of mixed blood like himself, in 1854.

The antislavery crusade in the North had entered upon a new and more militant phase by the time that Langston completed his undergraduate studies at Oberlin. With the annexation of Texas and the prospect of slavery's further expansion into the vast southwestern territory acquired by the Mexican War, abolitionists stepped up their demands for black emancipation and relied increasingly upon political action, rather than moral suasion, to achieve their ends. The Negro question, reintroduced into state and national politics by the late 1840s, seemed to offer black leaders an unparalleled opportunity to make their voices heard and encouraged the rise of a younger group of civil rights activists among the free blacks of the North. For a variety of reasons, however, the promise of effective interracial collaboration among reformers remained largely unfulfilled.

Many white abolitionists, to begin with, could not avoid a condescending attitude toward the blacks they were struggling to uplift. Themselves the products of a caste system, they tended to accept the black stereotype for the most part and held themselves aloof from any unnecessary social contact with the members of an unfortunate but degraded race. Basic disagreement over the scope and strategy of the reform effort further divided antislavery reformers along racial lines. Negro leaders demanded not merely the emancipation of the slave but the extension of full civil rights to the "half-free" black population of the northern states; white abolitionists, on the other hand, apart from William Lloyd Garrison and a few other moralists, took relatively little interest in the condition of the freedman, as opposed to the plight of the southern slave. Doctrinal disputes, as in any important social movement, shaded over at times into personal tests of power among the reforming elite, whose self-conscious posturing and sensitivity to the "verdict of history" added a final discordant note to the overall picture.[20]

In practice, then, black antislavery advocates conducted a largely independent campaign during the 1850s that sought to dramatize the effects of racial injustice on a national scale. They were aided to some extent by the existence of a ready-made organizational base in the black convention movement, which had begun as early as 1817 in certain states and localities. These conventions, meeting at irregular intervals, transmitted protests and petitions to the public concerning the needs of the American Negro, but otherwise their practical results had been meager. The State Convention of the Colored Citizens of Ohio, indeed, after an initial flurry of activity at the time of its formation in 1835, had lapsed into a semicomatose state from which it awakened only a decade later in response to a general upsurge of the reform spirit in state politics.

By 1848, with little prodding from any black pressure group, Ohio lawmakers approved a bill to make public education available to black children on a segregated basis (although little was done in the way of implementation until the mid-fifties), and the following year a coalition of Whigs and Free-Soilers forced the repeal of other Black Laws. Negroes were still deprived of the vote, and remained ineligible for jury duty or for admission to publicly financed poorhouses.[21] But limited gains were better than none, and black leaders had reason to hope that a more militant assertion of their rights might now hasten the removal of all remaining disabilities.

At this auspicious moment Langston began his public career. He attended his first convention in Columbus in the summer of

1849, on the eve of his graduation from Oberlin. The meeting in question marked a turning point in the development of the state organization as members pledged themselves to a more aggressive and sustained course of action for the future. Langston coauthored a Declaration of Sentiments for the group, which coupled threats of radical confrontation with professions of faith in the most conservative canons of bourgeois morality. Delegates agreed to "sternly resist" all forms of oppression or proscription and to disobey laws that curtailed the "natural rights of man," while concurrently promoting universal education, temperance societies, and better employment opportunities for blacks.[22] Both the sweep of the program and Langston's position as strategist proved characteristic of later developments.

Throughout the fifties J. Mercer (as he then styled himself) served on the State Central Committee, a group of less than a dozen men who acted as the permanent policymaking arm of the convention movement in Ohio. Under their joint direction plans were laid to mobilize the blacks of the state for the most comprehensive and energetic reform effort attempted anywhere in the North. Langston personally toured the state year after year, speaking to black and white audiences alike on the related issues of slavery and civil rights. As a rule he received no pay for his speeches and even found himself forced at times to defray all traveling expenses out of his own pocket.

The movement, which relied upon dues of fifty cents per person and occasional donations of larger sums, was singularly fortunate to count among its chief architects a persuasive young orator of independent means. Besides his Brownhelm farm (valued for tax purposes at more than $4,000 in 1853), Langston owned income-producing real estate in Columbus and Chillicothe, along with 160 acres of land in Winonia County, in the Minnesota Territory.[23] His investments gave him the economic security that enabled him to devote much time to reform activity even while pursuing his postgraduate studies at Oberlin, and as the Maecenas of the movement he supplied the funds to bail his coworkers out of financial crises on more than one occasion.

In his speeches he advocated no consistent policy for realizing black objectives but borrowed freely from all available models: Garrisonian moralism, nonviolent political lobbying, and direct action militancy. To William F. Cheek, the best-informed Langston scholar, this eclecticism mirrored his subject's rugged individualism and insistence upon being "his own man"—an explanation that J. Mercer himself would certainly have endorsed.[24] But it seems just as likely that, with no overriding plan of his own, he simply dealt with each issue on an ad hoc basis, in accordance with his pragmatic instincts. His law training, which began in 1850, must have demonstrated the value of such a flexible approach to problem solving. In any event, despite the occasional extremism of his rhetoric, he remained at heart a moderate reformer who devoted his best energies to obtaining the vote for the black residents of Ohio by peaceful means.

What the Negro race really needed, he declared in 1855, in a typical statement of priorities, was "political influence, the bridle by which we can check and guide to our advantage the selfishness of American demagogues. How important, then, it is, that we labor night and day to enfranchise ourselves."[25] When petitions to the legislature proved ineffective, he tried to organize the black masses of the state for more vigorous grassroots demonstrations. But all attempts to establish a mass base for the movement turned out disastrously. Of three separate organizations formed in the fifties to "go to the people," only one—the Ohio State Anti-Slavery Society of 1858—managed to continue in active operation for as long as two years, and it was practically a one-man show. Langston, who acted as president and general agent, donated his services and some funds, while his older brother Charles filled the position of recording secretary at a negligible salary. At the end of the decade the black convention movement in Ohio remained essentially what it had always been: a minority effort controlled by an educated black elite, with only two hundred delegates attending the most successful of its annual meetings.

The passivity of the masses, as reform leaders fully appreciated, stemmed from a variety of factors. Fear, ignorance, and indifference all played a part, as did a suspicion of black intellectuals and the conservative stance taken by most Negro churches. Langston and his associates did not despair of eventual success, despite the discouraging results of their recruitment drives, but in the meantime they were left in the uncomfortable position of generals with no troops behind them. As members of the Russian intelligentsia were concurrently discovering in their efforts to liberate the serfs of their homeland, there might be considerable difficulty in claiming to represent the will of a voiceless multitude. The very absence of adequate feedback from their constituents tended to force leaders at times into ex cathedra pronouncements that easily hardened into dogmas, and these in turn laid the foundation for personal quarrels among the elite over who best embodied the interests of an inchoate mass. The Russian analogy must not be pushed too far, but surely something of the tension between Herzen and Bakunin may be detected in the growing rivalry between Langston and the most prominent of all black militants, Frederick Douglass.

While the two Negro orators maintained friendly surface relations through the 1850s, their contrasting temperaments and attitudes gave promise of later bitterness. Douglass, who was twelve years older than Langston, was already an acknowledged leader of the antislavery cause before the young Oberlin graduate made his first public speech. Tall and broad-shouldered, with deep-set eyes and a leonine mane, Douglass impressed audiences with his virility even before he launched into one of his familiar tirades against the slave system. His mordant wit and highly charged prose roused the emotions of his listeners, whom he summoned to the immediate destruction of racist institutions by any means at hand, including large-scale violence. The passion that he introduced into antislavery discussions grew naturally out of his twenty years' experience as a slave—a record that Langston could not match, any more than he could pretend to Douglass's evident charisma.

Indeed, the physical dissimilarities between the two reformers were no less striking than their intellectual differences. Where Douglass resembled a tawny lion, Langston suggested the fox. Slender and wiry in build, the younger man moved with a cat-like grace that lent an added touch of elegance to his aristocratic bearing and finely molded features. Contemporaries habitually described him as a "gentleman" and called attention to his "high and well formed forehead," "full but not particularly striking eyes," and "mild and amiable countenance." His suavity of manner went hand in hand with a dandified taste in dress; on his lecture tours he appeared before audiences in a blue or brown frock coat, black doeskin pants, a fancy silk or satin vest, and a black cravat. When he proceeded to tell his listeners, "I stand here today with invisible manacles upon me," the effect was somewhat less than awe-inspiring.[26]

But Langston seldom relied on the personal touch to get his message across. Unlike Douglass, he sought to convert his opponents through appeals to their reason, buttressing his arguments with weighty factual data and keeping biblical and literary allusions to a minimum. His best speeches read like carefully constructed legal briefs that sacrificed belletristic embellishments to the overridding dictates of logic and clarity. They were probably most effective in winning some measure of sympathy from the hostile white audiences to whom he often spoke (although hecklers were quick to attribute his forensic skills exclusively to his white blood). Emphasizing the importance of gradual and piecemeal reforms, he offered the black community few of the thrills to be found in Douglass's apocalyptic visions, but his constructive self-help proposals improved the condition of black schools in Ohio and prompted the establishment of two black newspapers in Cleveland in the mid-fifties.

Only on rare occasions did he look beyond the techniques of peaceful protest toward more radical action. Once, in 1856, infuriated at the failure of Ohio legislators to dismantle the remaining caste system, he warned that the Negroes of the state would not tolerate the continued denial of their rights: "If we are deprived of education, of equal political privileges, still subjected to the same depressing influences under which we now suffer, the natural consequences will follow; and the State, for her planting of injustice, will reap her harvest of sorrow and crime. She will contain within her limits a discontented population—dissatisfied, estranged—ready to welcome any revolution or invasion as a relief, for they can lose nothing and gain much."[27] And in the case of the Fugitive Slave Law, which he believed to be unconstitutional as well as immoral, he urged his followers in explicit terms to forcible resistance.

"Let us swear eternal enmity to this law," he told a mass meeting convened in 1859 to protest the conviction of two Oberlin residents for their part in the rescue of fugitive John Price. "Exhaust the law first for these men, but if this fail, for God's sake let us fall back upon our own natural rights and say to the prison walls, 'come down,' and set these men at liberty."[28] No violence in fact grew out of the situation, for both prisoners were shortly released through the intervention of Governor Salmon P. Chase. But Langston practiced what he preached in the matter of civil disobedience by giving food and shelter to runaway slaves in the Oberlin area. He also reportedly helped to recruit two local blacks for John Brown's raid on Harper's Ferry, although he showed no disposition to join the force himself. The slave power could never be overthrown by isolated guerrilla actions, he maintained; only when a majority of northern whites came to recognize caste distinctions as a threat to their own liberties could a successful biracial offensive be launched.

"Slavery is no respecter of persons," ran the burden of one of his most famous speeches for the American Anti-Slavery Society; "in its far-reaching and broad sweep it strikes down alike the freedom of the black man and the freedom of the white one."

> This movement can no longer be regarded as a sectional one. It is a great national one . . . it must be evident to every one conversant with American affairs that we are now realizing in our national experience the important and solemn truth of history, that the enslavement and degradation of one portion of the population fastens galling, festering chains upon the limbs of the other. For a time these chains may be invisible; yet they are iron-linked and strong; and the slave power, becoming strong-handed and defiant, will make them felt. The identification of the interests of the white and colored people of the country, this peculiarly national feature of the anti-slavery movement is one of its most cheering, hope-inspiring and hope-supporting characteristics. This fact is encouraging because the white Americans cannot stand as idle spectators to the struggle, but must unite with us in battling against this fell enemy if they themselves would save their own freedom.[29]

To hasten the coming of Armageddon, Langston gave strong endorsement to white antislavery politicians and campaigned actively for the Free-Soil, and later the Republican, parties. He was instrumental in the founding of a "wide awake" Republican Club in Oberlin in 1860, and the following year—in the aftermath of the fall of Fort Sumter—he addressed a giant Union rally in support of Lincoln's call for 75,000 volunteers to suppress the southern "insurrection." The day of deliverance had dawned at last, it appeared, renewing his faith in a long-cherished vision of white and black Americans marching together to the battlefield to reaffirm the egalitarian principles of 1776. He was eager to join them, he told cheering crowds, either as "a common soldier or in a more exalted rank"—to "strike" for his country.

As matters turned out, Langston never shouldered a musket himself, although he helped to recruit three black infantry regiments for the Union army. Personal considerations, along with a shortsighted government policy toward the employment of black troops, kept him on the sidelines throughout a war that he genuinely believed to be an "irrepressible conflict" between the forces of freedom and despotism. The shabby treatment accorded black volunteer units by the War Department has been fully documented by twentieth-century historians, who have pointed to discriminatory pay differentials, degrading work assignments, and other illustrations of an ingrained racism that infected even the top echelons of the northern military machine.[30] While Langston urged enlistment upon the black masses as a means of reinforcing their claims to the full privileges of American citizenship, he proved unwilling to subject himself to the orders of white officers. Nothing less than a command position would do for him, he made clear to the secretary of war, in offering to raise and lead the nation's first all-black regiment. But the policymakers in Washington turned down his proposal and continued to appoint white men to the command of otherwise segregated fighting units.

Rebuffed in his bid for military preferment, Langston stepped up his agitation for an end to the second-class status of the Negro population at large. In October 1864 he helped to form the National Equal Rights League, a black lobbying group that aimed at securing full legal equality for all blacks. Through the rest of the war he and other civil rights leaders—including such figures as Frederick Douglass, Charles B. Ray, and George Vashon—lectured widely to northern audiences on the positive contributions of the Negro to American life and the indefensibility of existing caste legislation. Their efforts kept the issue of equal rights before the public and won for them the sympathy and encouragement of Charles Sumner and other Radical Republicans in Congress, who also called for a rejuvenated postwar democracy.

With the return of peace Langston devoted himself increasingly to the cause of the southern freedman and his prospective assimilation into the mainstream of American society. At the request of Republican party leaders he undertook the first in a series of "general trips of observation of the colored of the South" during the fall of 1865, touring the border states of Kentucky, Missouri, and Kansas, where he addressed state legislatures and freedmen's groups on the needs of the ex-slaves and the specific civil rights guarantees that should be incorporated into state constitutions. As always he gave top priority to the suffrage issue. "The colored man is not content when given simple emancipation . . . [but] demands absolute legal equality," he declared in a major speech before the Colored Men's Convention of Indiana in October.

> Shall those who are natives to the soil, who fight the battle of the country, who pledge to its cause their property and their sacred honor be longer denied the exercise of the ballot? It ought not, it cannot be. The great events that are coming to pass in this nation, the crumbling of slavery and the dissipation of prejudice, give prophecy of a different result. God and destiny are on our side, and it becomes the colored American to prepare himself at once for the complete investure of legal equality.[31]

Yet Langston frankly recognized the dangers that might flow from admitting four million illiterate blacks to the franchise and accordingly urged a crash program of education and character development upon the freedmen throughout the South. They must be "taught what is meant by being the owner of one's self," he insisted—a frame of reference that implied for him an uncritical acceptance of the values of an acquisitive society. Former slaves, in other words, had to be trained to the responsibilities of citizenship in a competitive democracy, but their transformation from chattels into persons—from objects to subjects—was to be accomplished within a nexus of white middle-class mores that left little room for the maintenance of alternate life-styles or attitudes.

> Ape the virtues of the white men [Langston told attentive audiences]. Freedom means that with the dollar [the black man] lifts himself out of degradation on to the platform of humanity and there stands with a dollar as his lever and protection. Now, then, my friends, get money, hold money. When the greenback leaves the palm of your hand let its stain rest there thereafter. Do not be "stingy;" do not be mean; but be economical and saving, recollecting that the higher your pile of greenbacks the loftier your position will be.[32]

From North Carolina to Louisiana he preached conformity to the Puritan ethic of thrift, hard work, and property accumulation. Much of what he said had the sententious ring of Poor Richard's maxims, as when he enjoined clean living and bourgeois propriety upon the freedmen of Mississippi and demanded that they put away at once their "filthy and expensive practices" of tobacco chewing and whiskey drinking. Like Franklin, too, he portrayed American society as essentially a meritocracy, in which the achievement of status depended upon individual character and accomplishment.

The black man had to earn his place in the postwar social structure, he warned, but his ultimate success was assured, provided he developed the proper work habits and motivation. Such an ascent from rags to riches presupposed, however, a more thoroughgoing form of cultural conditioning than had ever been required under the old slave system. Where once the black field hand had been forced to adjust to the production demands of a particular master (while retaining more or less unimpaired his distinctive attitudes and folkways in non-economic areas), he was now called upon to conform to the totality of the white cultural experience. Only by exchanging his African heritage for the get-rich-quick ethos of the Gilded Age could he satisfy the new role requirements set out for him by Langston: "We want to understand that we are no longer colored people, but Americans."[33]

To assist in the work of "elevating" the southern freedmen, Langston looked to the black bourgeoisie of the northern states. They should serve as cultural models and, wherever possible, as active participants in the reorientation program for ex-slaves, he declared. And he set the example himself by joining the Freedmen's Bureau as General Inspector of Schools in the spring of 1867. For more than two years he traveled through the South visiting black primary and secondary schools, consulting with local bureau officials on a variety of problems, and lecturing the freedmen on their duties to society, which included voting the Republican ticket in both state and federal elections.

The proselytizing element in Langston's talks was so blatant that a recent biographer has suggested that he may have taken the low-paying inspectorship position largely in the hope of mobilizing a black electorate behind his own political ambitions.[34] While his undeniable vanity (which grew more obsessive with each passing year), along with his demonstrated will to power, lends support to such a thesis, there is no concrete evidence that he attempted to build a black power base of his own in these years.[35] Although he worked tirelessly to promote Republican political control of the South, he seems to have been at least equally dedicated to the fulfillment of his less glamorous assignment: providing for the educational needs of the freedmen and their families. So much is clear from even a cursory reading of the voluminous and detailed reports that he regularly filed with bureau officials in Washington. And when in due course he was rewarded for his party loyalty, his advancement came with a novel educational twist. Impressed by his vigorous campaigning for Grant in the election of 1868 (and perhaps by his cultural conservatism as well), the trustees of Howard University invited him to take charge of their newly created Law Department. The position promised to utilize all of his varied talents—as scholar, lawyer, orator, reformer, and administrator—and he lost no time in accepting the offer.

Howard University was one of eight institutions of higher learning founded in the immediate postwar years to encourage the educational aspirations of the freedmen. Sponsored by a group of Congregational ministers and Radical Republican politicians, the school was originally envisaged as a training center for black ministers and teachers. By the time of its incorporation by act of Congress in March 1867, however, the design had been broadened to encompass all of the departments proper to a major university, including a prospective law school. General Oliver Otis Howard of the Freedmen's Bureau shortly succeeded to the presidency of the institution and personally selected a permanent site for the campus on a tract of one hundred fifty acres in northwest Washington. Undergraduate classes began on May 1, 1867, under an admissions policy that prohibited the exclusion of any student for reasons of race or sex. A year later school administrators, encouraged by favorable publicity and rising enrollment figures, embarked upon an ambitious expansion program that looked to the immediate development of law and medical faculties.

The Howard Law School officially opened its doors on January 6, 1869, when Langston was informed by the trustees that "a respectable number" of students had applied for admission. The number in fact turned out to be six, although an

additional fifteen persons showed up for classes by the end of
the term in June. At the time (and throughout Langston's seven-
year tenure as dean) there were no entrance requirements for
potential lawyers beyond "suitable age and good moral character." As a result, many individuals arrived from year to year
who were seriously handicapped by a lack of adequate prior
education. To meet this problem, which became all too
apparent with the very first batch of applicants, Langston and
his colleagues found it necessary to offer an introductory cram
course in remedial English, arithmetic, and other basic subjects
before moving into the regular law school curriculum. The first
genuine law classes did not, therefore, begin until September
1869. This pattern of a compulsory prelaw period continued for
three years, until the board of trustees ordered Langston to stop
duplicating the work of the college and to confine himself to a
strict two-year law program.

All classes at Howard Law School met in the evening, from
five to nine o'clock. The schedule enabled students to hold
down full-time government jobs during the day and with their
earnings to pay for their living expenses, textbooks, and the
annual tuition of forty dollars. The Grant administration,
which owed a great deal to the black vote in the South, went
out of its way to provide employment opportunities for Langston's pupils in the Freedmen's Bureau and other executive
agencies. Langston later boasted that at one point he had been
able to place one hundred law students in various government
positions, but the figure seems clearly inflated, since at no time
during his years at Howard did the total enrollment at the law
school exceed eighty-four persons.

Like the students, the faculty spent their daylight hours
working at nonacademic occupations that supplied the greater
part of their income. Langston, who received $3,000 a year
from the university in his dual capacity of law professor and
department head, also served on the Board of Health of the
District of Columbia from 1871 to 1877, and his two white sub-
ordinates relied even more strongly on outside sources of
support. Assistant Professor Albert Gallatin Riddle, a zealous
abolitionist and wartime congressman from Ohio, was a successful practicing attorney with a reputation as the "official
advocate of the Negroes of the Capital"; instructor Henry D.
Beam was the chief clerk of the Freedmen's Bureau. Together
with Judge Charles C. Nott of the United States Court of

Claims, who taught during the 1870-71 term, these men comprised the full faculty of Howard Law School in its formative period, meeting their first classes in a rambling red frame building on Georgia Avenue.

Their teaching methods, like those in vogue at other institutions, emphasized the importance of memorization and formal classroom drills on assigned subjects. Students were expected to master the basic legal principles set out in standard texts and to recite them by rote when called upon, while their teachers provided supplemental lectures to fill in the gaps. Members of the first-year class at Howard plowed their way through such old favorites as Walker's *Introduction to American Law*, Blackstone's *Commentaries*, Kent's *Commentaries*, and Smith on *Contracts*. Seniors read Greenleaf on *Evidence*, Hilliard on *Torts*, Washburn on *Real Property*, Williams on *Real Property*, Parsons on *Bills and Notes*, Stephen on *Pleading*, Adams on *Equity*, and Bishop on *Criminal Law*. The combination lecture-text approach made it possible for the Law Department to advertise that it offered its students "thorough instruction" in twenty-eight subjects ranging from international and constitutional law to equity and admiralty jurisprudence.[36]

One can gain some insight into the quality of early law lectures at Howard by turning to a small book titled *Law Students and Lawyers*, which Riddle had privately printed in 1873. It contains eight of the lectures that he delivered before the first graduating class, in which he expounded an instrumentalist view of the law as an equalizing force in American society. Written in a plain, straightforward style with no pretensions to erudition, his remarks centered on the practical difficulties that lay ahead for black practitioners and sought to bolster their confidence by offering detailed advice concerning courtroom pleading, public speaking, the location of their first practice, and related problems. In "The Philosophy of Political Parties" he presented a strong argument for continued Republican dominance; his "Observations on the Constitution" were predictably nationalistic; and his essay on "Government" defended the positive state, arguing that "government should do for a people whatever is necessary for their advancement and welfare, and which as individuals they cannot do for themselves."[37]

The emphasis on pragmatism and morale building that characterized Riddle's lectures found further expression in certain extracurricular student activities sponsored by the department. Every Thursday evening the junior class met with Dean Langston for "forensic exercises," which included instruction and practice in debating, extemporaneous public speaking, and the composition and delivery of formal essays on legal topics. Seniors drafted legal papers and argued moot court cases once a week under the direction of Henry Beam. And all law students were expected to attend Bible exercises between nine and ten o'clock each Sunday morning, at which time Langston usually gave a short lecture on professional ethics.

If a student survived two years of course work and related forms of group therapy, he was then ready for graduation—provided he first passed a stiff written examination of one hundred questions covering, in Langston's phrase, "the whole body of law, in theory and practice," and also prepared an acceptable dissertation on some legal topic, to be read or recited at commencement. The reason for these rigorous procedures lay in the fact that a diploma from Howard Law School until 1878 automatically entitled its possessor to practice before the D.C. courts, on the motion of Langston, Riddle, or any other lawyer in good standing.

Ten students made up the first graduating class in February 1871 and heard a stirring commencement address from Charles Sumner, who urged them to give top priority in their practice to civil rights litigation. "You are all free, God be praised!" Sumner told them,

> but you are still shut out from rights which are justly yours. Your-selves must strike the blow, not by violence, but in every mode known to the Constitution and law. I do not doubt that every denial of equal rights, whether in the school-room, the jury-box, the pub-lic hotel, the steamboat, or the public conveyance, by land or water, is contrary to the fundamental principles of republican government, and therefore to the Constitution itself, which should be corrected by the courts if not by Congress. See to it that this is done . . . Insist upon equal rights everywhere; make others insist upon them . . . I hold you to this allegiance; first, by the race from which you are sprung; and secondly, by the profession which you now espouse.[38]

Three more students received degrees in a special ceremony the following July, and for the next two years the number of graduates remained constant at fourteen. The Law Department was "prosperous," Langston reported to President Howard in 1873, and had begun to attract students from northern states and the West Indies as well as every portion of the South. In general they were an "obedient, teachable, and faithful" lot, with only one of their number expelled for misconduct during the previous twelve months. This optimistic prognosis, filed on the eve of the Panic of 1873, took no account of external pressures and circumstances that already threatened the future prospects of every department within the university.

The school's "time of troubles" began with the closing of the Freedmen's Bureau in 1872 amid charges of widespread corruption and misuse of funds. General Howard, under whose regime more than half a million dollars of bureau money had been transferred to the university, was twice called before congressional investigating committees to explain various irregularities in the management of the organization. Although he was ultimately acquitted of any personal wrongdoing, the hint of scandal clung to his name and perhaps had much to do with his decision to return to active military duty late in 1873. At that time he tendered his resignation as president of the university, but the faction-ridden board of trustees, unable to agree upon a suitable replacement, prevailed upon him to take an indefinite leave of absence instead. A new office—that of "vice president and acting president"—was created to oversee the administrative program of the university, and on Howard's personal recommendation the trustees elected Langston to the post by a vote of seven to two. So began a chain of events that led inexorably to one of the most bitter racial episodes of the decade.

By the time that Langston entered upon his executive duties the nation was in the grip of a major economic depression. The university's rapid expansion and unwise investment policies had already resulted in a deficit of more than $100,000. Now, in a period of frequent bank failures and the drying up of private philanthropic sources of revenue, there was little that an administrator could do except to cut back on expenses and wait for the storm to blow over. Under Langston's direction a vigorous economy drive was launched that substantially reduced salary levels throughout the academic community and looked to the elimination of all nonessential teaching and administrative personnel. In the law school, where he continued to serve as professor and dean, he and his colleagues relied exclusively upon student tuition fees for their pay—a form of remuneration that was uncertain at best and amounted to a virtual donation of their services as government job opportunities decreased and student enrollment fell off. (The graduating class from the law school in 1874 consisted of only seven students, or half the number of those graduating in previous years.)

Probably no college executive could have pushed through such a stringent retrenchment program without generating considerable opposition from some associates, but in Langston's case the predictable tensions were aggravated by personality factors. No sooner was he installed as vice-president than his customary imperiousness—or what Rayford Logan more charitably terms a "punctiliousness, probably stemming in part from his legal training"[39]—asserted itself. He demanded a written statement defining the full scope of his authority, to give binding force to Oliver Howard's informal assurance that he should be president "in all but name." The board of trustees passed a resolution that satisfied his legalistic scruples, but the incident—which seemed to impugn the board's good faith—did not sit well with some members. Those who questioned Langston's administrative pretensions soon found added grounds for mistrust in the circumstances surrounding the collapse of the Freedmen's Savings and Trust Company.

This well-publicized firm, of which Langston was a director, had been founded in 1865 to serve as a showcase for black economic achievement, just as Howard University was designed to demonstrate black intellectual advancement. There were close links between the two institutions: the university deposited some of its funds in the Freedmen's Bank, whose thirty-four branches in turn helped to recruit students for the school. When, therefore, the bank was forced to suspend operations in June 1874 as a result of incompetent management and occasional outright fraud by some officials, the repercussions of the scandal were felt within the university as well. White critics blamed the debacle upon the Negro's ineptitude in money matters (ignoring the fact that most of the plundering had been done by a dominant group of white trustees), and any black man who, like Langston, had played even a nominal role in the bank's affairs, became an object of public interest and scrutiny.[40]

Against this background of community-wide interrogation

and scandalmongering the fight for the control of Howard University moved toward a climax. In December 1874 President Howard again announced his resignation, and this time it was accepted. The board of trustees, at a meeting on Christmas Day, drew up a slate of five presidential candidates that included Langston, Frederick Douglass (who was also a Howard trustee), Erastus M. Cravath of Fisk University, and two white men. The election itself was postponed until the end of the academic year in June, with Langston agreeing to continue as acting president in the meantime.

Seventeen of the twenty-one trustees upon whose votes the presidential issue depended were white sectarians, affiliated with the Congregational church; the remaining four board members were blacks. Not surprisingly, racial feeling ran high on campus as the spring term progressed. At one point a group of twenty law students drafted a petition to the board in support of Langston's candidacy and pleaded that his "color [might] not operate as an invidious bar to his election." In the minds of many other observers, too, the election shaped up as a choice between black self-direction and white paternalism.

All four black trustees, along with eleven whites, attended the crucial board meeting of June 16, 1875, and cast a secret ballot for one of the presidential nominees. The Reverend George Whipple, secretary of the American Missionary Association and one of Langston's former professors at Oberlin, received a clear majority of ten votes. Langston came in second with four votes, while Douglass received one. The outcome, although not unexpected, was a blow to Langston's aspirations, and he did not accept his defeat with equanimity.

In a scathing postmortem of the election results that he published in the New York *Evening Post* some ten days later, he denounced the Congregationalist trustees for allegedly using their power to subvert the original goals of the university and make it conform to narrow sectarian purposes. These white liberals, he charged, had lost faith in the Negro's capacity for higher education. They no longer believed it desirable to train him beyond the normal-school level and so took little interest in the problems of the law, medical, or theological departments. Nor did they pay much greater attention to the legitimate grievances of individual black faculty members or trustees, whom they regarded as valuable chiefly for the symbolic effect they might have in attracting the attention of private philanthropists. While many worthy educational programs were being curtailed for lack of funds, the First Congregational Church of the District of Columbia continued to pay only 8 percent interest on its indebtedness to the university—a figure well below the current interest rate that the university was being charged on its own outstanding debts. Such sectarian exploitation of academic resources fully explained the outcome of the recent presidential contest, Langston concluded, implying that his four votes came exclusively from the bloc of independent Negro trustees. This interpretation of his voting strength, which he reiterated more dogmatically in his autobiography, remains uncorroborated by any positive evidence, however. The minutes of the board do not indicate who voted for whom, and Langston himself was not present at the election.

With charges of bad faith and duplicity being leveled at them in the press, Howard's white trustees retorted in kind. Besides denying Langston's general allegations, several university spokesmen accused him of trying to destroy the school to gratify his own frustrated ambitions. In an acrimonious debate that lasted for several weeks, the only significant new material was provided by Charles B. Purvis, the well-known black reformer, who reported on July 10 that Langston owed his defeat to the action of the black trustees, one of whom in particular had been working against him for months. Purvis did not name names, but his published statement suggests the interesting possibility that Douglass may have had a hand in deflating the ego of a rival race leader.

In view of the unsavory publicity generated by the entire episode, Whipple announced in mid-July that he would not accept the presidential post. His action left the university without an executive head for the next five months, until Edward P. Smith, a white trustee, agreed to take on the job in December. By that time morale within the academic community had sunk to an all-time low, and nowhere was the lack of leadership and direction more apparent than in the Law Department, where Langston's resignation as dean prompted the immediate withdrawal of the two remaining faculty members, Riddle and Beam.

Thereafter law classes continued on an ad hoc basis, with students meeting from time to time in the downtown offices of several white practitioners. As the range of available courses fluctuated erratically to suit the skills of a temporary staff, student patronage all but ceased to exist. Not a single person was graduated by the Law Department between 1877 and 1881, when a new era began with the appointment of Dean Benjamin Leighton. Under Leighton's guidance the law curriculum was thoroughly remodeled, a more competent and dedicated faculty assembled, and permanent off-campus quarters established at 420 Fifth Street, N.W. Rapid progress resulted from these improvements, and, especially after the civil rights activist William H. H. Hart joined the faculty in 1890, the Howard Law School took up with renewed vigor the libertarian mission prescribed for it by Langston and his associates.

One sympathetic observer, in commenting upon the potential of an early group of Howard law students, indicated as well the serious disabilities they were likely to face in their postgraduate careers. Some of Langston's pupils, noted the influential Republican journalist John W. Forney in 1871,

had only a year before been unable to read and write, and one bright, black fellow was especially patronized by the Professor, because six months before he did not know his alphabet. Nearly all had been slaves. There were oral and written arguments. The manner in which they spoke or read their productions displayed extraordinary talent. I thought I could detect in their flowing cadences and graceful gestures close copies of the old Southern statesmen, who in past years lorded it over both parties. There was scarcely an error of grammar or pronunciation. The logic and the appreciation of the subjects treated, which included landlord and tenant, titles to real estate, divorce, borrowing and lending, promissory notes, etc., proved not only careful study, but intense determination to succeed . . . I doubt whether the older and more extensive Law School connected with Columbia College, where the offspring of the other, and what is called the superior race, are educated, could show, all things considered, an equal number of graduates as well grounded and as completely armed for the battle of the future. There are colored lawyers in most of our courts, even in the highest judiciary. They are the pioneers of an interesting and exciting destiny. With them, unlike their more fortunate white brethren, the bitterest struggle begins when they receive their sheepskins. They go forth to war against a tempest of bigotry and prejudice. They will have to fight their way into society, and to contend with jealousy and hate in the jury-box and in the courtroom, but they will win, as surely as ambition, genius, and courage are gifts, not of race or condition, but of God alone.[41]

For all its tone of resolute optimism, Forney's account pointed unmistakably to the immense gap that separated academic training from professional success in an environment shaped by white practitioners, most of whom accepted the racial implications of Darwinian biology. We are thus led to the inevitable questions: How well in fact did the fifty-eight graduates trained by Langston and his colleagues between 1869 and 1875 measure up to the expectations of their teachers, and of such well-wishers as Sumner and Forney? How many even practiced law?

The record, unfortunately, is too fragmentary to permit anything like a comprehensive accounting, but we can pin down some relevant statistics. Langston himself kept tabs on the first group of graduates and reported at the end of June 1871 that nine out of ten were already engaged in active legal practice. Most of these had settled in various southern states: one in Louisiana, two in North Carolina, one in South Carolina, one in Arkansas, one in Mississippi, and one in Missouri, while two remained in the Washington area.[42]

A different picture emerges if we attempt to trace the immediate postgraduate occupations of all those who continued to live for a year or more in Washington. Of the thirty-two Howard law graduates listed in Boyd's annual *Directory of the District of Columbia*, only eight were practicing lawyers. A majority of the rest held clerical jobs in some government agency: six worked for the Treasury Department; three for the Post Office; two for the Land Office; one for the War Department; one for the Engineers; one for the Board of Public Works; one for the Freedmen's Bureau; and five simply styled themselves clerks. There was also one messenger, one doctor, one teacher, and one printer in the group. This breakdown, of course, reflects only a temporary situation; 50 percent of the individuals in question left Washington after a few years and may have established themselves in legal practice elsewhere.

Among those who did become practitioners, several made notable contributions to the cause of civil rights. D. Augustus Straker successfully defended the constitutionality of Michigan's public accommodations law before the state supreme court in the landmark case of *Ferguson* v. *Gies* (1890);[43] John Wesley Cromwell appeared before the Interstate Commerce Commission to protest segregation on interstate carriers; James M. Adams, one of Langston's few white students, built up a strong civil rights practice before his untimely death in 1892; Nathaniel

G. Wynn was murdered in Lake Village, Arkansas, while defending a black client. These are isolated instances, to be sure, but they do point to the possibility that a lost generation of black civil rights lawyers, largely Howard-trained, may have flourished in the last decades of the nineteenth century.

Straker suggested as much in 1891, when he published an admirable essay entitled "The Negro in the Profession of Law." In every state, he noted, the Negro lawyer was barred by "arbitrary custom" from representing the interests of white clients. Viewed exclusively as the advocate of his race, he occupied within the black community a special position of trust that entailed an obligation on his part to work untiringly for black civil rights.[44] And there is good reason to think that many besides Straker took that obligation seriously, at least during the rather tolerant decade of the eighties, when a Howard graduate like Josiah T. Settle (B.A. '72, LL.B. '75) could still be elected to the state legislature even in Mississippi. The subsequent enactment of repressive Jim Crow laws in the South and a general hardening of white racial attitudes across the nation by the turn of the century may well have cut short a promising experiment in peaceable social reform.

Certainly few black lawyers of the Gilded Age—or their exploits—are remembered today. Even Langston, who did so much to shape the sweeping provisions of the Civil Rights Act of 1875, has been largely ignored by posterity. So it is not surprising that when a new generation of civil rights activists arose in the South after World War II they found little evidence of any prior tradition of black legal reform. In Louisiana, reported a survey conducted by the Howard Law School in 1951, thirteen of the state's fourteen black lawyers had been in practice for only five years, and a substantial proportion of all Negro attorneys in Alabama, Florida, Georgia, and Virginia had been practicing less than ten years.[45] The lack of any strong connecting links with the past should not, however, be permitted to obscure the genuine, if limited, achievements of those nineteenth-century advocates whose collective experience forms an honorable and important chapter in the history of the American bar.

Despite discrimination and a continuing lack of professional opportunity, Straker remarked in 1891, the black lawyer could look back upon two decades of slow but steady progress, for which Langston and his Howard-trained disciples deserved much credit: "Today hundreds of colored and white lawyers bear the insignia [of the Howard Law School] through the energy of Mr. Langston's devotion to the Negro's advancement. We owe him gratitude for this, and he must be regarded as the pioneer of the colored lawyers in America, it may be he is the *paterfamilias* of the Negro lawyers in America. It is said he has not had any extensive practice, and cannot be rated as a great pleader, save in criminal cases; but he has otherwise done a great work, of which no just criticism can rob him."[46]

The profession of the law in this country,
though from its inherent arduous character,
and perhaps even yet somewhat from its traditional conservatism, more difficult of access
than business of other kinds, is nevertheless
practically free and open to all comers. So far
there is perhaps no reason to complain of the
results of the experiment, for the tone of the
American Bar is still as high and as honorable
as that of the English, and whether that were
so or not, it would be neither possible nor
desirable to give it those exclusive features
which have always been its distinctive character in England. Moreover, the [qualifying]
examination which is most strenuously advocated there, has in more or less public manner,
and with greater or less stringency, long
obtained in all the States of the Union; and it
is perhaps to this, as much as to anything else,
that we owe the learning and character of our
Bar.

J. T. M., "Legal Miscellany," *American Law
Register* (1863)

Conclusion

With the advent of American
independence a colonial bench and bar, accustomed to rely
upon English authorities in all doubtful cases, faced the task of
remodeling inherited legal doctrines and institutions to serve the
needs of a republican form of government. Although suspected
at times of reactionary tendencies (including a perverse design
to fleece the middle-class litigant), practitioners and judges
trained in the prewar years generally managed to exploit their
legal skills to good effect during the postrevolutionary era.
Peter Van Schaack's experience, in this respect, was not atyp-
ical. Many others who had been lukewarm, or even downright
hostile, to the Revolution were offered a place in the new state
governments because of their acknowledged expertise in
matters of social organization and conflict resolution.

Yet the conspicuous employment of legal talent in the young

Republic did not efface long-standing popular fears of the "law guild" and its arcane ways. Convinced that lawyer-politicians were enriching themselves at the expense of the commonweal, lay reformers early advanced proposals to democratize the bar and make it more responsive to the needs of the average citizen. Thus Benjamin Austin in 1786 urged the appointment of a salaried "Advocate-General" to represent without cost all persons accused of crimes within a state, while other reformers of the revolutionary generation looked to the emergence of a small subsidized bar, closely regulated by the state in the public interest. None of these schemes were realized, in part because they contradicted equally potent notions of rugged individualism and unfettered occupational mobility. But neither was the postrevolutionary legal profession permitted to develop into an autonomous, self-regulating body.

The revolutionary crisis itself had checked any incipient tendencies toward corporatism within the bar by disrupting existing organizations and driving many bar leaders into permanent exile. Thereafter, bar associations remained localized and inconsequential—token groups that typically met for social or other ceremonial functions. Rules governing the training and admission of new bar members emanated from the state legislatures, which gradually scaled down educational and apprenticeship requirements for all applicants. This leveling trend, so deplored by elite elements within the profession, in fact represented a logical response both to the competitive ideology of the nineteenth century and to public need. Far from bringing about the "degradation" of the antebellum bar, an open-door policy of recruitment and admissions enhanced popular respect for the legal system while insuring that the complex needs of a dynamic capitalist economy would be served by practitioners drawn from all social levels.

As early as 1815 the increasing size of the bar had become a matter for congratulation in the eyes of democratically minded commentators such as Richard Rush. The American people needed at least twice as many lawyers as their English counterparts, Rush asserted, because of the "habits, the manners, and the contentions, of the universally thriving and self-supported freemen on this side of the Atlantic":

Considering Burke's assertion in 1775 that nearly as many of Blackstone's *Commentaries* were sold in the American colonies alone at that period as in all England, we think it may be agreed that we set down the proportion at a safe rate. The noble definition of law, that nothing is so high as to be above its reach or so low as to be beyond its care, is probably true to a greater practical extent in this country than in any other. The cause obviously is, not our liberty alone, but an alliance between an active and restless spirit of freedom and the comfortable condition of all classes of the community, not excepting, relatively considered, even the poor. This encourages and provokes the disposition to go to law by supplying it almost universally with the means. We have honest blacksmiths suing banks for false imprisonment, and street cleaners fine gentlemen for assaults and batteries as the common occurrences of our courts.[1]

The complacent tone of Rush's argument reappeared in countless other legal writings of the nineteenth century, and there was a substantial measure of truth in what he said. At the outset of their national experience Americans did provide for a highly decentralized legal system, choosing to bring justice home to every man's door through a multiplication of local courts, a liberal allowance of appeals to higher tribunals, and the imposition of arduous circuit-riding duties (of the sort endured by Frederick Grimké in Ohio and William Pitt Ballinger in Texas) upon members of the bench and bar alike. While these efforts placed an intolerable burden upon appellate courts and led in time to a retaliatory insistence upon the exact observance of procedural niceties, they did effectively guarantee to the average property owner his day in court. By 1850 most non-poor white Americans enjoyed ready access to a lawyer whenever they needed one, and few individuals inside or outside the bar saw any need for the further extension of legal services to those below the poverty line.

The nation, after all, had been reared on a work ethic that sanctified individual economic achievement and regarded poverty as a temporary phenomenon, largely associated with recent emigrants from the caste-ridden societies of the Old World. Once the industrious poor discovered the opportunities for advancement that existed in a free society, asserted the democratic credo, they would speedily rise from their dependent status to a position of middle-class comfort if not of affluence. The major social theorists of the antebellum years, such as Tocqueville and Grimké, confirmed the fluid nature of class lines in America and reported that a significant number of rags-to-riches cases (along with a corresponding downward mobility trend) accompanied the workings of the capitalist system. Such an egalitarian work-and-win thesis, although largely disproved by twentieth-century statistical studies,[2] seemed axiomatic to most Americans for generations.

Surrounded by the mythology of rugged individualism, lawyers found added reason for not departing from their traditional role in society: the limited role of the advocate, the professional mouthpiece who represented his client's interests with single-minded dedication in adversary proceedings. From a common-law perspective, nothing more was required of a public-spirited practitioner. He discharged his duty to society by pleading his client's cause to the best of his ability. Responsible for maintaining the integrity of the legal process, he assumed no responsibility for the results of that process. Neutral principles supposedly dictated those results, once both sides had been fairly heard.

If a genuine public interest was to be served through the routine functioning of the attorney-client relationship, however, democratic theory demanded that suitors from every social stratum be allowed to share in the benefits of conflict resolution provided by the adversary system. For members of the middle and upper classes no problem existed; they could, if they chose, pay the fee that a lawyer charged for his services. But what of indigent clients? Antebellum attorneys acknowledged no right of the poor to legal representation; neither did they recognize the existence of any well-defined, and relatively permanent, pauper class (except in relation to measures of social control, such as the poor laws). In keeping with the pervasive self-help ideology of the time, they purported instead to deal with the impoverished on an individual basis, through voluntary engagement in pro bono work.

The very term *pro bono publico* suggests patrician connotations: activities undertaken for the good of the public, at the initiative of a benevolent elite. Lawyers who took the concept seriously professed a willingness to aid the "deserving poor" by providing them with free legal counsel in appropriate cases. There is no doubt that much good was accomplished in this offhand way. Practitioners as dissimilar in temperament and background as Sampson and Ballinger donated their services to needy clients on numerous occasions, and the tradition remains very much alive within the bar today. But uncoordinated volunteer efforts, no matter how well intentioned, could not begin to answer the legal needs of most low-income Americans or even to distinguish meaningfully between one type of hardship case and another. Since service to the poor was regarded as a charitable dispensation unrelated to a lawyer's normal work load, the criteria for identifying "worthy" lower-class clients varied erratically from practitioner to practitioner. Chance governed everything: an indigent who believed that his legal rights had been violated in some way had first to seek out an attorney and request his aid; such aid might be given or withheld, depending on the nature of the problem, the current demands of the attorney's income-producing business, the general impression made by the applicant, and other intangible factors. Lawyers who participated in pro bono work, moreover, typically showed little interest in questions of substantive law reform. Establishment-oriented, they tended to approach their poverty cases from a narrowly remedial perspective, seeking only to help clients assert rights that had been clearly granted by the existing power structure. Indeed, the leaders of the antebellum bar, such as Rufus Choate, specifically warned against tampering with the near-perfect institutions of representative government.

"We need reform enough, Heaven knows," Choate declared in a famous address delivered at the Harvard Law School in 1845,

> but it is the reformation of our individual selves, the bettering of our personal natures; it is a more intellectual industry; it is a more diffused, profound, and graceful, popular, and higher culture; it is a wider development of the love and discernment of the beautiful in form, in color, in speech, and in the soul of man,—this is what we need,—personal, moral, mental reform,—not civil—not political! No, no! Government, substantially as it is; jurisprudence, substantially as it is; the general arrangements of liberty, substantially as they are; the Constitution and the Union, exactly as they are,—this is to be wise, according to the wisdom of America.[3]

Admonitions of this kind carried great weight within a heterogeneous legal community beset by growing pains and uncertain of its future status in American society. As a politics of deference succumbed to cruder techniques for manipulating a mass electorate, antebellum lawyers found it ever more tempting to withdraw from public debate altogether, behind a wall of self-imposed professional neutrality. Unwilling to endorse the programs of popular legislative majorities but powerless to prevent their enactment, legal publicists claimed for the bar the right to concentrate exclusively upon the improvement of basic skills, without regard for the social consequences that might flow from such heightened technical proficiency.

There was one notable exception to a restrictive view of professional responsibility in the nineteenth century, and the impetus came, significantly, from a federal agency. On March 3, 1865, Congress created the Freedmen's Bureau in the War Department to help former slaves adjust to the conditions of life in a "free" society. For a time the bureau maintained its own network of courts throughout the South to adjudicate minor civil and criminal disputes involving blacks. Then, as regular civil courts were reestablished in every southern state, bureau officials recognized a continuing need to provide legal services for indigent freedmen if their newly acquired liberties were to be adequately protected. So was launched a pioneer legal aid program of impressive vigor and scope, the earliest attempt by Americans to respond in a systematic way to the legal problems of the poor.

In the District of Columbia and Maryland salaried "solicitors" were appointed by the bureau to represent black clients in all manner of cases—from debt collections, apprenticeship actions, and paternity suits to serious criminal prosecutions. A. K. Browne, a bureau solicitor in Washington, advertised his services in the newspapers and reported in October 1868 that during the previous fifteen months he had handled 592 civil cases and 291 criminal cases—a staggering work load for one man even by the standards of legal aid lawyers today. Browne also gave some attention to matters of law reform, urging changes in the harsh mandatory punishments attached to crimes of petty larceny and protesting violations of due process in the treatment of blacks by police and magistrates.

Elsewhere, in areas farther removed from the nation's capital, the bureau's legal aid activities were more circumscribed and makeshift. With no full-time legal staff at their disposal, bureau officials in the states south of Maryland relied upon members of local bars to represent freedmen on a case-by-case basis. The extent of such selectively subsidized litigation remains unclear, since no one has yet made an exhaustive search of bureau records from this perspective. But a recent ground-breaking inquiry by Howard C. Westwood has turned up more than three dozen instances of bureau-sponsored legal services in Mississippi, Florida, and South Carolina, while suggesting that bureau agents in North Carolina and Louisiana probably authorized similar legal action on occasion, pursuant to the instructions they received from Washington.[4] What mattered most in the long run, of course, was not the size of the program but its underlying rationale. For the first time the poor were recognized as having a *right* to legal services, and the power of government was used to help them gain access to courts and lawyers on equal terms with other social groups. Attorneys who worked for the Freedmen's Bureau implicitly rejected traditional canons of voluntarism and noblesse oblige in favor of a broader vision of professional duty, such as inspired the founders of Howard Law School.

Unfortunately, the new idealism made little impact upon the mass of practitioners who preferred private profit to social justice. And the nation's commitment to equal rights proved no less fragile. By the end of 1868 popular indifference to the plight of the freedman combined with ideological and cost factors to force the dismantling of most bureau programs. All forms of legal assistance were then terminated, after a trial period of only three and a half years. No comparable effort to mobilize federal funds and legal manpower on behalf of the disadvantaged occurred for another full century, until the Legal Services Program of the Office of Economic Opportunity began its operations in the fall of 1965.

Meanwhile the gap between private practice and public need steadily widened. With the rise of big business in the decades following the Civil War, specialization and stratification increased within the bar, as leading firms sought to preempt lucrative new fields of tort liability, patent law, and corporate reorganization procedures. The prestige that attached to a corporate clientele placed certain metropolitan lawyers at the head of their profession and marked a shift in emphasis from advocacy to counseling. Where the frock-coated courtroom warrior had set the tone of professional life in the mid-nineteenth century, he was now overshadowed by the "office man," the adviser to captains of industry, who was paid to keep his clients out of lawsuits, through the exercise of skills and tech-

niques—lobbying, legislative drafting, negotiating, public relations, arbitration—that transcended the narrow limits of the
adversary system. In a sense, then, the new-style bar leader of
the late nineteenth century was more policy-oriented than his
antebellum counterpart, since his managerial role forced him to
confront major public issues that threatened his client's welfare.
But the principle of loyalty to client continued to outweigh any
broader ethic of public interest, and the emergence of the
corporate state only enhanced the attractiveness of a price
model for legal services, as law schools and law firms began to
resemble factories where quality products were designed for
affluent customers.[5]

From the standpoint of professional training and recruitment,
two related developments of the 1870s did most to "modernize"
the American bar along conservative lines. At the beginning of
the decade Dean Christopher Columbus Langdell of the
Harvard Law School initiated a revolution in the study of law
by introducing the "case method" into his classes. Asserting that
law was a "science" whose principles were best discovered
through an analysis of appellate court opinions, Langdell
helped to formulate a more sophisticated, abstract jurisprudence and to shift the locus of legal study from the law office to
the university. In time his innovations produced a dangerous
cleavage between academic legal assumptions and objective
social conditions. To an extent unparalleled in the antebellum
years, the law lost touch with democratic mores and threatened
to become once more an occult force, beyond the comprehension or control of the layman.

While Langdell and his disciples worked to rid the law of its
doctrinal imperfections, others revived earlier efforts to tighten
bar admission standards and to exclude from the profession
those deemed unworthy by an elite leadership. Between 1870
and 1878 eight state bar associations—the first large-scale legal
pressure groups in America—were established, and a weak but
symbolic national organization, the American Bar Association,
also took shape. Such agencies, whose example soon inspired a
wave of further professional organizing, lobbied with increasing success for the kind of autonomous status that democratically minded legislatures had always refused to grant. Characteristically, too, the new state bars tended to oppose the
licensing of potential "people's lawyers": less-skilled black
applicants, ethnic graduates of urban night schools, and other

disadvantaged outsiders who might have served the legal needs of neglected lower-income clients.

Did such a stance represent a principled defense of professional values? Or did it serve to mask the self-seeking stratagems of a conservative elite? Were democratic aspirations and controls in fact compatible with the production of highly skilled legal technicians? What duty did a lawyer properly owe to his client? To his profession? To the larger society in which he lived and worked? How far could a free people be trusted to frame and enforce their laws? These issues, which had divided public opinion since the founding of the Republic, promised to be no less troublesome in the future, as the nation faced a new century of accelerating social and technological change.

Notes, Index

Notes

1. Peter Van Schaack and the Problem of Allegiance

1. No adequate modern biography of Van Schaack exists. I have relied for background details chiefly upon the following sources: Henry C. Van Schaack, *The Life of Peter Van Schaack, LL.D.* (New York, 1842), the standard account whose filiopietism is offset by the inclusion of much valuable manuscript material; Paul Mahlon Hamlin, "Peter Van Schaack," *Columbia University Quarterly*, 24 (March 1932): 66-105; and William Allen Benton, "The Whig-Loyalists: An Aspect of Political Ideology in the American Revolutionary Era" (Ph.D. dissertation, University of Pennsylvania, 1965). Benton's thorough analysis of Van Schaack's early relationship to the revolutionary movement has since been published as *Whig Loyalism: An Aspect of Political Ideology in the American Revolutionary Era* (Cranbury, N.J., 1968). See also, in general, Stanley N. Katz, *Newcastle's New York* (Cambridge, Mass., 1968).

2. Peter Van Schaack to Peter Silvester, August 1, 1768, Van Schaack Family Papers, Columbia University Library, New York.

3. Van Schaack's argument is reprinted in its entirety in Henry C. Van Schaack, *Memoirs of the Life of Henry Van Schaack* (Chicago, 1892), pp. 23-25.

4. Ibid., p. 15.

5. Van Schaack to Colonel John Maunsell, May 7, 1775, quoted in Van Schaack, *Life*, p. 38.

6. Van Schaack, *Life*, p. 28.

7. Van Schaack to James Duane (?), 1774, Van Schaack Family Papers.

8. Van Schaack to John Vardill, January 3, 1775, Van Schaack Family Papers.

9. Van Schaack to David Van Schaack, February 25, 1775, quoted in Van Schaack, *Memoirs*, p. 37.

10. Quoted in Benton, "Whig-Loyalists," p. 141.

11. *Historical Memoirs of William Smith*, ed. William H. W. Sabine, 2 vols. (New York, 1956-58), 1:221.

12. Van Schaack, *Life*, p. 56; Van Schaack, miscellaneous legal notes (undated), Van Schaack Family Papers.

13. David to Peter Van Schaack, April 28, 1775, quoted in Van Schaack, *Memoirs*, p. 44.

14. Elizabeth C. Van Schaack to Henry Cruger, Sr., September 7, 1775, Van Schaack Family Papers.

15. Van Schaack, *Life*, p. 65.

16. For a good account of wartime conditions in Kinderhook, see Edward A. Collier, *A History of Old Kinderhook* (New York, 1914), pp. 170-176.

17. Van Schaack, *Life*, p. 70.

18. Van Schaack to New York Provincial Convention, January 25, 1777, quoted in Van Schaack, *Life*, pp. 71-75.

19. Van Schaack, *Life*, p. 479.

20. Ibid., pp. 485-487.

21. Ibid., p. 110.

22. Van Schaack's memorandum, "Observations on the Banishing Act of

the Senate and Assembly of the State of New-York, 1778," is reprinted in full in Van Schaack, *Life*, pp. 111-116.

23. Theodore Sedgwick to Van Schaack, August 12, 1778, Van Schaack Family Papers.

24. Van Schaack to William Laight, January 26 (n.y.), Van Schaack Family Papers.

25. Van Schaack, *Life*, p. 162. Van Schaack's artistic norms were utilitarian, to say the least. He demanded that a work of art, like a good court decision, be didactic and convey some moral principle to which a man might recur for guidance on future occasions. Thus, in recommending the sentimental novels of Samuel Richardson to his son, he was careful to point out their supraliterary relevance: "How would a Sir Charles Grandison, how would a Clarissa have acted in this case?—will be a question every man and woman should put to themselves, in every difficult scene of life" (Peter to Henry [Harry] Van Schaack, January 11, 1780, quoted in Van Schaack, *Life*, p. 197).

26. Ibid., pp. 136, 239, 263.

27. Ibid., pp. 165-167. For an excellent discussion of refugee attitudes in general, see William H. Nelson, *The American Tory* (Oxford, 1961), pp. 153-169.

28. Van Schaack, *Life*, p. 241.

29. Ibid., pp. 259-260.

30. Ibid., pp. 262-263.

31. Van Schaack to Laight, January 26 (n.y.), Van Schaack Family Papers.

32. Van Schaack, *Life*, p. 263.

33. Van Schaack to John Jay, August 5, 1783, quoted in Van Schaack, *Life*, p. 309.

34. Van Schaack, *Life*, p. 165; Van Schaack to Jacob Walton, June 16, 1781, and Van Schaack to Thomas Hayes, March 2, 1784, Van Schaack Family Papers. For a discussion of Van Schaack's wartime allowance from the British government, see Lewis Einstein, *Divided Loyalties: Americans in England during the War of Independence* (Boston, 1933), pp. 264-265.

35. Peter to Henry [Harry] Van Schaack, December 22, 1779, quoted in Van Schaack, *Life*, p. 195.

36. Peter to Henry Van Schaack, January 5, 1783, quoted in Van Schaack, *Life*, p. 322.

37. Quoted in Collier, *Old Kinderhook*, p. 403.

38. Technically, Van Schaack's offense was "misprision of treason," a serious misdemeanor rather than a felony. The gist of the offense was that the accused had some knowledge of a treasonable plot which he did not divulge to the authorities, even though there was no evidence that he personally condoned or promoted the conspiracy in any way.

39. Van Schaack, *Life*, pp. 398-400. See also Anton-Hermann Chroust, *The Rise of the Legal Profession in America*, 2 vols. (Norman, Okla., 1965), 2:7, 10.

40. Peter to Henry Van Schaack, May 27, 1784, quoted in Van Schaack, *Life*, p. 356.

41. Van Schaack, *Life*, pp. 402-403.

42. Ibid., p. 403.

43. Van Schaack Family Records, Columbia County Historical Society, Kinderhook, New York. This small collection contains, besides Peter Van

Schaack's legal registers, some family account books which reveal the solid middle-class status of the Van Schaack clan. The estate of Cornelius Van Schaack alone amounted to more than £ 25,000, which was divided equally among his seven heirs, leaving each in comfortable circumstances.

44. Van Schaack, *Life*, pp. 364, 404, 414.

45. Ibid., p. 136.

46. Van Schaack to Robert Yates, March 13, 1786, quoted in Van Schaack, *Life*, p. 415.

47. Peter to Henry Van Schaack, January 2, 1769, quoted in Van Schaack, *Life*, p. 9.

48. Van Schaack to Henry Cruger, Jr., December 19, 1801, Van Schaack Family Papers.

49. Assets worth £ 3,100, of course, by no means constituted a princely fortune, even by the standards of 1809. In Kinderhook itself several individuals owned three times as much property as Van Schaack, whose economic position may best be described as modest. Still, in a community where 491 out of 594 persons (or 83 percent of the propertied classes) owned estates valued at *less* than £ 1,000—and where the average value of property holdings amounted to only a few hundred pounds—Van Schaack clearly qualified as a village nabob. The combined local assets of the Van Schaack family, moreover, totaled more than £ 9,000. For a complete picture of property distribution in Kinderhook, see the Kinderhook Assessment Roll of May 27, 1809, which appears in Collier, *Old Kinderhook*, pp. 112-124. Van Schaack's clerkship accounts, 1801-1814, are in the Van Schaack Family Papers.

50. Peter to Henry [Harry] Van Schaack, February 22, 1789, quoted in Van Schaack, *Life*, pp. 429-430.

51. Peter to Henry Van Schaack, July 12, 1783, quoted in Van Schaack, *Life*, p. 337.

52. Van Schaack to Henry Walton, June 3, 1788, quoted in Van Schaack, *Life*, pp. 425-426. Van Schaack's newspaper articles are, unfortunately, no longer available for study. The last known complete file of the *Hudson Weekly Gazette* was destroyed in the New York State Library fire of 1911.

53. Van Schaack to Henry Cruger, February 29, 1796, Van Schaack Family Papers.

54. Peter to Henry Van Schaack, January 27, 1769, Hawks Papers, New York Historical Society, New York City.

55. "Political Parties," Van Schaack Family Papers.

56. Loring Andrews to Peter Van Schaack, April 6, 1798, Peter Van Schaack Papers, Library of Congress, Washington, D.C. In the matter of repression Van Schaack's record was more than matched by that of his longtime acquaintance Theodore Sedgwick. As a rebel in the 1770s, Sedgwick had conspicuously defended the rights of "worthy" dissenters throughout the Revolution; as a Federalist congressman in 1798 he helped to draft both the Alien Friends Act and the Sedition Act and led the fight to push those measures through the House of Representatives. See Richard E. Welch, Jr., *Theodore Sedgwick, Federalist: A Political Portrait* (Middletown, Conn., 1965), pp. 193-195.

57. John C. Fitzpatrick, ed., *The Autobiography of Martin Van Buren*, in *Annual Report of the American Historical Association for the Year 1918*, 2 vols. (Washington, 1920), 2:19-20.

2.   Antilawyer Sentiment in the Early
Republic

1. Richard H. Major, ed., *Select Letters of Christopher Columbus* (London, 1847), p. 148.

2. John Robert Aiken, "Utopianism and the Emergence of the Colonial Legal Profession: New York, 1664-1710, A Test Case" (Ph.D. dissertation, University of Rochester, 1967). I am indebted to Aiken's perceptive study for many fresh insights into early legal utopianism. But cf. George Lee Haskins, *Law and Authority in Early Massachusetts* (New York, 1960).

3. Aiken, "Utopianism," pp. vii-viii.

4. "The Competitor, No. II," *Boston Magazine*, 2 (April 1785): 141.

5. "The Nursery, No. X," *Boston Magazine*, 2 (June 1785): 224. See also "Tamo Cheeki, the Creek Indian in Philadelphia, No. X," *The Time-Piece and Literary Companion*, 1 (May 12, 1797); "Principles of Government and Commerce," *American Magazine*, 1 (December 1787): 9-11; "The Savage and the Civilized State Compared," *South Carolina Weekly Museum*, 1 (April 15, 1797): 456-459.

6. Henry Cruger Van Schaack, *Memoirs of the Life of Henry Van Schaack* (Chicago, 1892), pp. 108, 114.

7. "Observations on Boston," *Monthly Miscellany and Vermont Magazine*, 1 (July 1794): 207, 209.

8. Peter DuPonceau to Anne L. Garesché, September 25, 1837, and July 9, 1839, Peter DuPonceau Papers, Historical Society of Pennsylvania, Philadelphia.

9. *Memoirs of William Sampson*, 2d ed. (Leesburg, Va., 1817), p. 337.

10. Williams's speech was reprinted in the *National Intelligencer* of January 13, 1805; for Strong's remarks, see *National Intelligencer*, January 29, 1806.

11. James Kent to Moss Kent, December 11, 1794, James Kent Papers, vol. 2, Library of Congress, Washington, D.C.

12. "A Poem, on the Happiness of America," *Boston Magazine*, 3 (August 1786): 306.

13. "Epistle from One Student of Law to Another," *Worcester Magazine*, 2 (December 1786): 464. The standard interpretation of the crisis in lawyer-community relations following the Revolution may be found in Charles Warren, *A History of the American Bar* (Boston, 1911), pp. 211-212; and Roscoe Pound, *The Lawyer from Antiquity to Modern Times, with Particular Reference to the Development of Bar Associations in the United States* (St. Paul, 1953), pp. 177-178. Anton-Hermann Chroust, while accepting the major premises of the argument, suggests that antilawyer prejudice always existed in the "rough-and-ready back country" (*The Rise of the Legal Profession in America*, 2 vols. [Norman, Okla, 1965], 2:4-5). Only very recently have students begun to take a fresh look at the whole problem and to reinterpret the available data from a more sophisticated interdisciplinary perspective. See, in particular, two first-rate unpublished studies: Charles R. McKirdy, "Lawyers in Crisis: The Massachusetts Legal Profession, 1760-1790" (Ph.D. dissertation, Northwestern University, 1969); and Gerard W. Gawalt, "Massachusetts Lawyers: A Historical Analysis of the Process of Professionalization, 1760-1840" (Ph.D. dissertation, Clark University, 1969).

14. "A Valedictory Address to the Young Gentlemen, Who Commenced

Bachelors of Arts, at Yale College, July 25th, 1776," *American Magazine*, 1 (January 1788): 101.

15. *Pennsylvania Gazette*, June 17, 1736. See, too, the succinct reference to "the quirks, quibbles, and the roguish part" of the law, in Carl Bridenbaugh, ed., *Gentleman's Progress, the Itinerarium of Dr. Alexander Hamilton, 1744* (Chapel Hill, 1948), p. 37.

16. "Monthly Chronologer for February, 1784," *Boston Magazine*, 1 (February 1784): 164; Horace Binney, "The Leaders of the Old Bar of Philadelphia," *Pennsylvania Magazine of History and Biography*, 14 (1890): 155.

17. [W. W. Fosdick,] "The Profession of the Law," *Western Law Journal*, 7 (1849): 101.

18. "The Republic of Beasts," *Columbian Magazine*, 2 (September 1788): 538.

19. *Columbian Magazine*, 2 (October 1788): 604, 605.

20. "Instructions of the Town of New-Braintree to its Representative," *Worcester Magazine*, 1 (June 1786): 106.

21. [Benjamin Austin,] *Observations on the Pernicious Practice of the Law* (Boston, 1786), pp. 25-26. See also "To the Legislatures of the Respective States, Letter Fourth," *National Intelligencer*, January 7, 1805; Chroust, *Rise of the Legal Profession*, 2:18-19.

22. See, for example, the complaints of middle-class litigants in contemporary America as reported in Murray Teigh Bloom's best-seller, *The Trouble with Lawyers* (New York, 1968).

23. "To the Legislatures of the Respective States, Letter Fourth," *National Intelligencer*, January 4, 1805.

24. Austin, *Observations*, p. 6.

25. Ibid., p. 34.

26. Ibid., pp. 17, 23-24.

27. [Jesse Higgins,] *Sampson against the Philistines*, 2d ed. (Philadelphia, 1805), pp. 24-25, 92.

28. Ibid., p. 66.

29. *Worcester Magazine*, 2 (November 1786): 382. See also "Proposal for a More Speedy and Less Expensive Method of Deciding Causes Judicially through the Commonwealth of Massachusetts, than What Is Now Practised," *Boston Magazine*, 1 (April 1784): 226-228; "The Politician, No. II," *Massachusetts Magazine*, 1 (August 1789): 500; "On the Gratuitous Administration of Justice," *American Monthly Magazine*, 1 (September 1829): 369-378; Higgins, *Sampson*, p. 31.

30. Philip Detweiler, "Early American Lawyers and the Public" (paper read at the Nineteenth Annual Meeting of the Southern Historical Association, October 14, 1953). Professor Detweiler's penetrating analysis of the public's ambivalence toward lawyers throughout the eighteenth century has done much to clarify my own thinking about the problem.

31. On this point, see especially Frederick P. Bowes, *The Culture of Early Charleston* (Chapel Hill, 1942), pp. 51-52.

32. "The Archer, No. II," *Monthly Register, Magazine, and Review of the United States*, 1 (1806): 308.

33. William F. English, *The Pioneer Lawyer and Jurist in Missouri*, University of Missouri Studies, 21, no. 2 (Columbia, Mo., 1947): 12-13; Chroust, *Rise of the Legal Profession*, 2:106-108.

34. "Western Eloquence," *Western Law Journal*, 5 (1847): 143. Although the quotation comes from a later period, the style was equally characteristic of frontier oratory in the early Republic. Elizabeth G. Brown, in "The Bar on a Frontier: Wayne County, 1796-1836," *American Journal of Legal History*, 14 (1970): 136, defends the caliber of pioneer practitioners to the extent of arguing that their alleged flamboyance was largely a matter of myth. More persuasive is Daniel H. Calhoun's evaluation of the early circuit system in the Cumberland River country of Tennessee: "For the whole period from the late eighteenth century through the middle of the nineteenth, the circuit bar seems to provide the type or image of frontier legal practice. Its essential features are personalism, organicism, and concreteness. Judges did not deal with lawyers as mere officers of the court who appeared when court opened, presented their briefs, then hastened back to offices to continue serious work. They dealt rather with men who were in literal attendance upon the court, who received clients in the courtroom or within sight of it, who prepared briefs (if any) and arguments while lingering so close to the proceedings that they could hear anything startling that developed. Both clients and students came to lawyers because they had seen them act the part of strong personalities in public quarrels or in the somewhat formalized disputes of court procedure, especially in criminal trials. Clients sensed in the emotional intensity of life at the bar a guarantee that the legal profession could never be completely removed from the feelings of ordinary men . . . Barter in fees, adventurous play with horseflesh—these stood for the live, tangible unity that was the bar itself" (*Professional Lives in America: Structure and Aspiration, 1750-1850* [Cambridge, Mass., 1965], p. 62).

35. D. Gardenier to Peter Van Schaack, August 3, 1787, Van Schaack Family Papers, Columbia University Library, New York.

36. "On the Multitude of Lawyers," *Massachusetts Magazine*, 1 (December 1789): 792.

37. Philip Shriver Klein, ed., "Memoirs of a Senator from Pennsylvania: Jonathan Roberts, 1771-1854," *Pennsylvania Magazine of History and Biography*, 62 (April 1938): 219, 223.

38. McKirdy, "Lawyers in Crisis," pp. 179-182.

39. Klein, "Memoirs of a Senator," p. 218; Elizabeth K. Henderson, "The Attack on the Judiciary in Pennsylvania, 1800-1810," *Pennsylvania Magazine of History and Biography*, 61 (April 1937): 113-136.

40. William Plumer, Jr., *Life of William Plumer* (Boston, 1857), pp. 153-154.

41. Ibid., p. 155.

42. Charles Watts to Henry Floyd-Jones, June 25 and August 29, 1821, Watts Papers, Columbia University Library, New York.

3.   William Sampson and the
Codification Movement

1. No adequate biography of Sampson has yet been written. He described his early career in *Memoirs of William Sampson*, 2d ed. rev. (Leesburg, Va., 1817) and provided additional details in his introduction to the American edition of William Henry Curran, *The Life of the Right Honorable John Philpot Curran, Late Master of the Rolls in Ireland* (New York, 1820). For the important American years one must rely principally upon a brief, eulogistic sketch

prepared by his daughter, Mrs. William Tone, for Richard R. Madden, *The United Irishmen, Their Lives and Times*, 7 vols. (London, 1842-1846), 2:335-388. This may be supplemented (and corrected in spots) by scattered manuscript materials. The David Baillie Warden Manuscript Collection at the Maryland Historical Society in Baltimore contains the largest number of Sampson letters (thirteen items) and is particularly useful in tracing the influence of his writings abroad during the 1820s. Also valuable are the few items found in the Peter DuPonceau Papers, Josiah S. Johnston Papers, Simon Gratz Collection, and Edward Carey Gardiner Collection, all at the Historical Society of Pennsylvania, Philadelphia. Sampson's correspondence with Thomas Jefferson (five letters in the General Correspondence Section of the Jefferson Papers, Library of Congress) is of minor interest, as is the Sampson-William Cullen Bryant correspondence in the Bryant-Godwin Collection of the New York Public Library. Irving Browne wrote a delightful account of Sampson's exploits at the New York bar in "William Sampson," *Green Bag*, 8 (1896): 313.

2. Madden, *United Irishmen*, 2:342. For a recent authoritative analysis of Irish politics in the late eighteenth century, see R. R. Palmer, *The Age of the Democratic Revolution*, 2 vols. (Princeton, 1959-1964), 1:287-294, 302-306.

3. *Memoirs of William Sampson*, p. 311.

4. Richard R. Madden, *The History of Irish Periodical Literature, from the End of the Seventeenth to the Middle of the Nineteenth Century*, 2 vols. (London, 1867), 2:225-235.

5. Sampson, *A Faithful Report of the Trial of Hurdy Gurdy* (1807), p. 10.

6. Curran, *John Philpot Curran*, p. xix.

7. *An Appeal from William Sampson, Esq., Barrister at Law, to the Public, with a Letter to His Excellency John Earl Camden, Lord Lieutenant of Ireland, &c. &c. and Another to Arthur Wolfe, Esq., His Majesty's Attorney General* (Dublin, n.d.).

8. Charles Ross, ed., *Correspondence of Charles, First Marquis Cornwallis*, 3 vols. (London, 1859), 2:368-369. For a more detailed account of the Irish Revolution of 1798, see Palmer, *Age of the Democratic Revolution*, 2:491-505; and Thomas Pakenham, *The Year of Liberty* (London, 1969).

9. *Memoirs of William Sampson*, pp. 66-67.

10. Ibid., p. 129.

11. Madden, *United Irishmen*, 2:374. Cf. Sampson's own statement in his private correspondence: "I have been charged with the affairs of all the French of mark in this country. The ex-King Joseph, Count Réal, Genl. Bernard, the Duke of Vience, the unfortunate Count Regnaud de St. Jean d'Angely, &c" (Sampson to David B. Warden, September 14, 1825, Warden Papers, Maryland Historical Society, Baltimore).

12. The court's ruling is printed in 1 Johnson (N.Y. Sup. Ct.) 528 (1806). For further details on the Emmet case, see 2 Caines (N.Y. Sup. Ct.) 386 (1805); and Charles Glidden Haines, *Memoir of Thomas Addis Emmet* (New York, 1829), pp. 84-87.

13. Sampson to Warden, July 18, 1808, Warden Papers. In the same letter Sampson remarks: "What you hear of Mrs. Sampson's having joined me is premature. But I hope before long it will be true." In fact he was not reunited with his family until October 1810.

14. Kent's remark comes from a handwritten necrology that he appended to the second volume of Johnson's *Reports* in his personal library, now in the

possession of the New York State Library, Albany. He went on to say that Sampson "was gentle & amiable & had wit and Genius." I am indebted to Professor Donald Roper for calling this reference to my attention.

15. Sampson's doggerel verse on Curran is reprinted in Curran, *John Philpot Curran*, p. xvii. The warning against Irish bombast occurs in David Hoffman, *A Course of Legal Study* (Baltimore, 1817), pp. 304-305.

16. *Trial of Capt. Henry Whitby . . . Also, the Trial of Capt. George Crimp* (1812).

17. For an interesting evaluation of Sampson's significance as an early court reporter, see Charles Currier Beale, "William Sampson," *Proceedings of the New York State Stenographers' Association at the Thirty-first Annual Meeting, Held at Albany August 23 and 24, 1906* (Albany, 1906), pp. 20-42. His reasons for publishing his reports are clearly spelled out in his correspondence. See, for example, Sampson to Mathew Carey, May 13 and June 3, 1820, Mathew Carey Papers, Edward Carey Gardiner Collection, Historical Society of Pennsylvania, Philadelphia.

18. Sampson's comments about fee taking are drawn from two of his letters to Warden, January 7, 1813, and August (n.y.), Warden Papers. The confession case has been reprinted in full as *The Catholic Question in America* (New York, 1813), while Sampson's championship of the Eskimos may be traced in the DuPonceau Papers. See, especially, the Reverend F. C. Schaeffer to DuPonceau, February 12, 1821.

19. The other two cases were Chotard v. Pope, 12 Wheaton 586 (1827) and Mason v. Matilda, 12 Wheaton 590 (1827). In the last case Sampson helped to defeat the efforts of a Negro slave and her three children to gain their freedom under Virginia law. His libertarian sympathies apparently stopped somewhat short of the color line, at least in this instance.

20. The Case of the Journeymen Cordwainers of the City of New-York, 1 Yates's Select Cases 142 (1811).

21. Sampson to Warden, January 13, 1824, and April 27, 1825, Warden Papers.

22. For Jefferson's ideas on legal history, see Julian S. Waterman, "Thomas Jefferson and Blackstone's Commentaries," *Illinois Law Review*, 27 (1933): 629.

23. *Sampson's Discourse, and Correspondence with Various Learned Jurists, upon the History of the Law, with the Addition of Several Essays, Tracts, and Documents, Relating to the Subject*, ed. Pishey Thompson (Washington, D.C., 1826), p. 32.

24. Ibid.

25. William T. Utter, "Saint Tammany in Ohio: A Study in Frontier Politics," *Mississippi Valley Historical Review*, 15 (December 1928): 321-340; Utter, "Ohio and the English Common Law," ibid., 16 (December 1929): 321-333; Erwin C. Surrency, "When the Common Law was Unpopular in Pennsylvania," *Pennsylvania Bar Association Quarterly*, 33 (1962): 291; Anton-Hermann Chroust, "The Dilemma of the American Lawyer in the Post-Revolutionary Era," *Notre Dame Lawyer*, 35 (1959): 48. Richard E. Ellis's *The Jeffersonian Crisis* (New York, 1971) admirably underscores the political dimensions of legal reform on both the state and national levels during the early years of Republican rule.

26. *Sampson's Discourse*, p. 38.

27. Ibid., p. 36.

28. Henry D. Sedgwick, "The Common Law," *North American Review*, 19 (October 1824): 427, 430; "The Common Law," *Port Folio*, 17 (April 1824): 296-299; "The Common Law," *Atlantic Magazine*, 1 (May 1824): 23-30; "On the Substitution of a Written Code, in the Place of the Common Law," ibid. (August 1824), pp. 283-298.

29. Sampson to Warden, April 27, 1825, Warden Papers.

30. Sampson to Warden, September 14, 1825, Warden Papers.

31. Sampson's principal American correspondents included Thomas Cooper and Governor John L. Wilson (S.C.), Charles Watts (La.), Senator Isham Talbot (Ky.), and George M. Bibb (Washington, D.C.). The debate over codification may be traced through such varied publications as the New York *American*, *National Intelligencer* (Washington, D.C.), New York *Evening Post*, Charleston *Mercury*, *National Advocate* (N.Y.), *North American Review*, *Southern Review*, *Atlantic Magazine*, and *United States Law Journal*.

32. See, for example, C. S. Daveis, "Common Law Jurisdiction," *North American Review*, 21 (July 1825): 104-141; "Verplanck's Essay on Contracts," *New York Review and Atheneum Magazine*, 2 (January 1826): 106-125; Henry D. Sedgwick, "Correspondence on the History of the Law," *North American Review*, 23 (July 1826): 197-201; Review of *Sampson's Discourse* and *Report from New York Commissioners*, *United States Literary Gazette*, 4 (August 1826): 345-348; "Aperçu de la situation intérieure des Etats-Unis d'Amérique et de leurs rapports politiques avec l'Europe, par un Russe," *Monthly Review* (London), n.s. 3 (September 1826): 45-59; Julien Bonnecase, *La Thémis (1819-1831): Son fondateur, Athanase Jourdan*, 2d ed. (Paris, 1914), pp. 158-159. The codification controversy also furnished material for several lively satires, including the novella "The Perfection of Reason" in James K. Paulding, *The Merry Tales of the Three Wise Men of Gotham*, rev. ed. (New York, 1839), pp. 105-169; and "Letter of Levinz Comberbach," *New York Review and Atheneum Magazine*, 2 (February 1826): 213-216.

33. *Sampson's Discourse*, p. 53.

34. Caleb Cushing, "Law Reports," *North American Review*, 18 (April 1824): 377.

35. *Sampson's Discourse*, p. 87.

36. Paul A. Palmer, "Benthamism in England and America," *American Political Science Review*, 35 (October 1941): 855-871.

37. Jeremy Bentham, *Supplement to Papers Relative to Codification and Public Instruction* (London, 1817), pp. 126, 130. See also Chilton Williamson, "Bentham Looks at America," *Political Science Quarterly*, 70 (December 1955): 543-551.

38. *Sampson's Discourse*, p. 59.

39. Ibid.; "On the Substitution of a Written Code, in the Place of the Common Law," pp. 287, 295.

40. "Letter on the Napoleon Code," *United States Review and Literary Gazette*, 1 (November 1826): 127.

41. Ibid., 128.

42. *Sampson's Discourse*, pp. 66-67, 191. A brief but colorful account of Réal may be found in Clarence Edward Macartney and Gordon Dorrance, *The Bonapartes in America* (Philadelphia, 1939), pp. 123-124.

43. Sampson to Warden, June 7, 1829, Warden Papers.

44. Quoted in Madden, *United Irishmen*, 2:387.

45. W. H. Gardiner, "Revision of the Laws of New York," *North American Review*, 24 (January 1827): 194; *Sampson's Discourse*, pp. 74, 103, 159-160; "Codification of the Laws of the United States of America," *Jurist* (London), 2 (1828): 47. In Louisiana, a stronghold of French legal thought, code commissioners had been appointed as early as 1821. Here Sampson's publicity campaign tended to provoke a vigorous anticode reaction by 1826 (see *Sampson's Discourse*, p. 162). The most famous Louisiana codifier, Edward Livingston, was an avowed Benthamite; significantly, his criminal code, which sought to approximate Bentham's standards, was not adopted by the Louisiana legislature, while a Civil Code and a Code of Practice, based upon French models, went into effect in 1825 (Eugene Smith, "Edward Livingston and the Louisiana Codes," *Columbia Law Review*, 2 [1902]: 24).

46. A good example of Rantoul's polemics may be found in his "Oration at Scituate" (1836), reprinted in *Memoirs, Speeches, and Writings of Robert Rantoul, Jr.*, ed. Luther Hamilton (Boston, 1854), pp. 251-296. See also Arthur M. Schlesinger, Jr., *The Age of Jackson* (Boston, 1950), pp. 322-333; and Chroust, *Rise of the Legal Profession*, 2:59-61, 69-72.

47. Erwin N. Griswold, *Law and Lawyers in the United States*, 2d ed. (Cambridge, Mass., 1965), p. 19; W. Raymond Blackard, "The Demoralization of the Legal Profession in Nineteenth Century America," *Tennessee Law Review*, 16 (1940): 314-318.

48. N. Haven, "English Common Law Reports," *North American Review*, 21 (October 1825): 377-388; "On the Substitution of a Written Code, in the Place of the Common Law," pp. 288-292, 295.

49. *The Principles of Moral and Political Philosophy*, 5th ed., 2 vols. (London, 1788), 2:411.

50. For a thorough account of Paley's influence in America, see Wilson Smith, *Professors and Public Ethics* (Ithaca, 1956), pp. 44-73. A nineteenth-century critique of Paleyan assumptions by a leading anticodifier may be found in Hugh S. Legaré, "Jeremy Bentham and the Utilitarians," *Southern Review*, 7 (August 1831): 261-296.

51. Charles Warren, *A History of the American Bar* (Boston, 1911), pp. 525-539.

52. "Revision of the Laws in Massachusetts," *American Jurist*, 13 (1835): 344. Perry Miller provides a stimulating, albeit highly personalized and impressionistic, appraisal of the codification movement to 1860 in *The Life of the Mind in America* (New York, 1965), pp. 239-265. A more comprehensive treatment of the subject may be found in Charles M. Cook, "The American Codification Movement: A Study of Antebellum Legal Reform" (Ph.D. dissertation, University of Maryland, 1974), which probes exhaustively into the goals and attitudes of the antebellum codifiers and contains many valuable insights. Two other studies that help to illumine the codification effort in individual states are Donald J. Senese, "Legal Thought in South Carolina, 1800-1860" (Ph.D. dissertation, University of South Carolina, 1970), pp. 167-226; and Gerard W. Gawalt, "Massachusetts Lawyers: A Historical Analysis of the Process of Professionalization, 1760-1840" (Ph.D dissertation, Clark University, 1969), pp. 166-187.

53. Two general surveys of American influence abroad in the early nineteenth century are outstanding: David Paul Crook, *American Democracy in English Politics, 1815-1850* (Oxford, 1965); and René Rémond, *Les Etats-Unis*

devant l'opinion française, 1815-1852, 2 vols. (Paris, 1962).

54. C. P. Cooper to DuPonceau, November 6, 1829, DuPonceau Papers.

55. Jabez Henry to Kent, August 8, 1829, James Kent Papers, vol. 5, Library of Congress, Washington, D.C. Kent's work was linked directly to the codification controversy by some magazine writers. In 1824, two years prior to the publication of the first volume of his *Commentaries,* a contributor to the *Atlantic Magazine* remarked that Kent's lectures on law were "worth more than all the codes as such, that could ever be formed" ("On the Substitution of a Written Code, in the Place of the Common Law," p. 298). Cf. Kent's own statement of purpose: "My object will be to discuss the law . . . as known and received at Boston, New York, Philadelphia, Baltimore, Charleston &c. and as proved by the judicial decisions in those respective states. I shall not much care what the law is in Vermont or Delaware or Rhode Island, or many other states. Cannot we assume American common law to be what is declared in the federal courts and in the courts of the states I have mentioned and in some others, without troubling ourselves with every local peculiarity? I shall *assume* what I have to say, to be the law of every state, where an exception is not shown, because I mean to deal in *general Principles* and those positive regulations, legislative and judicial, which constitute the basis of all American jurisprudence" (Kent to DuPonceau, December 29, 1826, DuPonceau Papers).

56. For further details on the society and its work, see *Monthly Law Reporter,* 7 (1844): 110; and Frances Hawes, *Henry Brougham* (London, 1957), pp. 285-286.

57. Browne, "William Sampson," p. 313: "He is known by tradition to all the old New York lawyers now living, to some of the middle-aged, and not at all to the young. Even when the roll of the lawyers who conferred glory on the New York Bar eighty years ago is called on festive occasions, his name is not mentioned."

4.   The Family in Antebellum Law

1. Alexis de Tocqueville, *De la démocratie en Amérique, avec notes par André Gain,* 2 vols. (Paris, 1951), 2:257-264. Tocqueville does suggest that the ties of economic interest that linked the children of aristocratic households may be replaced in democratic families by equally strong bonds of fraternal sympathy and affection (pp. 262-263).

2. George E. Howard, *A History of Matrimonial Institutions,* 3 vols. (Chicago and London, 1904), 2:389; Helen I. Clarke, *Social Legislation,* 2d ed. (New York, 1957), pp. 78-81. Clarke contends that even in the South, with the exception of Maryland, "the optional civil ceremony was legally or practically recognized under certain conditions" by the time of the Revolution (p. 80).

3. Lawrence M. Friedman, *A History of American Law* (New York, 1973), pp. 179-180. Otto E. Koegel, the author of a book-length monograph on the common-law marriage, concludes that the children of such unions were recognized as legitimate by English common-law judges prior to 1753 but that the marriage conferred no possessory rights on the parties or their issue; i.e., the children could not inherit property from their parents, nor did wives enjoy

any dower rights. In 1753 all "clandestine" marriages in England were expressly prohibited by an act of Parliament. (*Common Law Marriage and Its Development in the United States* [Washington, D.C., 1922], p. 9.)

4. Morris Talpalar, *The Sociology of Colonial Virginia* (New York, 1960), p. 194.

5. Joel F. Handler, ed., *Family Law and the Poor: Essays by Jacobus tenBroek* (Westport, Conn., 1971), pp. 33-34.

6. *The Lawes Resolutions of Womens Rights; or, The Lawes Provision for Women* (London, 1632), quoted in Julia Cherry Spruill, *Women's Life and Work in the Southern Colonies* (Norton Library ed., New York, 1972), p. 340.

7. Clarke, *Social Legislation*, pp. 58-67.

8. Richard B. Morris, *Studies in the History of American Law, with Special Reference to the Seventeenth and Eighteenth Centuries* (New York, 1930), pp. 126-133, 135.

9. Ibid., p. 143.

10. Spruill, *Women's Life and Work*, pp. 342-344; Nelson M. Blake, *The Road to Reno* (New York, 1962), pp. 34-47; Friedman, *History of American Law*, p. 181.

11. David H. Flaherty, "Law and the Enforcement of Morals in Early America," *Perspectives in American History*, 5 (1971): 203-253. See also Flaherty, *Privacy in Colonial New England* (Charlottesville, 1972); and Leo Kanowitz, *Women and the Law: The Unfinished Revolution* (Albuquerque, 1969), pp. 38-40.

12. Handler, *Family Law*, p. 34; Theodore F. T. Plucknett, *A Concise History of the Common Law*, 5th ed. (Boston, 1956), pp. 544-545.

13. *Commentaries on the Laws of England*, 1:447 (Cooley ed., 1899); Handler, *Family Law*, pp. 34-37.

14. George L. Haskins, *Law and Authority in Early Massachusetts: A Study in Tradition and Design* (New York, 1960), p. 81; Edmund S. Morgan, *The Puritan Family* (Boston, 1944), p. 78.

15. Stephen B. Presser, "The Historical Background of the American Law of Adoption," *Journal of Family Law*, 11 (1971): 443-516; Haskins, *Law and Authority*, pp. 81-83; John Demos, *A Little Commonwealth: Family Life in Plymouth Colony* (New York, 1970), pp. 71-75.

16. Handler, *Family Law*, pp. 5-26; Clarke, *Social Legislation*, pp. 465-472.

17. 18 Eliz. 1, c. 3, §IV (1575-1576), quoted in Handler, *Family Law*, p. 23.

18. Handler, *Family Law*, pp. 26-28.

19. 43 Eliz. 1, c. 2, §VI (1601).

20. Handler, *Family Law*, p. 32.

21. Stefan A. Riesenfeld, "The Formative Era of American Public Assistance Law," *California Law Review*, 43 (1955): 175-233.

22. David J. Rothman, *The Discovery of the Asylum* (Boston and Toronto, 1971), pp. 3-56.

23. Josiah H. Benton, *Warning Out in New England* (Boston, 1911), p. 54.

24. John Bach McMaster, *The Acquisition of Political, Social, and Industrial Rights of Man in America* (Cleveland, 1903), p. 38. Welfare recipients in colonial Virginia, according to Morris Talpalar, had to "wear a badge of a yellow color" (*Sociology of Colonial Virginia*, p. 155). For an incisive critique of Rothman's views, which charges him with constructing a "somewhat idealized portrait of seventeenth and eighteenth century colonial society," see

Gerald N. Grob, "Welfare and Poverty in American History," *Reviews in American History,* 1 (March 1973): 43-52.

25. Kent reiterated Paley's views on polygamy and cited Paley approvingly in his chapters on parent and child and inheritance laws (*Commentaries on American Law,* 2:81, 190, 195 [Holmes and Barnes ed., 1884], 4:397). Hoffman recommended Paley's *Moral Philosophy* as a basic text for beginning law students in his acclaimed *Course of Legal Study* (1817) and followed Paley's utilitarian argument concerning marriage and the parent-child relationship in *Legal Outlines,* 1:147-156 (1829).

26. William Paley, *The Principles of Moral and Political Philosophy,* 5th ed., 2 vols. (London, 1788), 1:86, 2:347.

27. Paley, *Principles,* 2:351, 395, 1:293-294.

28. Fenton v. Reed, 4 Johnson (N.Y. Sup. Ct.) 54 (1809); Kent, *Commentaries,* 2:87.

29. Newbury v. Brunswick, 2 Vt. 151 (1829); Pearson v. Hovey, 11 N.J. Law 12 (1829); Graham v. Bennett, 2 Cal. 503 (1852); Hargroves v. Thompson, 31 Miss. 211 (1856).

30. Dunbarton v. Franklin, 19 N.H. 257, 265 (1848).

31. 10 Tenn. 588 (1831). See also Milford v. Worcester, 7 Mass. 48 (1810); Bashaw v. State, 9 Tenn. 176 (1829).

32. Dumaresly v. Fishly, 10 Ky. 368, 372 (1821).

33. Rodebaugh v. Sanks, 2 Watts (Pa.) 9, 11 (1833).

34. State v. Samuel, 2 Dev. & Bat. (N.C.) 177 (1836); Malinda and Sarah v. Gardner, 24 Ala. 719 (1854); Johnson v. Johnson, 45 Mo. 595 (1870); Bishop, *Commentaries on the Law of Marriage and Divorce* (6th ed., 1881), 1:130-133.

35. Howard v. Howard, 6 Jones (N.C.) 235, 237 (1858).

36. 6 Mart. O.S. (La.) 559 (1819).

37. Free Frank and Lucy v. Denham's Adm'r., 15 Ky. 330 (1824).

38. Howard v. Howard, 238-239. See also John E. Semonche, "Common-Law Marriage in North Carolina: A Study in Legal History," *American Journal of Legal History,* 9 (1965):320-349; and Henry W. Farnam, *Chapters in the History of Social Legislation in the United States to 1860* (Washington, D.C., 1938), pp. 200-209.

39. Gilbert Thomas Stephenson, *Race Distinctions in American Law* (New York and London, 1910), pp. 67-75; Bishop, *Commentaries,* 1:138-139. Such Reconstruction legislation did not generally purport to cover racial inter-marriages. In a number of states, North and South, miscegenation statutes declared "null and void" any union of whites and nonwhites, and courts tended to enforce their provisions rigorously. See, for example, State v. Hairston and Williams, 63 N.C. 451 (1869); State v. Gibson, 36 Ind. 389 (1871); State v. Bell, 66 Tenn. 9 (1872); Carter v. Montgomery, 2 Tenn. Ch. 216 (1875); Green v. State, 58 Ala. 190 (1877). Cf. Dickerson v. Brown, 49 Miss. 357 (1873).

40. Roche v. Washington, 19 Ind. 53 (1862). See also Wells v. Thompson, 13 Ala. 793 (1848); State v. Ta-Cha-Na-Tah, 64 N.C. 614 (1870). For an excellent discussion of the underlying issue of "savagery," see Roy Harvey Pearce, *The Savages of America: A Study of the Indian and the Idea of Civilization,* rev. ed. (Baltimore, 1965).

41. 30 Mo. 72 (1860). Other decisions upholding Indian marriages include

Boyer v. Dively, 58 Mo. 510 (1875); Kobogum v. Jackson Iron Co., 76 Mich. 498 (1889); Earl v. Godley, 42 Minn. 361 (1890). See also Morgan v. M'Ghee, 24 Tenn. 13 (1844); and Wall v. Williamson, 11 Ala. 826 (1847).

42. Friedman, *History of American Law*, p. 186; Walker, *Introduction to American Law* (4th ed., 1860), pp. 254-255; "The Property Rights of Married Women," *North American Review*, 99 (July 1864): 34-64; Andrew Sinclair, *The Better Half: The Emancipation of the American Woman* (New York, 1965), pp. 86-88.

43. Billings v. Baker, 28 Barb. (N.Y. Sup. Ct.) 343 (1859).

44. Vallance v. Bausch, 28 Barb. (N.Y. Sup. Ct.) 633 (1859).

45. Naylor v. Field, 29 N.J. Law 287 (1861); Johnson v. Cummins, 16 N.J. Eq. 97 (1863). See also Friend v. Oliver, 27 Ala. 532 (1855); Junction Railroad Company v. Harris, 9 Ind. 184 (1857); Walker v. Reamy, 36 Pa. 410 (1860).

46. 8 Har. (Pa.) 308, 311 (1853).

47. 27 Miss. 830, 835 (1854).

48. 37 Maine 394 (1854). For further illustrations, see Rider v. Hulse, 33 Barb. (N.Y. Sup. Ct.) 264 (1860); Duncan v. Roselle, 15 Iowa 501 (1864); Bear v. Hays, 36 Ill. 280 (1865); Hoyt v. White, 46 N.H. 45 (1865).

49. Schindel v. Schindel, 12 Md. 108 (1858).

50. Schindel v. Schindel, 12 Md. 294, 299-300 (1858).

51. Ibid., 307-308.

52. Bishop, *Commentaries on the Law of Married Women* (1875), 2:341-342. See also Benjamin Vaughan Abbott, *Judge and Jury* (New York, 1880), pp. 146-157.

53. David Dudley Field to Sir Erskine Perry and others, Committee of the Law Amendment Society, January 29, 1857, Field Papers, Perkins Library, Duke University, Durham, North Carolina. Field was speaking specifically of conditions in New York, but his observation is valid for other states as well. See also Sinclair, *Better Half*, pp. 88-91.

54. Mercein v. People ex rel. Barry, 25 Wend. (N.Y. Ct. Err.) 64, 102-103 (1840).

55. People ex rel. Barry v. Mercein, 3 Hill (N.Y. Sup. Ct.) 399, 422 (1842).

56. See, for example, In re Kottman, 2 Hill (S.C. Law) 363 (1833); Tarking-ton v. State, 1 Car. (Ind.) 171 (1848); Bryan v. Bryan, 34 Ala. 516 (1859); State v. Richardson, 40 N.H. 272 (1860); Johnson v. Terry, 34 Conn. 259 (1867). Custody was awarded to the mother in Nickols v. Giles, 2 Root (Conn.) 461 (1796); Miner v. Miner, 11 Ill. 43 (1849); Bennet v. Bennet, 13 N.J. Eq. 114 (1860).

57. "Married Women," *Monthly Law Reporter*, 23 (1860): 362, 370.

58. Cromwell v. Benjamin, 41 Barb. (N.Y. Sup. Ct.) 558 (1863); Handler, *Family Law*, pp. 47-50. See also Pidgin v. Cram, 8 N.H. 350 (1836); Tomkins v. Tomkins 11 N.J. Eq. 512 (1858). Cf. Gordon v. Potter, 17 Vt. 348 (1845); Hunt v. Thompson, 4 Ill. 179 (1841).

59. Corey v. Corey, 19 Pick. (Mass.) 29 (1837); Lyon v. Bolling, 14 Ala. 753 (1848); Conovar v. Cooper, 3 Barb. (N.Y. Sup. Ct.) 115 (1848); Armstrong v. McDonald, 10 Barb. (N.Y. Sup. Ct.) 300 (1851).

60. Presser, "Historical Background," pp. 461-470.

61. Richard Wires, *The Divorce Issue and Reform in Nineteenth-Century Indiana*, Ball State Monograph no. 8 (Muncie, Indiana, 1967), pp. 2-6; Blake, *Road to Reno*, pp. 119-120.

62. Head v. Head, 2 Ga. 191 (1846); Friedman, *History of American Law*, p. 182.

63. Blake, *Road to Reno*, pp. 48-63.

64. Wires, *Divorce Issue*, p. 6; James Harwood Barnett, *Divorce and the American Divorce Novel, 1858-1937* (New York, 1968), pp. 71-73.

65. Martha Branscombe, *The Courts and the Poor Laws in New York State, 1784-1929* (Chicago, 1943), p. 29; Friedman, *History of American Law*, pp. 187-191.

66. John Cummings, "Poor-Laws of Massachusetts and New York," *Publications of the American Economic Association*, 10 (July 1895): 477-611; Fern Boan, *A History of Poor Relief Legislation and Administration in Missouri* (Chicago, 1941), p. 23; Aileen Elizabeth Kennedy, *The Ohio Poor Law and Its Administration* (Chicago, 1934), pp. 22-23. David Rothman points out that settlement laws were liberalized during the antebellum years in those states that favored the incarceration of paupers in almshouses. Settlement provisions did not disappear from state codes, however (*Discovery of the Asylum*, p. 186).

67. Trustees of Jefferson Twp. v. Trustees of Letart Twp., 3 Ohio 99, 102-103 (1827).

68. Trustees of Bloomfield v. Trustees of Chagrin, 5 Ohio 316 (1832).

69. Overseers of Vernon v. Overseers of Smithville, 17 Johnson (N.Y. Sup. Ct.) 89 (1819).

70. 7 Cow. (N.Y. Sup. Ct.) 760, 763-764 (1827).

71. 10 Vt. 436, 444 (1838).

72. Town of Londonderry v. Town of Acton, 3 Vt. 122, 125-126 (1830). For representative "dumping" cases, see Thomas v. Ross, 8 Wend. (N.Y. Sup. Ct.) 672 (1832); Kelly Township v. Union Township, 5 Watts & Ser. (Pa.) 535 (1843); Town of Charlotte v. Town of Colchester, 20 Vt. 91 (1847); Winfield v. Mapes, 4 Den. (N.Y. Sup. Ct.) 571 (1847). Courts protected family unity in Town of Northfield v. Town of Roxbury, 15 Vt. 622 (1843); Overseers of Paterson v. Overseers of Byram, 23 N.J. Law 394 (1852).

73. Sophonisba P. Breckinridge, *The Illinois Poor Law and Its Administration* (Chicago, 1939), p. 21; Commissioners of the Poor v. Gansett, 2 Bailey (S.C.) 320 (1831); Newton v. Danbury, 3 Conn. 553 (1821).

74. 1 R.I. 409, 411 (1850).

75. 30 N.H. 9, 15-16 (1854). See also Dover v. McMurphy, 4 N.H. 158 (1827). Cf. Templeton v. Stratton, 128 Mass. 137 (1880).

76. Howard v. Whetstone Township, 10 Ohio 365, 369 (1841). See also Rumney v. Keyes, 7 N.H. 571 (1835); Inhabitants of Monson v. Williams, 6 Gray (Mass.) 416 (1856).

77. 18 Barb. (N.Y. Sup. Ct.) 100, 101-102 (1854).

78. The *Norton* case was overruled by Goodale v. Lawrence, 88 N.Y. 513 (1882).

79. 6 Cow. (N.Y. Sup. Ct.) 234, 236-237 (1826).

80. 6 Blackford (Ind.) 83, 84 (1841). See also Demar v. Simonson, 4 Blackford (Ind.) 132 (1835); Reidell v. Morse, 19 Pick. (Mass.) 358 (1837); Baker v. Winfrey, 54 Ky. 499 (1854); Midgett v. McBryde, 3 Jones (N.C. Law) 21 (1855).

81. Presser, "Historical Background," pp. 470-489; Emil McKee Sunley, *The Kentucky Poor Law, 1792-1936* (Chicago, 1942), p. 148; Boan, *Poor*

Relief Legislation, pp. 20-21; Alice Shaffer, Mary Wysor Keefer, and Sophonisba P. Breckinridge, *The Indiana Poor Law* (Chicago, 1936), p. 39.

82. Farnam, *Chapters in the History of Social Legislation*, p. 206; W. McDowell Rogers, "Free Negro Legislation in Georgia Before 1865," *Georgia Historical Quarterly*, 16 (March 1932): 27-37.

83. Rothman, *Discovery of the Asylum*, pp. 57-236.

84. Presser, "Historical Background," pp. 465-516.

85. Friedman, *History of American Law*, p. 191. See also Rothman, *Discovery of the Asylum*, pp. 237-295.

5.   Upgrading the Professional Image

1. See chapter 2 for an extended discussion of this theme.

2. See, for example, Charles R. McKirdy, "Lawyers in Crisis: The Massachusetts Legal Profession, 1760-1790" (Ph.D. dissertation, Northwestern University, 1969), pp. 147-149.

3. Gerard W. Gawalt, "Massachusetts Lawyers: A Historical Analysis of the Process of Professionalization, 1760-1840" (Ph.D. dissertation, Clark University, 1969), pp. 86-87, 110-125.

4. Russel to Story, August 21, 1838, Joseph Story Papers, vol. 6, Library of Congress, Washington, D.C.

5. Charles Chauncey Binney, *The Life of Horace Binney* (Philadelphia, 1903), p. 37.

6. "Notes on the Early Jurisprudence of Maine," *Monthly Law Reporter*, 3 (1840): 126.

7. "Fairness and Formalism in the Trials of Blacks in the State Supreme Courts of the Old South," *Virginia Law Review*, 56 (1970): 64-100.

8. This chart and the one below have been compiled from lists found in Frederick C. Hicks, *Materials and Methods of Legal Research*, 2d ed. (Rochester, 1933), pp. 147-148, supplemented by material from Leonard A. Jones, ed., *An Index to Legal Periodical Literature* (Boston, 1888).

9. "Miscellany," *Monthly Law Reporter*, 1 (1838): 55.

10. Chandler to Joseph Story, December 1, 1838, Story Papers, vol. 6.

11. The generalizations that follow are based upon a survey of sixteen law magazines, selected with a view to geographical distribution and representing the least as well as the most successful publications.

12. Herbert Butterfield, *The Origins of Modern Science*: *1300-1800*, rev. ed. (New York, 1958), pp. 161-174.

13. George S. Hillard, "Biographical Sketch of James C. Alvord," *American Jurist and Law Magazine*, 2 (1840): 377-378.

14. "Obituary Notices," *Monthly Law Reporter*, 10 (1847): 383.

15. "Biographical Sketch of Chief Justice Ellsworth," *American Law Magazine*, 3 (1844): 271.

16. "The Death of Chief Justice Shaw," *Monthly Law Reporter*, 24 (1861): 10.

17. "Proceedings of the Bar upon the Occasion of the Death of Daniel Webster," *Monthly Law Reporter*, 15 (1853): 585.

18. John G. Cawelti, *Apostles of the Self-made Man* (Chicago, 1965), pp. 39-75.

19. "Inaugural Address of Hon. A. Caruthers, Professor of Law in Cumberland University, Lebanon, Tennessee," *United States Monthly Law Magazine,* 3 (1851): 542.

20. "Obituary Notices: Lewis Bigelow," *Monthly Law Reporter,* 1 (1839): 275.

21. "The Hon. John Holmes," *Monthly Law Reporter,* 6 (1843): 151, 154.

22. "Codification," *Monthly Law Reporter,* 7 (1844): 350.

23. "Obituary Notice," *Monthly Law Reporter,* 11 (1849): 527.

24. "Office Duties" *American Law Register,* 4 (1856): 193. Much the same utilitarian and antipolitical line was taken by apologists for another unpopular occupational group—the officer corps of the United States Army and Navy—during these years, and for similar reasons. Military journalists argued that a permanent cadre of trained professionals posed no threat to democratic institutions because their energies were wholly absorbed by the technical demands of their science, which gave them neither the time nor the inclination for political intrigues. See, for example, Sydney, "Thoughts on the Organization of the Army," *The Military and Naval Magazine of the United States,* 2 (December 1833): 193-198; and "The Wants of the Navy," *Army and Navy Chronicle,* 11 (December 17, 1840): 398-399. I am indebted to Professor William B. Skelton for bringing this analogy to my attention.

25. Perry Miller, *The Life of the Mind in America* (New York, 1965), pp. 99-265.

26. "Ways and Means of Professional Success; Being the Substance of a Valedictory Address to the Graduates of the Law Class, in the Cincinnati College, by T. Walker, Professor of Law in That Institution: Delivered March 2, 1839," *Western Law Journal,* 1 (1844): 545.

27. "A Letter of Judge Daggett," *Monthly Law Reporter,* 8 (1845): 94.

28. Richard F. Fuller, "Rufus Choate," *Monthly Law Reporter,* 25 (1863): 266-267.

29. "The Latimer Case," *Monthly Law Reporter,* 5 (1843): 497.

30. "Advancement of the Law by Lawyers," *Monthly Law Reporter,* 11 (1848): 150-151. For the details of several projects, see "Legislation in Maine," *Monthly Law Reporter,* 1 (1839): 276-278; J. Louis Tellkampf, "On Codification, or the Systematizing of the Law," *American Jurist and Law Magazine,* 8 (1842): 283-329; "National Jurisprudence," *United States Monthly Law Magazine,* 3 (1851): 125-134; "Legislation," *United States Monthly Law Magazine,* 5 (1852): 125-138; Joel Prentiss Bishop, "Law in the United States," *American Law Register,* 3 (1854): 60-61.

31. "The American Legal Association," *United States Monthly Law Magazine Advertiser,* 3 (1851).

32. The Library of Congress lists ten separate publications between 1850 and 1868. As editor of the *United States Monthly Law Magazine,* Livingston also devoted one composite issue (October-December 1851) to a reprinting of his complete *Law Register* for that year.

33. "Slavery in the States and Territories," *Monthly Law Reporter,* 23 (1860): 458.

34. A. O. P. Nicholson, *Address Delivered before the Two Literary Societies of the University of North-Carolina, June 1, 1853* (Raleigh, 1853), p. 28. See also Alfred Conkling, *Legal Reform* (Albany, 1856); Charles J. Stillé, *The Historical Development of American Civilization* (New Haven, 1863);

George M. Fredrickson, *The Inner Civil War* (New York, 1965), pp. 55-56. Cf. "Mr. Justice Story, as a Poet and Constitutional Writer," *Quarterly Law Review* (Richmond, Va.), 1 (1861): 70-71.

35. Wilkins Updike, *Memoirs of the Rhode-Island Bar* (Boston, 1842), p. 184.

36. Ibid., p. 120.

37. Stephen F. Miller, *The Bench and Bar of Georgia*, 2 vols. (Philadelphia, 1858), 1:46-47.

38. John Belton O'Neall, *Biographical Sketches of the Bench and Bar of South Carolina*, 2 vols. (Charleston, 1859), 1:257-258.

39. John Livingston, ed., *Biographical Sketches of Eminent American Lawyers Now Living* (New York, 1852), p. 389.

40. On Marshall's textbook reputation, see Ruth Miller Elson, *Guardians of Tradition: American Schoolbooks of the Nineteenth Century* (Lincoln, Neb., 1964), p. 210.

41. George Van Santvoord, *Sketches of the Lives and Judicial Services of the Chief-Justices of the Supreme Court of the United States* (New York, 1854), p. 482.

42. See, for example, [David Hoffman,] *Miscellaneous Thoughts on Men, Manners, and Things* (Baltimore, 1837), pp. 182-193, 213-215; "Reorganization of the Judiciary," *American Review*, 2 (November 1845): 474-493; Rufus Choate, "Speech on the Judicial Tenure," in *Addresses and Orations of Rufus Choate* (Boston, 1878), pp. 357-395.

43. Job R. Tyson, *Discourse on the Integrity of the Legal Character* (Philadelphia, 1839), pp. 13-14.

44. Bellamy Storer, *The Legal Profession* (Cincinnati, 1856), p. 8.

45. "Address . . . to the Law Class of the [Cumberland] University at Lebanon, February 15th, 1853," in *Speeches, Congressional and Political, and Other Writings of Ex-Governor Aaron V. Brown, of Tennessee* (Nashville, 1854), pp. 350-351.

46. Nicholson, *Address*, p. 27. See also "Establishment of Law Schools," *United States Monthly Law Magazine*, 2 (1850): 133-144; Joseph Story, "Value and Importance of Legal Studies," in William W. Story, ed., *The Miscellaneous Writings of Joseph Story* (Boston, 1852), pp. 504-535; and Choate, "The Position and Functions of the American Bar, as an Element of Conservatism in the State," in *Addresses*, pp. 133-166. Cf. W. P. Harris, *Address to the Graduating Class in the Department of Law, University of Mississippi, June 23d, 1869* (Jackson, 1869); and Edwards Pierrepont, *An Oration on the Influence of Lawyers upon Free Governments, and the Influence of Moral Forces upon the Prosperity of Governments* (New Haven, 1874).

47. *A Lecture, Read before the Worcester Lyceum, March 30th, 1831* (Worcester, Mass., 1831), pp. 14-15.

48. Timothy Walker, "Introductory Lecture Delivered before the Cincinnati Lyceum, 1831," Timothy Walker Papers, box 2, Cincinnati Historical Society.

49. Ibid. See also, in the same collection, "Notes of a Lecture for the Mechanics Institute, on the Practicability and Importance of a More General Diffusion of Legal Knowledge among Our Young Men, Nov. 12, 1836," and "Ultraisms of the Day: Outline of Speech for College of Teachers, Cincinnati, Oct. 7, 1841."

50. Robert T. Conrad, *The True Aims of American Ambition* (Philadelphia, 1852), pp. 25-26.

51. *The Duties and Responsibilities of the Rising Generation* (New York, 1848), p. 14.

52. *The Morals of Freedom* (Boston, 1844), pp. 18-19.

53. Timothy Walker, "Address before the Young Men's Mercantile Library Association, Nov. 30, 1847," reported in the *Cincinnati Gazette*, December 7, 1847. See also Joseph Story, "The Science of Government," in *Miscellaneous Writings*, pp. 624-636; Robert Rantoul, Jr., "The Education of a Free People," in Luther Hamilton, ed., *Memoirs, Speeches, and Writings of Robert Rantoul, Jr.* (Boston, 1854), pp. 112-140; Choate, "The Power of a State Developed by Mental Culture," in *Addresses and Orations*, pp. 106-132.

54. *On the Extra-Professional Influence of the Pulpit and the Bar* (New York, 1851), p. 16.

55. "The American Bar," *United States Magazine and Democratic Review*, 28 (March 1851): 197.

56. For a fuller discussion, see chapter 2.

57. Hugh Henry Brackenridge, *Modern Chivalry*, ed. Claude M. Newlin (New York, 1937), p. 20.

58. Ibid., p. 401.

59. Ibid., pp. 372, 553, 718.

60. Ibid., pp. 397, 459. For a detailed and informative biography of Brackenridge, see C. M. Newlin, *The Life and Writings of Hugh Henry Brackenridge* (Princeton, 1932).

61. William Littell, *An Epistle from William, Surnamed Littell, to the People of the Realm of Kentucky* (Frankfort, Ky., 1806), pp. 30, 38, 39.

62. [George Watterston,] *The Lawyer; or, Man as He Ought Not to Be* (Pittsburgh, 1808), pp. 55-56.

63. Ibid., p. 216.

64. Ibid., pp. 32-33.

65. *The Rhapsodist and Other Uncollected Writings*, ed. Harry R. Warfel (New York, 1943), p. 103.

66. [William Wirt,] *The Letters of the British Spy* (Richmond, 1803), p. 31.

67. *Sketches of the Life and Character of Patrick Henry* (Philadelphia, 1817), pp. 26, 28, 252. For an illuminating analysis of Wirt as mythmaker, see William R. Taylor, *Cavalier and Yankee* (London, 1963), pp. 67-94.

68. "Hotch-pot," *Monthly Law Reporter*, 9 (1847): 476.

69. Quoted in Charles H. Bohner, *John Pendleton Kennedy: Gentleman from Baltimore* (Baltimore, 1961), p. 182. Bohner's biography (pp. 180-185) provides an excellent account of the writing and reception of Kennedy's *Memoirs of the Life of William Wirt*, 2 vols. (Philadelphia, 1849).

70. [Frederick W. Thomas,] *Clinton Bradshaw; or, The Adventures of a Lawyer*, 2 vols. (Philadelphia, 1835), 1:17.

71. Ibid., 1:30.

72. Ibid., 1:114; 2:91.

73. Ibid., 1:147. Benjamin T. Spencer has suggested that the realistic elements in Thomas's work—the "disproportionate reliance on everyday urban customs and manners"—had much to do with its relative unpopularity (*The Quest for Nationality* [Syracuse, 1957], pp. 135, 137).

74. *Clinton Bradshaw*, 1:79-80; 2:174.

75. Ibid., 2:197.

76. Ibid., 2:271, 303-304.

77. Ibid., 2:328.

78. [Cornelius Mathews,] *The Motley Book: A Series of Tales and Sketches* (New York, 1838); [Augustus B. Longstreet,] *Georgia Scenes, Characters, Incidents, &c., in the First Half Century of the Republic* (New York, 1835).

79. Wesley Brooke [George Lunt], *Eastford; or, Household Sketches* (Boston, 1855), pp. 227-228.

80. For other representative magazine sketches, see "Pages from the Diary of a Philadelphia Lawyer—III," *Gentleman's Magazine*, 2 (April 1838): 248-250; Henry Stanhope Lee, "Quite a Pretty Property," *New York Mirror*, 17 (July-August 1839): 28, 36-37, 41, 52-53; "Modest Assurance; or, Some Passages in the Life of a Lawyer, by Lemuel Law," *American Review*, 3 (June 1846): 589-597.

81. Quoted in Elson, *Guardians of Tradition*, p. 26.

82. *Marco Paul's Adventures in Pursuit of Knowledge: State of Vermont* (Boston, 1843), pp. 54-55.

83. *Jonas a Judge* went through eight editions in the nineteenth century, while *Judge Justin* was reprinted once. See Carl J. Weber, *A Bibliography of the Published Writings of Jacob Abbott* (Waterville, Maine, 1948).

84. Harriet B. McKeever, *Woodcliff* (Philadelphia, 1864), pp. 401, 445-446.

85. *Ishmael; or, In the Depths* (reprint ed., New York, n.d.), pp. 295-296.

86. *Self-Raised; or, From the Depths* (Philadelphia, 1876), pp. 64-65, 625.

87. *All the Happy Endings* (New York, 1956), p. 133. See also Mary Noel, *Villains Galore: The Heyday of the Popular Story Weekly* (New York, 1954), pp. 161-165; and, in general, Regis Louise Boyle, *Mrs. E.D.E.N. Southworth, Novelist* (Washington, D.C., 1939).

88. Gilson G. Glasier, ed., *Autobiography of Roujet D. Marshall*, 2 vols. (Madison, Wis., 1923), 1:142-143.

89. Ibid., 1:143-144.

90. Even before leaving Cambridge, Force informed his father: "I have said nothing about politics, but I have not been silent from not having thought of it. I have observed that politics is a business as much as law or medicine; to succeed as a politician requires not only as much labor as the others, but, besides, some skill in intrigue, and some sacrifice of independence. That it is too expensive for a poor man; while to one who can afford it, the pursuit is an exciting and often disappointing amusement, like gambling or horse racing. If I should ever be sent to Congress by unsolicited votes, I should be glad of the honor. I should try to be useful, but would make no Bunkum efforts to keep my place or acquire popularity" (Manning F. Force to Peter Force, June 18, 1848, Manning F. Force Papers, University of Washington). Riddle's antipolitical views are set forth in his "Last Words: Advisory and Suggestive," in *Law Students and Lawyers, the Philosophy of Political Parties, and Other Subjects: Eight Lectures Delivered before the Law Department of Howard University* (Washington, D.C., 1873), pp. 104-127.

91. "Reconstruction: The Duty of the Profession to the Times," *Monthly Law Reporter*, 26 (1864): 278.

6.　Riot Control in Philadelphia

1. For the general urban background I am much indebted to the excellent

study of Sam Bass Warner, Jr., *The Private City: Philadelphia in Three Periods of Its Growth* (Philadelphia, 1968), pp. 3-123. See also Edward C. Carter II, "A 'Wild Irishman' under Every Federalist's Bed: Naturalization in Philadelphia, 1789-1806," *Pennsylvania Magazine of History and Biography,* 94 (July 1970): 331-346, which provides valuable statistical data on the incidence and character of Irish immigration to Philadelphia at the turn of the century; Dennis Clark, *The Irish in Philadelphia* (Philadelphia, 1974); Michael Jay Feldberg, "The Philadelphia Riots of 1844: A Social History" (Ph.D. dissertation, University of Rochester, 1970).

2. Selden Daskam Bacon, "The Early Development of American Municipal Police: A Study of the Evolution of Formal Controls in a Changing Society" (Ph.D. dissertation, Yale University, 1939), pp. 552-553; Howard O. Sprogle, *The Philadelphia Police, Past and Present* (Philadelphia, 1887), pp. 84-85. For a useful map of Philadelphia County prior to consolidation, see Henry Leffmann, "The Consolidation of Philadelphia," *City History Society of Philadelphia Publications,* 1 (1917): 26-40.

3. Edward P. Allinson and Boies Penrose, *Philadelphia (1681-1887): A History of Municipal Development* (Baltimore, 1887), pp. 34-36, 98-104; Bacon, "Early Development," pp. 501-517, 551-552.

4. Bacon, "Early Development," p. 548. Between 1833 and 1841 the city received an annual payment of approximately $28,000 for police expenses under the will of philanthropist Stephen Girard. After 1841, however, this fund was diverted to support the college that Girard had established in Philadelphia, and the entire cost of police administration fell upon the city's taxpayers (ibid., p. 533).

5. *Street Talk about an Ordinance of Councils, Passed the 11th July, 1844, Organizing a Military Force for the Government of Philadelphia* (Philadelphia, 1844), p. 20.

6. "The Spirit of Misrule," *Monthly Law Reporter,* 7 (1844): 209-221; "The Police," *United States Gazette* (Philadelphia), May 28, 1844; George Austin Ketcham, "Municipal Police Reform: A Comparative Study of Law Enforcement in Cincinnati, Chicago, New Orleans, New York, and St. Louis" (Ph.D. dissertation, University of Missouri, 1967), pp. 257-258. Horace Binney, on his first trip to Paris in 1836, well expressed the prevailing sentiments of American tourists: "There was one feature in Paris—I might say, in France —that was in most disadvantageous contrast with London and England. The day of Napoleon had passed, and a charter and a representative legislature had been substituted for the personal will of the Emperor, and also of the Bourbons; yet the metropolis and the country at large were obviously under military subjection. I do not mean that the government of the city or of the country was in the ordinary sense military, but everywhere military means seemed to constitute the principal reliance of the government for the execution of the laws . . . I do not know that I could at any time have looked a hundred yards ahead in Paris without seeing several, and often many, armed and uniformed men. Often in the country, when all within the reach of my eye was with one exception peaceful in the highest degree, the *gens d'armes* on horseback, armed to the teeth, seemed to show that the general rule was not only proved by the exception, but depended upon it . . . These ever-present soldiers did not impair the sense of my security, for I believed that their duty was to enforce just and equal laws, as far as the condition of things permitted such laws; but they made me feel unequal to my own defence, an uncomfortable

and belittling sensation, which no one feels in this country, and which I confess I never felt in any part of England" (quoted in Charles Chauncey Binney, *The Life of Horace Binney* [Philadelphia, 1903], pp. 165-166).

7. Quoted in Bacon, "Early Development," p. 537.

8. Warner, *Private City*, p. 151. See also Hugh J. Nolan, *The Most Reverend Francis Patrick Kenrick, Third Bishop of Philadelphia, 1830-1851* (Washington, D.C., 1948), pp. 305-306; Elizabeth M. Geffen, "Violence in Philadelphia in the 1840's and 1850's," *Pennsylvania History*, 36 (October 1969): 381-410; and, in general, David Grimsted, "Rioting in Its Jacksonian Setting," *American Historical Review*, 77 (April 1972): 361-397.

9. *Pittsburgh Gazette*, September 30, 1844, quoted in Henry A. Szarnicki, "The Episcopate of Michael O'Connor, First Bishop of Pittsburgh, 1843-1860" (Ph.D. dissertation, Catholic University of America, 1970), p. 188. The general background of Nativism is thoroughly canvassed in Ray Allen Billington, *The Protestant Crusade (1800-1860): A Study of the Origins of American Nativism* (New York, 1938), pp. 68-210. Gustavus Myers, *History of Bigotry in the United States* (New York, 1943), provides additional useful material.

10. *The Truth Unveiled; or, A Calm and Impartial Exposition of the Origin and Immediate Cause of the Terrible Riots in Philadelphia, on May 6th, 7th, and 8th, A.D. 1844, by a Protestant and Native Philadelphian* (Philadelphia, 1844), reprinted in *Records of the American Catholic Historical Society of Philadelphia*, 80 (June-September 1969): 160. This entire issue of the *Records* marked the 125th anniversary of the Philadelphia Riots by publishing valuable source materials, including several scarce manuscript accounts. See also Nolan, *Kenrick*, pp. 289-304, 310-312.

11. Warner, *Private City*, pp. 79-98; Billington, *Protestant Crusade*, pp. 118-125; *A Philadelphia Perspective: The Diary of Sidney George Fisher Covering the Years 1834-1871*, ed. Nicholas B. Wainwright (Philadelphia, 1967), p. 177.

12. Bacon, "Early Development," p. 539.

13. Gary B. Nash, "The Philadelphia Bench and Bar, 1800-1861," *Comparative Studies in Society and History*, 7 (1964-65): 203-220; John M. Campbell, "Biographical Sketch of Hon. James Campbell," *Records of the American Catholic Historical Society*, 5 (1894): 265-303.

14. *The Full Particulars of the Late Riots, with a View of the Burning of the Catholic Churches, St. Michael's and St. Augustine's* (Philadelphia, 1844), pp. 5-6. In my treatment of the riots I have tried to reconcile a number of divergent accounts, no two of which agree on important details. Besides the Nativist tract cited above, I have found the following works most helpful: Joseph L. J. Kirlin, *Catholicity in Philadelphia from the Earliest Missionaries Down to the Present Time* (Philadelphia, 1909); *Tremendous Riots in Southwark* (Philadelphia, 1844), reprinted in *Records of the American Catholic Historical Society*, 80:176-200; Nolan, *Kenrick*; Warner, *Private City*. These major sources have been supplemented, or corrected, by newspaper reports, eyewitness testimony, and unpublished manuscript material, as indicated in succeeding notes.

15. *Full Particulars*, pp. 9-10; Kirlin, *Catholicity*, p. 331.

16. Morton McMichael Manuscripts, quoted in *Records of the American Catholic Historical Society*, 80:71-73.

17. McMichael to Cadwalader, May 7, 1844; Brigade Order 13, May 7,

1844, in Cadwalader Manuscript Collection, George Cadwalader Section, Historical Society of Pennsylvania, Philadelphia; Kirlin, *Catholicity*, p. 319; Bacon, "Early Development," p. 543.

18. *Philadelphia Perspective*, pp. 167-168; Warner, *Private City*, pp. 145-146.

19. *Full Particulars*, p. 13.

20. Eli K. Price, *The History of the Consolidation of the City of Philadelphia* (Philadelphia, 1873), p. 115; Diary of Joseph Sill, Philadelphia businessman, in *Records of the American Catholic Historical Society*, 80:84; Sprogle, *Philadelphia Police*, pp. 85-86; Warner, *Private City*, pp. 147-148, 151.

21. Pleasanton to Cadwalader, May 20, 1844, Cadwalader Manuscript Collection, George Cadwalader Section. Pleasanton was relieved of his command on May 9 but was soon reinstated and played an active role in suppressing the Southwark Riots in July. See also *Philadelphia Perspective*, p. 165.

22. "The Police," *United States Gazette* (Philadelphia), May 28, 1844.

23. *Philadelphia Perspective*, p. 166. For a discussion of the legal powers of magistrates and militiamen in riot circumstances, see In re Riots of 1844, 2 Clark 275 (1844).

24. *Full Particulars*, p. 18.

25. Kirlin, *Catholicity*, pp. 321-322; *Truth Unveiled*, pp. 173-174.

26. "The Anti-Catholic Riots in Philadelphia in 1844," *American Catholic Historical Researches*, 13 (April 1896): 53.

27. Diary of Joseph Sill, p. 84; *Philadelphia Perspective*, pp. 165-166.

28. J. Hill Martin Papers, Historical Society of Pennsylvania, Philadelphia; *Full Particulars*, p. 22.

29. Binney, *Life of Horace Binney*, pp. 237-238. On Binney's preeminence in municipal affairs, see Nathaniel Burt, *The Perennial Philadelphians* (Boston, 1963), pp. 125-126.

30. The statements of Porter and Johnson are reported in *United States Gazette*, May 10, 1844, which also contains an account of the organization of the Peace Police. For additional details, see Kirlin, *Catholicity*, pp. 323-324.

31. *Full Particulars*, p. 24.

32. "Anti-Catholic Riots," p. 51.

33. *Philadelphia Perspective*, p. 167. Fisher noted on May 19, 1844: "A plan is now in agitation for the prevention of similar scenes of violence hereafter. It is proposed to organize a *volunteer* armed police of citizens, who are to form themselves into corps in each ward, to be officered & disciplined, and to hold themselves in readiness to assemble at a specified place whenever a riot occurs, & to act under the orders of the magistrates. Thus one of the results of a weak government is developed. The people are arming to protect themselves, because they see from experience that the law is not strong enough to protect them" (ibid., pp. 168-169). Although this vigilante force never materialized, the proposal received strong support from the city's elite.

34. The presentment of the grand jury is reported in *United States Gazette*, June 17, 1844. See also Nolan, *Kenrick*, pp. 324-325.

35. For Jones's charge, see *United States Gazette*, July 2, 1844.

36. The grand jury reported on June 1, 1844, that eighteen rioters—one-fourth of those indicted—had been committed to the county prison (*United States Gazette*, June 17, 1844). Conviction estimates are based on figures reported in the press through the fall of 1844. Among the defendants who

were found guilty of offenses connected with the Kensington Riots were Robert McQuillan, Henry Haughley, John Daley, John McAleer, Patrick Murray, John Bennett, John Paul, and Josiah Nichols. On the negligence charges against the magistrates, see In re Riots of 1844, 2 Clark 135 (1844).

37. *Address of the Catholic Lay Citizens, of the City and County of Philadelphia, to Their Fellow-Citizens, in Reply to the Presentment of the Grand Jury of the Court of Quarter Sessions of May Term 1844, in Regard to the Causes of the Late Riots in Philadelphia* (Philadelphia, 1844), reprinted in *Records of the American Catholic Historical Society*, 80:139-140.

38. *Truth Unveiled*, pp. 148-175.

39. Nolan, *Kenrick*, p. 328. Kenrick's proclamation is reprinted in *Records of the American Catholic Historical Society*, 80:107.

40. Morton McMichael Manuscripts, p. 74.

41. "Sheriff McMichael's Testimony before the Grand Jury Investigating the Southwark Riots," in *Records of the American Catholic Historical Society*, 80:95; Nolan, *Kenrick*, p. 329; *Tremendous Riots*, pp. 176-177; *Freeman's Journal* (New York), July 13, 1844; Warner, *Private City*, p. 148.

42. Cadwalader to Major General Robert Patterson, July 19, 1844, Cadwalader Manuscript Collection, George Cadwalader Section; "Sheriff McMichael's Testimony," pp. 95-98; *Tremendous Riots*, pp. 177-180; "Anti-Catholic Riots," pp. 58-61.

43. "Statement to Grand Jury by George S. Roberts," in *Records of the American Catholic Historical Society*, 80:85, 87.

44. Kirlin, *Catholicity*, pp. 334-335; Warner, *Private City*, pp. 149-150.

45. Morton McMichael Manuscripts, p. 78; "Sheriff McMichael's Testimony," p. 100.

46. "Anti-Catholic Riots," p. 62.

47. "Sheriff McMichael's Testimony," p. 101.

48. "Report of Major-General Robert Patterson in Relation to the Philadelphia Riots," *Journal of the Fifty-fifth House of Representatives of the Commonwealth of Pennsylvania*, 2 (1845): 13.

49. Cadwalader to Patterson, July 19, 1844; "Anti-Catholic Riots," pp. 62-64; Kirlin, *Catholicity*, pp. 335-336; "Statement to Grand Jury by George S. Roberts," p. 87; Warner, *Private City*, pp. 150-151.

50. *Tremendous Riots*, p. 187; *Philadelphia Perspective*, p. 173; Binney, *Life of Horace Binney*, p. 239; *Street Talk*, pp. 6-17. "What will justify firing upon a crowd?" queried the anonymous author of *Street Talk*. "We will not stop to discuss so large a question, but we may safely say that no pelting of the troops with eggs, or brickbats—no insults, however abominable—no threats, however diabolical—no mob obstinacy or stupidity, and mulish opposition to orders and entreaties, and even no actual attack upon the troops that does not endanger their own safety, or that of the public, can, according to any law known to this part of the world, justify the firing a single shot" (ibid., p. 17).

51. *Philadelphia Perspective*, p. 174; "Sheriff McMichael's Testimony," pp. 101-102; *Tremendous Riots*, pp. 187-190; Kirlin, *Catholicity*, p. 336.

52. *Tremendous Riots*, p. 191.

53. Autobiography manuscript, Binney Papers, Historical Society of Pennsylvania, Philadelphia.

54. Binney's address is reprinted in *Inquirer and National Gazette* (Philadelphia), July 12, 1844, which also provides good coverage of the entire proceedings at Evans' Hotel.

55. *Philadelphia Perspective*, p. 174; "The Sufferers by the Riots," *Inquirer and National Gazette*, July 13, 1844; Binney, *Life of Horace Binney*, p. 241.

56. For the complete text of the grand jury's presentment, see *Public Ledger and Daily Transcript* (Philadelphia), August 5, 1844.

57. Casualty figures vary greatly from commentator to commentator. For the May riots I have accepted the nine fatalities reported in *United States Gazette*, May 10, 1844, along with Nolan's estimate that "at least forty persons" were wounded in the fighting (*Kenrick*, p. 313). Elizabeth Geffen counts three dead and fifty wounded, while Kirlin's final tally shows forty dead and more than sixty "seriously wounded" (Geffen, "Violence in Philadelphia," p. 401; Kirlin, *Catholicity*, p. 325). See also *Full Particulars*, pp. 12, 19-20. Statistics relating to Southwark casualties reveal less divergence. Cf. *Tremendous Riots*, pp. 193-195; Kirlin, *Catholicity*, p. 336; Nolan, *Kenrick*, p. 331; Geffen, "Violence in Philadelphia," p. 403; "Report of Major-General Patterson," p. 15. On property damage and militia costs, see *Full Particulars*, p. 24; Kirlin, *Catholicity*, p. 325; Geffen, "Violence in Philadelphia," p. 401; "Report of the Select Committee of the House, Relative to Troops Ordered into Service during the Philadelphia Riots," *Journal of the Fifty-fifth House of Representatives of the Commonwealth of Pennsylvania*, 2:4. Indictments are reported in Minutes of Grand Jury, September 9-October 23, 1844, Philadelphia Courts Collection, Historical Society of Pennsylvania, Philadelphia. For compensation awards to riot victims, consult Nolan, *Kenrick*, pp. 335-338; Myers, *History of Bigotry*, p. 181. Myers sets the total compensation paid to riot victims at $245,750.

58. Thomas P. Roberts, *Memoirs of John Bannister Gibson, Late Chief Justice of Pennsylvania* (Pittsburgh, 1890), pp. 145-146; Theophane Geary, *A History of Third Parties in Pennsylvania, 1840-1860* (Washington, D.C., 1938), p. 92; Nolan, *Kenrick*, p. 337.

59. The original draft of Binney's bill is reprinted in *Harrisburg Argus*, February 17, 1845. For the public pressures behind it, see "A Reorganization of the Police," *Inquirer and National Gazette*, July 17, 1844; "A Strong Preventive Police," ibid., July 19, 1844; *Public Ledger and Daily Transcript*, August 5, 1844; *United States Gazette*, December 11, 1844; Binney, *Life of Horace Binney*, p. 241.

60. Bayard to McCall, February 15, 1845, Cadwalader Manuscript Collection, Peter McCall Section. See also the reported house debates in *Harrisburg Argus*, February 15 and 17, 1845. For the progress of the bill through the senate, see *Journal of the Senate of the Commonwealth of Pennsylvania*, 1 (1845):600, 664-665, 677, 690-691.

61. "An Act for the Better Regulation of Police in the City of Philadelphia, and the Adjacent Districts," *Laws of the General Assembly of the Commonwealth of Pennsylvania*, no. 255 (1845).

62. Bacon, "Early Development," pp. 546-547.

63. *Philadelphia Perspective*, p. 179. See also Warner, *Private City*, pp. 152-153; Leffmann, "Consolidation of Philadelphia," pp. 30-31.

64. For a full account of all changes in police organization and procedures between 1844 and 1854, see Allinson and Penrose, *Philadelphia*, pp. 104-106, 208-209; Bacon, "Early Development," pp. 555-567; Sprogle, *Philadelphia Police*, pp. 89-99.

65. Geffen, "Violence in Philadelphia," pp. 404-405; Geary, *Third Parties*, p. 104; Burt, *Perennial Philadelphians*, pp. 576-577. The decline of the Native

American party is traced to the moral repercussions of the Philadelphia Riots in Kirlin, *Catholicity*, p. 337; Nolan, *Kenrick*, p. 338; and Billington, *Protestant Crusade*, p. 234.

66. Geary, *Third Parties*, pp. 167-168, 218; Warner, *Private City*, pp. 153-156.

67. *Philadelphia Perspective*, p. 178.

7.   Frederick Grimké and the
Dynamics of Social Change

1. No adequate study of Grimké has yet been made. A perceptive pioneer essay by Arthur A. Ekirch, Jr., "Frederick Grimké: Advocate of Free Institutions," *Journal of the History of Ideas*, 11 (January 1950): 75-92, focuses primarily upon his book, which was reprinted in 1968 as part of the John Harvard Library series. For this new edition John William Ward wrote a helpful introduction that adds further background details and draws for the first time upon the unpublished correspondence between Grimké and his sister Sarah. Sadly, Adrienne Koch did not live to complete her study of the Grimké family through several generations, a major project that promised to provide a definitive account of Frederick's career. She did, however, publish two valuable interpretive essays: "Two Charlestonians in Pursuit of Truth: The Grimké Brothers," *South Carolina Historical Magazine*, 69 (July 1968): 159-170; and an extended review of the Ward volume in the same journal, 71 (July 1970): 197-211. I am much indebted to Professor Koch for sharing with me her personal insights into Grimké's character as well as her prodigious factual knowledge of all matters relating to the Grimké clan.

2. Grimké's aphorism may be found (along with fifty-nine others) in a letter to Sarah Grimké, November 16, 1850, in the Weld-Grimké Correspondence at the William L. Clements Library, Ann Arbor, Michigan. For the family's Carolina background I have relied chiefly upon Gerda Lerner, *The Grimké Sisters from South Carolina* (Boston, 1967), pp. 13-31; Catherine H. Birney, *Sarah and Angelina Grimké* (Boston, 1885), pp. 5-14; John Belton O'Neall, *Biographical Sketches of the Bench and Bar of South Carolina*, 2 vols. (Charleston, 1859), 1:39-42; and Anton-Hermann Chroust, *The Rise of the Legal Profession in America*, 2 vols. (Norman, Okla., 1965), 1:302-304. George C. Rogers, Jr., *Charleston in the Age of the Pinckneys* (Norman, Okla., 1969) provides an excellent overview of the urban environment in which Grimké grew up.

3. *CHE-LE-CO-THE: Glimpses of Yesterday* (Chillicothe, Ohio, 1896), pp. 167-168.

4. *Considerations upon the Nature and Tendency of Free Institutions* (Cincinnati and New York, 1848), p. 327.

5. William Greene to Abby B. Lyman, January 17, 1820, Greene Papers, Cincinnati Historical Society.

6. On the history of Chillicothe and its importance in the early nineteenth century, see Eugene H. Roseboom and Francis P. Weisenburger, *A History of Ohio* (Columbus, Ohio, 1953), pp. 58, 73, 113; *Chillicothe, Ohio's First Capital* (Chillicothe, Ohio, 1941), pp. 3-5, 31; *Ohio State Journal* (Columbus), February 22, 1827.

7. George I. Reed, ed., *Bench and Bar of Ohio*, 2 vols. (Chicago, 1897), 1:63. A good description of the leading Chillicothe lawyers may be found in John H. Keith, *They Cast a Spell* (Chillicothe, Ohio, 1943); see also Clement L. Martzolff, ed., "The Autobiography of Thomas Ewing," *Ohio Archaeological and Historical Quarterly*, 22 (January 1913): 126-204.

8. Alexander England of Charleston was one of these clients. See Grimké to William Greene, May 15, 1826, Greene Papers.

9. 3 Ohio 370, 372 (1828). Grimké's other reported cases were Baird v. Shepherd, 2 Ohio 261 (1826); Waddle and McCoy v. Bank of the United States, 2 Ohio 336 (1826); Adm'rs. of Hough v. Hunt, 2 Ohio 495 (1826); Ex'rs. of Decker v. Ex'rs. of Decker, 3 Ohio 157 (1827); Lessee of Taylor v. Boyd, 3 Ohio 337 (1828). On the nature of early court reporting in Ohio, see Carrington T. Marshall, ed., *A History of the Courts and Lawyers of Ohio*, 4 vols. (New York, 1934), 1:285-296.

10. Grimké to Greene, February 28, 1828, Greene Papers. This collection contains the largest number of unpublished Grimké letters as well as some of the most interesting. William Greene (1797-1883) came from a Rhode Island family that had been prominent in state politics for three generations. Following his graduation from Brown University in 1817, he studied law at Judge Tapping Reeve's famous Litchfield Law School in Connecticut. From 1819, when he moved to Ohio to pursue his legal career, until his return to Rhode Island in 1862, he played an active role in the civic and cultural life of Cincinnati. His Whig-Republican political orientation, while inimical to the Democratic views of Grimké, did not lessen their friendship (John Howard Brown, ed., *Lamb's Biographical Dictionary of the United States* [Boston, 1900-1903], 3:399).

11. *Scioto Gazette*, August 16, 1827. The latter half of the quotation is taken from a separate essay, "American Literature," which appeared in *Ohio State Journal*, January 19, 1826.

12. "The American Character," *Ohio State Journal*, March 22, 1827.

13. "American Parties," *Scioto Gazette*, February 14, 1828.

14. "Political," *Ohio State Journal*, November 30, 1826; "The Power of the United States over the Virginia Military Lands," ibid., December 7, 1826; "The Mill-Dam Case," *Scioto Gazette*, March 29, 1827. Grimké wrote under several pseudonyms: An American, Ohiensis, and A Citizen of Ohio. His remaining essays dealt with dueling (*Scioto Gazette*, February 21, 1828) and the privileges and immunities clause of the Constitution (*Scioto Gazette*, February 28, 1828).

15. Grimké, *Considerations*, p. 342.

16. Grimké to Greene, May 11, 1830, Greene Papers. On the common pleas courts and their operation, see Marshall, *Courts and Lawyers of Ohio*, 1:181-214; 2:365-403; F. R. Aumann, "The Development of the Judicial System of Ohio," *Ohio Archaeological and Historical Quarterly*, 41 (January 1932): 195-236; and lawyer William T. McClintock's reminiscences in "Centennial Celebraton of the Adoption of Ohio's First Constitution," ibid., 12 (1903): 8-10.

17. Grimké to Ebenezer Lane, March 1, 1836, Simon Gratz Manuscripts, Historical Society of Pennsylvania, Philadelphia.

18. Grimké to Greene, September 16, 1842, Greene Papers. For background on the Supreme Court of Ohio and its caliber in Grimké's time, see

Reed, *Bench and Bar*, 1:1-33, 49-50; Marshall, *Courts and Lawyers of Ohio*, 1:217-228.

19. [Timothy Walker,] "Grimké on Free Institutions," *Western Law Journal*, 6 (1848): 94.

20. Scott v. Fields et al., 7 Ohio 90, 96 (1836).

21. Flint v. Ohio Insurance Co., 8 Ohio 501 (1838); Smith v. Berry, 8 Ohio 365 (1838); Huber v. Huber's Adm'rs., 10 Ohio 371 (1841); State of Ohio v. Findley, 10 Ohio 51 (1840); State of Ohio v. Bowman et al., 10 Ohio 445 (1841); Glenn v. Bank of the United States, 8 Ohio 72 (1837).

22. Willyard v. Hamilton, 7 Ohio 111, 113 (1836); Lessee of Lloyd v. Giddings, 7 Ohio 50, 53 (1836).

23. Fulton and Foster v. Lancaster Ins. Co., 7 Ohio (Part 2) 5, 30 (1836).

24. Moore v. Brown, 10 Ohio 197 (1840); Lessee of Swazey's Heirs v. Blackman and Wife, 8 Ohio 1 (1837); Anderson v. Anderson, 8 Ohio 108 (1837); Fee's Adm'r. v. Fee, 10 Ohio 469 (1841).

25. 10 Ohio 31, 36 (1840).

26. 11 Ohio 96 (1841).

27. 8 Ohio 521 (1838).

28. Hutchinson v. Thompson and Gidings v. Thompson, 9 Ohio 52 (1839).

29. Grimké to Greene, June 25, 1844, Greene Papers.

30. Ibid.

31. Grimké to Greene, May 8, 1848, Greene Papers.

32. *Considerations upon the Nature and Tendency of Free Institutions*, 2d ed. (New York and Cincinnati, 1856), p. 1. This "corrected and enlarged" edition incorporated much new material, including an introductory chapter on the nature of civilization and others on the right of secession and the "ultimate destiny" of free institutions.

33. Grimké, *Considerations*, 1st ed., p. 312.

34. Ibid., p. 168.

35. Grimké, *Considerations*, 2d ed., pp. 79, 81-82.

36. Grimké, *Considerations*, 1st ed., p. 277.

37. Walker, "Grimké on Free Institutions," p. 94.

38. Grimké to Greene, January 12, 1846, Greene Papers.

39. Grimké, *Considerations*, 1st ed., p. 351.

40. Ibid., p. 354.

41. Ibid., p. 398.

42. Grimké, *Considerations*, 2d ed., p. 667.

43. *Scioto Gazette*, February 28, 1828.

44. Grimké, *Considerations*, 1st ed., p. 327.

45. Grimké to Greene, December 10, 1850, Greene Papers.

46. Grimké to Greene, February 19, 1856, Greene Papers. Grimké was mistaken, of course, in suggesting that "Republican" and "abolitionist" were synonymous terms. In fact the radical abolitionists, such as Garrison and Phillips, opposed political action at this time and took no part in the organization of the Republican party.

47. Grimké, *Considerations*, 2d ed., p. 485.

48. Grimké, *Considerations*, 1st ed., p. 263.

49. Grimké to Greene, November 30, 1849, Greene Papers.

50. Grimké to Greene, May 1, 1854, Greene Papers.

51. Grimké to Greene, September 27, 1856, Greene Papers.

52. Grimke to Sarah Grimké, January 20, 1861, Weld-Grimké Correspondence. Grimké expressed similar views to William Greene. See especially Grimké to Greene, June 6, 1858, and March 3, 1860, Greene Papers.

53. Grimké to Sarah Grimké, April 30, 1859, Weld-Grimké Correspondence. For a discussion of general trends in antebellum psychology, see Jay Wharton Fay, *American Psychology before William James* (New Brunswick, N.J., 1939), pp. 50-128.

54. *The Works of Frederick Grimké*, 2 vols. (Columbus, Ohio, 1871), 2:215. This third, and final, nineteenth-century edition of Grimké's writings was published several years after his death, in accordance with a stipulation contained in his will. Besides reprinting in full the enlarged version of his *Free Institutions*, it also included his Civil War articles and ten previously unpublished essays that dealt with various scientific and philosophical problems.

55. Grimké to Greene, March 4, 1862, Greene Papers.

56. *Works*, 2:47.

57. Elizabeth Waddle Renick, "A Memory," in *CHE-LE-CO-THE*, pp. 165-166. Miss Baskerville and her peculiarities are described in a separate unsigned essay in the same volume (pp. 155-163).

58. Lyle S. Evans, ed., *A Standard History of Ross County, Ohio*, 2 vols. (Chicago and New York, 1917), 1:170. Evans includes the following description of Grimké: "He was of medium height, rather meagre and angular, but of excellent health, strong and elastic of gait. His complexion was quite dark, his eyes black and overhung with heavy gray and black brows. His hair, originally dark, and always worn short, had become quite gray in his later years. His nose was thin and aquiline. In a quiet way he was very charitable to the poor. For years he was in the habit of taking long and rapid walks, or rides upon horseback, and he was almost ludicrously awkward in the saddle." For further details of Grimké's last illness and the community's response to his death, see *Scioto Gazette*, March 17, 1863.

59. William Whatley Pierson, Jr., "Foreign Influences on Venezuelan Political Thought, 1830-1930," *Hispanic American Historical Review*, 15 (February 1935): 27-28.

60. Grimké to Greene, June 21, 1847, Greene Papers. For an excellent general discussion of the related themes of "*Herrenvolk* democracy" and romantic racialism in antebellum writers, North and South, see George M. Frederickson, *The Black Image in the White Mind: The Debate on Afro-American Character and Destiny, 1817-1914* (New York, 1971).

8.   William Pitt Ballinger, Confederate Lawyer

1. No major biography of Ballinger has yet been written, nor have his voluminous diaries been published. One previous study exists: James L. Hill, "The Life of Judge William Pitt Ballinger" (M.A. dissertation, University of Texas, 1936). The diaries—which cover, with few exceptions, the years from 1854 to 1888—are available in both manuscript and typescript form and may be consulted in their entirety at the Rosenberg Library, Galveston, Texas, or the Barker Texas History Center on the campus of the University of Texas in Austin. Besides housing the bulk of the manuscript diaries, the archives of the

Rosenberg Library contain scattered business and personal papers of Ballinger, several early notebooks, and some family records. The major collection of Ballinger correspondence, including the records of Ballinger & Jack, is at the Texas History Center. For genealogical information and background data on Ballinger and his Texas contemporaries, I have relied upon William Pitt Ballinger, "Family Notes," Rosenberg Library; William S. Speer and John Henry Brown, eds., *The Encyclopedia of the New West* (Marshall, Texas, 1881); James D. Lynch, *The Bench and Bar of Texas* (St. Louis, 1885); Walter Prescott Webb and H. Bailey Carroll, eds., *The Handbook of Texas*, 2 vols. (Austin, 1952).

2. Quoted in Charles Fairman, *Mr. Justice Miller and the Supreme Court, 1862-1890* (reprint ed., New York, 1966), pp. 10, 13. Fairman's first chapter gives an excellent picture of Barbourville in the days of Ballinger's boyhood.

3. Ballinger to George W. Paschal, May 8, 1863, William Pitt Ballinger Papers, Barker Texas History Center, Austin, Texas. This document, a lengthy seven-page fragment that Ballinger apparently never completed, marks his most serious effort to analyze the motives that led him to support the Confederacy. Written as an apologia to an old friend and Unionist, it provides some penetrating autobiographical insights.

4. Diary, August 11, 1875.

5. The recommendations of Ballinger's committee, his attorney's oath, and a copy of his license may be found in the Ballinger Papers, Rosenberg Library Archives, Galveston, Texas. Unless otherwise indicated, all further references to Ballinger's papers will relate to the major collection in Austin.

6. For further information on the conditions of legal practice in the republic, see William Ransom Hogan, *The Texas Republic: A Social and Economic History* (Norman, Okla., 1946), pp. 245-289.

7. Earl Wesley Fornell, *The Galveston Era: The Texas Crescent on the Eve of Secession* (Austin, 1962), pp. 3-21, 36, 87-93.

8. Ballinger to James E. Harrison, March 3, 1854, Ballinger Papers, Rosenberg Library.

9. Diary, July 30 and August 4, 1854.

10. Ibid., August 6, 1854.

11. Ibid., January 6, 1859.

12. Ibid., April 26, 1860.

13. Houston *Telegraph*, March 24, 1865.

14. Diary, November 5, 1862.

15. See Betsy Webster v. T. J. Heard, 32 Tex. 686, 707 (1870), for Ballinger's own estimate of his efforts on Betsy's behalf.

16. Diary, June 21, 1860.

17. Quoted in Fornell, *Galveston Era*, p. 116.

18. Ballinger to Paschal, May 8, 1863, Ballinger Papers; Diary, November 16, 1860.

19. "Secession" (draft of a speech delivered by Ballinger on August 23, 1860), Ballinger Papers, Rosenberg Library.

20. Ballinger to Paschal, May 8, 1863, Ballinger Papers.

21. Ibid.

22. Ibid.

23. Diary, February 23, 1862.

24. Ibid., December 21, 1860.

25. The details that follow concerning Ballinger's mission are taken from his diary entries for August 7 through October 24, 1861.

26. Diary, May 17, 1862, and January 28, 1863.

27. For further information on the sequestration program, see William M. Robinson, Jr., *Justice in Gray* (reprint ed., New York, 1968), pp. 493-496, 626.

28. Diary, October 25-26, 1861.

29. Duer to Ballinger, November 28, 1861, Ballinger Papers.

30. Wilfred B. Yearns, *The Confederate Congress* (Athens, Ga., 1960), p. 196; Robinson, *Justice in Gray*, pp. 263-264.

31. Diary, September 17, 1863.

32. Robinson, *Justice in Gray*, pp. 263-264.

33. Webb to Ballinger, January 17, 1864, Ballinger Papers; Charles Rossignol to Ballinger, March 1, 1865, ibid.

34. Diary, April 2, 1863, and August 21, 1864.

35. Ibid., October 2, 1864.

36. Stockdale to Ballinger, January 13, 1865, Ballinger Papers. See also C. L. Cleveland to Ballinger, n.d., ibid.

37. For a more complete account of Murrah's activities and their results, see Ernest Wallace, *Texas in Turmoil* (Austin, 1965), pp. 118-125.

38. Diary, April 11, 1864.

39. Ibid., February 6, 1864.

40. Ibid., January 6 and March 7, 1865.

41. Houston *Telegraph*, April 26, 1865.

42. Diary, July 29, 1863.

43. Ibid., May 13, 1865.

44. Ibid.

45. Ibid., May 28, 1865.

46. For further details of the New Orleans negotiations, see the entries in Ballinger's diary from May 29 to June 14, 1865.

47. Diary, August 8, 1865.

48. Miller to Johnson, August 13, 1865, Ballinger Papers.

49. Houston *Telegraph*, April 28, 1865.

50. Diary, August 25 and September 1, 1865.

51. Ibid., August 27, 1865.

52. Ibid., October 25, 1865.

53. Ibid., January 24 and February 24, 1866. Ballinger itemized the returns from the Washington venture in diary entries of November 10 and November 23, 1865; his tax receipts and docket book are in the Ballinger Papers.

54. City Directory listings reveal no black lawyers prior to that date.

9.   John Mercer Langston and the Training of Black Lawyers

1. John Mercer Langston, *From the Virginia Plantation to the National Capitol* (Hartford, Conn., 1894), pp. 11-12. For the factual background of Langston's career, I have also relied upon William F. Cheek's careful studies: "Forgotten Prophet: The Life of John Mercer Langston" (Ph.D. dissertation, University of Virginia, 1961); and "John Mercer Langston: Black Protest Leader and Abolitionist," *Civil War History*, 16 (June 1970): 101-120. Few

manuscript sources exist. According to Langston's granddaughter, Mrs. Nettie L. Mathews, almost all of his papers were destroyed after his death by his son-in-law, James Carroll Napier. What remains is a meager collection of miscellaneous tax receipts, bills, a few early letters, and drafts of speeches at the Fisk University Library, Nashville, Tennessee; and some scrapbooks and other materials relating to his later career in the Moorland Room of Howard University, Washington, D.C.

2. Quoted in Charles Thomas Hickok, *The Negro in Ohio, 1802-1870* (Cleveland, 1896), p. 47. The lines were written by the black poet M. C. Sampson.

3. J. Reuben Sheeler, "The Struggle of the Negro in Ohio for Freedom," *Journal of Negro History*, 31 (April 1946): 209-211; James H. Rodabaugh, "The Negro in Ohio," ibid. (January 1946): 13-15.

4. Langston, *Virginia Plantation*, pp. 60-61.

5. Sheeler, "Struggle of the Negro," pp. 213-214.

6. Langston, *Virginia Plantation*, p. 67.

7. On the general background and educational objectives of Oberlin, see Robert Samuel Fletcher, *A History of Oberlin College*, 2 vols. (Oberlin, 1943).

8. Langston to Henry (?), April 10, 1854, John Mercer Langston Papers, box 1, Fisk University. A microfilm copy of the Langston Papers is available at the Amistad Research Center, Dillard University, New Orleans, Louisiana.

9. Draft of speech to the Union Society, May 23, 1848, Langston Papers, box 2.

10. Charles Sumner Brown, "The Genesis of the Negro Lawyer in New England," *Negro History Bulletin*, 22 (April 1959): 147-152; Martin Robison Delany, *The Condition, Elevation, Emigration, and Destiny of the Colored People of the United States* (Philadelphia, 1852), pp. 117-119. There are some amusing anecdotes about Morris and Bradley in Joseph A. Willard, *Half a Century with Judges and Lawyers* (Boston, 1895), pp. 243-245, 298-301.

11. Langston, *Virginia Plantation*, p. 110.

12. Ibid., pp. 107-108.

13. Quoted in Cheek, "Forgotten Prophet," p. 32.

14. Langston, *Virginia Plantation*, pp. 121-125. Relevant cases establishing the criteria for "white" citizenship in Ohio include Jeffries v. Ankeny, 11 Ohio 372 (1842); Lane v. Baker, 12 Ohio 237 (1843); Anderson v. Millikin, 9 Ohio (n.s.) 568 (1859). See also Hickok, *Negro in Ohio*, pp. 45-46.

15. Rental agreement, January 18, 1854, Langston Papers, box 1.

16. Langston, *Virginia Plantation*, p. 135.

17. Fitzhugh Lee Styles, *Negroes and the Law* (Boston, 1971), p. 119.

18. "List of Accounts Left with John Mercer Langston for Collection, Jany 1860," Langston Papers, box 2. See also two undated lists in box 3.

19. Langston to Caroline Wall, October 23, 1853, quoted in Cheek, "Forgotten Prophet," p. 47. Professor Cheek has informed me that these remarks, which he indicates in his dissertation were made by Langston to Caroline Wall, were in fact memoranda for a political speech which Langston had written on the back of a letter to Miss Wall.

20. On the tensions between white and black abolitionists, see Leon F. Litwack, "The Abolitionist Dilemma: The Antislavery Movement and the

Northern Negro," *New England Quarterly*, 34 (March 1961): 50-73; William H. Pease and Jane H. Pease, "Antislavery Ambivalence: Immediatism, Expedience, Race," *American Quarterly*, 17 (Winter 1965): 682-695.

21. Hickok, *Negro in Ohio*, p. 51; Sheeler, "Struggle of the Negro," pp. 222-223.

22. *State Convention of the Colored Citizens of Ohio, Columbus, January 10-13, 1849* (Oberlin, 1849).

23. For a more detailed picture of Langston's landholdings and personal wealth in the 1850s, see the miscellaneous tax receipts in Langston Papers, box 2.

24. Cheek, "Black Protest Leader," p. 115.

25. Quoted in Cheek, "Forgotten Prophet," pp. 49-50.

26. William Wells Brown, *The Rising Son* (Boston, 1876), p. 448. On Douglass's personality and oratorical style, see Benjamin Quarles, "Abolition's Different Drummer: Frederick Douglass," in John H. Bracey, Jr., August Meier, and Elliott Rudwick, eds., *Blacks in the Abolitionist Movement* (Belmont, Calif., 1971), pp. 17-24; Philip S. Foner, *Frederick Douglass* (New York, 1969), pp. 136-154. Although he initially supported the Garrisonian strategy of nonresistance and "moral suasion," Douglass had evolved into a full-fledged militant by the 1850s, when he publicly called for a massive slave revolt in the South and for the killing, if need be, of slave catchers in the northern states.

27. *Proceedings of the State Convention of Colored Men . . . 1856* (Cleveland, 1856).

28. Langston, *Virginia Plantation*, p. 189.

29. "The World's Anti-Slavery Movement," in John Mercer Langston, *Freedom and Citizenship: Selected Lectures and Addresses* (Washington, 1883), p. 65.

30. See, especially, Dudley Cornish's excellent and comprehensive study, *The Sable Arm: Negro Troops in the Union Army, 1861-1865* (New York, 1956).

31. "Citizenship and the Ballots," in Langston, *Freedom and Citizenship*, pp. 99, 121-122.

32. "Speech . . . before the Radical Union Club, St. Joseph, Missouri, 1866," undated newspaper clipping, Langston Scrapbook, Langston Papers, box 5.

33. Speech before Freedmen's Education Society, Cleveland, Ohio, August 1, 1866, reported in Cleveland *Daily True Democrat*, August 2, 1866.

34. Cheek, "Forgotten Prophet," p. 86.

35. Langston was mentioned as a possible vice-presidential candidate on the Republican ticket in 1868, but his sponsor, Colonel Charles E. Moss, a white Unionist from Missouri, intended no more than a symbolic gesture, and no one took the idea seriously. The mere suggestion, indeed, provoked an immediate outcry from representative white and Negro spokesmen alike. See Floyd J. Miller, "A Black Vice President," *New Republic*, 166 (April 29, 1972): 13.

36. *Howard University Law Department, 1870-71* (Washington, 1871), pp. 3-4. A more circumstantial picture of conditions at Howard University in its formative years may be found in Rayford W. Logan, *Howard University: The First Hundred Years, 1867-1967* (New York, 1969); Walter Dyson, *Howard*

University, the Capstone of Negro Education (Washington, 1941). See also A. Mercer Daniel, "The Law Library of Howard University, 1867-1956," *Law Library Journal*, 51 (1958): 203.

37. A. G. Riddle, *Law Students and Lawyers* (Washington, 1873), pp. 195-196.

38. "Address of Hon. Charles Sumner," in *Howard University Law Department*, pp. 14-15.

39. Logan, *Howard University*, p. 72. I have generally followed Logan's revisionist interpretation of campus politics, which is less favorable to Langston than earlier accounts.

40. The standard treatment of the Freedmen's Bank is Walter L. Fleming, *The Freedmen's Savings Bank* (Chapel Hill, 1927). See also Constance McLaughlin Green, *The Secret City: A History of Race Relations in the Nation's Capital* (Princeton, 1967), pp. 84, 94, 99, 113; Langston, *Virginia Plantation*, p. 343.

41. John W. Forney, *Anecdotes of Public Men* (New York, 1873), pp. 180-181.

42. "Annual Report of the Dean of the Department, June 30, 1871," in *Howard University Law Department*, p. 8.

43. 82 Mich. 358 (1890).

44. D. Augustus Straker, "The Negro in the Profession of Law," *A.M.E. Church Review*, 8 (October 1891): 180-182. Between 1870 and 1890, it has been calculated, 7,372 criminal prosecutions were brought under the civil rights laws, of which 5,172 were in the South. About 20 percent of these prosecutions resulted in convictions. Kenneth S. Tollett argues that black attorneys probably figured in many of these cases ("Black Lawyers, Their Education, and the Black Community," *Howard Law Journal*, 17 [1972]: 326).

45. George M. Johnson, "The Integration of the Negro Lawyer into the Legal Profession in the United States" (paper delivered at the Annual Conference of the Division of Social Sciences, Howard University, May 4, 1951). Johnson was dean of Howard Law School at the time. A mimeographed copy of his informative address is available at the Moorland Room of the university library.

46. Straker, "Negro in the Profession of Law," pp. 179-180. Very few cases involving Negro rights ever reached the Supreme Court, Straker pointed out: "Many other cases would have been carried to our Supreme Court but for the great expense consequent upon doing so. Our court costs are hinderances to many suitors seeking justice but not getting it" (p. 182). His analysis of the practical limitations imposed upon black lawyers in their professional efforts is corroborated by the experience of another Negro civil rights activist, Mifflin W. Gibbs (LL.B., Oberlin, 1869), who became a municipal judge in Little Rock, Arkansas, during the 1870s. See Mifflin W. Gibbs, *Shadow and Light* (reprint ed., New York, 1968). And, for a fictional treatment of the more systematic forms of repression employed against black professionals by the end of the century, read Charles W. Chesnutt, *The Marrow of Tradition* (Boston and New York, 1901). Chesnutt, who was himself a Negro lawyer, made a firsthand study of the facts surrounding the Wilmington, North Carolina, race riot of 1898, upon which his novel is based.

Conclusion

1. Richard Rush, *American Jurisprudence* (1815), reprinted in Perry Miller, ed., *The Legal Mind in America from Independence to the Civil War* (Ithaca, 1969), p. 44.

2. See, for example, Edward Pessen, "The Egalitarian Myth and the American Social Reality: Wealth, Mobility, and Equality in the 'Era of the Common Man,' " *American Historical Review*, 76 (October 1971): 989-1034.

3. "The Position and Functions of the American Bar, as an Element of Conservatism in the State," in *Addresses and Orations of Rufus Choate* (Boston, 1878), p. 143.

4. "Getting Justice for the Freedman," *Howard Law Journal*, 16 (1971): 492-537.

5. For an excellent discussion of changing concepts of professional responsibility from the nineteenth century to the present, see F. Raymond Marks et al., *The Lawyer, the Public, and Professional Responsibility* (Chicago, 1972). On the character of the bar in the late nineteenth and early twentieth centuries, see also Robert Stevens, "Two Cheers for 1870: The American Law School," in *Perspectives in American History*, 5 (1971): 405-548; Jerold S. Auerbach, "Enmity and Amity: Law Teachers and Practitioners, 1900-1922," ibid., 551-601.

Index

Studies in Legal History